Citizens and Communities

CIVIL WAR HISTORY READERS

Since 1955 the journal *Civil War History* has presented the best original scholarship in the study of America's greatest trial. In commemoration of the war's sesquicentennial, The Kent State University Press presents *Civil War History* Readers, a multivolume series reintroducing the most influential articles published in the journal.

Conflict and Command	Edited by John T. Hubbell
Race and Recruitment	Edited by John David Smith
On Lincoln	Edited by John T. Hubbell
Citizens and Communities	Edited by J. Matthew Gallman

CIVIL WAR HISTORY READERS
VOLUME 4

CITIZENS AND COMMUNITIES

Edited by
J. MATTHEW GALLMAN

THE KENT STATE UNIVERSITY PRESS
Kent, Ohio

© 2015 by The Kent State University Press, Kent, Ohio 44242
All rights reserved
Library of Congress Catalog Card Number 2015009653
ISBN 978-1-60635-247-2
Manufactured in the United States of America

LIBRARY OF CONGRESS CATALOGING-IN-PUBLICATION DATA
Citizens and communities / edited by J. Matthew Gallman.
   4 volumes ; cm. — (Civil war history readers ; volume 4)
   Includes bibliographical references and index.
   ISBN 978-1-60635-247-2 (pbk. : alk. paper) ∞
1. United States—History—Civil War, 1861–1865—Social aspects. 2. Confederate States of America—History—Social aspects. I. Gallman, J. Matthew (James Matthew) II. Civil war history.
   E468.9.C47 2015
   973.7'1—dc23

                    2015009653

Contents

Introduction   vii

VOLUNTARISM ON THE HOME FRONT
  Sanitary Fairs of the Civil War
    William Y. Thompson   3
  The Impact of the Civil War on Philanthropy and Social Welfare
    Robert H. Bremner   21
  The Woman's National Loyal League: Feminist Abolitionists
  and the Civil War
    Wendy F. Hamand   33
  "A Profound National Devotion": The Civil War Union Leagues
  and the Construction of a New National Patriotism
    Melinda Lawson   54

SCIENCE AND MEDICINE
  Yankees versus Yellow Jack in New Orleans, 1862–1866
    Jo Ann Carrigan   87
  Civil War Anthropometry: The Making of a Racial Ideology
    John S. Haller   101

COMMUNITIES AT WAR
  Sons and Soldiers: Deerfield, Massachusetts, and the Civil War
    Emily J. Harris   121
  Introduction to War: The Civilians of Culpeper County, Virginia
    Daniel E. Sutherland   137

FILLING THE RANKS
  Was It a "Poor Man's Fight"?
    Eugene C. Murdock — 159
  Confederate Volunteering and Enlistment in Ashe County, North Carolina, 1861–1862
    Martin Crawford — 164
  Which Poor Man's Fight? Immigrants and the Federal Conscription of 1863
    Tyler Anbinder — 187

WELFARE, DISSENT, AND NATIONALISM
  "The Cry of the Sufferers": The Problem of Welfare in the Confederacy
    Paul D. Escott — 217
  Dissent in the Confederacy: The North Carolina Experience
    Marc W. Kruman — 230
  Disaffection, Persistence, and Nation: Some Directions in Recent Scholarship on the Confederacy
    Gary W. Gallagher — 252

LITERATURE AND SOCIETY
  For the Good, the True, and the Beautiful: Northern Children's Magazines and the Civil War
    James Marten — 279
  The Sentimental Soldier in Popular Civil War Literature, 1861–65
    Alice Fahs — 301

Contributors — 330
Index — 332

Introduction

For just over sixty years, *Civil War History* (*CWH*) has stood as one of the best places to find top scholarship on "the middle period" in American history. Moreover, as John T. Hubbell—*CWH*'s editor for a miraculous thirty-five years—explained in the first volume of this retrospective series, the "journal was founded, at least in part to enlist the academy... into the mission of describing the Civil War to the public."[1] A journey through six decades of the quarterly journal, spanning over nine hundred scholarly articles, is a marvelous tour of both the evolving trends in academia and, perhaps, in the interests of that broader reading public.

I am pleased to have been invited to edit the *Civil War History* Bookshelf's volume on the home front. As expected, the task of selecting just sixteen essays proved formidable. *Home front* is a term that allows for multiple definitions. Often home front scholarship, a close cousin to social history, is defined by what it is not. The term generally refers to scholarship that is not military history, political history, economic history, or diplomatic history. Sometimes that scholarship asks how the Civil War affected civilians who stayed behind. Other work focuses specifically on the contributions of noncombatants to the war effort; thus, the folks at home are seen as presenting another "front" to the conflict. Much home front scholarship integrates many themes into a single narrative, often focusing on a particular community.

Sixty years of *Civil War History* are particularly interesting in this context, since the home front only emerged as a coherent field of inquiry in the early 1980s, or roughly halfway through the life of the journal (up to now). A glance at six decades of the journal reveals considerable attention to home front themes,

---

1. John T. Hubbell, introduction to *Conflict and Command* (Kent, Ohio: Kent State Univ. Press, 2012), vii.

long before the principle theoretical questions had emerged. In fact, readers who expect to find the early issues of *Civil War History* full of "traditional" military and political topics are likely to be surprised. In its first six years, the quarterly ran entire special issues on "humor," "theater," "music," and "religion," as well as an article titled "The Civil War in Fiction."[2] A half century later, the contents of *Civil War History* had changed considerably. The essays are longer and generally more theoretical. New questions and scholarly perspectives emerge. As scholars reexamined familiar questions and raise new ones, the boundaries between battlefield and home front blur, producing fine essays that defy received categories.

I approached the selection of these essays with an open mind. The initial list of candidates was long. I narrowed the field by excluding worthy essays on economic mobilization and on how each side made use of railroads or adjusted manufacturing to further the war effort. I did not include Mark Neely's wonderful essay "Total War," on the grounds that it is essentially a piece on military mobilization, not the home front. But at some point, those lines become arbitrary, reflecting the complexity of the issues themselves. I thought hard about matters of representation or collective balance. Are the six decades of the journal's history adequately represented? Does the book show a reasonable balance between Union and Confederate topics? Will readers get a taste of all the important questions that have framed the scholarship on the home front? In the end, I settled on the essays I could not live without and let the chips fall where they may. Some contributions have been central to my own work on the home front. Quite a few are essays I have admired for years, some authored by good friends. Others I only discovered as I prepared this volume. Several anticipated important monographs; others stand alone. When all the dust settled, the balance between Union and Confederacy, between old essays and new pieces, and across fields seemed close enough.

The essays that follow are arranged by topic, not by chronology. But most really touch many topics. That is the nature of home front studies. Readers are encouraged to browse and read as the spirit moves them.

Some of the most important early essays on the home front examined the scope and character of voluntary societies dedicated to assisting the war effort. The first two essays are true classics that have stood the test of time. In his 1958 essay on "Sanitary Fairs of the Civil War," William Y. Thompson presented an impressive piece of empirical research. The United States Sanitary Commission

---

2. No essay from these special issues appears in this collection, but specialists pursuing any of these themes would be rewarded by reading this early work.

(USSC) was a crucial Northern organization, dedicated to raising funds and distributing supplies and agents to regiments in the field. Midway through the war, the local branches of the USSC turned to fund-raising fairs to replenish coffers and stimulate patriotic enthusiasm. Thompson, who had previously published an article in *CWH* on the Sanitary Commission, packed in details about several dozen Northern sanitary fairs. Nearly a half century later, no scholar has improved upon Thompson's superb research.

Robert H. Bremner's 1966 essay on "The Impact of the Civil War on Philanthropy and Social Welfare" is, like Thompson's two essays on the Sanitary Commission, an absolutely foundational piece for students of the Northern home front. Bremner, one of the great historians of American philanthropy, asks how the Civil War affected Northern welfare organizations. This was a particularly important framework because Bremner explicitly considered the Civil War years within the longer historic context. Thus, he treats the war as an enormous event demanding massive institutional responses from patriotic and philanthropic civilians. During those four years, however, other charitable organizations unrelated to the war continued to grow, evolve, and compete for donations in an economy that was generally doing very well.

Wendy F. Hamand published "The Woman's National Loyal League: Feminist Abolitionists and the Civil War" a full generation later, speaking to a very different scholarly audience.[3] Founded by prominent abolitionists and woman suffrage advocates Elizabeth Cady Stanton and Susan B. Anthony, the Woman's National Loyal League (WNLL) organized a nationwide petition calling for a constitutional amendment banning slavery. Hamand's essay details the activities of this largely neglected organization, while also placing its work within the broader narrative of women's rights. As Hamand notes, historians had traditionally reported that the movement's leaders had set aside their political goals for the duration of the Civil War, but in fact the WNLL constituted a highly successful—and distinctly feminist—wartime organization that mobilized women as political actors in time of war. Hamand later incorporated these findings into her important book on women abolitionists and the Civil War.[4]

Melinda Lawson's "'A Profound National Devotion': The Civil War Union

---

3. Articles on women's history are not very numerous in the sixty years of *CWH*. One of the best of those not included here is Hamand's (then Venet) essay on Mary Livermore. Wendy Hamand Venet, "The Emergence of a Suffragist: Mary Livermore, Civil War Activism, and the Moral Power of Women," *Civil War History* (June 2002): 143–64.

4. Wendy Hamand Venet, *Neither Ballots nor Bullets: Women Abolitionists and the Civil War* (Charlottesville: Univ. of Virginia Press, 1991).

Leagues and the Construction of a New National Patriotism" considers wartime institutions dedicated to enhancing and guiding patriotism. The North's Union League Clubs emerged in several leading Northeastern cities and soon grew active in publishing and disseminating patriotic literature throughout the Union. Lawson, who explored these themes more fully in a book-length study, considers these organizations of powerful elites as major architects of a new sort of patriotic nationalism.[5]

The war years provide historians with a particularly valuable laboratory for studying the history of science and the history of medicine, because of the terrible challenges posed by the war and also because of the massive data collection that accompanied the conflict. The next two essays contribute to that vast literature. In "Yankees versus Yellow Jack in New Orleans, 1862–1866," Jo Ann Carrigan recounts the wartime battle against yellow fever in and around New Orleans. Carrigan's essay is a model for how a case study, set in a particular place and time, can illuminate the intricate interplay of disparate variables. In this case, the threat of yellow fever at the mouth of the Mississippi brought together familiar concerns about health and public policy, but as refracted through a new lens produced by a hostile army of occupation. Fans of Union General Benjamin Butler (if such readers exist) will be pleased with how this fascinating story unfolds.

The war years saw the creation of massive armies in sizes never before seen in North America. They, in turn, produced a treasure trove of quantitative data, assembled by various groups intent on keeping track of these men, or using the troops as subjects of larger quantitative studies. In 1864 the United States Sanitary Commission asked Benjamin A. Gould, the president of the American Association for the Advancement of Science, to take over a huge project assembling data on the physical measurements of Union soldiers. The resulting anthropometric data (and other comparable material on enslaved people) became the basis for sweeping studies of the human body, with particular emphasis on racial and ethnic differences. In "Civil War Anthropometry: The Making of a Racial Ideology," John S. Haller traces the history of this quasi-scientific field of inquiry and the racial theories that emerged from this Civil War data.

As the home front became a recognized field of historical inquiry, many scholars undertook community studies, asking new questions about how the Civil War affected communities of civilians. *Civil War History* published several of the most important of these essays, including the next two essays in this collection.

---

5. Melinda Lawson, *Patriot Fires: Forging a New American Nationalism in the Civil War North* (Lawrence: Univ. Press of Kansas, 2002).

Informed by the methods and insights of the New Social History, Emily J. Harris set out to understand the demographic traits that lead men to enlist in the Union Army. In "Sons and Soldiers: Deerfield, Massachusetts, and the Civil War," Harris combined traditional sources with a superb quantitative analysis of the Deerfield men who served in the Union army, compared with those who did not. This short essay, which was republished in a celebrated collection edited by Maris Vinovskis, has been cited hundreds of times as one of the first empirical essays that asked "who served?"[6]

Daniel E. Sutherland's beautifully written "Introduction to War: The Civilians of Culpeper County, Virginia" tells a very different story about a very different wartime place. But it shares Harris's core insight that sometimes we can learn the most about a very large topic through a close examination of a specific community. Whereas the citizens of Deerfield, Massachusetts, responded to the challenges of Civil War from a safe haven, hundreds of miles from the battle lines, the residents of Culpeper, Virginia, regularly found themselves in the thick of things. Sutherland tells an eloquent tale of civilians living in the midst of war. In doing so, he illustrates the limits to an excessively rigid understanding of terms like *battlefield* and *home front*.[7]

The intersection of military history and home front scholarship has often come when historians have tried to unravel what made some men enlist while others chose to stay home. The questions attract us because we know that the conscription laws in both the Union and the Confederacy offered blatant advantages to each society's wealthiest men, yet the opportunities for exemptions do not really get at the larger question. In one of the most important articles on the topic, Eugene C. Murdock asked the core question: "Was It a Poor Man's Fight?" Focusing on twenty-three districts in New York, Murdock compared local wealth with conscription data from the Provost Marshall's reports. The results are mixed, and the geographic scope of the study limited, but Murdock's preliminary data called into question the idea that the wealthiest individuals (or districts) were the most successful at avoiding service.[8]

Martin Crawford's "Confederate Volunteering and Enlistment in Ashe County, North Carolina, 1861–1862" returns to the community study for a close analysis of

---

6. Maris A. Vinovskis, *Towards a Social History of the American Civil War: Exploratory Essays* (New York: Cambridge Univ. Press, 1990).

7. Sutherland went on to publish a prizewinning book about Culpeper. *Seasons of War: The Ordeal of a Confederate Community, 1861–1865* (New York: Free Press, 1995).

8. Murdock wrote widely on Northern conscription, including Eugene C. Murdock, *One Million Men: The Civil War Draft in the North* (Westport, Conn.: Greenwood Press, 1980).

enlistment patterns in a mountain community in western North Carolina. Crawford finds subtle patterns beneath the aggregate data, reflecting family histories, economic circumstances, and individual inclinations. Like Sutherland's essay on Culpeper, Virginia, Crawford's study illustrates the deep links between the Civil War as a military experience and events and personal decisions on the home front.

Returning to the Northern states, Tyler Anbinder's contribution revisits the conscription question with "Which Poor Man's Fight? Immigrants and the Federal Conscription of 1863." Anbinder, a leading scholar of the politics of Nativism, asks how immigrants experienced the Union's draft laws. Working from a detailed—and immensely creative—analysis of data from thirty-nine Northern communities, Anbinder concludes that immigrants were surprisingly successful at avoiding forced service, even when conscripted. Despite familiar tales of poor immigrant men being drafted into military service in disproportionate numbers, Anbinder finds that foreign-born soldiers, like native-born recruits, were far more likely to have enlisted voluntarily.

Writing near the end of World War I, Randolph Bourne famously observed that "war is the health of the state."[9] The next three essays all consider the relationship that the new Confederacy had with its white civilian populace.

Prior to the Civil War, most public assistance to the poor and needy came from towns and communities. Individual state governments, particularly in the South, rarely budgeted for welfare assistance. In "'The Cry of the Sufferers': The Problem of Welfare in the Confederacy," Paul D. Escott combines a valuable survey of welfare policies across the Confederacy with a careful analysis of his own research from Orange County, North Carolina. The immense poverty that the war forced upon Southerners prompted important shifts in how people conceived of government responsibilities, even while material shortages undermined the success of any new policies. Escott notes that both the changing philosophies of government, and the overwhelming material needs, left important legacies for the postwar South.[10]

Marc W. Kruman's "Dissent in the Confederacy: The North Carolina Experience" returns us to the Tar Heel state to consider the other side of the coin. Several other *CWH* articles examined draft riots and moments of wartime conflict, but Kruman's essay is particularly valuable because it takes a broader approach,

---

9. Randolph Bourne, *War and the Intellectuals: Collected Essays, 1915-1919* (New York: Harper & Row, 1964).

10. Escott pursued these themes more fully in *Many Excellent People: Power and Privilege in North Carolina, 1850-1900* (Chapel Hill: Univ. of North Carolina Press, 1988).

considering dissent across the entire state throughout four years of war. While other scholars have described dissent as a response to unpopular wartime policies, or hostility to the war itself, Kruman argues that North Carolinians saw the rise of the wartime state as representing a distinct threat to their own personal liberties.[11]

Gary W. Gallagher's "Disaffection, Persistence, and Nation: Some Directions in Recent Scholarship on the Confederacy" is a very different sort of essay. In this sweeping historiographic essay, Gallagher, the author of a major work on Confederate nationalism,[12] surveys the scholarship on both conflict and consensus in the Confederacy. The result is an invaluable interpretive discussion of the vast scholarship on the Confederacy; the essay identifies points of general agreement as well as enduring controversies, where—as Gallagher notes—the wealth of diverse evidence allows for contradictory interpretations of the Southern nation at war.

This introduction began by noting that in its early years *Civil War History* published a series of special issues on various aspects of wartime culture. More recently, scholars have returned to the war's vast cultural output for new perspectives on Civil War society. The final two essays offer two excellent examples of the fruits of that labor.

James Marten, the leading scholar of children's literature during the Civil War, considers one slice of that large topic in "For the Good, the True, and the Beautiful: Northern Children's Magazines and the Civil War." Much like Bremner's essay on wartime philanthropy, Marten asks how the Civil War affected established wartime institutions (in this case, publications). Children's magazines had been offering boys and girls guidance on values and behavior for decades. As Marten notes, the war did not change their fundamental character, but the cultural demands for a patriotic citizenry did trickle down to children, as magazine stories grew more explicitly political and patriotic in some of their messages directed at young readers.[13]

For generations, scholars who worked on wartime literature focused on the works of the great and the near great, while ignoring the larger mass of popular literature. Five years after Marten introduced children's magazines as a source for serious investigation, Alice Fahs published "The Sentimental Soldier in Popular

---

11. For Kruman's book-length study of North Carolina politics, see *Parties and Politics in North Carolina, 1836–1865* (Baton Rouge: Louisiana State Univ. Press, 1983).

12. Gary Gallagher, *The Confederate War* (Cambridge: Harvard Univ. Press, 1999).

13. See James Marten, *The Children's Civil War* (Chapel Hill: Univ. of North Carolina Press, 1998).

Civil War Literature, 1861–65." Based on a chapter of her path-breaking book on wartime popular literature, Fahs explains how these authors produced the idea of the "sentimental soldier" as part of their literary construction of an "imagined war" that, Fahs argues, served the larger needs of a society at war.[14]

The essays that follow have been republished as they originally appeared in the pages of *Civil War History*, with the minor exception that the editor has corrected a handful of minor typographical errors.

---

14. See Alice Fahs, *The Imagined Civil War: Popular Literature of the North and South, 1861–1865* (Chapel Hill: Univ. of North Carolina Press, 2000).

Voluntarism on the Home Front

Sanitary Fairs of the Civil War

WILLIAM Y. THOMPSON

William Y. Thompson's name first appeared in these pages (June, 1956) over an article on the U.S. Sanitary Commission. He is a member of the Department of History of Louisiana Polytechnic Institute at Ruston, Louisiana.

One of the most neglected phases of Civil War history deals with the work of the civilian miles away from the front. Pen and ink have been liberally used to describe military and political exploits, but unexplored areas still remain in the activity behind the lines. An organization which did much to further the Northern cause was the United States Sanitary Commission, organized in June, 1861, by a group of patriotic and generally self-sacrificing civilians. This group purposed to improve the sanitary condition of the Union armies and to supplement government issue to the soldiers. This it succeeded admirably in doing as it contributed services and goods to the war effort estimated at a value of $25,000,000.

The problem of money to sustain its work was an ever-present one for the Commission. The most lucrative source of financial aid proved to be the Sanitary Fairs which began in the fall of 1863 and continued throughout the war. They originated in the West and, after experiencing success there, spread to all parts of the North. Generally the fairs were creations of the larger branches of the Commission, but many a small hamlet was caught up in the fervor.

The pioneer Sanitary Fair was held in Chicago from October 27 through November 7, 1863. Credit for its organization belonged to a pair of energetic feminine leaders, Jane C. (Mrs. A. H.) Hoge and Mary A. (Mrs. D. P.) Livermore. They wanted a means to replenish the treasury of the Northwestern Branch of the Sanitary Commission which had been so generous in its contributions to the work, and decided that a fair would refill the dwindling coffers.

On the morning of the 27th, after weeks of extended preparation, the Northwestern Sanitary Fair opened. The attention of all Chicago centered on the exposition since business for the most part was stopped, the courts closed, and the schools suspended. Chicago "for the time being [was turned] into a vast theatre of wonders." By nine o'clock "the city was in a roar," as a parade three miles long with roughly nine divisions began the activities. One division included wagons packed with singing children, lifting their voices together in "John Brown's Body Lies Mouldering in the Grave." Greatly cheered by the crowds were farmers bearing gifts for the fair. They came in "ricketty and lumbering wagons, made of poles, loaded with a mixed freight—a few cabbages, a bundle of socks, a coop of tame ducks, a few barrels of turnips, a pot of butter, and a bag of beans...."

Many contributions were made to the fair, some great, some small: "from the watchmaker's jewelry to horseshoes and harness; from lace, cloth, cotton, and linen, to iron and steel; from wooden and waxen and earthen ware to butter and cheese, bacon and beef...." Specific items included a steam engine "donated by the workmen of the Eagle Works Manufacturing Co., every man contributing something—not one Copperhead in the whole institution"; there were also mowing machines, reapers, "nails by the hundred kegs... cologne by the barrel, native wine in casks... a mountain howitzer, [and] a steel breech-loading cannon."

Buildings on the fairgrounds served for the purposes of sale or display. The main ones were Bryan Hall, "devoted to the exhibition and sale of fancy wares, needlework, musical instruments, silver ware, dry goods, glass ware, clothing, &c."; Lower Bryan Hall, a dining room, in which nearly 1,500 people were served daily; Manufacturers' Hall, for the display of heavy machinery; a trophy hall, housing, among other pieces, captured Confederate flags; an art gallery; and Metropolitan Hall, which was used for evening entertainment. For a reasonable expenditure of seventy-five cents, one could spend the day at the fair and partake of a meal at the dining room.

The great sensation of the fair was President Lincoln's gift of the original draft of the Emancipation Proclamation. In turning it over to the ladies, Lincoln wrote:

According to the request made in your behalf, the original draft of Emancipation Proclamation is herewith enclosed. The formal words at the top, and the conclusion, except the signature, you perceive, are not in my handwriting. They were written at the State Department, by whom I know not. The printed part was cut from a copy of the preliminary proclamation, and pasted on, merely to save writing. I had some desire to retain the paper; but if it shall contribute to the relief or comfort of the soldiers, that will be better.

The manuscript was purchased by T. B. Bryan at a price of $3,000, for the benefit of the Chicago Soldiers' Home. It was lithographed and copies sold by the board of managers of the Home for the purpose of establishing a permanent home for invalid soldiers. For his generosity, Lincoln was rewarded with a gold watch, donated by J. H. Hoes to the largest contributor to the fair.

On the last day of the fair, a dinner was given for soldiers in the Chicago area from Camp Douglas, local hospitals, and the Soldiers' Home. Some 600 were present at what was termed a great success.

The fair proved bountiful beyond the fondest expectations of its sponsors. Attendance was large, Bryan Hall averaging over 5,000 daily. The benevolence of the Northwest was tapped for $90,048.01 of which $78,682.89 was net profit. The Chicago Soldiers' Home was given $3,000, while $75,682.89 went to the treasurer of the Northwestern Sanitary Commission.

Another fair was held in Chicago in the early summer of 1865, intended for the benefit of the Sanitary Commission and the Chicago Soldiers' Home. The leaders were again Mesdames Hoge and Livermore. Initially, the pair was reluctant to embark again on such a project. One Fair experience was enough, said Mrs. Hoge, but the people seemed eager for another and "outlays for antiscorbutics & other necessities, ... [were] very large." It was decided to open the fair on February 27 and run through March 4. Preparations seemed to go well enough, even though, as Mrs. Livermore complained to the Reverend Henry W. Bellows, Unitarian minister and president of the Sanitary Commission, she had received no response from Henry Ward Beecher and Oliver Wendell Holmes to requests for an address and an ode for the benefit of the fair. "I suppose they both think a Western Fair must be a picayunish concern and very likely have altogether forgotten it by this time." Continuing at some length on the relationship of the clergy to the coming fair, Mrs. Livermore said:

> The most amusing thing in the whole aspect of affairs is the hearty cooperation of the Orthodox clergy. They were getting infested with the Christian Commission [the United States Christian Commission for the Army and Navy, a large, independent body, in some respects a rival of the Sanitary Commission] virus of the East, when the Fair was projected, when they turned a complete somersault into our ranks again, and are working for us like beavers. The Northwest swarms with agents of the Fair—*and every one is an Orthodox minister.* In order to undo the mischief they and the Christian Commission have been doing with their libels upon us and our work, they are compelled to distribute Sanitary Commission documents, . . . show that the Orthodox sects most heartily endorse us. . . .

While private sentiments were expressed behind the fair facade, formal preparations continued. The executive committee elected General Joseph Hooker honorary president. Mrs. Hoge and Mrs. Livermore journeyed to Washington to receive the assurance of Lincoln's presence at the fair as blueprints were drawn for the erection of the main building in Dearborn Park.

The fair suffered one postponement from its original February date and seemed likely to be postponed permanently when the end of the war and Lincoln's assassination occurred before its formal opening. It required superhuman efforts, Mrs. Hoge stated, to revive public enthusiasm. Everywhere the opinion circulated that the work of the Sanitary Commission was finished and the fair unnecessary. "The combined pressure of the churches & the press, was inconceivable." Ultimately the Christian Commission was brought into the fair and its adherence cemented to the enterprise by a promise of a portion of the proceeds. "Before this arrangement was made," remarked Mrs. Hoge, "we were as Nehemiah when he built the walls of Jerusalem, with the trowel in one hand and the sword in the other, work & fight, fight & work. . . ."

On May 30, the fair opened after months of frustrating delay. It was dedicated to the Union armies and their generals, with profuse praise polishing the brass to a new lustre. For instance, Benjamin F. Butler, the soldier-politician from Massachusetts, a man regarded with mixed opinions in both New Orleans and the North, was called by the *Chicago Tribune,* "our great Cromwell of a Butler." The war was over, but passions had not subsided in Northern breasts, if the temperament of the fair's newspaper can be taken as a barometer of public feeling. To the plantation bell of Jefferson Davis, on display at the fair, the paper said, "Your master will soon change the gown for the gallows, don the black cap instead of the bonnet, and lay off hoops for hemp." Of captured rebel flags the paper wrote:

And here, too, have come the foul and loathsome emblems of treason and slavery—the exponents of that hellish monster, begotten in perjury and fraud, conceived in wickedness, born in violence, rapine, plunder and cruelty, baptized in the blood of liberty's martyrs, and swaddled all over with a pestilent garment, whose warp was treason, whose woof was shameless lies.

On exhibition were such patriotic emblems as John Brown's ox yoke and the original Lincoln cabin built in Macon County, Illinois, in 1830. Northern pride and enthusiasm knew no bounds when Generals Ulysses S. Grant and William T. Sherman paid a brief visit to the fair on Saturday night, June 10. Lincoln of course was unable to carry out his pledge to Mrs. Hoge and Mrs. Livermore to attend, but young Tad Lincoln partially redeemed the promise of his late father by his appearance.

The fair closed on June 24 after a three-weeks' run. The net profits totaled around $85,000, with $50,000 going to the Christian Commission, and the rest divided between the Sanitary Commission and the Soldiers' Home. Mrs. Hoge told Bellows that it was a battle to secure half of the proceeds after the Christian Commission had been paid off. The argument that no more money was needed by the Commission had to be overcome. Charles J. Stillé, future historian of the Sanitary Commission, probably expressed the opinion of most when he labeled this second Chicago fair "an utter failure." No doubt a return to "normalcy" and a reaction to wartime benevolence and enthusiasm caused the last great Sanitary Fair to be anti-climactic and disappointing in its achievements. A colorful Civil War civilian crusade had come to a close.

The first fair in Chicago in 1863 set off a chain reaction in the Northern states. Cities large and small attempted to emulate this initial Midwestern endeavor as "Sanitary Fair" became a patriotic byword among loyal citizens.

Cincinnati's Western Sanitary Fair, December 21–January 9, 1864, proved more successful as a money maker than either of the Chicago expositions. Such was generally the case when one large fair opened on the termination of another and benefited from the tremendous enthusiasm being snowballed throughout all the Northern states.

An interesting feature of the Cincinnati fair was the sale of letters, documents, and manuscripts donated by well-known personalities. The value of the items varied considerably in the eyes of fair-goers, and the prices paid for some of them appear trivial indeed compared with their probable worth today. Schuyler Colfax's draft of his opening address as Speaker of the House brought $1.50.

William Cullen Bryant's autographed editorial manuscript, "Chesapeake Piracy and Murder," was purchased for sixty cents. A letter from General (at that time, Major) Robert Anderson to Governor Francis Pickens of South Carolina, dated January 9, 1861, and concerning the firing on the "Star of the West," sold for $3.00. William Lloyd Garrison's manuscript verse, "On Completing my Fifty-eighth Year," brought in seventy cents to the fair's treasury. Twenty-one dollars was paid for a letter from the Marquis de Lafayette to the mayor of New Haven. Lincoln's original amnesty proclamation, a five-page folio "with interlineations, corrections, and erasures" plus a frame thirty inches square, sold for $150.

Miscellaneous curios on exhibit were "a ferocious Bohemian boar's head," brass bullet molds and the powder horn of General Israel Putnam, a copper tea kettle transported over on the "Mayflower," cotton picked from the plantation of the President of the Confederate States,[1] and a piece of a coat worn by George Washington. Lectures, concerts, and gymnastic shows were still other facets of amusement and fund raising. The fair was closed by a public ball under the management of an independent committee of Cincinnati citizens. It was held despite the protests of some of the clergy. One wearer of the cloth wrote the chairman of the fair's executive committee asking whether "it would be wise for a *Sanitary* Fair to institute any form of social entertainment that would tempt ladies to an exposure to *sanitary* danger beyond such as all who unite or take part in the sales must necessarily meet from the nature of the principal building." Evidently the committee did not consider the "sanitary" risks involved too great for the ladies' health, for it refused to call off the ball.

The total amount raised by the Western Sanitary Fair was $235,406.72, establishing a high-water mark to date. Some discontent cropped up over the practice of raffling at the Cincinnati fair. The committee in charge, however, ruled that each individual organization represented must decide the matter for itself. No blanket regulation would be dictated from above. According to the *Sanitary Commission Bulletin,* the Commission in early 1864 laid down a general rule along the same lines—that while the board objected to raffling at the fairs it would leave the final decision on such matters to the managers of the fairs; that the Commission had established one rule in regard to the sources of its support: "to accept, without question and from all quarters, such gifts as were brought to its treasury."

The East meanwhile was picking up the challenge laid down by the West.

---

1. It appears that no fair was successful without something of Jefferson Davis.

Boston held its Sanitary Fair late in 1863, December 14-21. As became staid Bostonians, there was less fanfare here than elsewhere and less enthusiasm on the part of some of the Boston Sanitary Commission leaders. One of the Boston group, Miss Abby W. May, made some "desponding remarks" to Commission officials about the fair when it was in its preparatory stages, wondering if the endeavor was worth-while. Assistant Secretary Alfred J. Bloor went to work for the Commission to revive drooping New England spirits. He agreed that Miss May's skepticism of the fairs was not without foundation—that in a sense, as she had thought, they were similar to children's parties which left everyone limp and tired at the end of the day. Changing the simile from children's parties to revivals, he continued:

> Episcopalians and Unitarians being generally well cultured people do not as a common thing, fancy working out their religion at revivals, but the Methodists—who count, I suppose, twenty to one of the others—have a very particular predilection for them, and evidently cannot very well go to heaven without them. I am in hopes that these fairs all over the country may prove Sanitary revivals. You, who work constantly in the cause, feel no need of periodical incitements to it—but I think the multitude does....
>
> Besides one might as well try to dam up Niagra [*sic*] as to stem the succession of 'Fairs' which gathering their impulse at Chicago will now sweep over the whole country, carrying city, town and village in the current. Is it not better to accept what is thrown up on our shore by the top wave of passing excitement... than to refuse the spoil because the current which bore it along did not originate with and cannot be controlled by ourselves?

The Boston fair was suggested at a meeting of the finance committee of the New England Women's Auxiliary Association,[2] in May, 1863. Only one committee was set up to guide its organization, and its activities were carried on solely in the Boston Music Hall. Bloor attended the fair a few days after its opening and "found the crowd so dense that it was impossible to gather in the details, though enough could be seen, from advantageous stand points to give a vivid impression of ... elegance, profusion and costliness." The operation of the New England fair was without unusual or bizarre aspects. Total receipts amounted to $153,658.97; expenses were $4,771.92, excluding the rental for the Music Hall which was

---

2. A subsidiary of the United States Sanitary Commission.

$2,936.20, leaving $145,950.85 as net receipts. One-third of the receipts was turned over to the central treasury of the Commission, marking the first time any fair had so acted. Half a loaf, however, was not enough for Commission members of the central organization, who complained at this time and throughout the war over the retention of fair funds by the branches. The leaders of the Commission did not feel they were pursuing a selfish course in the matter. They simply thought that such large sums as were being raised by the fairs could best be supervised from the central office, which kept its eye on overall strategy and the allocation of funds. In addition, the fairs were given in the name of the Sanitary Commission, although a soldiers' home or a particular society sometimes shared star billing. As such, the funds promoted were theoretically tabbed for general use all over the country instead of for provincial distribution. Finally, the hierarchy believed that independently wealthy auxiliaries weakened the federal organization of the Sanitary Commission and promoted secession from the union. It was genuine and honest concern then which Bellows and his associates reflected.

Brooklyn continued the fair activity in the East with a highly profitable undertaking, February 22–March 11, 1864. This fair was the joint creation of the War Fund Committee of Brooklyn and County of Kings and the Woman's Relief Association of the City of Brooklyn.

Several of the fairs, including that at Brooklyn, were the recipients of handicraft from Confederate prisoners of war at Point Lookout, Maryland. In return for tobacco, the Southerners put idle hands and pocketknives to use in fashioning trinkets of various kinds. "It is a curious fact," commented a Commission agent, "that not withstanding all we have heard of King Cotton, his subjects have a more abiding and devoted affection for that more potent brother-monarch—King Tobacco." The managers of the Brooklyn fair received 75 fans, 130 inlaid and plain rings, and other articles, Confederate-made.

The "most novel and curious feature" of the Brooklyn fair was the New England Kitchen, "an attempt to re-produce the ancient manners and mode of living of the Puritans." The rest of the fair activities paralleled those of earlier ones. The net profits of the Brooklyn fair were $402,943.74. The managers of the fair were willing to surrender the entire sum to the central treasury. Bellows, however, authorized all proceeds over $300,000 to be used by the Woman's Relief Association of Brooklyn.

The most successful of all fairs from a financial standpoint was held in New York City, April 4–23, 1864. The leading female spirit was Mrs. Hamilton Fish; other prominent women connected with the fair as members of the Women's

Executive Committee were Mesdames Francis Lieber, John Jacob Astor, James B. Colgate, Alexander Hamilton, Jr., and Frederick Billings.

The main building of the New York fair was located between Fourteenth and Fifteenth streets. To the original structure were added other edifices to house such units as the Indian department, the arms and trophies museum, the restaurant, and the machinery department. Even though more space was needed, the building committee refused to approve further construction. The temporary buildings had already cost $60,000, and this was deemed to be the limit of expenditure. The Sanitary Commission, however, agreed to be responsible for additional structures and, furthermore, gained permission from city authorities to erect them in Union Square.

Supplementing the multitude of domestic gifts to the fair were those from abroad. From London came 1,000 tons of coals, the present of George Eliot. Union sympathizers and fair enthusiasts in Paris, Rome, Dusseldorf, Zurich, and Frankfort sent presents assessed at 40,000, 50,000, 12,000, 11,000, and 7,000 francs respectively. The Parisians also sent 30,000 francs in cash. Among the donations from the capital of France were a marble bust of William Henry Seward, a collection of paintings, and eighteen cases of champagne. The contribution of Newcastle was singular—a vessel loaded with coal. In St. Petersburg, loyal Americans raised money, then converted it into articles manufactured exclusively in Russia for the benefit of the fair. The Pope personally sent $500, while sympathizers in Smyrna, Copenhagen, Geneva, Hamburg, Lisbon, and Rio de Janeiro bestowed favors in varying degree. The European branch of the Sanitary Commission had hoped to have an "European table" at the New York fair, but its plans fell through.

When all was in readiness, the mayor of New York, C. Godfrey Gunther, issued a proclamation recommending that Monday, April 4, the opening day of the fair, be set aside as a holiday and that all business "except works of charity and necessity" be suspended. On Monday "Broadway lay white and brilliant under the spring sun, the sharp sky line of the roofs and the crimson stripes of the countless flags seeming to deepen the blue that hung over all." A great military display before which "the Prince of Wales' reception, heretofore regarded as offering the most august spectacle possible to New York, found its glory pale," opened festivities. Speeches of tribute and praise for the work behind the exposition were made by General John A. Dix and Joseph H. Choate. The *New York Times* termed the fair beginning "a memorable day . . . in the history of the City and of the country," a success which could only be achieved in the city of New York.

Several minor incidents served to ruffle conventional fair operation. Three pickpockets, all women, were arrested. Placards describing their avocations were put around their necks; then these disinterested fair visitors, escorted by police, were marched through the buildings before being ushered out. The Sanitary Commission understood that the Manhattan Gas Company had agreed to furnish gas for the fair at no charge. But the company "on account of the disloyal feeling of certain influential stockholders" backed out, the fair authorities maintained, and sent their bills without reduction. A group of Iroquois Indians was engaged for two weeks to exhibit the customs and rites of their tribe for the enlightenment of New Yorkers. Transportation, board, and lodgings were promised them while in town. The fair had been scheduled to start on March 28, but postponement until April 4 was necessary. It was rumored that during the week of delay the leader of the Indians "was kept continually upon the 'trail' through the waste places of the city grogshops, and . . . by next Monday was so worn down, by a series of pursuits and captures, that he found his after-toils but play in comparison."

The attraction receiving the most attention was the "sword voting" contest, in which a person attending the fair might vote for his military hero at $1.00 per ballot. The voting was hotly contested, particularly between Generals U. S. Grant and George B. McClellan. The latter led most of the way, but a flood of votes for Grant at the fair's conclusion made the Commander in Chief of the Union forces the winner. The final count among the leaders saw Grant with 30,291 votes, McClellan with 14,509, and a scattering of 163 votes. S. C. Rowan emerged victorious among maritime candidates with 462 votes, followed by Admiral David G. Farragut with 332, and a scattering of 128. The amount raised by the contest was $45,885.

Propagandizing the New York fair was a newspaper published from April 5 through April 23 and called the *Spirit of the Fair*. Its format was that of the standard fair paper except that it excluded commercial advertising and in some respects was more sedate than the average publication.

A flag was presented to General Dix, president of the fair, on the closing date, April 23. The presentation was to commemorate Dix's action in crisis-ridden January of 1861, when, as Secretary of the Treasury, he had sent this terse order to the Treasury agent in New Orleans: "If any one attempts to haul down the American flag, shoot him on the spot." His words were remembered during the war and honored at this time.

A report of the treasurer of the fair announced that well over $1,000,000 had been raised and that $1,000,000 had been given to the treasurer of the Sanitary Commission. The final report fixed the net proceeds of the fair at $1,183,506.23.

Philadelphia fell just short of its New York neighbor, as it reaped the second largest harvest from fair activity. Those working for the fair in the Quaker City were at first in doubt as to its outcome. One of Bloor's female correspondents of the branch in Philadelphia wrote:

> I fear that instead of [the success of the Boston fair] inciting to perseverance those who were moving in the matter here, it will have a tendency to discourage them. The stolid Dutch population of Pennsylvania will not take hold, as did the people throughout New England; and without such assistance, Philadelphia could accomplish but little, taxed as she has been, since the commencement of the war, by her hospitals, refreshment saloons, etc. So please don't expect too much of us.

Trying to stir up enthusiasm in Harrisburg was not without difficulty for another female worker. She said that some people were against any assistance to the fair because they claimed Philadelphians were doing all they could to take the capital away from them. Other opposition was based on the grounds that the Philadelphia fair was supposed to offer liquor, dancing, and raffling. Bloor himself said that the fair would net as much as any of the others "if it were not that Phila. is the headquarters of the C. C. [Christian Commission]." Virtually all misgivings, however, were soon dispelled by the enthusiasm which the fair generated.

Opening on June 7, 1864, the fair stretched two miles in length and contained "miracles as many as Faust saw in his journey through the world of magic." It was thought that the fair was of such proportions as to warrant a visitors' guide, which was duly published. To visit the ninety departments of this wonderland cost an adult $2.20, a fairly steep fee according to conventional fair prices. Philadelphia did not deviate to any great extent from the standard fair framework and operation in its sales and exhibits.

The fair restaurant seemed quite formidable with a range 26 feet long, 12 boilers with a 360-gallon capacity, and 30 cooks. A glimpse at the bill of fare indicated that even the most demanding appetite could be satisfied.

The high light of the Philadelphia fair was the visit of the President of the United States and his family on June 16. The price of admission was doubled for the day, but crowds were still large. In a brief speech President Lincoln praised the work of the Sanitary Commission and the Christian Commission. He spoke of the worthy purposes of the Sanitary Fairs which had been held in Chicago, Boston, Cincinnati, Brooklyn, New York, Baltimore, St. Louis, Pittsburgh, and now Philadelphia. Often, stated Lincoln, he had been asked when the war would end. Only when the "object" had been obtained, and that object was "restoring the national authority over the whole dominion." The American people would go through on this objective even if it took three more years. But President Lincoln expressed the view that Grant would not be dislodged before Richmond. General Lew Wallace also addressed the crowd. He paid tribute to both Lincoln and Grant in their war pursuits and maintained that Grant would lead the Northern forces on to victory. Continuing, he prophesied:

> . . . Mr. Lincoln's appreciation lies in the future. Midst the hurry, rush, and tumult of events, we have not time to fix our minds upon any one man or circumstance. Those who will come after us, and who will write the history of the past and present of this war, are the men who will give him the full credit he is entitled to, and describe him as he really is.

A third speaker was Edward Everett, but his remarks were not recorded.

The net proceeds of the Philadelphia fair were determined at $1,035,398.96. Stillé called the fair a great success, which he attributed to two of Bellows' ideas: first, making the fair a grand spectacle and, second, confining all executive power in the hands of a small and well-defined body.

Other large fairs were held in Pittsburgh, St. Louis, Baltimore, Cleveland, and Albany. Plans for the Pittsburgh fair were possibly made in ignorance of the coming fair at Philadelphia, and the simultaneous holding of the two fairs no doubt worked to the detriment of both.[3] Pittsburgh netted around $300,000. The St. Louis exposition, titled the Mississippi Valley Sanitary Fair, ran May 17–June 18, 1864. It was the longest fair on record although its last days of operation were devoted more to raffling than the customary sales and exhibitions. The St. Louis fair was under the control of the Western Sanitary Commission rather than the United States Sanitary Commission, and its proceeds went to the former organization. It was a big spectacle, the lone fair undertaking of the Western Sanitary Commission, and nothing was spared to insure its success.

---

3. The Pittsburgh fair ran June 11–18; the fair at Philadelphia, June 7–28.

The structure of fair operation in St. Louis did not differ greatly from that of the other fairs: the selection of an important military personage—in this case, General William S. Rosecrans—as president of the fair, a general city holiday proclaimed by the mayor, on opening day, a long parade, and inaugural ceremonies to initiate activities. The St. Louis fair claimed superiority over that of New York in the commodious arrangement of its buildings which offered more elbow room to fair visitors. A point of pride was the main building. It measured 114 by 525 feet, was opened by many exits, and lighted by 3,000 gas jets supplied through one mile of pipe. The architectural center of attraction was an octagon-shaped floral temple in the main building, supported by eight pillars wound with evergreen and dotted with white lilies. Inscribed on the arches between the pillars or columns were the names of Union officers and their moments of glory: Grant at Vicksburg, Rosecrans at Stone River, Porter at Memphis, Osterhaus at Chattanooga, Sherman at Shiloh, Lyon at Wilson's Creek, Hancock at Spottsylvania, and Sigel at Pea Ridge.

The "sword voting" contest which had proved so popular in New York was conducted in St. Louis. General Winfield S. Hancock with 2,403 ballots won easily, more than doubling the votes of all his opponents.[4] Raffling was wide open, popular, and profitable to many. The prize package, the "Smizer farm" valued at $40,000, was sought by the holders of 50,000 one-dollar chances. Little Nellie Grant, the General's daughter, was blindfolded to draw the winning number. Other lucky participants at this raffle took home eleven prizes, including a billiard table, buggy, grand piano, and Turkish rifles. Total receipts of the St. Louis fair were $618,782.28. Expenses were $64,191.28, leaving $554,591 for the work of the Western Sanitary Commission.

Baltimore's fair for the benefit of the Sanitary and Christian Commissions was honored by the presence of President Lincoln at its opening, April 18, 1864. In a speech at the inauguration ceremonies, Lincoln commented on the change which had come over the city since Union troops were attacked there three years ago. He was impressed with the loyalty and devotion of the people of Maryland to the cause. Lincoln chose this time to make public his views on the alleged massacre at Fort Pillow. There had been grumbling that the government was not

---

4. The also-rans were McClellan, Butler, Grant, and Sherman, in that order. While it is difficult to explain Hancock's popularity, it is, perhaps, not so difficult to explain Grant's lack of it. Grant was having a great deal of trouble with Lee in Virginia. His recent losses at Cold Harbor (June 3) were enormous and were thought by many to have been unnecessary. McClellan, always popular in many areas, soon was to become the Democratic presidential candidate.

doing its duty in this affair, but when the facts were established, the President stated, the government would act if retribution was called for. The Maryland fair closed on April 30 and $40,234.54 was turned over to the central treasury of the Sanitary Commission.

Cleveland offered its Northern Ohio Sanitary Fair for the benefit of the local Soldiers' Aid Society, February 22–March 10, 1864. Fronting the impressive spectacle as honorary officers were the governor of Ohio, an ex-governor, the mayor of Cleveland, and some of Ohio's favorite sons—General James A. Garfield, Salmon P. Chase, and Benjamin F. Wade. The fair was housed in "buildings erected on the Public Square ... cover[ing] 64,000 square feet, [and] forming a Greek cross, the center rising in a rotunda and enclosing the Perry statue." The fair was a popular undertaking in Cleveland and throughout the state. A successful run of over two weeks netted $78,551.33. Of this, $50,000 was invested within a short time in United States securities.

Albany, New York, operated its Sanitary Fair from Washington's birthday through the 10th of March. It was called the Albany Army Relief Bazaar and focused its activities in the city's Academy Park. Here a large building was erected in the shape of a double cross, "the Eastern nave, about 200 feet in length, the Western one, 160 feet; the transepts, 205 feet; the width of nave and transepts, 60 feet; height of roof at eaves, 13 feet, and at apex, 28 feet." Fair operations were launched by a eulogistic speech from Governor Horatio Seymour and proved lucrative throughout the seventeen-day run. An unofficial report fixed the gross receipts at $111,493.49, expenses at $29,584.99, and net receipts at $81,908.50. The proceeds were tabbed for delivery to the central treasury.

Surprisingly enough, the Sanitary Fair in the nation's capital was a dismal failure. Publicity and support were feeble and proceeds scant, but $3,031.07 for the Sanitary Commission. Only two prefair notices were carried by the *Washington Evening Star*. One announced that a fair for the benefit of the Christian and Sanitary Commissions was to be held shortly in a building being erected on the corner of Pennsylvania Avenue and Seventh Street; the other announced the opening of the fair. Even the expected presence of President Lincoln, Vice-President Hannibal Hamlin, Schuyler Colfax, Salmon P. Chase, and other Washington notables was not realized. Only Senators Samuel C. Pomeroy, of Kansas, and Henry S. Lane, of Indiana, representing capital officialdom, spoke in behalf of the fair on opening night.

Information obtained by Bloor some time later from a wife of a member of Congress gave an insight into the failure of the fair. It mirrored also the attitude toward the Sanitary Commission held by some groups in the capital. The feeling among the latter was that the Commission had grown unlawfully beyond the limits of its jurisdiction and that a dangerous situation resulted when much money passed into the hands of these persons outside the government and not directly responsible to it. Consequently, before the Sanitary Fair had begun, all the prominent women withdrew, in favor of a Christian Commission Fair.

> carrying off the sources of supply, & the sympathy of the money-spending community; and abandoning it, thus deprived of the elements of success, to a handful of ladies of little social position.... During its continuance, where it was not ridiculed or contemned it was ignored by the "better classes."

Other fairs were held throughout the country.[5] Poughkeepsie raised $16,192.27, with Matthew Vassar playing a leading role in donating the use of a "spacious four-story building"; Kalamazoo, Michigan, $1,400; Irvington, New York, $1,717.39; Dubuque, Iowa, $90,000; Burlington, Iowa, $25,000; Taylorsville, California, $3,744.12; Chelsea, Massachusetts, $3,263.10; Carlisle, Pennsylvania, $1,000; New Castle and Damariscotta, Maine, $216.69; and Bridgeport, Connecticut, $200. In the financial report of the Sanitary Commission, the following fairs and results are recorded: Yonkers, New York, $12,000;[6] Flushing, Long Island, $3,934.32; Schuyler County, New York, $1,287.43; Warwick, Orange County, New York, $1,432.73; Hornellsville, New York, $800; South Adams, Massachusetts, $3,087.04; and Wheeling, Virginia, $2,500.[7]

From the fairs of which records are available, an approximate total of $4,392,980.92 was raised. This figure does not represent the amount of money turned over to the Sanitary Commission headquarters and to the national officers, nor was all of this money used for Commission work. In many cases, fairs which raised large cash sums turned over all of the money to the branches of the Commission sponsoring the fairs. In other instances, in case of joint operation with the Christian Commission or an aid society, proceeds were divided, with

---

5. The list given in this paper of cities and hamlets which sponsored Sanitary Fairs is not exhaustive. No doubt fairs were also held in other places, but because records and sources are not accessible, they were "born to blush unseen" except in their immediate localities.

6. About $2,000 was kept by the Yonkers Ladies Union Aid Society for its own use.

7. Net proceeds used when available. Cities in which fairs were held but for which no figures of success or failure are available are Dayton, Ohio(?); Elmira, N.Y.; and Springfield, Mass.

A fair, raising around $40,000, was held in Buffalo, February 23-March 2, 1864, but since it was sponsored by the Christian Commission and not the Sanitary Commission, its proceeds are not listed in the grand total above. The fair of the Western Sanitary Commission at St. Louis, however, is included. See the *Buffalo Morning Express*, February 23-March 3, 1864.

some of the money going into work other than that of the Sanitary Commission. This is not to imply that there were no benefits derived from such fairs by the national organization. But in such cases certain difficulties and misconceptions did arise. The total amount received by the central treasury from the Sanitary Fairs was $2,736,868.84.[8]

Though the Sanitary Fairs appeared to be fruitful and endless fountains of money, they were not without their disadvantages. In a letter to Henry Ward Beecher, President Bellows explained some of the difficulties the Commission was experiencing which were not generally known to the public. He stated that even with the fairs, the Commission was not much better off financially than it had been in earlier years. Women in many parts of the North were now engaged in making dolls and fancy things for the fairs. The sale of such articles would only raise money to buy supplies which the women had formerly made themselves; and with the depreciation of money, it would be a more expensive process to buy supplies than to have them homemade. Bellows also pointed out that in spite of the millions secured through the Sanitary Fairs, the Commission actually lacked sufficient money to keep its machinery functioning. Generally, the fairs sent money raised to the branch treasuries, who spent it for supplies. The supplies were forwarded to the central depots of the Commission, but the whole cost of distribution fell on the central treasury. "The more money the branches have," said Bellows, "the more supplies we have; and the more supplies we have, the more it costs to forward them, distribute and supply them to our vast army, scattered over our wide country."

These sentiments were echoed by J. Foster Jenkins, successor to Frederick Law Olmsted as general secretary, when he said in 1864:

> The fairs had arrested the flow of sanitary stores to such an extent that the receipts in kind had for some months been fifty per cent less than in the corresponding

---

8. *Commission Financial Report;* James Ford Rhodes, *History of the United States from the Compromise of 1850* (9 vols.; New York: The Macmillan Co., 1893-1922), V, 258. Rhodes uses only the round numbers, $2,736,000. Besides those fairs noted immediately above in the financial report, the following fairs contributed to the central treasury: Boston, $50,000 (out of $145,950.85); Brooklyn, $305,513.83 (out of $402,943.74); New York, $1,184,487.72 (all); Philadelphia, $1,035,398.96 (all); Baltimore, $40,234.54 (all?); Poughkeepsie, $16,192.97 (all); and Albany, $80,000 (out of $81,908.50). Fairs not contributing to the central treasury were those at Chicago, Cincinnati, Pittsburgh, St. Louis, Cleveland, Kalamazoo, Irvington, Dubuque, Burlington, Taylorsville (although here the proceeds may have been absorbed as part of the general donation from the state to the central treasury), Chelsea, Carlisle, New Castle and Damariscotta, Bridgeport, Dayton, Elmira, and Springfield.

period of 1863. Even if the commission had received all the money raised by the various fairs, it would still be straitened [*sic*] by the falling off in the supply of supplementary stores.

The Sanitary Fairs, taken as a whole, proved beneficial to the Commission both as publicity and as a source of supply in cash and kind. There were difficulties and drawbacks attending them—jealousies from within and hostility from without, the deviations which they caused in the regular and systematic efforts at supply—but these were overbalanced by the salutary results.

An analysis of the large body of source material on the fairs gives one the impression that they served to draw Northern cities together in a common goal—victory for the Union armies. Starting in the fall of 1863, when the tide had begun to turn militarily for the North, the fairs launched a tremendous wave of enthusiasm for "the cause"—pocketbooks, though pinched by two years of war, were opened again, arms folded in an attitude of peace without victory were unclasped to work for the soldiers. This nationwide surge of vitality and common trust did not slacken materially until Lee surrendered at Appomattox.

SOURCES

Albany Evening Journal, February 23, 1864.
Annals of Cleveland—1819-1935; A Digest and Index of the Newspaper Record of Events and Opinions in Two Hundred Volumes . . . Cleveland: 1936-1938, Vol. 47.
Baltimore American, April 19, 1864.
Chicago Daily Tribune, November 9, 1863; May 30, 1865.
Final Report of the Treasurer and Finance Committee of the Metropolitan Fair, in Aid of the United States Sanitary Commission, Held in New York, April, 1864. New York: 1864.
Final Report of the Western Sanitary Commission, from May 9th, 1864 to December 31st, 1865. St. Louis: R. P. Studley & Co., 1866.
Goodrich, Frank B. *The Tribute Book; A Record of the Munificence, Self-Sacrifice and Patriotism of the American People during the War for the Union*. New York: Derby & Miller, 1865.
Henshaw, Sarah Edwards. *Our Branch and Its Tributaries; Being a History of the Work of the Northwestern Sanitary Commission and Its Auxiliaries* . . . Chicago: A. L. Sewell, 1868.
History of the Brooklyn and Long Island Fair, February 22, 1864. Brooklyn, 1864.
History of the Great Western Sanitary Fair. Cincinnati: C. F. Vent & Co., 1864.
History of the North-Western Soldiers' Fair, Held in Chicago, the Last Week of October and the First Week of November . . . Chicago: Dunlop, Sewell & Spalding, 1864.
Hoge, Mrs. A. H. *The Boys in Blue; or Heroes of the Rank and File*. New York: E. B. Treat & Co., 1867.
Livermore, Mrs. Mary A. *My Story of the War: . . . Four Years Personal Experience . . . in the . . . Sanitary Service of the War*. Hartford: A. D. Worthington & Co., 1888.

Newberry, J. S. *The U.S. Sanitary Commission in the Valley of the Mississippi during the War of the Rebellion, 1861-1866; Final Report of Dr. J. S. Newberry* . . . Cleveland Fairbanks, Benedict & Co., 1871.

Presentation to Major-General John A. Dix, President of the Metropolitan Fair in Aid of the United States Sanitary Commission; New York, April 23, 1864. New York: 1864.

Randall, James G. *The Civil War and Reconstruction.* New York: D. C. Heath & Co., 1937.

A Record of the Metropolitan Fair in Aid of the United States Sanitary Commission, Held at New York, in April, 1864. New York: Hurd & Houghton, 1867.

Report of the Duchess County and Poughkeepsie Sanitary Fair Held at Sanitary Hall, in the City of Poughkeepsie, from March 15 to March 19, 1864. Poughkeepsie, 1864.

Report of the Ladies Relief Society, of Bridgeport, Conn., Commenced August 1, 1863, for the Aid of Sick and Wounded Soldiers Belonging to the Army of the United States; Completed Its Work July, 1865. Bridgeport, [1864?]

Rhodes, James Ford. *History of the United States from the Compromise of 1850.* 9 vols. New York: The Macmillan Co., 1893-1922. Vol. 5.

St. Andrews' Society, Memorial of the Great Sanitary Fair, Held in the City of Albany, New York . . . *February and March, 1864.* Albany, 1864.

St. Louis Daily Missouri Democrat, May 17, 18, 1864.

"The Sanitary Commission," (in) *The North American Review,* Vol. 98, 1864.

The Sanitary Commission of the United States Army: A Succinct Narrative of Its Work and Purposes. New York: 1864.

Statement of the Receipts and Disbursements of the United States Sanitary Commission, from June 27th, 1861, to May 14, 1878. (New York Public Library, Manuscript Division)

Stillé, Charles J. *Memorial of the Great Central Fair for the U.S. Sanitary Commission, Held at Philadelphia, June 1864.* Philadelphia: U.S. Sanitary Commission, 1864.

United States Sanitary Commission. *Archives.* New York Public Library, Manuscript Division, Box Nos. 571 Cu, 619, 639, 640, 641, 642, 812, 839, 840, 1001, 1003, 1004, 1017, 1019.

United States Sanitary Commission. *Bulletins.* New York: 1866. 3 vols.

United States Sanitary Commission. *The Sanitary Reporter, to Promote the Health, Comfort and Efficiency of our Army and Navy.* 2 vols. Louisville: 1863-1865.

The Visitor's Guide to the Great Central Fair, for the U.S. Sanitary Commission, Held in Logan Square, Philadelphia, June, 1864. Philadelphia. [1864.]

Washington Evening Star, January 13, 27, 1864.

The Impact of the Civil War on Philanthropy and Social Welfare

ROBERT H. BREMNER

> "Philanthropy, in its broadest sense, has always found its widest sphere of activity in war time."
> —Linus P. Brockett

Many authors who come late and ill-prepared to the study of the Civil War confess to having thought of it as something that happened between the first and second parts of the American history survey course. Of course, they had often heard the war described as the central drama of American history; but to many it seemed more like the half-time ceremonies of an athletic contest, an intermission during which the real teams temporarily surrendered the field to symbolic performers—bandsmen, drum majors, and pom-pom girls. The present writer, after having agreed to write a book about the impact of the Civil War on philanthropy and social welfare, came to live with the war and, not surprisingly, began to regard it, at least within the contexts here considered, as a link rather than a break in American social development.

As opposed to what Walt Whitman called the real war, the war of the combatants, attention here has been fastened on the response of the civilian population to the demands of war and on efforts to maintain and advance civilian welfare

Civil War History, Vol. XII No. 4 © 1966 by The Kent State University Press

during wartime. If not the "real war," these sideline skirmishes among noncombatants were part of the larger struggle. Because the larger struggle was a civil war, its impact on social welfare and reform in both the Union and the Confederacy must be considered. To say the least, that makes generalization difficult.

One generalization that can be made is that despite, or because of, sectional animosity, partisan rivalry, social tension, and religious and ethnic prejudice, the ten or twelve years just before the Civil War was a period of lively activity in humanitarian reform. In every section of the country states built or enlarged institutions for the insane, deaf, and blind. Public agencies and voluntary associations shared a concern for youth and often collaborated in providing for orphaned, homeless, or wayward children. The epidemics, disasters, and economic vicissitudes of the 1850's gave Americans frequent opportunities to display and develop their talent for organizing emergency relief campaigns. Meanwhile, the mission, tract, Bible, and Sunday school societies, plus a variety of reform organizations, developed systematic methods of tapping the benevolent resources of the country. These large-scale operations, combined with local, regional, and national disaster-relief programs, led to considerable refinements in the arts of fund raising. Practically every charitable fund-raising device later employed in the Civil War was already in use in the 1850's. Well before the war, however, Americans had grown accustomed to giving service as well as money to charitable work. Women took active, sometimes leading roles in prewar benevolent and civic enterprises. Thus, while the male-dominated Washington Monument Society floundered in discord, the Mount Vernon Ladies Association succeeded in purchasing Washington's home and tomb as a national shrine. Children, too, engaged in philanthropy, contributing pennies and dimes to such causes as the building of packet ships to serve mission stations in the South Seas.

It would be a mistake, however, to paint the prewar charitable scene in too rosy colors. The rancor and extremism, no less than the vigor and expansiveness of the times, left their marks on efforts to do good. The main problem was that while Americans of the 1850's lived in an age of high aspiration and rising expectation, they also lived, as their forefathers had lived, in an economy of scarcity. When almost any goal seemed attainable, good causes proliferated, some of a highly specialized nature—a nursery for children of wet-nurses, for example. Yet in the best of times the scant surplus available for philanthropic purposes was insufficient to meet all demands on public and private bounty. Competition among rival charitable, benevolent, and reform organizations was therefore intense. Some agencies regularly directed their appeals to sentiment, impulse, particularism, and prejudice. Countering them were other societies and reformers who, for a generation before 1860, had denounced "thoughtless liberality" and "careless relief," and attempted to make philanthropy an instrument of preventing rather than simply of alleviating need. The effect of the war on these contradictory tendencies in philanthropy is a subject full worthy of scholarly interest.

In December, 1860, the superintendent of the Eastern Kentucky Lunatic Asylum wrote Dorothea Dix: "States as well as individuals are feeling the pressure of the times, and if the 'irrepressible conflict' is to go on I fear that our means will be demanded for other than charitable purposes."[1] Throughout most of 1861 the superintendent's prediction seemed likely to be realized. The excitement of war and mobilization pushed civilian needs into the background. Construction of buildings and additions to state institutions authorized before 1861 continued, but after the outbreak of the war projects for new state schools, prisons, and asylums were set aside. Ohio, for example, defeated an appropriation for a new school for the deaf, and cut salaries of teachers and staff at the school for the blind by as much as 19 per cent.[2] Established private charities also suffered in the uncertain months just before and immediately after the start of the war. Receipts of the American Bible Society, ordinarily the best supported of the great benevolent societies, declined in 1860-1861 and fell lower in 1861-1862. In September, 1861, the American Board of Commissioners of Foreign Missions, anticipating a period of hard times, ordered expenditures in Near Eastern missions reduced by one-third.[3] The New York Children's Aid Society also experienced a drop in receipts in 1861 and, in consequence, had to discharge four of its six visitors and close several of its industrial schools.[4]

Once the shock of the first months of the war had passed, the people of the North, much to their surprise, entered a period of unprecedented prosperity. This was, it seems, the nation's first prolonged and fairly general experience

---

1. W. L. Chipley to Dorothea Dix, Dec. 19, 1860. Dix Papers, Houghton Library, quoted by permission of the Harvard College Library. This article was originally presented at the Dec., 1965, meeting of the American Historical Association in San Francisco. The author will treat the subject in greater detail in *Philanthropy and Social Welfare in the Civil War Era*, a volume in the "Impact Series," edited by Allan Nevins, to be published in 1967 by A. A. Knopf.

2. Blake McKelvey, *American Prisons* (Chicago, 1936), p. 32; Roger Morton, "The Impact of the Civil War on the Ohio Institutions for the Deaf and Blind, 1853-1877" (Seminar Paper, Ohio State University, 1963); Nancy Lee Smith, "The Impact of the Civil War on Philanthropic Work with the Mentally Ill" (Seminar Paper, Ohio State University, 1963).

3. *Fifty-fifth Annual Report of the American Bible Society* (New York, 1871), p. 148; Henry Harris Jessup, *Fifty-three Years in Syria* (Chicago, 1910), I, 304-305.

4. Children's Aid Society, *Ninth Annual Report* (New York, 1862), pp. 19-24.

with the phenomenon of war-induced prosperity. Wonderingly, and usually in tones of self-congratulation, northern newspapers and relief agencies described the condition of the population as singularly comfortable. "In the most gigantic civil war the world has yet seen," asserted the New York *Times*, "the people of the North were never better fed, sheltered, or clothed."[5] Charity agents in eastern cities reported that the war had not brought "the terrible calamities to our needy classes which might have been expected"; on the contrary, there had been less destitution and fewer cases of suffering from poverty than in times of peace.[6] High employment and moderate winters which permitted work during months when labor was ordinarily idle took many families out of the charity market. Bounties and public assistance financed by special state and county tax levies eased the hardships faced by families whose breadwinners entered military service. There remained, however, a residue of poor people—self-employed women, the aged, and the handicapped—who, because of rising living costs, were worse off in the affluent war years than in less prosperous times. As the war dragged on, war-widows and orphans, distressed families of servicemen, disabled veterans, loyal refugees from the South, and sufferers and survivors of wartime epidemics swelled the ranks of the needy.[7]

After 1862 civilian charitable societies in the North recorded large increases in contributions for their various activities. "Indeed," observed Charles Loring Brace, an experienced and aggressive almoner, "it seems easier for people to support charitable institutions now ... than before the war. They have learned to levy on their own pockets, to pay voluntary as well as involuntary taxes."[8] In the midst of domestic tribulations, northern workmen, merchants, and financiers found the means to send supplies valued at $350,000 to distressed textile workers in Lancashire.[9] Orphan homes, asylums for the aged and indigent, hospitals, and dispensaries were among the beneficiaries of blood-bought prosperity. Churches burdened with debt at the start of the war burned their mortgages in the course of it. Receipts of the major benevolent societies—usually an accurate barometer

---

5. *New York Times*, Mar. 1, 1864.

6. Children's Aid Society, *Tenth Annual Report* (New York, 1863), p. 4; New York Association for Improving the Condition of the Poor, *Twenty-first Annual Report* (New York, 1864), pp. 74–76. Lowell (Mass.) *Missionary Society, Nineteenth Annual Report* (Boston, 1864), p. 3; Boston Provident Association, *Twelfth Annual Report* (Boston, 1863), p. 9.

7. Lowell Missionary Society, *Twentieth Annual Report* (Boston, 1865), p. 5; Boston Provident Association, *Fourteenth Annual Report* (Boston, 1865), pp. 6–7; New York A.I.C.P., *Twenty-second Annual Report* (New York, 1865), p. 31.

8. Children's Aid Society, *Tenth Annual Report* (New York, 1863), p. 35.

9. *London Times*, Dec. 12, 1864.

of philanthropic pressure—rose to new highs in 1864 and 1865. Colleges and theological schools added a million and one half dollars to their endowments during the war, Yale alone garnering more than $400,000. Declared William E. Dodge, one of the most active and generous philanthropists of the period: "I say it is a most remarkable fact that we have not only sustained this war, but the institutions of this country as they never were sustained before."[10]

Northern public institutions, although benefiting less than private charities, shared in the largesse of war prosperity. In 1864 the Ohio legislature, reversing its action of 1861, appropriated funds for a costly new school for the deaf. State officials interpreted this action as proof that Ohio was not only first among her sisters in military efforts, but queen of the states in "designs and deeds of philanthropy."[11] Between 1861 and 1864 admissions to northern state hospitals for the insane either declined slightly or remained at prewar levels.[12] After 1863, however, expenditures of the state hospitals began to increase, partly as a result of higher operating costs and partly because of the introduction of amenities such as gas lights, bowling alleys, workshops, and chapels. As in prewar years some of these improvements were paid for out of gifts and legacies from private donors.[13] While the war was in progress New York set an example for other states by opening the first special institution for confinement of the criminal insane, and both New York and Massachusetts took steps toward founding asylums specifically for the chronically insane.[14] The latter move represented an advance over the customary practice of returning "incurables" to county poorhouses in order to make room in state hospitals for new and presumably "curable" patients.

Commitments of male offenders to state prisons fell off sharply during the war. According to one warden the reason was that in wartime the penalty for crime was "to enlist in the army and get a large bounty."[15] From the wardens'

---

10. William E. Dodge, *Influence of the War on Our National Prosperity* (New York, 1865), p. 24 *et seq*; see also Linus P. Brockett, *The Philanthropic Results of the War in America* (New York, 1863), pp. 26-27.

11. *Laying of the Cornerstone of the New Building for the Ohio Institution for the Education of the Deaf and Dumb, October 31, 1864* (Columbus, 1864), p. 7.

12. U.S. Census Office, *Tenth Census, 1880*, XXI (Washington, 1888), 166-167.

13. *Ibid*, 158-159. W. S. Chipley to Dorothea Dix, Apr. 29, 1863; Isaac Ray to Dorothea Dix, May 1863, Dix Papers, Houghton Library. "Reports of American Asylums," *American Journal of Insanity*, XVIII (1862), 103-104; XX (1864), 476; XXI (1864), 236.

14. "Reports of American Asylums," *ibid.*, XIX (1862), 102; XXII (1866), 521. H. H. Hunt, *The Institutional Care of the Insane in the United States and Canada* (Baltimore, 1910), II, 675-676.

15. Enoch C. Wines and Theodore W. Dwight, *Report on Prisons and Reformatories of the United States and Canada* (Albany, 1867), p. 312.

point of view the decline in prison population was unwelcome because prisons did not "pay" unless they furnished contractors with abundant and cheap convict labor. Consequently most northern prisons operated in the red during the war years.[16] In Massachusetts' state almshouse, and no doubt in numerous county poor farms, shortages of able-bodied male labor also interfered with efforts to make the institutions self-supporting.[17]

While the Union, quickly recovering from the commercial and industrial stagnation of 1860–1861, literally rejoiced in the philanthropic by-products of economic and military mobilization, the Confederacy, after an early spurt, sank into depression. Between 1862 and 1865 the people of the South experienced all the hardships and privations traditionally associated with war: devastation; depredations by invaders and defenders alike; ruinous inflation; and shortages of food, clothing, and medicine. Under the circumstances, maintaining public institutions such as asylums for the insane would seem to have been an impossible task. In some instances it apparently was impossible; in others, as in the venerable asylum at Williamsburg, Virginia, the fortunes of war brought the institution under the control and support of Union forces. Behind Confederate lines in the Southeast, however, the insane continued to be admitted to asylums. When legislative appropriations were inadequate, superintendents and trustees begged or borrowed funds to keep their institutions operating. Thus, at the State Hospital for the Insane in Columbia, South Carolina, the number of patients declined by only about one-fourth between 1862 and 1865, but the expense of operating the institution increased five-fold.[18] In February, 1865, when Sherman's army burned Columbia, the asylum escaped destruction and became a refuge for the homeless people of the city.[19] After the war its doughty superintendent boasted to Dorothea Dix that the hospital was the only public institution in South Carolina which survived the war.[20]

For the Confederacy, no less than for the Union, one of the first lessons of the war was the necessity of maintaining morale and a sense of well-being among the civilian population. In 1862 a Mississippian warned the governor of his state: "Another army besides that in the field must be supported—*the army at*

---

16. *Ibid.*, p. 267.

17. *The American Annual Cyclopedia and Register of Important Events of the Year 1863* (New York, 1864), III, 627.

18. U.S. Census Office, *Tenth Census, 1880*, XXI, 158–159, 172–173.

19. Hunt, *Institutional Case of the Insane*, III, 598–599.

20. Dr. F. W. Parker to Dorothea Dix, May 5, 1868, Dix Papers, Houghton Library.

home.... Their preservation and their comfort are as essential to our success as that of soldiers in the field."[21] To assist indigent families of servicemen several of the southern states adopted public relief programs which had no precedent in southern history and which, in comparison to available resources, dwarfed similar efforts in northern states. Beginning with laws which permitted counties to pass tax levies for needy families of soldiers, southern legislatures proceeded to appropriate state funds for relief; as the value of currency fell legislatures imposed taxes in kind, and finally, near the end of the war, they authorized requisition and impressment of supplies for relief of servicemen's families.[22] Probably no system of public assistance would have been adequate to meet the needs of a people as sore-stricken as those of the Confederacy. None of the methods employed eased the suffering of woe-and-war-begone women like those in North Carolina who cried: "We have not drawn nothing but want in three months and without help we must starv."[23] However unsatisfactory the results, the great expansion of activity in welfare on the part of southern state governments was certainly one of the major, and unexpected, consequences of the war.

During the Crimean War and the Franco-Austrian War of 1859 civilians had contributed to the relief of troops in camps, hospitals, and on battlefields. But the outpouring of goods, services, and money for the succor of Union and Confederate soldiers surpassed all previous endeavors in military relief. "No war in history," declared a contemporary observer, "was embellished by such matchless exhibitions of benevolence... as this. Never before were the people so immediately related to an army in the field, so intimately identified with its fortunes, or so profoundly solicitous for its comfort."[24]

Since neither the Union nor Confederate government was prepared for war, opportunities for voluntary efforts to supply fighting men with necessities and comforts were virtually unlimited. In both sections the early months of the war witnessed a "chaos of philanthropy" as local soldiers' aid societies multiplied and their members worked zealously but without plan or direction. Throughout the war most of the local societies, whether in North or South, wanted their contributions to go to men from their own communities or states. In the South

---

21. W. H. Hardy to Gov. John J. Pettus, Dec. 2, 1862, quoted in Charles Ramsdell, *Behind the Lines in the Southern Confederacy* (Baton Rouge, 1944), p. 30.
22. *Ibid.*, pp. 62–68, 82.
23. Francis B. Simpkins and James W. Patton, *The Women of the Confederacy* (Richmond, 1936), p. 126; Charles P. Roland, *The Confederacy* (Chicago, 1960), p. 153.
24. *Sanitary Commission Bulletin*, II (1864), 781.

military conditions and state rights sentiments precluded the formation of Confederacy-wide military relief organizations-, even state-wide co-operation among voluntary associations was exceptional, and where it developed, as in Georgia and South Carolina, the central agencies depended in large part on subsidies from the state treasury.[25] State-oriented and state-supported military relief operations—whatever their justification and occasional advantage—inevitably resulted in unequal treatment of men supposedly enlisted in a common cause.[26] Local, state, and regional particularism was probably as prevalent among civilians in the Union as in the Confederacy; but the North could afford the luxury of maintaining competing relief agencies. Moreover, the North developed organizations like the Sanitary and Christian Commissions which attempted, and in some measure succeeded, in directing the flow of patriotic philanthropy into national channels. The two great commissions, both voluntary associations organized on a Union-wide basis with regional branches and hundreds of local auxiliaries, approached the task of military relief from different angles. The Sanitary Commission was interested in saving lives, the Christian Commission in saving souls. The leaders of both organizations regarded the collection and distribution of supplemental relief supplies for the army as incidental to their principal objectives. The charitable public, however, remained more interested in getting material assistance to volunteers than in preventing disease or in promoting religion among troops. Relief, therefore, became an essential activity for each commission, not only as a form of service, but as a means of attracting and holding home-front supporters.[27]

From the standpoint of philanthropy, the war, especially in its later phases, involved a contest between the rival commissions for supplies, funds, and public recognition. Perhaps the most pertinent comment on such rivalries was William Greenleaf Eliot's observation: "The most hateful of all jealousies and controversies are those among philanthropic or charitable associations."[28] The

---

25. E. B. Coddington, "Soldiers' Relief in the Seaboard States of the Southern Confederacy," *Mississippi Valley Historical Review*, XXXVII (1950), 23-24.

26. Frank L. Owsley, *State Rights in the Confederacy* (Chicago, 1925), pp. 120, 126-127, contrasts the prosperous condition of North Carolina troops at the end of the war with the destitution of Lee's army.

27. Henry W. Bellows, "The U.S. Sanitary Commission," *Johnson's New Universal Cyclopaedia* (New York, 1877), IV, 73, 75-76; Mrs. Wm. E. Boardman, *Life and Labours of the Rev. W. E. Boardman* (New York, 1887), pp. 119-126; Lemuel Moss, *Annals of the United States Christian Commission* (Philadelphia, 1868), p. 651.

28. William Greenleaf Eliot, "Loyal Work in Missouri," *The North American Review*, XCVIII (1864), 529. Eliot was the founder of the Western Sanitary Commission, another rival of the U.S. Sanitary Commission.

contest would have little interest were it not that the two commissions represented different strains in the character of the northern people. Support for the rival commissions cut across class, denominational, and geographic lines. The Sanitary Commission, founded in the first months of the war, grew out of the determination of society women and the medical profession in New York City to put "system and order" into soldiers' aid work in the metropolis. Under the leadership of the Unitarian clergyman, Henry W. Bellows, and generally reflecting the views of the social and professional elite of the Eastern Seaboard—particularly of New York City—the Sanitary Commission built up a strong and enthusiastic following in the Midwest and derived its greatest financial contributions from California and other states and territories in the Far West. The Christian Commission, originating at a meeting of Y.M.C.A. workers in November, 1861, chose as its head George Hay Stuart, a Philadelphia dry goods merchant who was chairman of the central committee of the Y.M.C.A. The management of the Christian Commission resembled an interlocking directorate of Y.M.C.A.'s, Bible, tract, Sunday school, and temperance societies. The "Christians," as they called themselves, attracted powerful support among religious (Methodist and Episcopalian bishops), business (Jay Cooke and William E. Dodge), and political (Schuyler Colfax) leaders.[29] Its rank and file came from the pulpits and membership of orthodox Protestant churches. Like the Sanitary Commission, the Christian Commission had loyal adherents on the West Coast. Bellows reported in the summer of 1864 that in San Francisco "a Society of 300 women of all the evangelical sects . . . meet 3 times a week to gossip over the infidelity and wicked character of the U.S. Sanitary Commission, & to roll up their eyes over the holiness of the Christian Commission."[30]

Rivalry between the Christian and Sanitary Commissions might have been less intense had the agencies not differed so widely in ideology. The Christian Commission embraced the traditional views of charity as a religious obligation, alleviative in nature, and particularly sanctified when directed toward spiritual ends. The Sanitary Commission, adopting a more secular attitude, made prevention its watchword; suspicious of "spontaneous benevolence," it sought to discipline the nation's charitable impulses and turn them toward practical goals. While the "Christians" tended to see even such deeds as providing the thirsty with water as matters of prayerful self-congratulations, "Sanitarians" cautioned

---

29. Moss, *Annals of the Christian Commission*, pp. 216–217.
30. Henry W. Bellows to Standing Committee of the U.S. Sanitary Commission, June 22 and Aug. 11, 1864; Bellows to George T. Strong, June 30, 1864, Bellows Papers, Massachusetts Historical Society.

against "gratuitous superfluity" in gifts to soldiers—not out of parsimony but as a matter of principle—lest "'imprudent benefactions" create *"a system of alms-giving and alms-taking"* and dry up the springs of public assistance.³¹

Space does not permit cataloguing here the deeds of field agents of the two commissions. Their activities are well known and have been duly celebrated. Without intending to slight the useful work performed by the Christian Commission, by other agencies like the Western Sanitary Commission, and by mavericks like Clara Barton who operated independent of any commission, the opinion of the present writer is that the United States Sanitary Commission rendered the greatest service to the general cause of philanthropy. Much of the energy of Sanitary Commission leaders went into watchful, critical, perhaps officious surveillance of the conduct of the Medical Bureau and the Department of War. Resolutely refusing to assume functions properly belonging to the army, the commission acted as a goad to make the Medical Bureau accept and discharge the obligations the government owed to its fighting men. In preparing plans for pavilion hospitals, in temporarily operating sanitary hospitals, transports, and in developing an improved railway hospital car, the commission inaugurated and demonstrated useful services subsequently adopted by military authorities. Through these activities the Sanitary Commission clarified the role of modern philanthropy in peace as in war. The task of philanthropy, as Katharine Prescott Wormeley learned from her experience on hospital transports, was to *"lead the way."*³² Quartermaster General Montgomery C. Meigs, a friend of the Sanitary Commission and a champion of the army, accurately defined the commission's function as that of providing leaven for the government's "large lump of dough."³³

Any conflict as immense as the American Civil War was bound to have diverse results. At the start of the centennial observation Robert Penn Warren said the war

---

31. Attitudes of Christian Commission "Ambassadors for Jesus" can be seen in Moss, *Annals of the Christian Commission*, pp. 541-638, *passim*; George R. Crooks, *The Life of Bishop Matthew Simpson of the Methodist Episcopal Church* (Boston, 1891), p. 405; and in the daybooks of Christian Commission stations in the U.S. Christian Commission Papers, National Archives, Record Group 94. For attitudes of the Sanitary Commission see Bellows, "U.S. Sanitary Commission," *Johnson's New Universal Cyclopaedia*, IV, 75-76; Laura E. Richards (ed.), *Letters and Journal of Samuel Gridley Howe* (Boston, 1909), p. 498; and Elisha Harris, "The Sanitary Commission," *The North American Review*, XCVIII (1864), 178-179.

32. Katharine Prescott Wormeley, *The United States Sanitary Commission. A Sketch of Its Purposes and Its Work* (Boston, 1863), p. 92.

33. M. C. Meigs to Henry I. Bowditch, Oct. 30, 1862, in U.S. War Dept., *The War of the Rebellion: A Compilation of the Official Records of the Union and Confederate Armies* (Washington, 1880-1901), Ser. III, II, 702-703.

gave the South "the Great Alibi" and the North "the Treasury of Virtue."[34] The first student of the philanthropic results of the war, writing in the midst of the struggle, reported that war had aroused eagerness in all classes "to taste the luxury of doing good."[35] In civilian welfare, especially for families of servicemen, the war brought a temporary liberalization of poor-law practice both in the North and in the South, and a great increase in public assistance to the poor. Military relief by public and voluntary agencies was on such a scale and involved the participation of such a large portion of the civilian population that it confirmed and seemingly vindicated divergent attitudes and approaches to philanthropy. A southerner, transforming necessity into virtue, and with a characteristic mixture of sorrow and pride, could justify the parochialism of southern relief efforts by boasting:

> We had no Sanitary Commission in the South. . . . We were too poor; we had no line of rich and populous cities closely connected by rail, all combined in the good work of collecting and forwarding supplies and maintaining costly and thoroughly equipped charities. With us, every house was a hospital. . . . [36]

At a final meeting held in February, 1866, in the chamber of the House of Representatives, members of the Christian Commission looked backward with pride and forward with confidence:

> The Christian Commission [intoned Bishop Matthew Simpson] has led a noble life. It was baptized in prayer, worked amid suffering and affliction, leaned on the affection of the wise and pure, received aid from all classes, and ministered to multiplied thousands.[37]

Stretching before leaders and supporters of the commission were paths of usefulness in foreign and domestic missions, especially missions to Indian tribes, religious evangelism, vice crusades, and education of freedmen.

No fanfare marked the end of the Sanitary Commission's labors. For these workers the end of the war meant the start of new and the continuation of old campaigns for public health, reform of public charities, and a more systematic

---

34. Robert Penn Warren, *The Legacy of the Civil War: Meditations on the Centennial* (New York, 1961), p. 54.
35. Linus P. Brockett, *The Philanthropic Results of the War in America*, p. 14.
36. Alexander Hunter, *Johnny Reb and Billy Yank* (New York and Washington, 1905), p. 347.
37. Crooks, *Life of Bishop Matthew Simpson*, p. 404.

organization of private philanthropy. In later life veterans of the commission would remember their war experiences in much the same light as veterans of the armies. "This expedition, if it has done no other good, has made a body of life-long friends," wrote one to a companion in the service.

> We have a period to look back upon when we worked together under the deepest feelings, and to the extent of our powers, shoulder to shoulder, helping each other to the best of our ability... I can never look back to these months without feeling that God has been very good to let me share in them and see human nature under such aspects. It is sad to feel that it is all over.[38]

---

38. Katharine Prescott Wormeley, *The Other Side of War* (Boston, 1889), p. 205.

The Woman's National Loyal League
Feminist Abolitionists and the Civil War

WENDY F. HAMAND

In the summer of 1862, Ellen Wright penned a letter to her close friend Lucy McKim. Both of these young women were the daughters of well-known abolitionists and both would later marry sons of William Lloyd Garrison. Writing from her home in upstate New York, Ellen Wright expressed her disappointment at being unable to play an active role in what she regarded as the war to liberate the slaves. "Think how our boys are all going!" she wrote. "Is it not stifling, irksome work, to remain quietly at home."[1] Her letter demonstrated the exuberance and impatience of youth, but she also touched upon something more far-reaching. Many women felt a sense of frustration during the war. Fully aware of the importance of the conflict about antislavery and the future of democratic government, many longed to take a more active role in the war than the traditional female tasks of nursing, sewing, and bandage rolling.

---

1. Ellen Wright to Lucy McKim, Aug. 15, 1862, Garrison Family Papers, Smith College. Ellen Wright, daughter of Martha Wright and niece of Lucretia Mott, married William Lloyd Garrison, Jr., on Sept. 14, 1864. See Walter M. Merrill, ed., *The Letters of William Lloyd Garrison*, 6 vols. (Cambridge: Belknap Press, 1979), 5:190. Lucy McKim and Wendell Phillips Garrison were married Dec. 6, 1865. Several months before Ellen Wright penned the above letter, McKim had accompanied her father to Port Royal, S.C. Miller McKim was heading a relief effort to help the newly freed slaves there. A trained musician, she collected slave songs, some of which were published in 1862. *Slave Songs of the United States*, which she co-edited in 1867, became the standard book on slave music. Edward T. James et al., eds., *Notable American Women*, 3 vols. (Cambridge: Belknap Press, 1971), 2:23-24.

Civil War History, Vol. XXXV No. 1 © 1989 by The Kent State University Press

When the Emancipation Proclamation became law January 1, 1863, some abolitionist women rejoiced, but most were skeptical of the measure. Amy Post, a Rochester activist, summarized the views of many when she wrote that the proclamation was "more than I feared but much less than I hoped." Abolitionists also complained about the president's motives. "The ugly fact cannot be concealed from history," wrote the novelist and pamphleteer Lydia Maria Child, "that it was done reluctantly and stintedly . . . merely a war-measure."[2]

The proclamation failed to arouse wide public enthusiasm, which was another reason for abolitionist disillusion. Many had predicted optimistically that when emancipation became an official war aim, Northerners would embrace abolition and the war would end quickly. "The War does not seem to end, with the *1st* Jan.," Ellen Wright complained in a letter to her cousin. "How great has been the punishment which we must bear, for Slavery!"[3]

Many abolitionists concluded that the people must be inspired to send a clear message to Congress and the president demanding immediate emancipation for all slaves. Although women abolitionists had aided the cause early in the war through their speeches, fund-raising, and letter writing, their efforts had never been collectively organized. In the winter of 1863, two determined and energetic reformers, Elizabeth Cady Stanton and Susan B. Anthony, decided to form an organization of women united against slavery. Stanton, who had helped to launch the formal woman's rights movement at Seneca Falls in 1848, was an abolition crusader as well. Anthony had also engaged in a wide range of reform activities. Although both women had come to regard feminism as their first priority, Stanton insisted they must stop holding woman's rights conventions in order to concentrate on the issue of emancipation for the slaves.[4]

Together Stanton and Anthony founded the Woman's National Loyal League, which, they hoped, would collect a mammoth petition to Congress carrying one million signatures from every Union state. The petition would provide senators and congressmen with irrefutable proof that Americans favored the complete and immediate abolition of slavery.

---

2. Amy Post to Isaac Post, Jan. 13, 1863, Post Family Papers, Rochester University Library; Lydia Maria Child to Sarah Shaw, Oct. 30, 1862, in Milton Meltzer et al., eds., *Lydia Maria Child, Selected Letters 1817–1880* (Amherst: Univ. of Massachusetts Press, 1982), 419.

3. Ellen Wright to Laura Stratton, Jan. 7, 1863, Garrison Family Papers, Smith College.

4. Blanche Glassman Hersh, *The Slavery of Sex: Feminist Abolitionists in America* (Urbana: Univ. of Illinois Press, 1978), 95–99, 106–10; see also Elisabeth Griffith, *In Her Own Right: The Life of Elizabeth Cady Stanton* (New York: Oxford Univ. Press, 1984), 110.

Recruiting and organizing women for the league was a challenging proposition. In the decades before the war, women across the Northern states had participated widely in religious revivals, in Bible and tract societies, and in charity fund-raising on behalf of orphaned children and fallen women—even in temperance agitation. Only a very small number became active in antislavery or feminist societies.[5] When the war broke out, many women joined local soldier's aid groups, some of which were affiliated with the United States Sanitary Commission. But the Loyal League was not a benevolent society; it did not call upon women to knit socks, roll bandages, or make jams and jellies for the wounded soldiers. Instead the league was an organization dedicated to a radical principle—the abolition of slavery—and was based on the idea of female participation in the political sphere. Stanton and Anthony hoped to legitimize feminist activity in the political arena, and in so doing to further the goal of gender equality in the postwar period.

Stanton and Anthony had several precedents with which to work. Union Leagues were founded in many Northern cities in 1863. These male groups served as booster clubs for the Republican party and as pressure groups aimed at refuting Copperhead or peace sentiment. The existing network of antislavery societies, founded in the thirty years preceding the war, could be called upon for assistance in the petition drive. In at least one state, Connecticut, local female leagues had already been founded—at Hartford, Rockville, and East Winsor Hill. The president of Hartford's league was Isabella Beecher Hooker, half sister of Harriet Beecher Stowe. Several antislavery petitions signed by women had also been introduced into Congress by abolitionist senator Charles Sumner of Massachusetts. On April 16, 1862, he presented a petition, 700 feet long, signed by 15,200 women. In May, he introduced another petition signed by 8,000 women. Senator Edgar Cowan of Pennsylvania presented a similar document signed by members of the Fallowfield Monthly Meeting of Women Friends.[6]

Elizabeth Cady Stanton wrote an appeal "To the Women of the Republic"

---

5. See Keith E. Melder, *Beginnings of Sisterhood: The American Women's Rights Movement, 1800–1850* (New York: Schocken Books, 1977).

6. James M. McPherson, *The Struggle for Equality: Abolitionists and the Negro in the Civil War and Reconstruction* (Princeton: Princeton Univ. Press, 1972), 123. McPherson's book is the best single source on Civil War abolitionists. Because of the scope of this book, the treatment of women is limited. Elizabeth Cady Stanton, *Eighty Years and More: Reminiscences of Elizabeth Cady Stanton* (New York: European Publishing Co., 1898), 235–36; *Connecticut Courant*, 4, 11 April 1863; *Congressional Globe*, 37th Cong., 2d sess., 1862, 104, 2327: Among the records of the Senate Select Committee on Slavery and Freedmen are the aforementioned petitions. Records of the U.S. Senate, RG 46, 38th Cong., Petitions Referred to the Select Committee on Slavery and Freedmen, National Archives.

announcing the first Loyal League convention. It was printed in anti-slavery journals and in several other newspapers as well. Hoping to reach many more women than those already involved in antislavery societies, Stanton's goal was a massive, nationwide, democratic surge of support for abolition. Her argument was based on several premises. First she appealed to women's sense of patriotism. Confederate women, she said, "see and feel the horrors of the war; the foe is at their firesides; while we, in peace and plenty, live and move as heretofore." In addition, she invoked the doctrine of separate spheres. Nineteenth-century industrialization inaugurated an era of rising affluence and materialism, of smaller families and more leisure time for the middle class. Many social commentators believed that women, while "innately weaker" than men, were divinely gifted with the virtues of piety, purity, domesticity, and submissiveness. Arguing that women were traditionally the moral and religious teachers of the family, Stanton claimed that slavery was a moral issue and therefore it fell within women's rightful sphere to discuss it. She concluded by recalling another traditional argument, republican motherhood. Even in the era of the American revolution against British tyranny, she declared, republican mothers such as Abigail Adams voiced their opinions on the subject of freedom and liberty.[7]

The convention of the Woman's National Loyal League met on May 14, 1863 at Church of the Puritans in New York. Convention officers included Lucy Stone, a well-known feminist abolitionist, who presided; Elizabeth Cady Stanton, Angelina Grimké Weld, Fannie Willard, Mary Cabot, Mary White, Mrs. E. O. Sampson Hoyt, Eliza Farnham, and Mrs. H. C. Ingersol as vice presidents; Martha Wright and Lucy Colman as secretaries; and Susan Anthony, Ernestine Rose, Antoinette Brown Blackwell, Amy Post, and Annie Mumford who composed the business committee.[8]

---

7. *Liberator,* Apr. 17, May 1, 1863; *Independent,* Apr. 16, 1863; *National Anti-Slavery Standard* [hereafter *Standard*], Apr. 25, May 2, 1863; *New York Tribune,* Apr. 24, 1863; Elizabeth Cady Stanton et al., eds., *History of Woman Suffrage,* 3 vols. (Rochester: Charles Mann, 1889), 2:51-53. See also Barbara Welter, "The Cult of True Womanhood, 1820-1860," *American Quarterly* 18(Summer 1966): 151-74; Mary Beth Norton, *Liberty's Daughters: The Revolutionary Experience of American Women, 1750-1800* (Boston: Little, Brown, 1980); and Linda K. Kerber, *Women of the Republic: Intellect and Ideology in Revolutionary America* (Chapel Hill: Univ. of North Carolina Press, 1980).

8. Woman's National Loyal League [hereafter WNLL], *Proceedings of the Meeting of the Loyal Women of the Republic, Held in New York, May 14, 1863* (New York: Phair & Co., 1863), 4; *Standard,* May 23, 1863; Stanton, *History of Women Suffrage,* 2:53. The Woman's National Loyal League was occasionally referred to as the Woman's Loyal National League or the Loyal Women's National League. To avoid confusion I have adhered to the title Woman's National Loyal League throughout this article. Stanton and Anthony used this name in the *History of Woman Suffrage.*

Susan Anthony read a series of resolutions, including one which praised President Abraham Lincoln's Emancipation Proclamation while urging him to initiate a more comprehensive abolition decree. When Anthony also read a resolution demanding civil and political equality for all Americans regardless of sex or race, she shocked many of the delegates. This specifically feminist resolution passed only after heated debate and did not receive the unanimous vote accorded to all other resolutions.[9]

Mrs. E. O. Sampson Hoyt of Wisconsin spoke for those delegates who opposed the inclusion of woman's rights at the convention. Arguing that "Woman's Rights as an *ism* has not been received with entire favor by the women of the country," she claimed that thousands of Northern women would refuse to participate in league activities if feminism were associated with the organization. A majority of delegates disagreed, however, and applauded Ernestine Rose when she rebutted Hoyt. Rose, a Jewish immigrant from Poland, noted that "if it had not been for Woman's Rights, that lady would not have had the courage to stand here and say what she did."[10] Feminism would remain an integral part of the Woman's National Loyal League.

Stanton's "Address to President Lincoln" was presented to the convention for its approval. The address was supportive in tone. "We come not to criticise or complain ... We come to strengthen you with earnest words of sympathy and encouragement." At no point in the nation's history was the time more propitious for rectifying the one mistake made by the founding fathers. After approving the Address to President Lincoln and providing for a permanent league office in the Cooper Institute, the convention adjourned.[11]

Following the May meeting, Stanton and Anthony began the arduous task of organizing the league. Although Lucy Stone had presided at the convention, Stanton was elected president of the organization, while Anthony devoted her energies to the position of secretary. Anyone who contributed one dollar or more could become a voting member; any contribution at all made one an honorary member. League members often wore a breast pin, which depicted a slave breaking his chains and bore the league motto, "In Emancipation is national unity."[12]

9. WNLL, Proceedings, 15; Stanton, *History of Woman Suffrage*, 2:57; *Liberator*, May 29, 1863; *Standard*, May 23, 1863; *New York Tribune*, May 16, 1863.

10. WNLL, *Proceedings*, 20–21, 27.

11. Ibid., 32–35, 53–54. The published *Proceedings* of the convention included more than thirty pages of reprinted letters from Northern women who supported the league but who could not attend the convention. Stanton, *History of Woman Suffrage*, 2:67–69, 73–78; *Standard*, May 30, 1863.

12. Elizabeth Cady Stanton to Elizabeth Smith Miller, Sept. 1, 1863, in Theodore Stanton and

Stanton and Anthony were assisted in their organizational efforts by several prominent women. Angelina Grimké Weld emerged from semi-retirement to help the league. A Southerner who renounced slavery after converting to the Quaker faith, Weld and her sister Sarah Grimké became the first professional women abolitionists when they gave lectures throughout New England in the 1830s. Other women such as Lucy Stone and Amelia Bloomer also decided to participate. Stone, one of the most popular prewar lecturers had, like Weld, retired from public work when marriage and motherhood made demands upon her time. Amelia Bloomer, who had once edited a reform newspaper called *The Lily*, moved west in the 1850s, but sent a letter in support of the league from her Council Bluffs, Iowa, home.[13]

Although leadership of the Loyal League was always female, the membership voted on June 11, 1863 to allow male signatures on the petition. Male and female signatures were tabulated separately to encourage a friendly gender rivalry and the states were encouraged to compete for signatures as well. Soon, every state in the North had an organized movement for the collection of petition signatures. The original Woman's National Loyal League petition simply requested that Congress pass an act "emancipating all persons of African descent held to involuntary service or labor in the United States." When Garrisonian abolitionists of the American Anti-Slavery Society began to insist on a constitutional amendment freeing the slaves, Stanton and Anthony decided to follow. In 1864 league members added to their petitions the specific demand for a constitutional amendment.[14]

Black women and men were eligible for membership in the Loyal League, but there is no evidence that large numbers of them joined, nor is there evidence that Stanton and Anthony actively recruited black members or officers.

Harriot Stanton Blatch, *Elizabeth Cady Stanton As Revealed in Her Letters, Diary and Reminiscences*, 2 vols. (New York: Harper and Brothers, 1922), 2:95-96; Susan B. Anthony to Mrs. Drake, Sept. 18, 1863, Anthony Collection, Vassar College.

13. Katherine Du Pre Lumpkin, *The Emancipation of Angelina Grimké* (Chapel Hill: Univ. of North Carolina Press, 1974), 216. During the war, Weld composed "A Declaration of War on Slavery," reported to be "one of the most powerful things she ever wrote." Sadly, it is no longer extant. Gerda Urner, *The Grimké Sisters From South Carolina: Pioneers for Woman's Rights and Abolition* (New York: Schocken Books, 1975), 355; Elinor Rice Hays, *Morning Star: A Biography of Lucy Stone 1818-1893* (New York: Harcourt, Brace and World, 1961), 177-78; Stanton, *History of Woman Suffrage*, 2:886.

14. Records of the United States Senate, RG 46, 38th Cong., Petitions Referred to the Select Committee on Slavery and Freedmen, NA; *Liberator*, 2, 16 Oct. 2, 16, Nov. 6, 1863; *Standard*, June 20, 1863; WNLL form letter in Anthony's hand, June 20, 1863, Anthony Collection, Library of Congress; Stanton, *History of Woman Suffrage*, 2:50; McPherson, *The Struggle for Equality*, 125-26. See also American Anti-Slavery Society, *Proceedings of the American Anti-Slavery Society at its Third Decade* (New York: American Anti-Slavery Society, 1864; reprint, New York: Arno Press and the New York Times, 1969).

Frederick Douglass, the runaway slave, abolitionist, and newspaper editor, did give lectures on behalf of the league, but on balance, black participation in this essentially white, middle-class organization appears to have been minimal.

Stanton and Anthony worked well as a team. Anthony acted as the league's chief strategist, organizer, and promoter. In September 1863, she wrote confidently to a friend that "we, the League, are *alive* and planning a most vigorous prosecution of *our war* of *ideas*—not bullets & bayonets." When one male league member sent her a completed set of petitions containing more than two hundred names, Anthony congratulated the gentleman while admonishing him that "it will not do for the friends of freedom to slacken in any of their efforts." Ellen Wright, who had complained about women's limited role in the war to her friend Lucy McKim, was also drawn into league activities by Susan Anthony. "Women as well as men must take up their packs & wander & work for their country," she wrote to her mother on May 21, 1863. Ellen Wright's mother was also put to work, after Susan Anthony sent her "half an acre of petitions" in June 1863.[15] Anthony also asked that each petition collector obtain contributions of a penny or more from each signer of the petition. The *National Anti-Slavery Standard* occasionally printed lists of these contributions, which totaled about three thousand dollars. These lists give an indication of the breadth of the league's appeal. Scores of Americans from all across the Northern states contributed money and signed the petitions. Although contributions acknowledged by the *Standard* ranged from twenty-five cents to one hundred dollars, most contributors gave fewer than two dollars each. The small size of these contributions and the broad geographical range of the communities would seem to indicate that Stanton and Anthony were succeeding in their plan to establish a broad-based organization.[16]

Susan Anthony appealed to the male leadership of the American Anti-Slavery Society for help in fund-raising. William Lloyd Garrison and Wendell Phillips encouraged the women's group with a donation of money from the Hovey Fund, an abolitionist charity. Charles Sumner, one of abolition's most persuasive spokesmen in Congress, allowed league members the use of his franking privilege in sending out petitions. Henry Ward Beecher collected two hundred

---

15. Susan B. Anthony to Samuel May, Sept. 21, 1863, Anthony to "my dear Friend," July 1, 1863, Anthony to Edmund G. Galen, Dec. 14, 1863, Anthony Collection, Vassar College; Ellen Wright to Martha Wright, May 21, 1863, Martha Wright to Ellen Wright, June 22, 1863, Garrison Family Papers, Smith College.

16. Alma Lutz, *Created Equal: A Biography of Elizabeth Cady Stanton 1815–1902* (New York: John Day Co., 1940), 127; *Standard*, Sept. 19, Oct. 10, Nov. 21, 1863.

dollars from his parishioners at Plymouth Church in Brooklyn. Ticknor and Fields, the Boston publishers of Harriet Beecher Stowe and others, agreed to allow a league contribution box in their offices.[17]

Elizabeth Cady Stanton was the Loyal League's philosopher and orator as well as its president. In her speeches and newspaper articles she emphasized several themes. First, she wanted to refute those who argued that the Emancipation Proclamation effectively ended the slavery question. Second, she believed that the Slave Power had too long dominated the American government by corrupting the political parties, by threatening churches and schools as well. The war was a democratic struggle which must culminate in the destruction of the Slave Power.[18]

Angelina Grimké Weld used similar logic in writing an address to the "Soldiers of our Second Revolution." In the present conflict, Weld argued, black men were the immediate victims, but workingmen of every color were also threatened by the Southern slavocracy. "The nation is in a death-struggle. It must either become one vast slavocracy of petty tyrants, or wholly the land of the free." The Civil War was not a war of races, as the South contended. Instead, it was a conflict of principles, a struggle in which all who favored freedom of speech, freedom of suffrage, freedom to work, and freedom of education "are driven to do battle in defense of these or to fall with them, victims of the same violence that for two centuries has held the black man a prisoner of war." Finally, Stanton, Weld, and others argued that America's republican experiment was clearly threatened. With European nations eagerly following the Civil War and "plotting our downfall," patriotic Americans must fight to preserve America's republican institutions.[19]

In an effort to educate the American public on the subject of slavery, New York league members organized a lecture series in the fall of 1863. At the first such meeting, Henry Bellows, head of the Sanitary Commission, addressed the group at Cooper Institute. Horace Greeley also delivered a brief address, as did

---

17. *Liberator*, July 10, 31, 1863, Apr. 1, 1864; Susan B. Anthony to Elizabeth Cady Stanton, Oct. 10, 1863, Stanton Collection, Library of Congress; Lydia Mott to Amy Post, Oct. 25, 1863, Post Family Papers, Rochester University Library; McPherson, *Struggle for Equality*, 125; Elizabeth Cady Stanton to Fanny and Frank Garrison, May 25, 1863, Stanton Collection, Boston Public Library; Susan B. Anthony to Samuel May, July 1, 1863, Anthony Collection, Vassar College; *Standard*, Dec. 12, 1863; *Independent*, Aug. 6, 1863, Apr. 7, 1864.

18. Elizabeth Cady Stanton, "What Can Women Do for the War?" (New York, 1861-1864); "Address Before the Woman's Loyal League," 1863, Stanton Collection, Library of Congress.

19. WNLL, *Proceedings*, 51-53; *Liberator*, Oct. 2, 1863; *Chicago Tribune*, May 30, 1863; Lumpkin, *The Emancipation of Angelina Grimké*, 217-19; Elizabeth Cady Stanton, "The Future of the Republic" (1861-1865?), Stanton Collection, Library of Congress.

Frances D. Gage, who had begun to work with freedmen in South Carolina. Congressman William D. Kelley of Philadelphia spoke to the league November 21; Frederick Douglass, Theodore Weld, Anna Dickinson, and Wendell Phillips each addressed the league in the ensuing months.[20]

The abolitionist press encouraged the Loyal League by giving favorable coverage to its petitioning activities and public lectures. The *Liberator,* the *National Anti-Slavery Standard,* and the *Independent* published detailed articles about the league. The *Commonwealth,* edited by the well-known abolitionist minister Moncure Conway, offered these words of encouragement in October 1863: "God speed these patriotic women in their labor of love."[21]

Even when, as in New York, attendance at league meetings fluctuated greatly, the general press accorded the women considerable coverage. The *New York World* was always critical, accusing league members of behaving in an unwomanly fashion. The *World* wrote that women, who were traditionally the moral teachers of the family, should not stoop to the level of advocating emancipation by force. The *World* had labeled the league's founding convention "a genuine 'witches Sabbath,'" while the *New York Herald* complained that league members had "mixed up the questions of anti-slavery and woman's rights." The *Springfield* (Massachusetts) *Republican* questioned the constitutionality of the league petitions and the femininity of the women who spread them. "All the maiden philanthropists, of whatever age or sex, may find all the employment they need in ... works of charity and mercy," one reporter wrote. "But they should also be told, if they do not already know it, that by asking the government to violate the Constitution in order to manifest a sacred animosity to slavery, they are really doing injury to the cause of the Union."[22]

The *New York Times* and *Tribune* reported news of league activities in a more sympathetic manner. Horace Greeley's *Tribune* applauded the Loyal League for "undertaking to do what never has been done in the world before, to obtain one million of names to a petition." At the same time, the *Tribune*'s editor may have been slightly nervous about Stanton and Anthony's tendency to interject feminism

20. *Standard,* Nov. 21, 1863, Jan. 9, 16, Feb. 13, 1864; *New York World,* Nov. 21, 1863; *New York Times,* Nov. 22, 1863; *New York Tribune,* Nov. 19, 21, 1863; Ida H. Harper, *Life and Work of Susan B. Anthony,* 2 vols. (Indianapolis: Bowen-Merrill, 1899), 1:232-33; Ellen Wright to William Lloyd Garrison, Jr., Apr. 29, 1863, Garrison Family Papers, Smith College.

21. Frank Luther Mott, *A History of American Magazines,* 4 vols. (Cambridge: Harvard Univ. Press, 1938), 2:536; *Liberator,* Oct. 16, 1863; *Independent,* Apr. 7, 1864.

22. *New York World,* May 15, 16, July 25, 1863; *New York Herald,* May 15, 16, 1863; *Springfield* (Mass.) *Republican,* n.d., reprinted *Standard,* Jan. 2, 1864, and *Liberator,* Jan. 8, 1864.

into the league, for the newspaper offered this cautious praise in one article. "The Women of the Loyal League have shown great practical wisdom in restricting their efforts to one object." After recording, in April 1864, that the league had fifteen thousand petition forms in circulation, Greeley's newspaper strongly urged its readers to sign and return the documents without delay.[23]

The tenor of these newspaper comments—support for the league's antislavery stance but uneasiness with its feminism—reflected the unique character of the league. Woman's rights and abolitionism were inseparable. In the winter of 1863 Stanton, recalling the appeals of prewar feminists and abolitionists, urged women to join the league's petition drive because the right to petition was the only political right given to women under the Constitution.

While praising women for their work on behalf of the Sanitary and Freedmen's organizations, Stanton continually urged her readers not to restrict their activities to women's traditional role in benevolent societies. "Let it not be said that the women of the Republic, absorbed in ministering to the outward alone, saw not the philosophy of the revolution through which they passed; understood not the moral struggle that convulsed the nation—the irrepressible conflict between liberty and slavery," she wrote in February 1864. "Remember the angels of mercy and justice are twin sisters, and ever walk hand in hand." Stanton was clearly looking forward to the resumption of overtly feminist agitation after the war when she wrote, "by our earnestness and zeal in the exercise of this one right, let us prove ourselves worthy to make larger demands in the readjustment of the new government."[24] Just as the newly arrived freedmen living in Washington's refugee camps were demonstrating their ability to live quietly and respectably, just as black men were proving their manliness and courage by volunteering for duty in the Union army, so women could prove their readiness for enfranchisement by patriotically supporting the war effort, by becoming informed on political questions, and by exercising their political right of petition on behalf of the slave.

Though Stanton and Anthony made a concerted effort to appeal to women on terms they would find acceptable, the feminist bias of the league was undeniable and it probably hampered recruitment. Whether Stanton liked it or not, American women were more interested in tending sick soldiers and singing patriotic anthems than they were in participating in an organization devoted to

---

23. Stanton, *History of Woman Suffrage*, 2:50–51; Susan B. Anthony to William Lloyd Garrison [1863 or 1864], Anthony Collection, Vassar College; *New York Tribune*, Apr. 13, 1864. See also *New York Times*, May 24, 1863.

24. *Standard*, Dec. 26, 1863, Jan. 9, Feb. 27, 1864.

emancipating slaves and women. Although several hundred thousand women would sign the petitions, only five thousand would join the organization.

The women's periodical press provides a case in point. During the war, women's magazines had a combined circulation of approximately 250,000. Although women's magazines did not ignore the war, many urged women to participate in nursing and other charitable activities, while suggesting they avoid reckless extravagance in dress. Only a few of the more religious and reform oriented journals, those with rather limited circulation, went so far as to urge the abolition of slavery.[25] Women's magazines apparently found the Loyal League's platform too radical, for no journal endorsed or even mentioned the activities of the Woman's National Loyal League.

Although league headquarters was in New York, western abolitionists participated in numerous activities. Hannah Tracy Cutler, whose first husband died after being attacked by a proslavery mob, lectured throughout Illinois in 1862. The following year, she became a paid agent of the league. Josephine Griffing of Ohio, another agent, embarked on an extensive tour of Michigan and Illinois in August 1863, lecturing for the league and working for freedmen's relief. She was later appointed General Agent of the National Freedman's Relief Association in Washington, distributing food and opening schools where black women received vocational training. These efforts helped to inspire formation of the Freedman's Bureau in 1865.[26]

Illinois proved to be fertile ground for the Loyal League. The *Galesburg Free Democrat* urged its readers to sign the league's "mammoth petition." In Chicago, every Methodist minister in the city pledged to preach a sermon on the duty of Congress to pass an antislavery amendment and to circulate the Loyal League petitions. When Frederick Douglass gave a benefit lecture for the league in Chicago, the *Tribune* reported that "Bryan Hall was crowded with a large and appreciative audience." Douglass reiterated the abolitionist plea that the antislavery fight was far from over and he argued persuasively in favor of granting the vote to black men.[27]

---

25. Kathleen L. Endres, "The Women's Press in the Civil War: A Portrait of Patriotism, Propaganda, and Prodding," *Civil War History* 30(Mar. 1984):31–53.

26. *Liberator*, May 23, 30, June 13, July 4, 1862; *Standard*, Aug. 8, 1863; Autobiography of Hannah Tracy Cutler in *Woman's Journal*, Sept. 19, 26, Oct. 3, 10, 1896. In 1869, at the age of fifty-three, Hannah Tracy Cutler received her M.D. degree from Women's Medical College in Cleveland, Ohio. She was active in the crusade for woman suffrage after the war. James, *Notable American Women*, 1:426–27; Jeriah Bonham, *Fifty Years Recollections* (Peoria, Ill.: J. W. Franks and Sons, 1883), 22–47; Stanton, *History of Woman Suffrage*, 2:26–39.

27. *Liberator*, Oct. 16, 1863; *Standard*, Nov. 28, 1863; *Chicago Tribune*, Feb. 11, 26, 1864.

By 1864 the Woman's National Loyal League was ready to present its first installment of petitions to Congress. One hundred thousand signatures had been collected on six thousand petition forms. Glued end-to-end and rolled into bundles, the petitions were mailed in a trunk to Senator Charles Sumner. "These signatures represent, mothers wives sisters & daughters of honest men who have fought and died for our country," Stanton and Anthony said. "Through you they now ask that the cause be made worthy [of] their terrible sacrifice." Furthermore, the women emphasized that since "the 'Right of Petition' is woman's only political right under our government, it is the sacred duty of her representatives to give this petition earnest careful consideration."[28]

On February 9, 1864, two tall, stalwart black men entered the Senate chamber and carried the first installment of league petitions to the desk of Charles Sumner (see table 1). The senior senator from Massachusetts arose to address his colleagues. "This petition is signed by one hundred thousand men and women," he declared, "who unite in this unparalleled number to support its prayer.... They are from the families of the educated and uneducated, rich and poor.... Here they are," he said, "a mighty army, one hundred thousand strong, without arms or banners, the advance guard of a yet larger army." At the conclusion of his speech, which became known as the "Prayer of One Hundred Thousand," Sumner asked that the petition be referred to his Select Committee on Slavery and Freedmen. This committee was created at Sumner's request in January 1864. Sumner expected a plethora of petitions in the new year, notably those of the Loyal League, and he wanted a format from which to advertise them. "I hope very soon to report... an amendment of the Constitution abolishing slavery throughout the U. States," he wrote confidently to the Duchess of Argyll the day before introducing the league petitions.[29] New York and Illinois vied for the most signatures. As late as January 29, the president's home state was in the lead, but New York eventually surpassed it. The *Chicago Tribune* reflected this state rivalry in its story on the petition totals. The *Tribune* printed Illinois' total first, burying New York's higher total in the middle of the column.[30]

---

28. WNLL to Charles Sumner, Feb. 4, 1864, Sumner Collection, Houghton Library, Harvard University. This letter, expressing the sentiments of Elizabeth Cady Stanton and Susan B. Anthony, was written by Charlotte Wilbour, corresponding secretary of the league.

29. *Congressional Globe*, 38th Cong., 1st sess., 1864, 536; *Liberator*, Apr. 1, 1864; *Independent*, Feb. 18, 1864; *New York Tribune*, Feb. 10, 1864; *New York Herald*, Feb. 10, 1864; *Philadelphia Daily News*, Feb. 10, 1864; Stanton, *History of Woman Suffrage*, 2:78–80; Charles Sumner to the Duchess of Argyll, Feb. 8, 1864, quoted in David Donald, *Charles Sumner and the Rights of Man* (New York: Alfred A. Knopf, 1970), 148–49.

30. *Congressional Globe*, 38th Cong., 1st sess., 1864, 536; Stanton, *History of Woman Suffrage*, 2:79;

Table 1
Petition Totals by State

State	Men	Women	Total
New York	6,519	11,187	17,706
Illinois	6,382	8,998	15,380
Massachusetts	4,249	7,392	11,641
Pennsylvania	2,259	6,366	8,625
Ohio	3,676	4,654	8,330
Michigan	1,741	4,441	6,182
Iowa	2,025	4,014	6,039
Maine	1,225	4,362	5,587
Wisconsin	1,639	2,391	4,030
Indiana	1,075	2,591	3,666
New Hampshire	393	2,261	2,654
New Jersey	824	1,709	2,533
Rhode Island	827	1,451	2,278
Vermont	375	1,183	1,558
Connecticut	393	1,162	1,555
Minnesota	396	1,094	1,490
West Virginia	82	100	182
Maryland	115	50	165
Kansas	84	74	158
Delaware	67	70	137
Nebraska	13	20	33
Kentucky	21	—	21
Louisiana (New Orleans)	—	14	14
U.S. Citizens living in New Brunswick	19	17	36

The degree of Loyal League organization in the individual states varied greatly. New York, which produced the greatest number of signatures, included strong efforts in New York City and in Rochester, where Amy Post mobilized the local Ladies Anti-Slavery Association. Because organization in Illinois was good, that state produced a high proportion of signatures despite its relatively small population. The Philadelphia Female Anti-Slavery Society, led by Sarah Pugh and Abby Kimber, enthusiastically embraced the league petition campaign, and their efforts produced several thousand signatures. Sometimes individual efforts were successful. Tiny New Hampshire had no formal league organization but

Liberator, Jan. 29, 1864; *Chicago Tribune*, Feb. 15, 1864. Sumner may have rounded his numbers. *The New York Times*, Feb. 10, 1864, reported the total as 100,698.

two Concord women initiated a petition drive that contributed more than 2,500 signatures. One widow from rural Wisconsin, whose husband and two sons died in the war, collected 1,800 signatures and also recorded names of those who refused to sign, so that "they may be handed over to the future scorn they so well deserve."[31] More than forty thousand signatures came from the states of the Old Northwest, indicating that the league had been successful in spreading an essentially eastern organization into the western states. Of the total signers, roughly two-thirds were female. Despite the invaluable help that Stanton and Anthony received from men, their organization remained a female operation.

After the initial introduction of petitions in February, league members stepped up their abolition campaign. In a letter to Sumner commenting on his "most excellent" speech, Susan Anthony expressed her gratitude to New York printers for donating both paper and services free of charge. Their generosity enabled her to mail twenty-five thousand petitions to league members around the country, accompanied by a broadside proclaiming the *"Constitutional right of the Government,"* as well as the *"moral duty of the people,* to abolish slavery."[32]

The anniversary meeting of the Woman's National Loyal League convened in New York on May 12, 1864. The league could boast a successful year. With a national membership of five thousand, the league's two thousand active petition collectors had rolled up 265,314 names on twenty thousand petitions during the past year. In the aftermath of Sumner's speech, members had doubled their petition totals. They had also printed numerous copies of Sumner's "Prayer of One Hundred Thousand" address for distribution across the country. League-sponsored lectures helped to educate the people about the importance of immediate emancipation.[33]

At the first league convention in 1863, Stanton and Anthony had adopted a conciliatory attitude toward President Lincoln. By May 1864, both women had joined other radical abolitionists in supporting the presidential bid of Republican maverick and abolitionist general John C. Frémont. Perhaps bowing to pressure from league members who supported Lincoln's reelection, Stanton and

---

31. Nancy A. Hewitt, *Women's Activism and Social Change: Rochester, New York 1822–1872* (Ithaca: Cornell Univ. Press, 1984), 196–97; Philadelphia Female Anti-Slavery Society Minute Books for Sept. 10, Oct. 8, Nov. 12, Dec. 10, 1863, and Feb. 11, 1864, include brief references to league petitioning activities. Pennsylvania Abolition Society Collection, Historical Society of Pennsylvania. Concord (N.H.) *Independent Democrat,* n.d., reprinted *Standard,* Jan. 9, 1864; *Standard,* Dec. 26, 1863.

32. Susan B. Anthony to Charles Sumner, Mar. 1, 1864, Sumner Collection, Houghton Library, Harvard University; published broadside, "Office of the Women's Loyal National League, Room No. 20, Cooper Institute, New York, March 12, 1864," signed by Susan B. Anthony, Cornell University Library.

33. Stanton, *History of Woman Suffrage,* 2:80–83.

Anthony did not turn the second league convention into a platform from which to promote Frémont's candidacy. They made little attempt to hide their antipathy for President Lincoln, however, as resolution after resolution which passed the convention condemned the administration. The league stated emphatically that the United States government "*still* upholds slavery by military as well as civil power." They demanded for black soldiers, sailors, and laborers pay equal to their white counterparts and the right of suffrage as well.[34]

The feminist tone of the anniversary meeting was far stronger than that of the first convention. In circulating petitions, league members had complained that women occasionally refused to sign because they believed that slavery and other weighty matters should be debated only by Congress. Stanton and Anthony worked hard to dispel the notion of deference toward elected officials, a belief strong among women. They argued that the national crisis called for a new type of woman, one who would continue to aid the Sanitary and Freedmen's organizations but one who would also be an active participant in the "broader, deeper, higher range of thought and action than has yet been realized." By lifting politics into the "sphere of morals and religion . . . it is the duty of women to be co-workers [with men] . . . in giving immortal life to the new nation." Stanton and Anthony argued in favor of the concept of gender equality and also addressed the specific issue of pay equity. They demanded that female nurses, at least those who had received formal medical training, should be paid on the same scale as male medical personnel.[35]

On April 8, 1864, the Senate passed the Thirteenth Amendment abolishing slavery. Immediately, the Woman's National Loyal League had sent out an additional fifteen thousand petition forms to be returned directly to the Senate Select Committee on Slavery and Freedmen.[36] In this manner they hoped to build on the momentum created by the Senate's action. Their strategy did not produce the desired effect, for, month after month, the House failed to approve the antislavery amendment.

---

34. Ibid., 2:85. Although Stanton and Anthony did not endorse Frémont's candidacy at the May 12 meeting, they did help to organize the first "Freedom and Frémont" club which opened for business in the Cooper Institute offices of the WNLL. See Elizabeth Cady Stanton to Susan B. Anthony, Aug. 22, 1864, in Stanton and Blatch, *Elizabeth Cady Stanton,* 2:100.

35. Stanton, *History of Woman Suffrage,* 2:82–87; WNLL broadside advertising the anniversary meeting, May 12, 1864, Anna Dickinson Collection, Library of Congress; *New York Herald,* May 13, 1864; *New York Tribune,* May 12–13, 1864; see also *Standard,* May 28, 1864; *Independent,* May 19, 1864.

36. *Liberator,* Apr. 22, 1864; *Standard,* June 4, 1864. Lyman Trumbull and the Judiciary Committee drafted the Thirteenth Amendment.

Charles Sumner continued to be the Loyal League's chief congressional sponsor. By presenting petitions on at least a bimonthly basis throughout the winter, spring, and summer of 1864, Sumner kept hammering at the point that emancipation by constitutional amendment was the will of the American people. After presenting the first installment of league petitions February 9, 1864, he followed with more petitions on February 11, March 15 and 23, April 14, 15, 25, 27, and May 9. By June he was presenting petitions at a rapid rate: June 1, 2, 6, 7, 14, 15, 16, 20, 22, 23, 24, 27, and July 1. In a speech on April 15, introducing 41,218 names, Sumner read the petition aloud. On April 25, another 12,276 names were added. By June, after Stanton had mailed an additional 85,000 signatures, the total climbed to 300,000 many of them, Sumner was proud to report, from the working classes. The state of Illinois led all states by 2,000 signatures. By the time Congress recessed for the summer, league petition totals neared 400,000.[37]

The House of Representatives finally passed the Thirteenth Amendment in January 1865. By year's end, three-fourths of the states ratified the amendment. Although members of the Woman's National Loyal League never came close to their goal of one million signatures on the "mammoth petition," their achievement was nevertheless a notable one.

While antislavery petitioning was hardly new, the league's campaign encompassed every Northern free state and involved the political participation of an unprecedented number of women. While many people, including some abolitionists, believed that the Emancipation Proclamation ended the antislavery controversy, the Loyal League pushed incessantly for stronger measures to secure universal emancipation on a constitutional basis.

Based on the 1860 census, the white adult population of the Northern free states was approximately 9.5 million. In other words, roughly one in twenty-four Americans in the free Northern states signed an abolition petition circulated by

---

37. Elizabeth Cady Stanton to Charles Sumner, June 23 [1864] and [June 1864], Sumner Collection, Houghton Library, Harvard University; *Congressional Globe*, 38th Cong., 1st sess., 1864, 536, 581, 1107, 1247, 1607, 1635, 1840, 1887, 2170, 2621, 2651, 2751, 2777, 2920, 2962, 3001, 3086, 3156, 3188, 3218, 3285, 3412.

Although the Loyal League petition is extant (Records of the U.S. Senate, RG 46, 38th Cong., Petitions Referred to the Select Committee on Slavery and Freedman, NA), very little manuscript material has survived concerning activities at the local level. Illinois was the state with the greatest number of signatures. Civil War manuscripts housed at the Chicago Historical Society burned in the great fire of 1871. Scattered letters on league letterhead written by Anthony and others are extant. See, for example, her letter to R. W. Lyman, Dec. 14, 1863, George Dunlap Lyman Collection, California Historical Society; league form letter dated June 20, 1863, Maine Historical Society.

the Woman's National Loyal League. It was the largest number of signatures ever introduced on a congressional petition up to that time, and Senators Charles Sumner and Henry Wilson assured the women that the petitions constituted the bulwark of their drive for legislative action to end slavery. Although Sumner ceased to introduce antislavery petitions after the summer recess of 1864, league activity did not stop. Elizabeth Cady Stanton commented in a letter to Susan Anthony, December 8, 1864, that she had recently organized two local leagues, in addition to distributing tracts and making speeches. League activists may have exerted pressure on their state legislatures to ratify the Thirteenth Amendment.[38]

Once the Thirteenth Amendment had been ratified, the Woman's National Loyal League disbanded, a move feminist abolitionists soon had reason to regret. With the end of the war, the defeat of the South, and the liberation of the slave, Congress turned its attention to the question of black male suffrage. Radical Republicans in Congress, intent upon directing the course of Reconstruction, favored black enfranchisement for both humanitarian and tactical reasons. They needed the votes of Southern blacks to ensure their dominance in the South and their national political hegemony. The Fourteenth Amendment, introduced late in 1865, defined national citizenship. It also stipulated that states of the Confederate South, before being readmitted to the Union, must grant the vote to black men or lose Congressional representation proportionately. The Fourteenth Amendment made no provision for woman suffrage.[39]

Not only did Radical Republicans in Congress support the Fourteenth Amendment, but many abolitionists praised the measure, which was written by no less a figure than Charles Sumner. In 1866, abolitionists and feminists joined ranks to found the American Equal Rights Association, an organization dedicated to furthering the political rights of blacks and women. With prominent male abolitionists in leadership positions, AERA support for the amendment became inevitable. These men might sympathize with the cause of universal suffrage, but freedmen's rights must take precedence during the "Negro's Hour." Elizabeth Cady

---

38. According to the 1860 census, the white population of men and women over the age of twenty in the Northern states was 9,558,531. U.S. Census Office, 8th Census, 1860, *Population of the United States in 1860; Compiled from the Original Returns* (Washington, D.C.: GPO, 1864), 592–93. Adults over the age of eighteen could sign league petitions. McPherson, *Struggle for Equality*, 126; Susan B. Anthony, "Woman's Half-Century of Evaluation," *North American Review* 175 (15 Dec. 1902): 807; Elizabeth Cady Stanton to Susan B. Anthony, Dec. 8, 1864, in Stanton and Blatch, *Elizabeth Cady Stanton*, 2:102–3.

39. Ellen Carol DuBois, *Feminism and Suffrage: The Emergence of an Independent Women's Movement in America, 1848–1869* (Ithaca: Cornell Univ. Press, 1978), 57–60.

Stanton, furious with one longtime ally, wrote to him testily, "do you believe the African race is composed entirely of males?"[40]

Summoning Susan Anthony, who had traveled to Kansas to visit her brother and his family, Stanton made a frantic effort to stop the Fourteenth Amendment from excluding women. "This is not the Negro's hour," she declared. "We have passed from him to the broader question of the life of the Republic. . . . Abolitionists have demanded suffrage for women for the last ten years & why do they injure the question now?" The two indefatigable women wrote a petition to "prohibit the several States from disfranchising any of their citizens on the ground of sex." It was the first woman suffrage petition presented to Congress instead of the state legislatures. By the end of the 1865-66 congressional session, Stanton and Anthony had collected 10,000 signatures on petitions, a notable achievement in a relatively short time, except when compared with the Loyal League's 400,000 signatures on the antislavery petition.[41]

Because Sumner had deserted them, Stanton and Anthony approached the Democrats for help. Senator Gratz Brown of Missouri spoke on their behalf in the Senate, arguing that women had put aside their own cause during the war and now feared "the same Constitutional amendment which may carry civil rights to the emancipated classes may prohibit those rights, either directly or by implication, to women." Brown failed to persuade his colleagues. Radical Republican support for the Fourteenth Amendment was unshakable and the amendment was ratified in 1868. Anthony complained that "the Republicans are very cowardly," while Stanton feared that the woman suffrage cause might be set back fully one hundred years because of passage of this amendment.[42]

After the May 1869 convention of the Equal Rights Association, where delegates clashed over the question of black versus female suffrage, Stanton and Anthony broke with their male colleagues in the abolition movement and the

---

40. Elizabeth Cady Stanton to Wendell Phillips, May 25, 1865, in Stanton and Blatch, *Elizabeth Cady Stanton*, 2:105; James Brewer Stewart, *Wendell Phillips, Liberty's Hero* (Baton Rouge: Louisiana State Univ. Press, 1986), 282-83; Griffith, *In Her Own Right*, 125.

41. Elizabeth Cady Stanton, "Speech on Reconstruction," [1866?] Stanton Collection, Library of Congress; Stanton wrote a letter to the *Standard* on Jan. 2, 1866. "Petition of Elizabeth Cady Stanton and other women for Amendment of Constitution to prohibit disfranchisement on account of sex," Jan. 29, 1866, Records of the U.S. House of Representatives, RG 233, 39th Cong., Committee on the Judiciary; Stanton, *Eighty Years and More*, 243-44; DuBois, *Feminism and Suffrage*, 60-61.

42. *Standard*, Feb. 10, 1866; Susan Anthony to Caroline Dall, Jan. 30, 1866, Dall Collection, Massachusetts Historical Society; Eleanor Flexner, *Century of Struggle: The Woman's Rights Movement in the United States* (New York: Atheneum, 1974), 144.

Republican party by founding their own feminist organization, the National Woman Suffrage Association. Moderates led by Lucy Stone and her husband Henry Blackwell promoted passage of the Fifteenth Amendment, which went one step further than the Fourteenth in guaranteeing adult male suffrage. Once the black man had been enfranchised, they argued, then the Republican party might turn its attention toward woman's rights. They founded a separate organization called the American Woman Suffrage Association.[43]

Traditionally, historians have argued that feminist activity ground to a halt during the Civil War period,[44] and yet this was clearly not the case. Although woman's rights conventions were not held during the war, the league was implicitly feminist because Stanton and Anthony encouraged female participation in the political process, urged them to think ahead to postwar possibilities for women, and even discussed specific concepts such as gender equality and equal pay for equal work. The issue of female labor was addressed by several newspapers during the war. The *New York Independent* printed articles under the banner "Woman's Right to Labor" and the *New York World* ran a similar series.[45] Though it was a subordinate concern to abolitionism, feminist activity was never totally eclipsed by the Civil War emphasis on Negro rights.

The postwar period may, with some justification, be interpreted as the nadir of the nineteenth-century woman's rights movement. The Fourteenth and Fifteenth Amendments gave the vote to black men, in theory if not in fact. Women made no such gain. Many female activists, in addition to having participated in the wartime emancipation crusade, had labored for decades before that time on the slave's behalf, and yet citizenship's most treasured privilege still eluded them.

Angered by congressional action, Elizabeth Cady Stanton and others resorted to racist rhetoric. Increasingly they referred to blacks as "Sambo." In the monumental *History of Woman Suffrage*, published in the 1880s, feminists lamented that, "in the enfranchisement of the black man," women "saw another ignorant class of voters placed above their heads." This bigotry may have been more rhetorical than substantive. In 1866, during the intense debate over the Fourteenth Amendment, Elizabeth Cady Stanton invited the black abolitionist Sojourner Truth to be a guest in the Stanton home. Her invitation was accepted. Even if her racist

---

43. Griffith, *In Her Own Right*, 136-37; DuBois, *Feminism and Suffrage*, 163-64.
44. Flexner, *Century of Struggle*, 142; DuBois, *Feminism and Suffrage*, 52; see also Hays, *Morning Star*, 175-76.
45. *Independent*, Mar. 3, 24, 1864, Jan. 12, 1865; *New York World*, Dec. 3, 5, 1863.

rhetoric was mere invective, Stanton and other feminists were becoming more narrow in their reform outlook, concentrating on white, middle-class issues.[46]

The schism in the Equal Rights Association divided and therefore hurt the woman's rights movement. Although there had always been differences of opinion in the feminist ranks, the divisions produced by the debate over the Fourteenth and Fifteenth Amendments were deep and long lasting. Not until 1890 did the National and American Woman Suffrage Associations reunite with Elizabeth Cady Stanton as president of the combined group.

There were gains as well. The schism of 1869 benefited the feminist movement in at least one way. By severing their ties with the abolition movement and the Republican party, Stanton and Anthony came to the realization that only through the agitation of women could emancipation be achieved. Thereafter they carried out their suffrage activities independent of any political party or other reform group.[47]

Another gain for postwar women activists was an improved public image. Although women had given speeches and signed petitions for a variety of causes before the war, they were almost universally condemned as unladylike except by a small group of reform-minded citizens. The public response to the activities of the Loyal League, however, was positive. "The leading journals vied with each other in praising ... the executive ability, the loyalty, and the patriotism of the women of the League," Elizabeth Cady Stanton recalled in her memoirs, "and yet these were the same women who, when demanding civil and political rights ... for themselves, had been uniformly denounced as 'unwise,' 'imprudent,' 'fanatical,' and 'impracticable.'"[48]

Undoubtedly this change in public opinion carried into the postbellum period. Abolitionist orators and writers such as Lucy Stone, Susan Anthony, Mary Livermore, Anna Dickinson, and Julia Ward Howe spoke on feminist concerns after the war. Even though they encountered public opposition to their views, they encountered far less opposition to the public expression of those views than had prewar feminist abolitionists.

---

46. Stanton, *History of Woman Suffrage*, 2:88; Harriot Stanton Blatch, *Challenging Years: The Memoirs of Harriet Stanton Blatch* (New York: G. P. Putnam's Sons, 1940), 17.

47. DuBois, *Feminism and Suffrage*, 164, 182–84. Dubois also contended that Stanton and Anthony altered their tactics from "agitation" to "organizing, from radicalism to a more temperate appeal," after they ceased to be associated with Garrisonian abolitionism. Stanton's and Anthony's WNLL activities indicate they learned to temper their radicalism long before the split with Garrison. Their printed broadsides and speeches were painstakingly worded and designed to encourage female political participation based on woman's traditional role as moral and religious teacher of the family.

48. Stanton, *Eighty Years and More*, 240.

Stanton herself helped to win respectability for women speakers. A successful lyceum lecturer, she traveled extensively, addressing audiences on all manner of topics from child rearing to divorce reform. In her later years she looked like the quintessential grandmother and her rosy-cheeked face appeared in advertisements for women's facial soap, hardly an indication of a "disreputable" woman. At the age of seventy-five she was characterized by the *Washington Star* as "looking as if she should be the Lord Chief-Justice, . . . her amiable and intellectual face marked with the lines of wisdom."[49] Though Stanton had gained respectability in the eyes of the public, her views were as radical as ever. She championed such causes as woman suffrage and divorce reform until her death at eighty-six in 1902.

The postwar period was a negative one in many ways for women. They were not included in the Fourteenth and Fifteenth Amendments. And yet there were gains, albeit less tangible ones, which resulted from the Civil War and in part from women's abolition work during the war. Women had long been accepted as nurses and seamstresses and charity organizers. Their Civil War work in these areas, while significant, was not path-breaking. The petitioning, public speaking, and political organizing Northern women performed during the war helped to gain new acceptance for women in the public sphere after the war. Although suffrage would not be granted to women until the second decade of the twentieth century, woman's rights advocates in the postbellum period did not face the same degree of ridicule that they faced before the war. Becoming the champions of the black slave and the patriotic supporters of the Union cause had clearly helped to give legitimacy to woman speakers and political organizers. Elizabeth Cady Stanton, Susan B. Anthony, and their lieutenants had helped win the war. In the years to come, they would continue to battle for woman's rights.

---

49. Ibid., 259-82; Harper, *Life and Work of Susan B. Anthony*, 2:665. Griffith, *In Her Own Right*, 161-62. Stanton's likeness was used in advertisements for Fairy Soap manufactured by the N. K. Fairbank Company. A reprint of one ad, dated June 10, 1899, may be found in Andrew Sinclair, *The Better Half: The Emancipation of American Woman* (New York: Harper & Row, 1965).

"A Profound National Devotion"
The Civil War Union Leagues and the Construction of a New National Patriotism

MELINDA LAWSON

In December 1863, the *Atlantic Monthly* carried an unusual and striking narrative. The anonymous article told of the life and recent death of Philip Nolan, a young officer in the Western Division of the early-nineteenth-century army. An accomplice in the schemes of Aaron Burr, Nolan was convicted of playing a minor role in a treasonous plot. At his sentencing he was asked if he had anything to say that might suggest his abiding loyalty to the United States. But the young officer was tired of the service; he was tired of orders; he was tired of the trial, which seemed to drag on and on. In a "fit of frenzy," Nolan cried out, "Damn the United States! I wish I may never hear of the United States again!"[1] The presiding colonel was terribly shocked. He withdrew from the room. Returning minutes later "with a face like a sheet," the colonel granted Nolan's wish. He would never, by the authority of the court, hear the name of the United States again. Nolan spent the next fifty-five years on a series of naval vessels. The crews on those ships were forbidden to speak to him of the United States; the ships never docked at home until he was transferred to a new vessel. Deprived of a homeland, Nolan slowly and painfully learned the true worth of his country. He missed it more

---

This article was adapted from *Patriot Fires: Forging a New American Nationalism in the Civil War North*, by Melinda Lawson (Lawrence: Univ. Press of Kansas, 2002), and is used by permission of the publisher.

  1. Edward Everett Hale, *The Man Without a Country* (reprint, Boston: Roberts Brothers, 1893), 23.

than his friends or family, more than art or music or love or nature. Without it, he was nothing.²

On his deathbed in 1863, Nolan was visited in his cabin by an officer on board the vessel. As the officer later reported, the cabin had been transformed into "a little shrine." The stars and stripes were draped around a picture of Washington. Over his bed Nolan had painted an eagle, with lightening "blazing from his beak" and his claw grasping the globe. At the foot of his bed was a dated map of the old territories. Turning to his visitor, Nolan smiled. "Here, you see, I have a country!"³ Thus Philip Nolan became "the man without a country," and Civil War Americans learned a new way to envision their relationship with the nation: only through a collective national identity could one realize "self and freedom." Or, as the Reverend Joseph Fransioli argued in an 1863 sermon that later became a widely circulated pamphlet, "Deny the duty of loving your country, and you deny your own feelings; you deny mankind itself."⁴

As some but not all readers later discovered, there was no Philip Nolan. The article was in reality a short story written by Edward Everett Hale, Unitarian minister, member of the Boston Union Club, and executive board member of the New England Loyal Publication Society. Distressed by the war weariness and defeatism that had descended on the North, Hale had written the story to teach his readers the importance of loyalty to country. He intended that the story be read as fact and was upset when, through an editorial oversight, his name appeared in the index. Fiction or nonfiction, Hale's message struck a chord for a people struggling to understand the place of the nation in their lives. Within a year of its original publication, reprinted editions of "A Man Without a Country" sold half a million copies, and the story quickly earned a reputation as a minor classic.⁵

Although Hale was the sole author of this patriotic parable, his message was part of a larger mission assumed by the elite metropolitan Union Leagues in

---

2. For quote see Hale, *The Man Without a Country*, 23.

3. Hale, *The Man Without a Country*, 88.

4. Anthony D. Smith, *Nationalist Movements* (New York: St. Martin's Press, 1977) writes that nationalism holds that the only genuine identity "is a national one, and every man, be he peasant or worker, merchant or intellectual, can only rediscover self and freedom through that new collective identity." Cited in Wilbur Zelinsky, *Nation into State: The Shifting Symbolic Foundations of American Nationalism* (Chapel Hill: Univ. of North Carolina Press, 1988), 6; Rev. Joseph Fransioli, "Patriotism, A Christian Virtue: A Sermon Preached . . . at St. Peter's (Catholic) Church, Brooklyn, July 26th, 1863," New York Loyal Publication Society pamphlet no. 24, *Pamphlets Issued By the New York Loyal Publication Society* (New York: The Society, 1864-66).

5. John R. Adams, *Edward Everett Hale* (Boston: Twayne Publishers, 1977), 27; Jean Holloway, *Edward Everett Hale* (Austin: Univ. of Texas Press, 1956), 139.

Philadelphia, New York, and Boston. Begun as gentlemen's clubs in the midst of the social chaos generated by sectional conflict and civil war, these leagues quickly acquired a more complex character. The leagues brought an embattled intellectual and professional elite together with powerful business interests in a coalition to rally support for the Union and strengthen the national state. They constructed a new national patriotism on two distinct levels. First, through the creative appropriation of an upper-class institution, League founders hoped to cultivate a nationalist patriotism among the metropolitan elite, forging a cohesive upper class in the process. They created exclusive gentlemen's clubs whose chief criteria were loyalty to the nation and support of the national administration. Second, for Northerners who did not qualify as elites, League members had a different approach: they sponsored and wrote literature for their associated organizations, the publication societies. These societies produced pamphlets designed to rally Northerners behind the war, tame an increasingly unruly working class, and inculcate a preeminent national loyalty. They employed a multitude of arguments, battling partisanship, painting the North as a free labor Mecca, and—like Hale's "The Man Without a Country"—portraying the nation-state as an organic entity central to the fulfillment of self and freedom.

The Union Leagues' wartime activities were part of a much larger effort to cultivate loyalty and national identity throughout the Civil War North. Americans were a young people when the war began. They held powerful loyalties to their towns, their states, and their regions; their loyalty to the nation was as yet untested. Americans' suspicions of concentrated power contributed to the formation of a weak national government, one that left domestic governance almost entirely to the states. The federal government exercised little control over the states and had little visible presence in its citizens' lives. With the exception of national elections and trips to the post office, most Americans had almost no interaction with their national government.[6]

Notions of rights and consent laid the groundwork for a patriotism that historian Merle Curti has labeled as "contractual": Americans believed that the

6. For Democrats and the role of the state see Marvin Meyers, *The Jacksonian Persuasion* (Stanford: Stanford Univ. Press, 1957), Jean H. Baker, *Affairs of Party: The Political Culture of Northern Democrats in the Mid-Nineteenth Century* (Ithaca: Cornell Univ. Press, 1983), 143-46, and Joel Silbey, *A Respectable Minority: The Democratic Party in the Civil War Era, 1860-1868* (New York: Norton, 1977). For Whigs see Daniel Walker Howe, *The Political Culture of the American Whigs* (Chicago: Univ. of Chicago Press, 1979); Merrill D. Peterson, *The Great Triumvirate: Webster, Clay, and Calhoun* (New York: Oxford Univ. Press, 1987), 68-84. For Republicans and support of the national state for the market revolution, see Eric Foner, *Free Soil, Free Labor, Free Men* (New York: Oxford Univ. Press, 1970), 186-225.

national state was formed by a contract that guaranteed them a body of rights and bound their country to an ideal. If the state violated those rights, or failed to represent that ideal, the contract could be broken. This notion stood in sharp contrast to an old world loyalty to country in which attachment to a monarch or land was preeminent. American patriotism was not, as Alexis de Tocqueville testified in 1835, that "instinctive, disinterested, and undefinable feeling" rooted in customs and traditions that characterized European nations—a feeling that could help a citizenry become "capable of making the most prodigious efforts" to save the state in times of crisis.[7]

It is not that Americans did not entertain a genuine, even ardent, affection for the Union. By the eve of the war, white Northerners and Southerners alike described an attachment to Union that historians have labeled as mystical or spiritual. To the extent that Americans felt themselves to be a nation, however, it was the people—not the national state—who were considered to embody the virtues, ideology, and destiny of America. This limited nationalism carried the nation through both the War of 1812—before universal white male suffrage placed more importance on citizens' attitudes toward the state—and the Mexican War, a small-scale war that neither threatened the existence of the Union nor demanded much from the average citizen.

For a time during the Civil War, it appeared that even this limited nationalism might be sufficient to rally Northerners, who responded to the attack on Fort Sumter with an eruption of enthusiastic patriotism.[8] But popular enthusiasm soon subsided. As the war progressed American national identity encountered a major challenge. In the North, a rapidly expanding national state taxed and drafted the people, suspended the writ of habeas corpus, and moved to abolish slavery. For the first time, the federal government confronted the need for widespread, protracted support and sacrifice. With no official public relations office

---

7. Merle Curti, *The Roots of American Loyalty* (New York: Columbia Univ. Press, 1946), 175; Paul C. Nagel, *One Nation Indivisible: The Union in American Thought* (New York: Oxford Univ. Press, 1964), 31-41; George M. Fredrickson, *The Inner Civil War: Northern Intellectuals and the Crisis of the Union* (New York: Harper & Row, 1965), 132; Alexis DeTocqueville, *Democracy in America*, vol. 1, ed. Phillips Bradley (New York: Vintage Books, 1945), 250-51.

8. Zelinsky, *Nation into State*, 218-19; Nagel, *One Nation Indivisible*, 69-103. For the effect of the War of 1812 and the Mexican War on American nationalism, see Curti, *Roots of American Loyalty*, 16-29, 152-56; David Potter, *The Impending Crisis: 1848-1861* (New York: Harper & Row, 1976), 12-14. E. J. Hobsbawm, *Nations and Nationalism Since 1780: Programme, Myth, Reality* (Cambridge: Cambridge Univ. Press, 1990), 83, discusses the effect of universal suffrage on nation building. For the North's reaction to the attack on Fort Sumter, see James M. McPherson, *Battle Cry of Freedom: The Civil War Era* (New York: Oxford Univ. Press, 1988), 274-75.

to rally the people behind the war—equivalent, for example, to the Committee on Public Information that operated during World War I—the job of defining the war in patriotic terms fell largely to private individuals or associations, each with its own motives and methods. Thus, throughout the war, Northerners produced and distributed diverse and at times contradictory ideas about the meaning of patriotism and of their nation. These ideas laid the groundwork for a new American nationalism, rooted in history and tradition and celebrating the preeminence of the nation-state.

Through their wartime campaigns, the Union Leagues contributed to the construction of this new nationalism. The Leagues cultivated a national loyalty that superceded local, state, and regional loyalties; they enveloped the nation-state in a mystical aura, assigning a spiritual meaning not only to the nation but also to the newly empowered nation-state. The nationalism that the Leagues helped to construct looked beyond the notion of contract, beyond the limits of a subjective national idea, more closely resembling the European patriotism Tocqueville described as "instinctive, disinterested" and "capable of making the most prodigious efforts" to save the state in times of crisis.[9]

The Union League movement was a nationwide phenomenon that took shape as war weariness and defeatism threatened not only the fate of the Union but the fate of the Republican party as well. In the fall of 1862, hundreds of clubs began to form in cities and towns across the North; by 1864 the movement claimed almost one million members. All the leagues shared a founding premise of cultivating loyalty to the nation, but outside Philadelphia, New York, and Boston, the leagues had a more popular, distinctly partisan nature. These partisan leagues were established as secret societies with passwords and rituals. Members held meetings in lodges, storefronts, and halls in the dark of night. They lit candles, chanted oaths, and burned incense. League agents traveled across the North administering the League's oath to local Republican leaders and providing new councils with League charters.[10]

The Union League to which Hale belonged stood in marked contrast to such societies. These were gentlemen's clubs, with limited membership, lavish quarters,

---

9. Tocqueville, *Democracy in America* 1:250-51.
10. Clement Silvestro, "None But Patriots: The Union Leagues in the Civil War and Reconstruction" (Ph.D. diss., University of Wisconsin, 1959), 7, 27-72, 93-97, 102, 122-216; Guy Gibson, "Lincoln's League: The Union League Movement During the Civil War" (Ph.D. diss., Univ. of Illinois, 1957), 14, 19-20, 106.

abundant treasuries, and a focus on a nationalist, rather than partisan, patriotism. Although the Philadelphia League made a weak and somewhat abortive effort to organize leagues in its immediate environs, for the most part the elite clubs did not participate in the spread of the League throughout the North and, in fact, were often at odds with or embarrassed by the popular Leagues. The Boston organization chose the name "Union Club" to distinguish itself from the Union Leagues, and for several years officials in the New York City Union League Club considered changing the name of their association so that they would not be confused with the popular Leagues of the same name in New York City and New York State.[11]

That they concerned themselves with differentiating their organization from the other Leagues should come as no surprise: a concern to maintain the distinct authority of the upper class informed both the establishment and operations of the elite metropolitan leagues during the war. The antebellum years had witnessed a series of challenges to urban upper-class political power. Industrialization and immigration reshaped class relations, populations exploded, and universal white manhood suffrage empowered the masses. Many of the older elite withdrew from political office or were displaced by a new breed of politician wielding the weapons of political democracy and party machines. If the merchant elite withdrew from office holding, however, they did not withdraw from politics. Their survival as a class depended on political power, which implied the ability to enact duties, issue permits, expand infrastructure, secure land grants, impose taxes, and grant franchises, charters, or monopolies. Merchants and politicians initially worked hand-in-glove: the politicians organized the electorate and sought office, while the merchants financed their efforts and served on councils. By the 1850s, however, further changes in the cities' class and political structure had undermined this "amicable division of labor." Increasingly, politicians looked directly to the masses for support, and in exchange, protected the voters'—not the merchants'—interests. As urban elites watched their control over the new professional politicians slipping away, their influence over the masses waned as well. During the 1840s and 1850s, all three cities witnessed anti-abolitionist, anti-black, nativist, and/or labor riots.[12]

11. According to Frank Klement, the elite Union Leagues had "more spontaneity and less calculation, less partisanship and more social emphasis." See his *Dark Lanterns: Secret Political Societies, Conspiracies, and Treason Trials in the Civil War* (Baton Rouge: Louisiana State Univ. Press), 1984, 42; Charles Eliot Norton to G.W. Curtis, Feb. 26, 1863, in Sara Norton and M.A. DeWolfe Howe, eds., *Letters of Charles Eliot Norton* (Boston: Houghton Mifflin, 1913), 261; Will Irwin, Earl Chapin May, and Joseph Hotchkiss, *A History of the Union League Club of New York City* (New York: Dodd, Mead, 1952), 19.

12. For differing visions of this phenomenon, see Robert Dahl, *Who Governs? Democracy and*

Threatened by professional politicians, fearing anarchy in an age of class politics, the embattled elite soon found themselves rocked from within, as slavery and secession divided the cities' upper and middle classes. In Philadelphia, secession and the war for Union drove a wedge between men with familial or business ties to the South and the conservative Whig-Republicans who otherwise dominated the city's elite. In New York, cultural and economic concerns united many of the cities' professionals, merchants, industrialists, and bankers behind the war, but fueled a simmering feud between an older patrician class troubled by the "experience of commerce" and one segment of the rising merchant class. In Boston, the battle over slavery jeopardized a longstanding Brahmin-Whig hegemony, pitting Cotton Whigs against Conscience Whigs.[13]

The toll the war took on urban upper- and middle-class solidarity was clearly illustrated by the fate of urban gentlemen's clubs, which, in mid-nineteenth-century America, all but constituted "society." With club members assuming opposing positions on the sectional conflict, previously congenial social gatherings were now riven with conflict. In Philadelphia the Wistar Party, a sixty-three-year-old association evolved from the tradition of weekly entertainments at the home of Dr. Caspar Wistar, disbanded shortly after the war began. The Philadelphia Club continued its meetings, but they became increasingly tense and unpleasant, as did meetings of the Somerset and Forest Clubs in Boston and those of the old Union Club of New York City. Although the rush to patriotic unity muted many of these conflicts early in the war, by autumn 1862 battlefield defeats, the burgeoning role of the federal government, and the change in war aims heralded by the preliminary Emancipation Proclamation had loosened wartime restraints on

---

Power in an American City (New Haven: Yale Univ. Press, 1961); Sam Bass Warner, *The Private City: Philadelphia in Three Periods of Its Growth* (Philadelphia: Univ. of Pennsylvania Press, 1968); Frederic Cople Jahar, *The Urban Establishment: Upper Strata in Boston, New York, Charleston, Chicago, and Los Angeles* (Urbana: Univ. of Illinois Press, 1982); Amy Bridges, *A City in the Republic: Antebellum New York and the Origins of Machine Politics* (New York: Cambridge Univ. Press, 1984). Tocqueville, *Democracy in America* 1:186-87; William Dusinberre, *Civil War Issues in Philadelphia 1856-1865* (Philadelphia: Univ. of Pennsylvania Press, 1965), 19-32; J. Robert Mendte, *The Union League in Philadelphia: 125 Years* (Devon, Pa.: W. T. Cooke, 1987), 39; Iver Bernstein, *The New York City Draft Riots: Their Significance for American Society and Politics in the Age of the Civil War* (New York: Oxford Univ. Press, 1990), 186-87; Oscar Handlin, *Boston's Immigrants* (Cambridge, Mass.: Belknap Press, 1959), 76, 186-206.

13. Maxwell Whiteman, *Gentlemen in Crisis: The First Century of the Union League in Philadelphia* (Philadelphia: The League, 1975), 5-6, Dusinberre, *Civil War Issues*, 113; Sven Beckert, "The Making of New York City's Bourgeoisie, 1850-1886" (Ph.D. diss., Columbia University, 1995), 119-204; Bernstein, *New York City Draft Riots*, 125-61; Jahar, *Urban Establishment*, 55-56; Daniel Walker Howe, *The Unitarian Conscience: Harvard Moral Philosophy, 1805-1861* (Cambridge, Mass.: Harvard Univ. Press, 1970), 295.

expressions of discontent. As defeatism escalated, the elite in each of these cities confronted its particular divisions in distinct yet similar ways.[14]

In Philadelphia, the discontented were by no means in the minority. Given Pennsylvania's geographical proximity to the South, many of Philadelphia's most prominent families were of Southern origin. They maintained close ties to their Southern kin and sent their sons to Southern schools. Philadelphians were linked to the South economically as well: their banks floated the money for the cotton that left Charleston for Liverpool; they discounted the bills of exchange for Virginia tobacco. Moreover, the South provided a market both for the foreign goods that passed through Philadelphia's ports and for the city's own manufactured products. Whatever their political affiliations prior to the sectional struggle, most men and women with close Southern ties allied with the Northern Democratic party when the war began; a minority went further, and announced their support for the Confederacy.[15]

For wealthy Philadelphians without Southern ties, politics prior to 1854 meant membership in the Whig party, for that party best represented the interests and ideals of a manufacturing city's elite. With secession, Philadelphia's unionists believed that the very foundation of their prosperity as a class had been placed in jeopardy. The perpetuation of the nation on Northern terms was necessary to the continued existence of the commercial and manufacturing interests. Though for years those interests had taken the Union, with its lawful environment, internal improvements, and tariffs for granted, with the war, Philadelphia's business elite could no longer afford that luxury. Morton McMichael, editor of the *Philadelphia North American*, spoke for many when he argued that the South's secession was "a question of simple law and order against anarchy. It is a question which vitally concerns every man's safety in business." Two days later he reiterated this theme: "We ... live under the national law. If that is broken down, our interests, our property, and our lives may be lost in the disorder which will ensue. ... Do our merchants expect to preserve their business when the authority of the Union is gone in the Mississippi Valley ... ? Can their trade to any state be of value if

---

14. Whiteman, *Gentlemen in Crisis*, 15–16; George Parsons Lathrop, *History of the Union League of Philadelphia, From Its Origin and Foundation to the Year 1882* (Philadelphia, J.B. Lippincott and Co., 1884), 26–27; Gibson, "Lincoln's League," 79.

15. Whiteman, *Gentlemen in Crisis*, 5–6; Kenneth M. Stampp, *And The War Came: The North and the Secession Crisis* (Baton Rouge: Louisiana State Univ. Press, 1950), 123–25; Eric Foner, *Free Soil, Free Labor, Free Men*, 186–87.

there are no courts or laws to aid the recovery of debts? Nothing but ruin awaits all business interests of ours . . . if the doctrines of the Secession leaders are to prevail." McMichael warned those "who have obtained to such prosperity in the United States" that if they were to "remain in peace and prosperity at all, . . . there must be a powerful and united effort made now to sustain the government." Thus the *North American* supported a war to strengthen the national state and combat Southern political power.[16]

As the war escalated, the tensions between the two factions of the Philadelphia elite intensified as well. The publication in 1862 of Charles Ingersoll's pro-Southern pamphlet, "Letter to a Friend in a Slave State," marked the end of the elite dissenters' restraint. As defeatism spread from meetings and rallies into the social clubs of the wealthy and renowned, the Unionist patriciate expressed dismay. Judge J. I. Clark Hare, a prominent Whig jurist, bemoaned the rising status accorded the disloyal in Philadelphia. "The thought that seemed to move Judge Hare the most," reported George Boker, secretary of the Philadelphia Union League, "was that while we, the inhabitants of a loyal city, were thus cast down before the ill fortunes of our country, men who were almost leagued with the Southern traitors were walking with high heads among our people, openly exalting in our discomfiture, and eagerly waiting for the day of our utter overthrow." As a director of that League later explained, "The thoroughly aroused loyalists of Philadelphia had to establish and maintain their social position," and, in the process, protect the prosperity that that position both reflected and enabled.[17]

Consequently, the Unionist elite laid plans for a new kind of social club. If previous clubs had looked primarily to social status to determine eligibility, this club would be different: the chief criterion for membership would be support for the Northern war effort. With fidelity to the Union as its cornerstone, this fashionable club would wage a battle for the loyalty of the upper class through the manipulation of powerful symbols of status and prestige. If successful, it would weld that class into a cohesive force, strengthening the Unionist faction at home in their battles for political power and social control, as well as throughout the nation, where the irresoluteness of the people seemed to threaten an end to the Union as the elite knew it.

In November 1862, McMichael, Clark Hare, George Henry Boker—poet, play-

---

16. *Philadelphia North American and United States Gazette*, Apr. 9, 1861; Apr. 11, 1861; Apr. 16, 1861.

17. Lathrop, *Union League of Philadelphia*, 15-18; Whiteman, *Gentlemen in Crisis*, 14; George Boker, cited in Lathrop, *Union League of Philadelphia*, 27; Union League of Philadelphia, *Chronicle of The Union League of Philadelphia*, 1862-1902 (Philadelphia: Fell, 1902), 32-33.

wright, and son of a Philadelphia financier—and Benjamin Gerhard, a wealthy businessman, met to discuss plans for an association that would honor the nation and exclude the disloyal. The new club called for "unqualified loyalty to the Government of the United States and unwavering support of the suppression of the rebellion." Membership was by invitation only; those eligible must meet the founders' requirements for social standing as well as for patriotism. Philadelphians who could not meet these requirements would be refused social and business relations with club members, for the time had arrived when "sympathy with (armed rebellion) should in social and commercial life meet the frown of the patriotic and the true. Disloyalty must be made unprofitable." The original draft called for associates to refrain from "all social intercourse and dealings with disloyal persons." Thus the "primary object" of the organization would be "to discountenance and rebuke by moral and social influences, all disloyalty to the Federal Government."[18]

To enhance the social appeal of the Philadelphia Club, large sums of money were invested in elegant quarters. "No effort nor reasonable expense has been spared in the Reading Room, the Telegraphic News and the Restaurant, to make our house an inviting centre of instruction and convenience," noted Boker of the Chestnut Street clubhouse. Those expenses included the purchase (at a reduced price) of Thomas Sully's equestrian portrait of George Washington, originally commissioned for Congress in 1842. Further adding to the club's attraction was the fact that it was modeled closely on the style of the Wistar party, the prestigious gentlemen's club that had disbanded with the onset of the war. The "cards of invitation" issued by the new club were almost replicas of the Wistar's. Appearing only eighteen months after the demise of that prestigious association, the Union Club appeared to be assuming the role of successor. But it was ostracizing—even blacklisting—anyone who entertained Southern sympathies. The excluded were outraged: a local Democratic paper printed the names and addresses of club members, suggesting that those gentlemen's houses would soon be destroyed.[19]

. . .

18. "Address by the Union League of Philadelphia to Citizens of Pennsylvania, in favor of the Re-Election of Abraham Lincoln," MSS, Union League of Philadelphia (hereafter cited as MSS, ULP), Union League of Philadelphia, Philadelphia; "Articles of Association of the Union Club," in *Chronicle of The Union League of Philadelphia*, 52–53; M. A. DeWolfe-Howe to George Boker, Feb. 17, 1863, MSS, ULP; "Original draft of *Articles of Association of the Union League of Philadelphia*," MSS, ULP; Statement, "Union League Of Philadelphia," MSS, ULP.

19. George Boker, *First Annual Report of the Board of Directors of the Union League of Philadelphia* (Philadelphia: King and Baird, 1863), 2–13; Whiteman, *Gentlemen in Crisis*, 20, 28; Lathrop, *Union League of Philadelphia*, 28–31. Shortly into the life of the Philadelphia Union Club, a motion was made to enlarge the club into a league, open to more than the original fifty-five members. The

As the Union Club took shape in Philadelphia, plans for a similar club were being made in New York City, where a small but vocal segment of the city's commercial and manufacturing class opposed the evolving war aims and measures of the Lincoln administration. This largely Democratic contingent did support the war for the Union. But they argued against emancipation and a transformation of the South's political economy, fearing both the impact of the disruption of Southern labor relations on the production and export of agricultural products and the implications of black suffrage for the Democratic party. Often recent arrivals to New York, these men worked closely with the city's politicians, catered to the immigrant masses, advocated free trade, and supported the kind of "international republicanism" typified by the "Young America" movement, which sympathized with liberal revolutions in Europe and called for aggressive westward expansion. August Belmont, a prominent financier and Democratic party leader, was a spokesperson for this faction.[20]

The New York League was rooted in a political and cultural critique of Belmont and his national vision. Its chief founders were professionals and intellectuals, including Henry Bellows, prominent Unitarian minister; Frederick Law Olmsted, Sanitary Commission Secretary and Central Park superintendent; George Templeton Strong, lawyer; and Wolcott Gibbs, physician. Like their counterparts in Philadelphia, these men understood the centrality of the state to the continued prosperity of the nation. Moreover, they faced challenges both to their political influence and to their vision of a moral, cohesive society. In their view, laissez-faire and mass democracy represented perhaps the greatest threats to that vision. They hoped that new institutions might help bind a society in decay. In the war they saw an opportunity to restore their power and enact their vision, in part through the strengthening of the national state and national identity. All four men were already members of the United States Sanitary Commission, an association designed to coordinate the volunteer and medical war efforts, but whose "animating idea," according to Bellows, was the "nation as super-eminent above the states."[21]

Philadelphia Union Club formed the nucleus of—and continued to exist as an autonomous unit within—what ultimately became the Union League of Philadelphia.

20. Beckert, "The Making of New York City's Bourgeoisie," 166-67; Bernstein, *New York City Draft Riots*, 132-48.

21. Beckert, "The Making of New York City's Bourgeoisie," 119-204; Bernstein, *New York City Draft Riots*, 148-61; Fredrickson, *Inner Civil War*, 23-35, 98-112; Henry W. Bellows, *Historical Sketch of the Union League Club of New York* (New York: Club House, 1879), 6. See also Jeanie Attie, *Patriotic Toil: Northern Women and the American Civil War* (Ithaca: Cornell Univ. Press, 1998), 51-86. For conflicts between Belmont and Olmsted's circle prior to the war, see Roy Rosenzweig and

Thus, League founders hoped that the New York club would assert the authority of the older mercantile class against that of Belmont and the "arrivistes." Writing to physician Wolcott Gibbs in November 1862, Olmsted outlined his hopes for a nationalist gentlemen's club in New York. Its members, the "hereditary natural aristocracy," would be distinguished from the "parvenus; we are rich, they are vulgar." Olmsted pointed specifically to August Belmont and Henry G. Stebbins (a member of the Belmont clique) as examples. Olmsted's club, an association of the "legitimate descendants and arms bearers of the old dukes of our land," would define loyalty in such a way as to exclude Belmont and Stebbins, even if they professed support for the war.[22]

Olmsted's vision of the club as a weapon in a war for class survival had yet another dimension. In his view, the new generation of young wealthy men did not understand the obligations and duties of an elite upper class. In an elaborate membership plan, Olmsted expressed his hopes that the club might attract "promising young men," and indoctrinate them to the ways of the nationalist elite. "Gentlemen in the European sense," these young men were "men of leisure" who "don't understand what their place can be in American society." As a result, they were "greatly tempted to go over to the devil, (boss devil)."[23]

The Union League had to teach young rich Americans where their allegiances must lie, in the process constructing a self-consciously nationalist elite to govern. Olmsted hoped that in the Leagues the youthful rich might be "sought for and drawn in and nursed and nourished with care." "Established men," he added, could "fraternize with them, to welcome and hold every true man of them in fraternity." Such fraternization would not only help to shape a nationalist mind-set, it also would help socialize a new generation of wealth to the ways of the nationalist upper class, helping to perpetuate that class while cultivating a political governing elite from the youthful rich: "so soon they may govern us if they will." To accomplish this task, "good rooms with something to do is

---

Elizabeth Blackmar, *The Park and the People: A History of Central Park* (Ithaca: Cornell Univ. Press, 1992), 143–45, 184, 218.

22. Frederick Law Olmsted (FLO) to Oliver Wolcott Gibbs (OWG), Nov. 5, 1862 in Jane Turner Censer, *The Papers of Frederick Law Olmsted*, vol. 4 (Baltimore, Johns Hopkins Univ. Press, 1986), 466–70.

23. FLO to OWG, Nov. 5, 1862, Censer, *The Papers of Frederick Law Olmsted*, 466–70. C. Wright Mills argues the power of urban clubs both to socialize new members to the ways of the elite and to clarify class lines when they have become blurred. See, *The Power Elite* (New York: Oxford Univ. Press, 1956), 47–70.

alone essential.... Billiards and reading and smoking at least." In Olmsted's estimation, luxurious, well-appointed facilities would reinforce young members' social standing while making them amenable to the nationalist prescriptions of their elders. The Union Club, then, would both shore up the patriotism of the wavering elite by virtue of its status and serve as a forum within which the upper class could know and form one another.[24]

To be effective in uniting the city's elite behind the war and against the views of Belmont's circle, the New York League's founders understood that they needed a coalition of professionals like themselves with the cities' commercial, financial, and manufacturing classes. "Leading merchants are essential to our success," Strong wrote in his diary. With "a very respectable catalogue of moneyed men ... we may make the thing work." Such a coalition was not at all unrealistic. Before the war the city's merchants, bankers, and industrialists had differed in their approach to the sectional crisis; many merchants and bankers feared losing the benefits that Southern markets and the cotton trade provided, and favored compromise at any cost, while industrialists viewed slavery as a threat to Northern workers' right to rise, and thus opposed compromise. But when the war came, the majority of these men rallied behind the Union and the Republican administration. They understood that the national state represented court-enforced contracts, tariffs, and an expanding infrastructure. Moreover, as the war progressed, New York City's elite assumed a disproportionately heavy portion of the government's debt. As they poured individual or corporate savings into war bonds, their stake escalated in the war and the nation it was being fought to preserve. As New York's Chamber of Commerce noted in its annual report of 1863-64, the war had engendered a "vast pecuniary obligation" to suppress the rebellion.[25]

The New York Union League was founded to unite the city's business elite with its professionals and intellectuals behind a strong national state and a vigorous prosecution of the war. The club took shape in the early spring of 1863 as Bellows, Strong, Olmsted, and Gibbs refined their project and began screening potential members. On March 20 the organization held its first official meeting and elected officers. In its choice of officers the New York club revealed its reliance upon the commercial class: Robert B. Minturn, head of the second largest

---

24. FLO to OWG, Nov. 5, 1862, Censer, *The Papers of Frederick Law Olmsted*, 466-70.

25. George Templeton Strong, in Allan Nevins and Milton Halsey Thomas, *The Diary of George Templeton Strong*, vol. 3 (New York: Macmillan, 1952), 302-3, 307; Beckert, "The Making of New York City's Bourgeoisie," 133-204, 161 (chamber quotation).

shipping and shipbuilding firm in the nation, was elected president. Among the vice presidents were William H. Aspinwall, banker and shipping and commission merchant, Moses Taylor, shipping and sugar merchant, and Alexander T. Stewart, dry goods merchant. In his diary, Strong expressed his delight in finding "strong representatives of capital and commerce . . . interested and active."[26]

In keeping with Olmsted's vision, the New York League vowed to make their clubhouse "in its appointments, as complete as any in the world." They rented an unoccupied family home—"one of the most splendid mansions of the metropolis"—on the corner of 17th and Broadway, facing Union Square, for $6,000 a year. Another $20,000 was set aside to furnish and carpet it. The house contained a meeting room, committee rooms, two billiard rooms, and a bar. Temporarily, meals would be catered, but plans were made to build a restaurant "upon a scale commensurate with the dignity of what ought speedily to become the largest and most influential club in America."[27]

As it did in Philadelphia, the New York club caused some consternation among the excluded. Their discomfiture made Strong gleeful as he observed, "It is delightful to perceive that 'respectable' Copperheads begin to be aware of this club, and to squirm as if it irritated them somehow." Describing an encounter at the opera with a gentleman who claimed he disapproved of a club founded on a political basis and had therefore chosen to decline an offer of membership, Strong wrote, "Very funny; for in all our talk about organization and tests of admission, the name of William Butler Duncan has been familiarly used as a convenient . . . specimen of the class we would not admit on any terms."[28]

If in New York and Philadelphia the impetus for the Union Clubs came in part from an attempt to secure the moral and social advantage for a faction of the cities' elite, in Boston the club served to bring two upper-class factions closer, if only temporarily. For much of the antebellum period, Boston Brahmin society was noted for its cohesiveness and its ability to withstand challenge. In *The Unitarian Conscience*, Daniel Walker Howe described the alliance between Harvard moralists and Boston businessmen: the moralists provided a rationale for capitalism, the merchants granted them positions of cultural and moral leadership. In the

---

26. Bellows, *Union League Club of New York*, 6, 50; Strong, *Diary*, 302-3, 307.
27. "Report of Executive Committee," Bellows, *Union League Club of New York*, 19-21; Strong, *Diary*, 307; Bellows, *Union League Club of New York*, 53; Irwin, *A History of the Union League Club of New York City*, 27-28.
28. Strong, *Diary*, 319.

1830s, when textile manufacturing engendered a new economic elite, the old merchant elite adapted by financing the new industry, forging business alliances, and intermarrying. The sectional conflict called commitments and interests into the open. As Cotton Whigs fretted over the potential loss of Southern markets and business connections, Conscience Whigs insisted that slavery would expand no farther. After the attack on Fort Sumter, Boston's formerly Whig and now Republican elite had closed ranks once again, but the Emancipation Proclamation and plans for black troops presented yet another challenge.[29]

To conservative Bostonians, the war appeared to be taking a dangerously radical turn. In the Somerset Club, "the state of feeling was more conspicuously critical than patriotic," wrote Martin Brimmer, graduate of Harvard Law School and son of a wealthy former mayor of Boston. "Some privately denounced the war in all its aspects; some attacked indiscriminately all the acts of the government . . . ; some were indifferent; some were wavering; some, with the best intentions, were made doubtful or timid by the tone of people about them. For those, and there were happily many of them, who were unhesitating in their support of the war, there was no common centre, no rallying place."[30]

In February 1863, a committee of fourteen of Boston's elite, including Harvard scholar Charles E. Norton and John Murray Forbes, railroad magnate and United States Sanitary Commission founder, issued invitations to membership in a society of "clubbable men." In its desire to serve as a place for diverse members of the upper class to meet, the club officially eschewed political action and elected Edward Everett, an antebellum conservative Whig and John Bell's running mate on the 1860 Constitutional Union ticket, as League president. The membership rolls of the Boston Union Club bear testimony to its success in this endeavor: members of the city's mercantile and manufacturing elite joined—the Lowells, the Lawrences, the Appletons, and the Brookses—as did many of New England's most prominent intellectual and literary men, including Ralph Waldo Emerson, Edward Everett Hale, Oliver Wendell Holmes, and James Russell Lowell.[31]

Much as it had in Philadelphia and New York City, the Union League in Boston set the tone for the elite of the city, establishing national patriotism and fidelity to the administration as the standard of behavior in high society. As Oliver Wendell

---

29. Howe, *The Unitarian Conscience*, 140–41; Jahar, *Urban Establishment*, 55–56.

30. Cited in S. Lothrop Thorndike, *A Brief Sketch of the History of the Union Club of Boston* (Boston: Union Club of Boston, 1893), 6; Gibson, "Lincoln's League," 79–81.

31. Thorndike, *A Brief Sketch*, 7; S. Lothrop Thorndike, *The Past Members of the Union Club of Boston* (Boston: Union Club of Boston, 1893), passim.

Holmes observed, the club would both serve as a locus for ardent supporters of the administration and attract those whose chief concerns were social: "once a rallying point is given for all who mean hearty loyalty, the weak brethren who do not know what they believe will walk in with their white cravats and vacuous features, and leave the malignants in the only position they are ashamed of—that of being in the minority."[32]

As a result of the metropolitan Union Leagues, patriotism became mandatory for many of the urban upper and middle classes. As one contemporary later noted, the League's "effect was to make patriotism fashionable. Its political power consisted . . . in informing the rich and fashionable that they would lose caste if they became Copperheads." By the end of the Leagues' first year, membership in Philadelphia had grown to 985. The membership list of the New York club read like a *Who's Who* in New York City with a total of 528 members, and the Boston club boasted more than 400 members. Democrats and Republicans alike belonged. Those who were not members pretended to be. According to Strong, Charles Gould told William C. Russell "that the Union League Club was a most praiseworthy institution which every loyal citizen of New York ought to join at once. He [Charles Gould] had done a great deal to set it going and worked for it until he saw it fairly established and likely to succeed, and then he had resigned because he had so many engagements that he really couldn't—and so forth. Whereas Charles Gould and Prosper M. Wetmore have from the first been recognized as embodiments of corrupt, mercenary, self-seeking sham-patriotism, and as representing a dirty set of false-hearted hack stump orators and wire-pullers, vigilantly to be excluded."[33]

The promise of status and profit coaxed the wavering elite into the metropolitan Union Leagues, but once there, it was clear that though these clubs offered luxurious meeting rooms, elegant restaurants, and elite company, they were not ordinary gentlemen's clubs. The Leagues organized Committees on Enlistments, which raised tens of thousands of troops for the Union, sponsored speakers who addressed national topics, celebrated national anniversaries "which could be turned to account in affecting public sentiment," and appointed committees to carry out

---

32. Oliver Wendell Holmes to John Murray Forbes, Feb. 5, 1863, in Sarah Forbes Hughes, ed., *Reminiscences of John Murray Forbes*, vol. 2 (Boston: George H. Ellis, 1902), 218–19.

33. Cited in Lathrop, *History of the Union League of Philadelphia*, 42. Whiteman, *Gentlemen in Crisis*, 26, 66; Irwin, *A History of the Union League Club of New York City*, 24; Thorndike, *Past Members*, passim; Strong, *Diary*, 319.

various other war-supporting measures. League members also participated in electoral races. Setting aside its claim to nonpartisanship, the Philadelphia League campaigned in the 1863 gubernatorial race; both the Philadelphia and New York Leagues staunchly supported Lincoln in 1864. Through their publication societies, examined below, the Union Leagues advocated the national loan, income taxes, the draft, emancipation, and enlistment of black troops. Charting the course for the metropolitan elite to follow, they suggested that loyalty to country entailed championing a vigorous war effort, sustaining the war administration, and supporting the unprecedented growth of the national state.[34]

Perhaps the most striking statement that the Leagues made concerning the meaning of national patriotism for the upper class lay in their support for emancipation and their active role in the mustering of African American troops. This was, after all, a class of men whom, as Sven Beckert points out in a study of the New York City bourgeoisie, had agitated for compromise with the South at any cost prior to the war. Their support of such measures as the Fugitive Slave and Kansas-Nebraska acts was rooted in a strong desire to see the South, with its markets and cotton production, remain as a part of the Union. Similarly, their vehement opposition to secession and support of the Northern war effort were in large part responses to the threat to the authority of a national state that protected and fostered their business concerns.[35]

The Leagues were not, then, abolitionist organizations, though individuals ethically committed to the abolition of slavery did join. The members found common ground in their deep concern about the fate of the national state; hence many supported both emancipation and the deployment of black troops chiefly as war measures. Moreover, with the Emancipation Proclamation, anti-black sentiment stood to undercut support for the national cause. In Philadelphia and New York, the campaigns undertaken by the Leagues to raise and then showcase black troops were designed to aid the nation in its battles against both Southern secession and Northern resistance to increasingly radical war measures.

In June 1863, following months of campaigning on the part of its more abolitionist-minded members, the Union League of Philadelphia organized the Supervisory Committee for the Enlistment of Colored Troops and began raising money and recruiting men. Sentiment in Philadelphia was initially hostile:

---

34. Bellows, *Historical Sketch*, 53–84; Lathrop, *History of the Union League Club of Philadelphia*, 45–63, 70–81; Boker, *First Annual Report of the Board of Directors*, 3–9.

35. Beckert, "The Making of New York City's Bourgeoisie," 119–204.

Democrats in particular condemned the League for undertaking a reckless, even dangerous project. But supporters of the endeavor persevered. Working with leaders of Philadelphia's black community, they held mass meetings for the recruitment of black troops, issued circulars, and brought Frederick Douglass in to address League members on the training of black recruits. In July, the 3d United States Regiment, Colored Troops, joined the national forces. On October 3, the black troops paraded through downtown Philadelphia and then marched for review in front of Gen. George Cadwalader, who observed the parade from the steps of the Union League house. Though many feared a violent reaction from the city's racist contingent, a loud, "secretly hostile or openly jubilant" crowd thronged the streets; the parade was reportedly without incident.[36]

The New York League also recruited black troops and staged a similar parade only eight months after the draft riots had exposed the deep frustrations and anti-black sentiment of the Irish working class. One account, perhaps apocryphal, suggests that it was during those riots, as they sat armed behind locked doors and barricaded windows, that League members devised their plans. "If they got out of this thing alive, they would make the club defy public sentiment by raising and equipping a regiment of Negro troops and sending them to the front. More than that, they would march these freed men through the city streets." Particularly after the draft riots, it was important that Americans learn that loyalty was more important than color. Over the winter the regiment was assembled, and the soldiers trained on Riker's Island.[37]

On March 5, 1864, the regiment marched from the dock at the East 26th street wharf to the League building at Union Square, where an estimated 100,000 people viewed the presentation of colors to the new regiment. In a dramatic and symbolic gesture, the "Mothers, Wives, and Sisters of the Members of the Union League Club" stood on a grandstand erected in front of the clubhouse and presented the troops with their flags and an address signed by 189 prominent society women. This list included Mrs. John Jacob Astor and Mrs. John Jay, wives of men who symbolized both the elites' wealth and their patrician lineage. The address first recognized the Union League for its "liberality and intelligent patriotism," then turned to a truly remarkable tribute to the troops:

---

36. Lathrop, *History of the Union League of Philadelphia*, 75–81; Whiteman, *Gentlemen in Crisis*, 46–52.

37. Irwin, *A History of the Union League Club of New York City*, 30–37; Bellows, *Historical Sketch*, 56–57; Bernstein, *New York City Draft Riots*, 65–68.

"When you look at this flag and rush to battle ... remember that it is also an emblem of love and honor from the daughters of this great metropolis to her brave champions in the field, and that they will anxiously watch your career, glorying in your heroism, ministering to you when wounded and ill, and honoring your martyrdom with benedictions and with tears." Following an elaborate reception, the troops paraded through New York City as planned, accompanied by flag bearers, a hundred policemen and a military band.[38]

What was particularly remarkable about this tribute was its dramatic transgression of mid-nineteenth-century, white cultural norms. The intermingling of white women and black men spoke to Northerners' deepest racial fears. Yet here were the city's most elite white women, vowing to love and honor the black soldiers, to nurse those who were wounded back to health, and to weep over those who died. It was a striking statement of the role that emancipation and the arming of blacks had assumed in the League's understanding of patriotism.

Although Union League support for black troops was rooted in a desire to see the nation strengthened and preserved, the result broadened the definition of patriotism in America. Loyalty, not race, defined a patriot. While this message was intended in part for the participants of the city's recent draft riots, it held meaning for elites as well: if the upper class men who flocked to the Leagues were to enjoy its perquisites of social prestige, they would have to embrace its policies toward African Americans as well.[39]

Thus, through the appropriation of gentlemen's clubs, League leaders rallied their class behind the war. As the cities' most prominent professionals, businessmen, and intellectuals followed the lure of status and profit into the Union Clubs, patriotism, which began with the swearing of unwavering loyalty, soon meant support for the vigorous prosecution of the war, an expanding national state, emancipation, and black troops. Moreover, by bringing the upper class's wealth, power, and prestige to the problem of wartime support, Union League leaders modeled their brand of loyalty and displayed their credentials to govern. Claiming the exclusive mantle of patriotism, they reclaimed some of the cultural and social authority that had escaped them prior to the war. Support from the cities' elite alone, however, would not win the war. If defeatism within the up-

---

38. Irwin, *A History of the Union League Club of New York City*, 30–37; Bellows, *Historical Sketch*, 56–57; Bernstein, *New York City Draft Riots*, 65–68; *Address to the 20th Regiment, U.S. Colored Troops on the Occasion of the Presentation of a Stand of Colors by the Ladies*, March 5, 1864, in Bellows, *Historical Sketch*, 187.

39. Bernstein, *New York City Draft Riots*, 67.

per classes could be mitigated through the manipulation of status ambition, a different approach was required for the great majority of Americans.

For the founders of the Union League, the masses had always presented a special problem. As a group, League founders had little respect for the common man and disdained democracy. Representatives of their cities' intelligentsia as well as their professional and capitalist classes, some feared unfettered democracy for its impact on culture, or the "training and refinement of . . . tastes, ideas, and manners;" others recognized it as a threat to property. Most, however, agreed that popular assertiveness threatened social stability. Charles Eliot Norton, the editor of the Boston Loyal Publication Society, argued that the masses were without "counsel, restraint or education." "It is not, then," he advised, "to the people that we look for wisdom and intelligence . . . they could not, if they would, rescue themselves from evil;" hence, the upper class must accept its role as guardian. Strong likened the people to a contagious disease: "Neither the blind masses, the swinish multitude that rule us under our accursed system of universal suffrage, nor the case of typhoid, can be expected to exercise self-control."[40]

Elite fears of democratic passions were temporarily assuaged when the populace rallied following the attack on Fort Sumter. Labor union branches closed, labor meetings were canceled, and strikes were called off as workers rushed to enlist in the Union cause. As the war progressed, however, Union defeats, a burgeoning national state, and increasingly revolutionary war aims fed growing disillusionment with the war and its Republican advocates. Economic tensions further antagonized the people: mounting taxes and wartime inflation denied workers the prosperity the nation as a whole seemed to be enjoying. Eggs increased from fifteen to twenty-five cents in a two-year period; potatoes and bread nearly doubled. In Pennsylvania, prices rose 110 to 200 percent between March 1861 and November 1862 while wages lagged.[41]

In the early months of the war, workers did little in the way of organizing to combat high prices and stagnant wages. By late 1862, as business and industry flourished, organization appeared necessary. Skilled and semi-skilled tradesmen

---

40. Jahar, *The Urban Establishment*, 43; Kermit Vanderbilt, *Charles Eliot Norton: Apostle of Culture in a Democracy* (Cambridge, Mass.: Belknap Press of Harvard Univ. Press, 1959), 1, 30, 44; Strong, *Diary*, 272. See also the writings of Francis Lieber in Frank Freidel, *Francis Lieber: Nineteenth-Century Liberal* (Baton Rouge: Louisiana State Univ. Press, 1947), 160.

41. Phillip Shaw Paludan, *"A People's Contest": The Union and the Civil War 1861–1865* (New York: Harper & Row, 1988), 182; Arnold M. Shankman, *The Pennsylvania Antiwar Movement 1861–1865* (Rutherford: Fairleigh Dickinson Univ. Press, 1980), 97.

began to demand higher wages. By early 1863, labor was experiencing what Philip Foner has called "a revival of trade unionism." New unions were established; old unions grew; strikes abounded. In 1862 New York City witnessed thirteen trade-wide strikes. That number rose to twenty-nine in 1863 and forty-two in 1864. Noting the sudden upsurge of labor unrest, in June 1863, *Fincher's Trade Review* ran a series on "The Upheaving Masses in Motion!"[42] Such upheaval was anathema to the founders of the Union League, who feared that, in addition to jeopardizing the social order, labor's assertions would undermine the war effort. Even Forbes, who, almost alone among the Leagues' elite, claimed that "true democracy" was "a particular hobby," feared the impact of "wak(ing) up the laboring classes" on the war."[43]

In fact, most workers remained surprisingly loyal. Although some were Democrats and some Republicans, the vast majority continued to support the government. League members, however, who feared for the loyalty not only of eastern labor but of the midwestern masses, were convinced that Northern anarchy and Southern victory were certain if popular discontent enjoyed free reign. Democratic victories in the 1862 fall elections served as a tocsin to the unionist elite across the country. Thus, long before the July 1863 draft riots appeared to give shape to their fears, the Unionist upper classes embarked on a campaign to remind the masses for whom the war was being waged, and to instruct them in a more deferential patriotism.[44]

In the early months of 1863, leading intellectuals, industrialists, and merchants in Philadelphia, New York, and Boston founded publication societies to produce and distribute pro-Union literature. In Philadelphia, wealthy businessman Benjamin Gerhard joined forces with prominent merchant William Ashurst and lawyer Joseph B. Townsend to head the Board of Publication of the Union League of Philadelphia. In New York, the Loyal Publication Society placed Columbia University political scientist Francis Lieber at the helm, and in Boston, railroad magnate John Murray Forbes and Harvard scholar Charles

---

42. Philip S. Foner, *History of the Labor Movement in the United States*, vol. 1 (New York: International Publishers, 1947), 339; David Montgomery, *Beyond Equality: Labor and the Radical Republicans 1862-1872* (Urbana: Univ. of Illinois Press, 1981), 96-97; Paludan, *"A People's Contest,"* 187; *Fincher's Trade Review*, June 20, 1863.

43. JMF to William Pitt Fessenden, Jan. 29, 1863, in Hughes, *Reminiscences* 2:214-15; Thomas C. Cochran, *Railroad Leaders 1845-1890: The Business Mind in Action* (New York: Russell and Russell, 1965), 180.

44. On the loyalty of labor, see Foner, *History of the Labor Movement*, 331-37; Montgomery, *Beyond Equality*, 91-134.

Eliot Norton established the New England Loyal Publication Society. Edward Everett Hale, who would author "The Man Without a Country," was on the Boston society's board of directors. In all three cities, the publication committees were financed by members of the Union Leagues, in collaboration with the cities' leading capitalists.[45] The publication societies solicited pro-Union literature from Northern writers and culled nationalist articles from Union newspapers. They printed pamphlets and broadsides, then distributed these publications across the North. They sent them to smaller Union Leagues for distribution in local communities; to postmasters who delivered them to local authorities, businesses, and libraries; and to newspaper editors for inclusion in local papers. All told, millions of pamphlets and broadsides were produced and distributed by the publication societies.[46]

From the beginning, the publication societies directed their efforts at the masses. As a member of Philadelphia's Board of Publication reflected years later, "Those devoted loyalists realized to the full the imperative necessity for stimulating a healthy national sentiment among the class from which recruits were chiefly to come ... and then there was the 'average man' to be looked after; toned up in his conception of duty."[47] Stimulating a "healthy national sentiment" among a discouraged people in the midst of a long war was a challenge. The pamphlets and broadsides brought a variety of approaches to this task. To bolster the spirits of a war-weary public, they placed the war in historical perspective, pointing to the precedents of long wars ending in national honor, such as the Peninsular War, wherein the British had persevered for seven years

---

45. Boker, *First Annual Report of the Board of Directors*, 6–7; "Minutes of the Union League of Philadelphia," Feb. 17, 1863, MSS, ULP; Lathrop, *History of the Union League of Philadelphia*, 48; Whiteman, *Gentlemen in Crisis*, 273–77; Loyal Publication Society, *Report of Proceedings at the First Anniversary Meeting of the Loyal Publication Society* (New York: The Society, 1864), 8–12; Silvestro, "None But Patriots," 127; George Winston Smith, "Broadsides for Freedom: Civil War Propaganda in New England," *The New England Quarterly* 21 (Sept. 1948): 292. As a result of the long gap between the discussions of a New York League and the formation of the League itself, the Loyal Publication Society actually predated the New York League. Both the New York and the Boston Publication Societies appear to have been associated with, but not necessarily direct products of, the Union Leagues.

46. Whiteman, *Gentlemen in Crisis*, 30–42; Union League of Philadelphia, *Chronicle of the Union League of Philadelphia*, 106; Frank Freidel, "The Loyal Publication Society: A Pro-Union Propaganda Agency," *Mississippi Valley Historical Review* 17 (Dec. 1939): 359–63; Smith, "Broadsides for Freedom," 292; James B. Thayer to William E. Junior, Esq., Feb. 1, 1864, MSS, New England Loyal Publication Society, Boston Public Library, Boston.

47. Freidel, *Lieber*, 365; JMF to WCN, July 28, 1862, in Sarah Forbes Hughes, ed., *Letters and Recollections of John Murray Forbes*, vol. 1 (Boston: George H. Ellis Co., 1905), 324–25; Union League of Philadelphia, *Chronicle of the Union League of Philadelphia*, 103.

before triumphing over the French. Many pamphlets invoked the voice of the soldiers to instill resolve in readers. After all, if the soldiers who bore the brunt of the suffering could resist defeatism, what right did the people have to succumb? Others painted the nation as the foundation of America's wealth and prosperity, discouraged the elevation of party above country, and addressed Northerners' complaints about the growing nation-state and its increasingly radical policies. Describing the benefits that these new policies would bring to Northern whites, many pamphlets depicted the war as one for free labor. As Forbes explained in a March 1863 letter to Norton, "I think we can do most good by showing how completely this is the war of a class, and a small one, against the people everywhere. . . ." In December he reiterated: "the North will never be firmly united until the truth is more widely spread that this is a war of slave aristocracy versus the people North and South."[48]

Once the masses understood that the war had been undertaken on their behalf, it remained only for them to be "toned up in [their] conception of duty." Duty varied, as Henry Bellows was reported to have told a camp of Union soldiers, according to "one's position and surroundings." Strong had acknowledged the difficulties of unconditional loyalty during deliberations on qualifications for League membership: "No one can be expected to pledge himself to uphold whatever any set of men at Washington or elsewhere may hereafter think proper to do. . . ." No such understanding was granted the masses. The marches of black soldiers down the streets of Philadelphia and New York may have broadened the definition of patriotism by removing race as a factor, but they offered another prescription in its place. Iver Bernstein argues that "through their open association with the black poor, merchants sought to counteract working class disloyalty publicly by exhibiting an ideal relationship between classes." The Union League

---

48. For the war in historical perspective, see New York Loyal Publication Society (NYLPS) Pamphlet #11, *Pamphlets Issued By the New York Loyal Publication Society;* Board of Publication of the Union League of Philadelphia (BPULP) Pamphlet #4, MSS, ULP. For the soldiers, see NYLPS Pamphlets #13, #4, #9, *Pamphlets Issued By the New York Loyal Publication Society*. For the nation's wealth and prosperity, see New England Loyal Publication Society (NELPS) clipping # 15, Manuscript Papers, New England Loyal Publication Society (MSS NELPS), Boston Public Library, Boston; NELPS clipping # 91, MSS NELPS; NYLPS Pamphlets #45, #48; *Pamphlets Issued By the New York Loyal Publication Society* BPULP Pamphlet #37, MSS, ULP. For partisanship see BPULP Pamphlet #41, MSS, ULP; NYLPS Pamphlet #16, *Pamphlets Issued By the New York Loyal Publication Society.* For defense of government policies, see BPULP Pamphlet #12, MSS, ULP; NYLPS Pamphlet #22, *Pamphlets Issued By the New York Loyal Publication Society.* For the war for free labor, see NELPS Clipping #144, MSS NELPS; John Murray Forbes (JMF) to Charles Elliot Norton (CEN), March 22, 1863, MSS NELPS; JMF to CEN, Dec. 26, 1863, MSS, NELPS.

could "uphold the city's blacks as a model deferential working class because of their indisputable status as victims."[49]

The true patriot, then, was deferential and unquestioning. "A man must be either for his country or against his country," averred Maj. Gen. Benjamin Butler, in a widely circulated pamphlet. "He cannot be throwing impediments all the time in the way of the progress of his Government under pretense that he is helping some other portion of his country...." Even if dissension was considered acceptable in times of peace—a claim which many League members disputed—war demanded silence and support: "We are in the midst of a civil war," a pamphlet on financial war measures reminded Americans. "Men and money are necessary for (the nation's) protection, ... the national life must be preserved.... Sir, with all my objections to the financial system of the country, I feel it to be my duty to support that system *until the war is over.*"[50]

Many pamphlets spoke to the discontent that Americans might feel but must not express: "the present Government was not the Government of my choice" acknowledged Butler as he addressed soldiers in the field. He added: "I did not vote for it, or any part of it, but it is the Government of my country ... and as long as I believe that Government to be honestly administered, I will throw a mantle over any mistakes that I think it has made, and support it heartily.... I am a traitor and a false man if I alter in my support ... ; no man who opposed his country in time of war ever profited." A New England broadside argued that even a democratic government could not survive if its members were not willing to cease discussion when called upon to do so by the crisis of the nation and the authority of the government. Americans were not, it pointed out "living together as a debating club."[51]

That wartime patriotism implied unquestioning support of the government's policies was a common theme in the pamphlet literature, but for some Union Leaguers, unqualified loyalty should not be limited to times of war. Like Philip Nolan in "The Man Without a Country," these men argued, Americans were singularly unappreciative of the nation and the role it played in their lives. During the war, a handful of Northern intellectuals set out to cultivate a new form of patriotism—an old world "loyalty"—among Americans, whose ideas of consensual

---

49. Strong, *Diary*, 178, 293; Bernstein, *New York City Draft Riots*, 57.
50. NYLPS Pamphlet #7, #45, *Pamphlets Issued by the New York Loyal Publication Society*; NELPS Clipping #46, MSS NELPS.
51. BPULP Pamphlet #15, MSS, ULP; NELPS clipping # 46, MSS NELPS. See also NYLPS Pamphlet #15, *Pamphlets Issued By the New York Loyal Publication Society*.

government informed contractual views of their duties as citizens. According to these men, the contractual premise was flawed: the nation was not the product of a contract, but an organism whose growth was natural and good. Loyalty to such a nation must be unconditional, much like the love a mother gives her child. As historian George Fredrickson has explained, "Americans needed to think of themselves as subjects, having the blind duty to uphold a traditional way of life, rather than as free individuals claiming their rights under the constitution."[52]

The idea of an organic society was not unique to the Union League. This tenet had roots both in German political theory—Francis Lieber, who had studied Hegel, held that the Constitution was "an organism of national life . . . not a mere league of independent states or nations"—and in Unitarianism. According to historian Daniel Walker Howe, Unitarians in the early nineteenth century believed that the "ideal commonwealth was an organic unit, composed, like a living body, of interrelated parts, each contributing its essential function." It existed as an "aid to the expression of human purposes." Unitarians rejected the notion of a social compact, arguing that emotional attachment was more important to the stability of society than self-interest. But if "social cohesion depended on emotional appeals, it was obviously necessary to envelop institutions in some kind of mystical aura."[53]

It is not surprising, then, to find New England Loyal Publication Society's editor Charles Norton, son of the prominent Unitarian Andrews Norton, arguing, "Our nation was never, in truth, founded . . . it was not made by man; it is no discovery or invention, but a natural growth." Boston League member Alexander H. Bullock was an elegant spokesman for such organicism. For him a nation was not an aggregate of individuals, but "a power and a life," "the agency and instrumentality among the providence of God and the designs of his glory. We are indeed a part of it, but only for a moment. . . . The organism of a nation! It enfolds and blesses races; it perpetuates traditions, ideas, examples, principles . . . it is government!"[54]

---

52. Fredrickson, *Inner Civil War*, 138, 130-65; Curti, *Roots of American Loyalty*, 172-99; Peter Dobkin Hall, *The Organization of American Culture, 1700-1900: Private Institutions, Elites, and the Origins of American Nationality* (New York: New York Univ. Press, 1982).

53. Curti, *Roots of American Loyalty*, 173-81; Freidel, *Lieber*, 302-3; Bernard Edward Brown, *American Conservatives: The Political Thought of Francis Lieber and John W. Burgess* (New York: Columbia Univ. Press, 1951), 44-46; Howe, *Unitarian Conscience*, 125-31.

54. Charles Elliot Norton, "American Political Ideas," *North American Review* 101 (Oct. 1865): 550-66; Alexander H. Bullock, *The Relations of the Educated Man with American Nationality: Address of Alexander H. Bullock, before the Literary Societies of Williams College, August 1, 1864* (Boston: Wright and Potter, 1864), 1-32. For Bullock as a League member see Thorndike, *Past Members*, 27.

A citizen's obligation to such a nation was profound, transcending the notions of patriotism that had characterized the American polity. Americans' attitudes toward their leaders in particular required revision. In a sermon titled "Unconditional Loyalty," the Unitarian minister Henry Bellows argued, "The Head of a Nation is a sacred person.... There is something in the chief magistrate infinitely more important than his personal qualities, his judgment, his intelligence, his rectitude. It is his office, his representative character as the National Head. He can truly say with Louis XIV, 'The State—it is I. Dishonor me, and you disgrace the nation.' ... To rally 'round the President—without question or dispute—is the first and most sacred duty of loyal citizens."[55]

Bellows's sermon, delivered early in 1863, was published as a pamphlet by the New York society later that year. It also appeared in numerous Northern newspapers and was republished by the Board of Publication in Philadelphia in September. That same month, the Philadelphia board published another sermon with a similar tone: "I hold that the President of the United States, according to the scriptures, is the minister of God," the Reverend William B. Stewart proclaimed. "The President, with the constitution in his hand, can say to those who denounce him ... as Louis XIV of France said to his opponents, 'The Government, it is I.'"[56]

Harsh as it may have seemed, such silent obedience was not without its rewards. In fact, for those who considered this tenet in its entirety, the maxim of unquestioning loyalty to a nation and the state which embodied that nation represented the sole path to freedom—to the realization of self. True liberty "requires a *country*," Lieber insisted. It was only through identification with and obedience to the nation that the mystical spirit of a people could be fulfilled. Embracing the implications—if not the philosophical foundations—of both Hegelian romanticism and Unitarian organicism, League members called for Americans to recognize the nation as the sole route to freedom. They enveloped the nation-state with the Unitarian "mystical aura" in prose: "We live not our lives merely," wrote Bullock," but we live a *state* consciousness that runs back and prefigures among the eternities, blending with the ages past and bidding the next ones hail." Without that state, "in obeyed and felt majesty, there is no development for man, no mission for woman, no sleep for children. How sublime the life of a nation!"[57]

---

55. Henry W. Bellows, "Unconditional Loyalty" (New York, 1863), in Frank Freidel, ed., *Union Pamphlets of the Civil War, 1861-1865* (Cambridge: Belknap Press of Harvard Univ. Press) 1967.

56. BPULP Pamphlet #41, MSS, ULP.

57. Freidel, *Lieber*, 302; Brown, *American Conservatives*, 44-45; Bullock, *The Relations of the Educated Man with American Nationality*, 1-32 (emphasis added).

Though popular in elite intellectual and literary circles, it is doubtful that this notion of freedom through patriotic obedience gained much acceptance among a people whose revolutionary heritage defied old world precepts of hierarchy and authority. But the same ideas, when set forward without political science preachments or philosophical anachronisms, could evoke Americans' deepest fears of atomization, of the individual, in Tocqueville's words, confined "entirely within the solitude of his own heart."[58]

In Edward Everett Hale's "The Man Without a Country," the organic vision was made palatable to Americans. Hale's emotional, firsthand—albeit fictional—account of the spiritual cost of disloyalty provided a concrete counterpoint to the theoretical patriotism of League sermons and tracts. Compelling in its detail, fantastic yet believable, the narrative aimed to tap its readers' emotions. Hale himself professed, "my own tears blotted the paper of the original manuscript."[59] "The Man Without a Country" was inspired by exiled Copperhead Clement Vallandigham's bid for the Ohio governorship in the fall of 1863 and, more specifically, by Vallandigham's assertion that he "did not want to belong to a nation which would compel by arms the loyalty of any of its citizens; he did not want to belong to the United States." Although Hale campaigned to get the story published before the Ohio gubernatorial election so that he might influence the outcome, the story appeared in *Atlantic Monthly* in December 1863, two months after Vallandigham's defeat.[60]

The story is narrated by Frederic Ingham, an old shipmate of Philip Nolan's, and begins as Ingham discovers Nolan's death notice in the paper. Nolan, a privileged wealthy Westerner, a "gay, dashing, bright young fellow," had been one of Aaron Burr's accomplices. Though his role was small, though his fellow conspirators escaped with minor sentences, Nolan's crime is his irreverence, and for this he is exiled not to another country, but to an endless journey on the seas. It is during that journey that Nolan learns what it means to be without a country. Through Ingham, Hale relates a series of incidents which reveal Nolan's evolving, and eventually obsessive, patriotism. Taking turns reading aloud to

---

58. Tocqueville, *Democracy in America*, vol. 2, ed. Phillips Bradley (New York: Vintage Books, 1945), 106.

59. Edward Everett Hale, "Introduction," *The Man Without a Country and Other Stories* (Boston: Little, Brown, 1898), 12.

60. Adams, *Edward Everett Hale*, 8; Hale, "Introduction," 4-5; Edward Everett Hale, *Memories of a Hundred Years*, vol. 2 (New York: Macmillan, 1902), 217-18; William Sloane Kennedy, "Edward Everett Hale," *The Century Illustrated Monthly Magazine* 29 (Jan. 1885): 341.

pass the time on the ship, the sailors unwittingly hand a book of poems to Nolan just at the point in Sir Walter Scott's "The Lay of the Minstrel" where he is to read a tragically ironic passage:

> Breathes there a man with soul so dead
> Who never to himself has said
> This is my own, my native land
> Whose heart has ne'er within him burned
> As home his footsteps he hath turned
> From wandering on a foreign strand?
> For him no minstrel raptures swell;
> High though his titles, proud his name,
> Boundless his wealth as wish may claim,
> Despite these titles, power and pelf,
> The wretch, concentrated all in self . . .

Nolan turns white while reading the passage, "gags" and "chokes," then flings the book into the ocean and retires to his cabin, from which he does not emerge for two months.

When a great ball is held on board the ship, Nolan hopes it may be his chance to hear the news from home. There is a celebrated Southern beauty on board; perhaps she has not heard of his sentence. Bowing to the woman, he asks for a dance. Because the dance is a contra-dance, there is little time for talk, but there is, as Hale avers, "chances for tongues and sounds, as well as for eyes and blushes." Nolan woos the Southern beauty with flattery and casual conversation, then, "a little pale," he asks what she has heard from home. He is instantly rebuffed. The object of his failed seduction is not romantic love but word from the states: country is a more primal need than love or sex.

In the South Atlantic in the first days after the slave-trade treaty, Nolan's ship overhauls a small schooner with slaves aboard. Acting as a Portuguese interpreter, Nolan tells the slaves that they are free and will be taken to Cape Palmas. The slaves protest, and Nolan must translate their emotional protestations: they want to go home to their own beloved countries. Returning to the ship in a dinghy, Nolan turns to the young Ingham: "Remember, boy, that behind all these men you have to do with, behind officers and Government and people even, there is the 'Country Herself,' your country, and that you belong to her as you belong to your own mother."

Nolan's dying wish is to hear what has become of his beloved country. His deathbed visitor violates the terms of Nolan's sentence and at last shares with Nolan the events of the previous fifty years. He fills Nolan's dated map in, and describes the glory that has become the United States. He tells him of "old Scott and Jackson," of steamboats and railroads and inventions, of West Point and the Smithsonian and the Capital and Lincoln, of "the grandeur of his country and its prosperity." He has not the heart to tell him of the war. Nolan dies within the hour and is buried at sea.

"The Man Without a Country" was an instant success. It remained in print throughout the war, and was reprinted intermittently for years afterward. In spite of this success, Hale regretted that his hopes for anonymity were not realized. He had hoped that the public would believe his story was true. Told in a first person narrative, the story is peppered with statements that lead the reader to that assumption: "this I know" or "this I have been told" precede many of the narrator's revelations. A myriad of historic details adds to the story's verisimilitude. The ship on which Nolan dies is named after a real vessel that had been lost at sea just two years before the story's publication. The sailors and captains had names similar to real historic figures. Even the ship's alleged longitude and latitude at the time of Nolan's death, which, claimed Hale, initially placed the Levant at the top of the Andes as a hint to the clever of the story's fictional nature, was changed before publication—perhaps, Hale admitted, by himself—to place the ship not far from where she had in fact disappeared.[61]

In spite of the fact that Hale's name appeared in the index, many readers assumed the story was factual. Many wrote to say they had known Nolan or Ingham. Some expressed horror that the government would effect such a cruel punishment. Retired sailors wrote Hale to say they remembered Ingham, and a rumor that Nolan had actually been pardoned circulated.[62]

Years later, Hale reflected that he had set out to teach Americans "that the country is in itself an entity. It is a Being," and to show how meaningless life outside of that entity must be. Nolan does not miss friends or family or art or women. He is not even called by name. Because his buttons bore no insignias, the sailors called

---

61. Adams, *Edward Everett Hale*, 27; Nancy Esther James, "Realism in Romance: A Critical Study of the Short Stories of Edward Everett Hale" (Ph.D. diss., Pennsylvania State University, 1969) 17, 178-85; Hale, "Introduction," 9-12; Edward Everett Hale to Charles Hale, Nov. 28, 1863, in Edward Everett Hale MSS, New York State Library, Albany, New York; Holloway, *Edward Everett Hale*, 136-37.

62. Holloway, *Edward Everett Hale*, 135-36.

him "Plain Buttons." He has been completely stripped of all identity, because without country, there is no identity.[63]

Like Philip Nolan, Civil War Northerners stood to lose their country and little comprehended the enormous cost. If intellectual tracts did not resonate, Nolan's suffering was palpable. The pathos of his tale was an admonition: infidelity to country could mean loss of country, an awful fate not even poor Nolan deserved. Hale's story dramatized this maxim, and brought it into living rooms, reading rooms, and libraries across the North. It was a provocative notion for a people who appeared at times to have more invested in their state, local, or even partisan identities than they did in their role as members of a nation.

---

63. Edward Everett Hale, "Introduction" in "The Man Without a Country," *The Outlook*, May 14, 1898, 116. Nolan's nickname "Plain Buttons" and its relation to the loss of identity are discussed in James, "Realism in Romance," 17, 178–85.

Science and Medicine

Yankees versus Yellow Jack in New Orleans, 1862–1866

JO ANN CARRIGAN

From the late eighteenth century until the first year of the Civil War cases of yellow fever appeared annually in New Orleans. Several times in each decade the disease ravaged the city in violent epidemic form, disrupting all normal social and economic activities, inciting panic and mass exodus from the vicinity, and burdening the remaining inhabitants with problems of widespread sickness and death. Throughout the first half of the nineteenth century each of the recurring pestilential attacks seemed even more virulent than the last. The decade of the 1850's witnessed four great epidemics, worse than anything the Crescent City had ever suffered—and it had suffered much. In 1853, 1854, 1855, and 1858 yellow fever claimed a total mortality of about eighteen thousand in New Orleans alone, plus additional thousands in the gulf ports, river towns, and interior communities to which the disease was transmitted from its original focus.[1]

Since the early 1800's Yellow Jack's repeated incursions had earned for New Orleans a reputation throughout the country as an exceedingly insalubrious location. The horrors of the 1850's only intensified the city's notoriety. It was

---

Jo Ann Carrigan is a member of the history faculty at Louisiana State University in Baton Rouge and editor of *Louisiana History*, the journal of the Louisiana State Historical Association.

    1. Edward Hall Barton, *The Cause and Prevention of Yellow Fever, Contained in the Report of the Sanitary Commission of New Orleans* (Philadelphia, 1855), pp. 41-44 and comparative table preceding p. 1; *New Orleans Medical and Surgical Journal*, new ser., VI (1879), 699.

also a well-known fact that newcomers to New Orleans, especially European immigrants and Northerners, always bore the brunt of the fever's attacks and swelled the mortality lists, while native and long-resident New Orleanians exhibited considerable resistance or immunity to its ravages.[2] Had New Orleans been visited by the scourge during the period of Federal wartime occupation, the Northern forces would undoubtedly have suffered severe losses and disorganization—at least for a period of two or three months, the usual duration of a yellow fever epidemic. Ironically, at the very time the city might have considered Yellow Jack more friend than foe, that disease remained conspicuously absent.

In its annual report for 1861 the Louisiana State Board of Health recorded a total annual mortality much lower than the usual figure for New Orleans, and also announced the astounding fact that for the first time in more than a half century not a single death from yellow fever had occurred in the Crescent City. This incredible phenomenon was attributed to the Federal blockade, "partial though it may have been," which together with Louisiana's quarantine restrictions had cut down the possibilities of introducing disease from foreign ports.[3] This year of complete exemption from the pestilence marked the beginning of a brief interregnum in yellow fever's century-long reign in New Orleans, while an entirely different species of force moved in to dominate the city—Yankee troops.

In late April, 1862, the Crescent City fell to the Union forces and remained under military occupation throughout the war. Particularly during the first year of wartime occupation, yellow fever was a subject much in the minds of both the conquerors and the conquered—a source of great fear and dread to the one, of hope and encouragement to the other. General Benjamin F. Butler, in command of the Federal occupation forces during the first year, later wrote: "I learned that the rebels were actually relying largely upon the yellow fever to clear out the Northern troops, the men of New England and the Northwest . . . whom they had learned from experience were usually the first victims of the scourge." Furthermore, he had also heard "that in the churches [of New Orleans] prayers

---

2. This phenomenon, so noticeable that yellow fever was sometimes called "the stranger's fever," was at that time explained on the basis of acclimation. It was believed, in other words, that natives and long-term residents had become adjusted to the climate and were thereby rendered less susceptible or even immune to yellow fever. The real explanation is that these New Orleanians had probably suffered mild, unrecognized cases of yellow fever in childhood, which gave them lifelong immunity. Yellow fever's erratic activities remained a mysterious and highly controversial problem to theorists until 1900-1901, when the U.S. Army Commission under Walter Reed in Cuba demonstrated the fever's mode of transmission to be the *Aedes aegypti* mosquito.

3. *Report of the Louisiana State Board of Health for 1861* (Baton Rouge, 1861), p. 4.

were put up that the pestilence might come as a divine interposition on behalf of the brethren."[4]

Although he found this difficult to believe, Butler noticed "many things that render[ed] it almost probable." It seemed to him that New Orleanians deliberately cultivated a "condition of perfect nastiness" as if in the hope of generating the fever. If they did go so far as to offer up prayers, he wrote, they did not do so aloud in the churches because Federal soldiers attended their services. But "in the course of liturgy the clergyman always gave out at a certain point ... an opportunity for silent prayer," the General reflected, "and then the people either prayed for the yellow fever, or Jefferson Davis to come there victorious; neither of which was comforting to the Yankee worshiper. . . ."[5] These observations, although perhaps slightly exaggerated, were not entirely a product of Butler's imagination. A New Orleans physician, writing after the war, remarked that "the hostile population of New Orleans . . . [had] confidently anticipated that if the enemy should take New Orleans, the yellow fever would take the enemy."[6]

Apparently the hopeful expectation of a Yellow Jack epidemic which would wipe out the Yankees in the Crescent City was not confined solely to New Orleanians. One newspaper in Virginia consoled the people of the Confederacy over the Union capture of New Orleans with this thought: "They have got the elephant, it is true, but it is a prize which will cost them vastly more to keep than the animal is worth, if his Saffron Majesty shall make his usual annual visit to the city and wave his sceptre in the hospitals there."[7]

Northern soldiers, aware of the terrors of that fatal pestilence for which New Orleans was infamous, were also well-acquainted with stories of the fever's obvious preference for the unacclimated stranger. Not for one moment were the forces of occupation allowed by the residents of New Orleans to forget this fact. Wishing to intensify fear among the troops, two citizens armed with measuring tape and notebook set off on a sardonic mission. Approaching a group of Federal soldiers, the morbid pranksters began to measure the height of the Northerners and take down notations of the same. When asked the meaning of this action, they replied that a contract had been obtained for making ten thousand coffins which would

---

4. Benjamin F. Butler, *Butler's Book* (Boston, 1892), p. 396.
5. Benjamin F. Butler, "Some Experiences with Yellow Fever and its Prevention," *North American Review*, CXLVII (1888), 530.
6. *New Orleans Medical and Surgical Journal*, XXIII (1870), 568.
7. Howard Palmer Johnson, "New Orleans under General Butler," *Louisiana Historical Quarterly*, XXIV (1941), 478.

be needed ultimately for the steady stream of Yankee replacements sent in as, one by one, yellow fever carried them off. Even the children of the Crescent City participated in the harassment of the United States troops. In late May and early June of 1862 they jeeringly chanted at the soldiers in the streets that

"Yellow Jack will grab them up
"And take them all away."[8]

For once it seems that the citizens of New Orleans would have welcomed the arrival of the Saffron Scourge. According to General Butler, all their conversations in the presence of his officers included descriptions of past epidemic horrors, especially the disaster of 1853 when yellow fever had claimed eight thousand victims in New Orleans. Under a constant barrage of this demoralizing propaganda, Butler's men soon began to evidence its effects. Many of the officers were panic-stricken, depressed; some requested transfers to different areas; others offered every conceivable excuse for leaves. But the General held firm and proceeded to study the problem of yellow fever in order to circumvent the coming of an epidemic. He asked an old New Orleans physician about ways and means to prevent the fever. No means existed, he was told, and no way to prevent its spread once under way. The physician admitted that quarantine of incoming vessels might be useful, but pointed out that the presence of unacclimated troops together with the city's unsanitary condition made it likely that the disease, if it broke out at all, would rage with great fury. Butler then obtained some books on the subject and a map of New Orleans indicating the localities where Yellow Jack usually prevailed. Upon investigation of those places, he found them uniformly "filthy with rotting matter."

After much reading, investigating, and thinking on the questions relating to the pestilence, General Butler finally developed his own fever theory. He concluded that exhalations from putrid animal matter produced typhus fever and that exhalations from rotting vegetable matter produced congestive fevers. Upon breaking out, yellow fever would spread through that portion of the atmosphere contaminated by *both* the animal and the vegetable effluvia. In Butler's opinion, the disease was not indigenous to New Orleans as so many believed, but rather its "seeds" had to be imported. It was possible, he thought, for these seeds to last

---

8. Elisabeth Joan Doyle, "Civilian Life in Occupied New Orleans, 1862-65" (Ph.D. dissertation, Louisiana State University, 1955), pp. 56-57.

through the winter hidden away in woolen clothing and protected from the frost. Without the dual contamination of the atmosphere, however, he believed the seeds, whether imported fresh or preserved through the winter months, would be unable to propagate.

Having settled upon three indispensable factors involved in the production of an epidemic, Butler set out to deal with them without delay. First of all, since he believed the seeds to be imported, he decided to enforce a strict quarantine on the Mississippi River below New Orleans. Secondly, he realized it would be impossible to dispose of all decaying vegetable matter because of the dense growth around the city. But if a *combination* of animal and vegetable elements was required to produce an epidemic atmosphere, the disposal of either one of the two elements would suffice. He was convinced that putrid animal matter and filth could be cleared away. After neatly outlining the problem in his mind, General Butler set to work to accomplish the two indicated objectives: instituting an effective quarantine system and cleaning up the city of New Orleans. Interestingly enough, his theory represented a composite of practically all the epidemiological concepts which had been floating around for centuries, and his program of prevention combined the two suggestions so long debated by yellow fever philosophers—quarantine and sanitation.

Although previous attempts had been made to institute such measures, never before had sanitation and quarantine been so rigorously enforced in the Crescent City as under Butler's iron hand. He established a firm, uncompromising guard at the state's regular quarantine station seventy miles below New Orleans where, in his words, "thirty-two and sixty-eight pound shots should be the messengers to execute the health orders." His quarantine regulations and means of enforcement stood in striking contrast to the lax, inconsistent, and easily evaded system previously attempted by Louisiana health authorities. By Butler's order, all vessels entering the river were required to stop below Fort St. Philip, about five miles downriver from the quarantine station, for initial inspection by a duly-appointed health officer. This gentleman then reported to the General the sanitary condition of the vessel, its passengers, crew, and cargo. If the quarantine officer extended a clean bill of health and Butler in turn telegraphed his consent, then and only then could the vessel proceed upriver to the city. "If any vessel attempted to evade quarantine regulations and pass up without being examined," recalled Butler, "the vessel was to be stopped if there was power enough in the fort to do it." Unlike Louisiana's lawmakers who had drafted the state's quarantine legislation, Butler accepted the literal meaning of the term quarantine and required any ship with any infectious sickness on board to remain at the detention station for forty days, after which another thorough inspection was necessary. Furthermore, all vessels from ports where yellow fever was prevailing had to spend forty days in quarantine, whether they arrived with a clean bill of health or not.[9]

General Butler obtained the services of a competent physician to administer the inspection and to report on the condition of incoming vessels, and paid him well for performing these duties as health officer. The General threatened to invoke the death penalty, however, should this physician make false reports and allow an infected ship to come up to New Orleans. According to Butler's own account, only on one occasion during his command in 1862 did Yellow Jack slip through the stringent quarantine, and this was not because of negligence on the part of the appointed physician. Butler himself had allowed a tug carrying much-needed provisions from New York to come upriver without undergoing the forty-day detention, accepting the captain's oath that coal, and only coal, had been taken on at the Nassau stop where yellow fever prevailed. Several days later two cases of fever appeared in the French Quarter in the persons of two passengers from Nassau who had come in on the tug. The military took over immediately and surrounded the square where the cases were located. Under Butler's order certain acclimated persons went in to attend the patients and came out only after being thoroughly cleansed. Fires fed with tar and pitch burned day and night at the four corners of the square. When the two patients died, everything in and around the building which Butler thought might harbor yellow fever seeds was burned; even the bodies were cremated. No other cases developed, but the deceitful captain of the tug spent three months in jail and paid a fine of five hundred dollars.[10]

On first assuming control of New Orleans, General Butler had not planned to institute full military government, but intended to leave the administration of ordinary civil functions in the hands of the duly constituted municipal government. He soon realized, however, the necessity of public sanitation reform on his part against what he considered the causative forces of yellow fever.[11] After having established quarantine regulations, Butler proceeded to the "Herculean task" of cleaning up the city of New Orleans early in June, 1862. In a message to the military governor and the New Orleans city council, Butler directed that

---

9. *Butler's Book*, pp. 398–401, 407–408.
10. *Ibid.*, pp. 403, 408–410. Writing on another occasion, Butler mentioned only one case of yellow fever imported from Nassau. See Butler, "Some Experiences with Yellow Fever," 531, 536–37, and *Medical and Surgical History of the War of the Rebellion*, Ser. III, I (Washington, 1888), 675–76.
11. James Parton, *General Butler in New Orleans* (New York, 1864), p. 295.

the city employ a force of two thousand men, fully provided with the necessary tools and supervision, for a period of at least thirty working days, to clean the streets, squares, and unoccupied lands of the city. Seeking the full cooperation of the council, Butler played upon their sentiment in this manner: "The epidemic so earnestly prayed for by the wicked will hardly sweep away the strong man, although he may be armed, and leave the weaker woman and child untouched." Reminding them of the presence of many women and children who ordinarily left New Orleans during the summer months, he suggested that "The miasma which sickens the one [the troops] will harm the other."[12]

One squad from the cleansing force was sent to the French Market with an order, "accompanied by a few bayonets," that the area be cleaned. The superintendent in charge of the market said he could not have it done; nevertheless, the clean-up crew proceeded with the task, scraped up the filth, sent it down the river, and charged him with the expense. It is not at all surprising that General Butler gave top priority to the cleansing of this particular area. On first inspecting the place he had been shocked by its filthy state. "In the French market," he wrote, "the stall women were accustomed to drop on the floor around their stalls all the refuse made in cleaning their birds, meat, and fish." Furthermore, he added, "Here it was trodden in and in. This had been going on for a century more or less."

The remaining sanitary detail then went through the streets, clearing away all putrefying animal matter, scraping and sweeping out every drain and ditch in the city. The city water works was ordered to flush the street with all its pumps, and as the water flowed through the freshly scraped drains and ditches into the canals leading to Lake Pontchartrain, the accumulated filth was forced out into the lake and eventually into the Gulf.[13]

Detailed orders were issued to the people of New Orleans on the subject of cleanliness. The head of every household was forced to have his premises cleaned inside and out to meet the approval of military inspectors. It was directed that all refuse from each household be deposited in a box or barrel acceptable to the inspector, and on two or three specified days a week that the receptacle be placed at the end of the street. From that point the refuse would be collected and hauled off in wagons drawn by mule teams. Those in charge of the wagons were directed to disinfect the containers with chloride of lime. In addition, all persons were expressly forbidden to throw anything of any kind into the streets, alleys, or any open spaces, including their own back yards.

12. *Butler's Book*, pp. 403–404.
13. *Ibid.*, pp. 400, 406–407; Butler, "Some Experiences with Yellow Fever," 536.

One might suppose that such regulations would have been extremely difficult to enforce. But according to Butler it was a fairly simple task, and he provided several examples to illustrate his point. One citizen of New Orleans, deliberately testing the orders, walked along the street and called a policeman to watch him throw down a small piece of white paper. Informed of this wilful disobedience, Butler sent for the man, who freely admitted the act and insisted it was his privilege to toss paper on the street. The General replied that "the streets were made to pass through, and when he took his privilege I would take mine and pass him through the streets into the parish prison to stay three months." Another case involved a "high-toned woman" who tried to ignore the sanitary regulations. This "fashionable lady" of New Orleans adamantly refused to clean her back yard, which contained a box of excrement not yet hauled off from the privy. She informed the military inspector that her back yard was "as I choose to have it, and it won't be altered at the order of any Yankee." When the inspecting officer told her to gather up whatever clothes and articles she wanted to take along to jail, she burst into tears and agreed to accept another opportunity to comply with the regulations. By the next afternoon "the yard was in apple-pie order."[14]

Even Butler with all his efforts apparently was unable to obtain a perfect state of urban purity. In August, 1862, the editor of the *Daily True Delta* complained of the filthy gutters. Having observed several with green scum on the water "thick enough to bear the weight of a small-sized bird," he recommended that the authorities attend to the removal of all such pestilential influences.[15] Nonetheless, General Butler must be given credit for whipping New Orleans into what was perhaps a better sanitary condition than it had ever enjoyed before. In November, 1862, the *Picayune* declared that only once before had the Crescent City been so clean: a relatively pristine condition had prevailed for a short time immediately after the disaster of 1853 when the city government had been aroused temporarily to action. And after the Civil War even the most acrimonious rebel was willing to admit that Ben Butler at least had been "the best *scavenger* we ever had among us."[16]

When the Union forces occupied New Orleans in the spring of 1862, not one of Butler's surgeons had ever seen a case of Yellow Jack or possessed the vaguest notion of how to combat the "hideous foe." In July, after the inauguration of sanitation and quarantine measures, a pamphlet was prepared with the assistance

14. *Butler's Book*, pp. 404–406.
15. New Orleans *Daily True Delta*, Aug. 20, 1862.
16. Johnson, "New Orleans under General Butler," 478.

of several New Orleans physicians for the instruction of Union surgeons in the Department of the Gulf. It outlined in detail the symptoms for diagnosis and prognosis as well as a specific course of treatment for yellow fever. The pamphlet stated that every precaution had been taken to prevent the fever's occurrence, but emphasized the ever-present possibility of an outbreak as well as the duty of an army surgeon to be prepared for all emergencies.[17] Fortunately for the Yankees, the first year of the Federal occupation of New Orleans passed with only two known deaths from yellow fever—the two passengers from Nassau who had slipped in on the tug. The mortality records are imperfect, however, and it is entirely possible that several other cases occurred. The significant fact is that in spite of the appearance of a few cases the pestilence did not spread to any noticeable extent.[18]

In November of 1862 General Nathaniel P. Banks was appointed to replace "Beast" Butler as Major-General Commanding the Department of the Gulf. When Butler left New Orleans in December he stated in his farewell address to the citizens of the Crescent City that "I have demonstrated that the pestilence can be kept from your borders.... I have cleansed and improved your streets, canals, and public squares...."[19] One Creole of New Orleans took a slightly different view of the matter, according to a story printed in the *Picayune* several years later. When asked to admit that Butler had demonstrated great ability in preserving the Crescent City from pestilence while in command there, the New Orleanian supposedly said: "By gar, vat you take me vor? You no believe in a God? You no believe zere is mercie? Yellow fever and G-e-n-e-r-a-l Butler at the same time!!!"[20]

During the remainder of the occupation sanitary regulations were administered and enforced through the cooperative efforts of General Banks, the military governor, the mayor of the city, the provost-marshal, the medical director of the department, and specially appointed sanitary inspectors. Quarantine regulations continued in force, although never quite as strictly administered as under General Butler.[21] Among the civilian population of New Orleans, two yellow fever deaths were reported in 1863, six in 1864, and one in 1865. In 1863 and

---

17. *Some Practical Observations on Yellow Fever, Published for the Use of Surgeons of the Volunteer Forces in the Department of the Gulf* (New Orleans, 1862); *Butler's Book*, p. 398.
18. *New Orleans Medical and Surgical Journal*, XXIII (1870), 569.
19. Parton, *General Butler in New Orleans*, p. 605.
20. New Orleans *Daily Picayune*, Nov. 14, 1867.
21. Elisha Harris, "Hygienic Experience in New Orleans during the War: Illustrating the Importance of Efficient Sanitary Regulations," *Southern Journal of the Medical Sciences*, I (1866), 25-30; Doyle, "Civilian Life in Occupied New Orleans," pp. 66-67.

1864 the disease broke out on several vessels of the United States river fleet and spread to the Naval Hospital—approximately one hundred cases in 1863 and two hundred in 1864. But, although clearly present in the vicinity of New Orleans, Yellow Jack strangely failed to develop into a raging epidemic.[22]

Under wartime occupation, Louisiana's Board of Health had been converted into a military bureau with the medical director of the Department of the Gulf serving as president. Not until April, 1866, was the Louisiana State Board of Health reorganized on its prewar basis, with six members appointed by the governor and three by the New Orleans city council. Almost immediately the board encountered its traditional problems: no power, no funds, no cooperation from the municipal authorities.[23] These problems had not existed for the military command.

Provost-Marshal James Bowen, who served in New Orleans for two years during the war, had predicted that with the return of the "usual lax administration" of sanitary regulations by the civil authorities New Orleans would again be visited by pestilence.[24] As if to fulfill his prophecy, both yellow fever and Asiatic cholera appeared in New Orleans in 1866. While cholera claimed more than twelve hundred victims, the Saffron Scourge struck lightly that year, resulting in only 185 fatalities. But the following year, 1867, witnessed a two-fold increase in the city's total mortality over that of 1866 and a yellow fever epidemic which caused over three thousand deaths.[25]

In the years following the war New Orleans physicians occupied themselves evaluating the health measures of the war period in an attempt to reconcile prevailing theories with the facts, or vice versa. In the spring of 1866 Dr. Erasmus Darwin Fenner reviewed the subject of health in New Orleans under military rule to determine what lessons might be learned for future application. He praised the tremendous efforts exerted by the army authorities throughout that period toward the problem of sanitary reform. "Such efforts were never made here before," he declared, "although so often urged by the medical profession in previous years." But, Dr. Fenner added, "perhaps, it may be said *such motives* were never presented before." In spite of the war and the dark side of its balance sheet, he felt that New Orleans should be grateful for "this great sanitary experiment." Compared

---

22. *New Orleans Medical and Surgical Journal*, XXIII (1870), 569-574.
23. *Report of the Louisiana State Board of Health for June 1866-January 1867* (New Orleans, 1867), pp. 3-4; New Orleans *Daily Picayune*, July 24, 1866.
24. Harris, "Hygienic Experience in New Orleans," 30.
25. *Report of the Louisiana State Board of Health for June 1866-January 1867*, pp. 6, 12-13; *Report of the Louisiana State Board of Health for 1867* (New Orleans, 1868), pp. 18, 20.

to its previous condition, the city had been kept unbelievably clean throughout the period. "It was a Herculean task," said Fenner, "and, in our humble opinion, nothing short of military despotism would have accomplished it."

To Dr. Fenner the great lesson of the episode consisted in the validation of his own theory of fever causation. He had long held the opinion that filth and atmospheric contamination produced diseases of all sorts, including yellow fever, and from the premise of local causation, he had always reasoned that sanitary measures would best serve to prevent disease. In contrast to this view, many persons attributed the freedom of New Orleans from epidemic pestilence during wartime occupation to the rigorous quarantine measures. Fenner disagreed. Although quarantine had been enforced rather strictly through most of the period, he said he knew definitely of one case imported from Key West and believed there were others as well. Admitting the likelihood of several imported cases of Yellow Jack each year during the period, he thought it extraordinary that the disease had not become epidemic in the city. It could only be explained by the consistent enforcement of sanitary regulations, Dr. Fenner insisted. And, as he reasoned further, how could quarantine be expected to afford complete protection against a disease which was so obviously indigenous to New Orleans?

The "sanitary experience" of the period between 1862 and 1866 had provided "useful instruction," and Fenner felt it should not be overlooked by the citizenry. Suggesting that Generals Butler and Banks deserved much credit for their achievements in the Crescent City, he maintained that "we may yet have occasion to mingle some thanks among the many curses that have been heaped upon their heads for their unnecessary severity upon the citizens of New Orleans." For twenty years or more, some physicians of New Orleans had preached the gospel of cleanliness without appreciable effect. But, said Fenner, "In the mysterious course of events the hand of the tyrant has been brought to our aid, and the results are marvelous." Now that the true path of sanitary reform had been clearly demonstrated, not only by logic but also by the Yankee experiment in not-so-gentle persuasion, Dr. Fenner hoped that New Orleanians would not fall by the wayside.[26]

Dr. Stanford E. Chaillé, eminent New Orleans physician, editor, and medical educator, also studied the facts relating to yellow fever and sanitation during wartime occupation and arrived at conclusions somewhat different from those of Dr. Fenner. Writing in 1870, Chaillé observed that many persons attributed

---

26. E. D. Fenner, "Remarks on the Sanitary Condition of the City of New Orleans, during the period of Federal Military Occupation," *Southern Journal of the Medical Sciences*, I (1866), 22-25.

the relative freedom from yellow fever during the war to the sanitation measures, but, although a true believer in the desirability of sanitary reform, he felt that the conclusion regarding yellow fever was "not logically deducible from the true premises." He then pointed to the years when New Orleans had been incredibly filthy and yet had suffered no epidemic.[27] More skeptical than most, Dr. Chaillé was not quite willing to concede that the military health measures which coincided with a period of exemption from epidemic visitations had really proved anything. In his opinion, there were many yet-unanswered questions about the irregularities of the pestilence. And so the arguments proceeded among both medical thinkers and laymen of the Crescent City. Some felt that quarantine had been the decisive factor; others gave sole credit to the sanitary measures; still others compromised and allowed that it was the combination effect of the two.

It is impossible to determine exactly how much the rigid enforcement of quarantine and sanitary measures had to do with the city's exemption from a Yellow Jack epidemic during the war. Quarantine, when literally and absolutely enforced, would have held out the disease, but after Butler the detention period was generally reduced and the regulations became somewhat less severe. Moreover, yellow fever was definitely imported on several occasions, but failed to spread extensively. Sanitary regulations undoubtedly reduced the incidence of certain endemic diseases and certainly eliminated some of the offensive, if not pestilential, odors of the city. Such measures would hardly have affected the yellow fever mosquito, however, which chose cisterns and indoor water receptacles as breeding places in preference to gutters, stagnant pools, and swamps. Many factors, some affected by chance, are necessary for the production of a full-scale yellow fever epidemic.[28] In addition, there is the problem of the not-yet-fully understood virus itself, known only by its activities and evidencing a considerable amount of variability and irregularity in those activities from year to year.

---

27. *New Orleans Medical and Surgical Journal,* XXIII (1870), 589-92.

28. Yellow fever virus is transmitted from person to person by the female *Aedes aegypti.* The mosquito must feed on the blood of a fever patient within the first few days of his illness. An incubation period of ten to twelve days is then required, after which the mosquito can pass the disease on. Obviously a rather delicate balance of circumstances is necessary for the development of an epidemic where yellow fever is not endemic (that is, present constantly). The lethal insects must be present in sufficient numbers, and the weather must be warm enough to encourage their activity. A sufficient concentration of susceptible persons must exist, and the virus must be introduced into the area either by a previously infected mosquito or person. At New Orleans the coming of winter always put a stop to mosquito activity, and also the disease—but it was reintroduced almost every summer from Latin America, where it prevailed as an endemic malady.

It could be argued that without Butler's careful isolation of the two imported cases in 1862 they might well have sparked a great epidemic in the city. On the other hand, they might not have resulted in another single case. Wartime conditions and the blockade, by diminishing the normal extent of Latin American trade and travel, also reduced the numerical possibilities for yellow fever's introduction. Yet when all the circumstantial factors exist in the required space-time arrangement, one imported case of yellow fever can initiate a devastating epidemic. In spite of the several cases which did occur in New Orleans, no epidemic materialized. Hence, one can only speculate as to whether or not a yellow fever epidemic would have occurred without the conscientious efforts of the Union commanders to prevent such a development.

At any rate, General Benjamin F. Butler deserves considerable credit for his comprehensive sanitation and quarantine programs, a kind of double-barreled shotgun against Yellow Jack's mysterious cause—an unknown, unseen target. By combining the prophylactic measures advocated by the two competing schools of yellow fever theorists (the local causationists and the importationists), he did all that could have been done within the limitations of the epidemiological and etiological knowledge of the period, and a great deal more than had ever been attempted before. And his successor, General Nathaniel P. Banks, for the most part followed his example.

The long range significance of the military health regulations lies in the resulting impact on medical and lay opinion in New Orleans and the future development of public health activity. If New Orleanians were somewhat disappointed that Yellow Jack had not appeared to save them from Yankee domination, they were nevertheless tremendously impressed by the simultaneity of three factors during the war years: strictly enforced sanitary measures, rigid quarantine, and the absence of a yellow fever epidemic. As a result, many were thoroughly convinced that either quarantine or sanitation or both had prevented the occurrence of an epidemic. Medical opinion, although still divided, began to incline toward the wholehearted support of quarantine as well as sanitary reform, which had long had its advocates.[29] In spite of the faulty logic involved in evaluating the circumstances, the coincidence was a striking one, and public opinion moved one small step closer to recognizing the validity of regulatory measures consistently enforced to preserve the health of a city. Although the general apathy and official negligence which had characterized the first half of the nineteenth century were

29. *New Orleans Medical and Surgical Journal*, XXIII (1870), 563-564.

to return as a negative force again and again, and the public health movement by no means progressed in an even line without setbacks, an attitude slightly more favorable to the idea had undoubtedly developed out of the events of the wartime occupation of New Orleans.

Civil War Anthropometry
The Making of a Racial Ideology

JOHN S. HALLER

The Civil War in America stands as a watershed in nineteenth-century anthropometric developments. The body measurements collected during the war years marked the culmination of efforts to measure the various "races" or "species" of man and derive a semblance of understanding as to specific race-types. Both the office of the Provost Marshal General's Bureau and the United States Sanitary Commission, a semiofficial organization made up of "predominantly upper-class ... patrician elements which had been vainly seeking a function in American society" during the Civil War, became the pioneer forces in the wide scale measurement of the soldier during the war years.[1] The war marks a watershed, not so much because its conclusions were new, but because nearly all subsequent late-nineteenth-century institutionalized attitudes of racial inferiority focused upon the war anthropometry as the basis for their belief. Ironically, the war which freed the slaves also helped to justify racial attitudes of nineteenth century society. The direction and conclusions of the Civil War anthropometric evidence buttressed the conservative ethos of American social order and stability while, at the same time, encouraged a new "scientific" attitude.

The reason the Civil War became such an important catalyst in the development of anthropometry stemmed from two particularly troublesome wartime

---

1. George M. Fredrickson, *The Inner Civil War: Northern Intellectuals and the Crisis of the Union* (New York, 1965), p. 100.

situations. First, as a result of the embarrassing Union defeat in the first battle of Bull Run, Lincoln authorized on June 13, 1861, the creation of the United States Sanitary Commission. Its function was to make a study of the physical and moral condition of Federal troops, carry out anthropometric examinations of soldiers, and offer suggestions and aid for improvements in army life. The life insurance companies of America underwrote a large portion of the Commission's expenses, since they were willing to subsidize almost any program that could work out statistical averages on the physical condition of the population.[2] Members of the Commission included Henry W. Bellows, Unitarian minister of New York, Alexander Dallas Bache of the Coast Survey, Dr. Wolcott Gibbs of Massachusetts, Dr. Samuel Gridley Howe, educator and philanthropist, Dr. William H. Van Buren of New York and Charles J. Stillé, lawyer and historian of the Sanitary Commission. Frederick Law Olmsted became the general secretary of the Sanitary Commission, and while it operated independently of the Federal Army, it was subject to the prerogatives of the Secretary of War, Edwin Stanton. A second situation, and one which became extremely important to the anthropometric section of the Sanitary Commission, grew out of the July 17, 1862, Congressional authorization for Lincoln "to employ as many persons of African descent as he may deem necessary and proper for the suppression of the Rebellion." The Act permitted Lincoln to use the Negroes in "any military or naval service that they may be found competent." Eventually over 180,000 Negroes were inducted into the Federal service.[3]

European anthropologists had made studies on groups of individuals before the American Civil War, but their findings were not very comprehensive. John Towne Danson (1817-1898) took measurements of some 733 Liverpool prisoners of all ages, James David Forbes (1809-1868) on Scottish students at Edinburgh, and Franz Liharzik (1813-1866) on 300 Viennese men.[4] There were also extensive measurements made during the Crimean war. But both the European anthropological societies as well as the interested numbers of American scientists looked upon the creation of the Sanitary Commission, and the induction of Negroes into the Union Army, as an opportune means of investigating

---

2. Charles J. Stillé, *History of the United States Sanitary Commission* (Philadelphia, 1866), p. 84.

3. Quoted in Sanford B. Hunt, "The Negro as a Soldier," *Anthropological Review* VII (Jan., 1869), p. 41; "The Sanitary Commission," *North American Review*, XCVII (Jan., 1864), 167; also *ibid.*, (Apr., 1864), 370-419; Benjamin A. Gould, *Investigations in the Military and Anthropological Statistics of the American Soldier* (Washington, 1869), p. 14.

4. Gould, *Investigations*, p. 119; Royal Statistical Society of London, *Journal*, XXV (1862), 24.

race differences on a scale never before achieved. Somatological differences, which previously had been ascertained from random measurements upon small numbers and with a variety of measuring devices, could now be taken on a wide scale, with planned experiments and uniform measuring instruments.

The Sanitary Commission based its anthropometric investigations upon the statistical methodology of the Belgian philosopher, Lambert Adolphe Jacques Quetelet (1796-1874). Quetelet had made several statistical analyses of human physiognomy, including examinations on 900 men enrolled for the draft in Brussels, 9,500 Belgian militia, 69 convicts in a penitentiary at Vilvarde, and 80 students at Cambridge, England. In 1846 Quetelet applied his theory of probability to "moral and political science," and his results were given wide audience by Sir John Herschel. Herschel's extended article in the *Edinburgh Review* on Quetelet's methodology "led the way to examination of the subject in Great Britain, and, later, in the United States."[5] The whole basis of Quetelet's researches was the creation of an "average man" as representative of specific groups, and an analysis of that specimen "in his various relations, physical, social, and moral."[6]

Drawing statistics and relationships out of a multitude of examinations on soldiers, the Sanitary Commission sought to construct Quetelet's average man. In finding him among the "native American," British American, English, Irish, German, "foreigner," Negro, Indian, and "college student," the Commission determined profiles of an abstract man to whom they assigned a statistical intellect, capacity, judgment and tendency. It was a study oriented from its very inception upon a proper understanding of the varieties of man—a reflection of the reformer's zeal in the early years of anthropology in America.

> Indeed the external form of this average man may legitimately be adopted as a standard of beauty and a model for art. The eminent scientist already named [Quetelet] has shown that we may discover not merely the outward semblance of this abstract being, but his needs, capacities, intellect, judgment, and tendencies;

---

5. J. H. Baxter, Statistics, *Medical and Anthropological, of the Provost-Marshal-General's Bureau, derived from Records of the Examination for Military Service in the Armies of the United States During the Late War of the Rebellion, of Over a Million Recruits, Drafted Men, Substitutes, and Enrolled Men* (Washington, 1875), I, lxxvii; E. B. Elliott, *On the Military Statistics of the United States of America* (Berlin, 1863), pp. 14-15.

6. Gould, *Investigations*, p. 244; Howard Becker and Harry E. Barnes, *Social Thought From Lore to Science* (Washington, 1952), I, 563; L. A. J. Quetelet, *A Treatise on Man and the Development of His Faculties* (Edinburgh, 1842), p. 74; Franz Boas, "Remarks on the Theory of Anthropometry," American Statistical Association, *Publications*, III (Dec., 1893), 569-75.

and Quetelet may thus be regarded as the founder of statistical anthropology, indeed of social science, in the true significance of the word, according to which science depends upon the investigation of laws, not upon the consideration of isolated facts, nor the dissemination of correct principles.[7]

In July, 1864, the Sanitary Commission invited Benjamin A. Gould, a member of the National Academy of Sciences, and president of the American Association for the Advancement of Science, to assume direction on extension of the anthropometric statistics undertaken in 1863 by Ezekiel B. Elliott, the Commission's first actuary.[8] In the reports of the Sanitary Commission, published in 1869, Gould admitted freely to a variety of difficulties encountered in the investigations. For one thing, Secretary of War Stanton had continually declined to assist the Commission in its efforts to obtain information. He denied them use of the War Department records and hindered plans for more extensive investigations. Part of the explanation for Stanton's attitude was that a similar military anthropometric study had been inaugurated by the Provost Marshal General's Bureau in 1861. Perhaps Stanton declined to aid the Commission because of departmental pressure from the Provost Marshal.[9] In any case, Gould took every opportunity in the published reports to remark on Stanton's unwillingness to help them. Other difficulties that the anthropometric section members experienced grew from the lack of intelligent classification. This situation became evident in their unsuccessful attempts to define adequately various mixtures of Negro blood, in the realizations that they had made statistical studies of only an Iroquois tribe, yet they were speaking of the Indian in general, that they were unaware of the number of mixed-blood Iroquois they had examined, and that quite often accidental errors occurred in examination procedures. This latter procedural error was most evident in the confusion surrounding their use of the facial angle instrument. Unfortunately, much of the

---

7. Gould, *Investigations*, p. 246; Edward B. Tylor, "Quetelet on the Science of Man," *Popular Science Monthly*, I (May, 1872), 45–55. Due to the very nature of the classifications used by the Civil War anthropologists, the statistics accumulated became tools not only for determining the qualitative differences between the Negro and Caucasian, but also the quality of foreign immigration. Later immigration restrictionists like N. S. Shaler and F. A. Walker drew upon the Civil War examinations. See F. A. Walker, "Restriction of Immigration," *Atlantic Monthly*, LXXVII (June, 1896), 824; N. S. Shaler, "American Quality," *International Monthly*, IV (July, 1901), 52–53.

8. Gould, *Investigations*, v; Erving Winslow, "Sketch of Professor Benjamin A. Gould," *Popular Science Monthly*, II (Mar., 1882), 683–87; Elliott, *Preliminary Report on the Mortality and Sickness of Volunteer Forces of the United States Government During the Present War* (New York, 1862); "Death of E. B. Elliott," *Science*, XI (June 1, 1888), 261.

9. Gould, *Investigations*, p. 298.

statistical data taken during the Civil War "was carried out under unfavorable circumstances and by men many of whom had no previous knowledge of these matters, and who received no instruction except by circulars."[10]

The instruments used by the Commission—andrometer, spirometer, dynomometer, facial angle, platform balance, calipers, and measuring tape—were intended to include "the most important physical dimensions and personal characteristics." Fortunately for the Commission, Joseph Henry (1797–1878), first Secretary of the Smithsonian Institution, had undertaken similar studies a few years earlier. The Sanitary Commission utilized the design of Henry's apparatus in order to facilitate a uniformity in instruments and procedure. The Coast Survey office built the remaining instruments under the guidance of Professor Alexander Dallas Bache, Vice President of the Commission and Superintendent of the Coast Survey.[11]

In the first year of its operations, the anthropometric section examined 8,004 white Union and Confederate troops. Of that number, the Commission accepted 7,904 as valid examinations for statistical analysis. In July, 1864, the Commission suggested modifications in both the apparatus and the form (Form E) containing the statistical data requested in the examination. The newly modified form (Form EE) clearly reflected the Commission's recognition of Lincoln's call for Negro soldiers. "No examination of the negro troops seems to have been made yet," the Commission argued, "and the importance of such inspections needs no comment." By modifying the form, information concerning the Negro in America could be ascertained "with advantage."[12]

As a result of the suggestions of the Commission, the statistical section added six more measurements to the original form: (1) distance from tip of middle finger to level of upper margin of patella, (2) height to knee, (3) girth of neck, (4) perinaeum to most prominent part of the pubes, (5) distance between nipples, and (6) circumference around hips. The Commission also made corrective modifications in the apparatus. With the aid of Louis Agassiz, Jeffries Wyman, William H. Holmes, and J. H. Douglas, the instruments were further refined for closer and more exact measurements.[13]

During the second phase of examination, which lasted until the end of the war, a staff of twelve examiners drew statistics from 15,900 examinations, of which

10. *Ibid.*, pp. 146, 384–97; Ales Hrdlicka, "Physical Anthropology: Its Scope and Aims; Its History and Present Status in America," *American Journal of Physical Anthropology*, I (Apr.–June, 1918), 172.
11. Gould, *Investigations*, p. 218; "Alexander D. Bache," *Appleton's Cyclopaedia, 1867* (New York, 1872), pp. 78–79; Elliott, *On the Military Statistics of the United States of America*, p. 10.
12. Gould, *Investigations*, p. 221.
13. *Ibid.*, pp. 218–27.

15,781 were accepted as valid. The total consisted of 10,876 white soldiers, 1,146 white sailors, 68 white marines, 2,020 full-blooded Negroes, 863 mulattoes and 519 Indians. The examination of Indians, mostly Iroquois, was made while they were held for a time as prisoners of war near Rock Island, Illinois. There were, in addition to these measurements, statistics taken from the examination of three dwarfs and two captured "Australian children." These latter were made almost as an afterthought and had no bearing on the main body of materials, though, surely, they reflected the avid curiosity of nineteenth-century anthropologists for specimens of atavism and savagery.[14]

Bridging a variety of topics, the results of the Sanitary Commission measurements far surpassed any collection previously made. The records of the Commission report compared and contrasted the various nationalities, college students, Indians, and Negroes according to body dimensions, head size, strength, teeth, vision, respiration and pulmonary capacity. The evidence offered an immediate refuge for both hereditarians and environmentalists among the anthropologists. For one thing, the report showed that there were perceptible differences between the free and slave state Negroes with respect to head size, height, and weight.[15] In its report on the mulatto, the statistics were interpreted as corroboration of earlier racialist assertions that the product of miscegenation was physiologically inferior to the original stocks, and therefore, mixing races was no real remedy to the racial inferiority of the Negro.

> The curious and important fact that the mulattoes, or men of mixed race, occupy so frequently in the scale of progression a place outside of, rather than intermediate between, those races from the combination of which they have sprung, cannot fail to attract attention. The well-known phenomenon of their inferior vitality may stand, possibly, in some connection with the fact thus brought to light.[16]

Those characteristics which most marked the races, according to the report, were, for the whites, "the length of the head and neck and the short fore-arms;" for the Indian, "the long fore-arms and the large lateral dimensions, excepting at the shoulders;" and for the blacks, "the wide shoulders, long feet, and protruding heels."[17] The length of the fore-arm was important to the anthropometrist.

14. *Ibid.*, pp. 312-15.
15. *Ibid.*, pp. 147, 297, 347, 379, 568.
16. *Ibid.*, p. 319.
17. *Ibid.*

It was the measurement the Commission added to the original statistical form for the benefit of the Negro and Indian examinations. The measurement applied to the difference found in the distance from the finger-tip to the knee-pan. Here, the full Negro was but three-fifths and the mulatto five-sixths the average distance for the white soldier. This difference was due to the greater arm length and shorter body length of the full black, and marked the Negro as that much closer to the anthropoid in development.[18] The report went on to compare chest size and concluded from its statistics that "the difference between the mulattoes and the full blacks is here very conspicuous . . . the blacks in their turn falling below the Indians, and these vastly below the whites, of whatever class."[19]

After the war, the Sanitary Commission, in an effort to continue uniformity in anthropometrics, distributed its apparatus among colleges and institutions for continued research. Also distributed were the modified forms and instructions. Although the Commission admitted to defects in the apparatus, forms, and procedures of examination, it felt that the program was a step forward, rendering American anthropometric investigations more uniform than any yet performed, and providing a useful, singular guide for future race study.[20]

In 1875, J. H. Baxter brought out *Statistics, Medical and Anthropological of the Provost-Marshal-General's Bureau*. Though varying at times from the conclusions of Gould's Sanitary Commission reports, Baxter's investigations, carried on between 1861 and 1865, generally corroborated on a much larger scale the earlier findings. One of the interesting elements of the Army study was a questionnaire sent to the military medical doctors requesting their observations of Negro recruits—their physical build, intelligence, and ability to render military service. A large number of doctors refrained from answering the portion relating to the Negro since many of them had few or no Negro recruits upon which to base judgment. Those who did offer remarks gave surprisingly similar conclusions. The Negro in America, because of his contact with a higher civilization, had lost most of his "grosser peculiarities." This factor, along with his good physical endowment, made him a capable soldier.[21] His only apparent physical deformation was his flat feet.[22] Though a good soldier, and perhaps a good citizen, wrote Dr. E. S.

---

18. *Ibid.*, p. 347.
19. *Ibid.*, p. 359; "The Negroes and Indians of the United States," *Anthropological Review*, IV (Jan., 1866), 40-42.
20. Gould, *Investigations*, p. 231; Joseph Henry, "Report of the Secretary," Smithsonian Institution, *Annual Report for 1865*, pp. 47-48.
21. Baxter, *Statistics, Medical and Anthropological*, I, 370, 384, 394, 465.
22. *Ibid.*, pp. 394, 311.

Barrows of Iowa, the Negro "never can be as well qualified as he who by nature possesses greater physical perfection and greater mental endowments."[23] The smaller facial angle of the Negro recruit, wrote a New Jersey doctor, denoted a physical organization of "brute force rather than intellectual pre-eminence," a situation which relegated him to the lower tasks of society.[24]

Like the conclusions of Gould's Sanitary Commission reports, Baxter's questionnaire to the Union doctors confirmed the prevailing belief in the physical inferiority of the mulatto. Negroes of mixed blood were incapable of enduring hardship and were weaker than either the pure black or the white. As a class, wrote Dr. J. H. Mears of Pennsylvania, the colored race "furnished a larger proportion of men who have passed the examination than any other." On the other hand, however, those rejected were invariably mulattoes.[25] Though imitative, the powers of the mulatto were a good deal less than the full black and he exhibited a greater tendency to scrofulous disorders.[26]

In 1869, Sanford B. Hunt, who was a surgeon in the United States Volunteers, published an article in the London *Anthropological Review* entitled, "The Negro as a Soldier." The article was a copy of a report he made to the United States Sanitary Commission, and whose publication in the *Review* had been made with the permission of Dr. William A. Hammond, Surgeon-General of the United States Army. The conclusions which Hunt felt could now be ascertained about the Negro concerned such things as his "capacity to learn tactics," personal hygiene, "powers of resistance to hunger and fatigue," diseases, morale, courage, obedience, cheerfulness, and "his comparative intellectuality." The "well known imitative faculty" of the Negro, along with "his natural fondness for rhythmical movement," made him a good recruit for the drill-master. "The habit of obedience inculcated by the daily life of the slave," added to the Negro's ability to become a worthy soldier. His "large, flat, inelastic foot . . . almost splay-footed," gave him an advantage in marching over rough terrain."[27]

"It would be grossly unfair to subject the negro," argued Hunt, "to a comparison of intellectual capacity based on his present manifestations of mental acuteness." Held in ignorance by the southern planter, he was barred from education and

---

23. *Ibid.*, p. 461.
24. *Ibid.*, p. 285.
25. *Ibid.*, pp. 394, 403.
26. *Ibid.*, p. 285.
27. Sanford B. Hunt, "The Negro as a Soldier," *Anthropological Review*, VII (Jan., 1869), pp. 42–43.

all paths of competition. Hence, his inferiority, being of an environmental sort, blunted any mental test that might be used to define his relative position in the scale of races. For this reason, Hunt suggested three different modes for determination: (1) by "external measurements of the cranium," (2) by ascertaining a direct ratio "between the mental and the cubic capacity of the cerebral mass," attempted before the war by Samuel George Morton, and (3) by determining the "weight of the brain by post-mortem examinations." Of the three possible methods, Hunt chose the last as being more reliable. All three methods, he admitted, "presupposed that the size and weight of the brain is the measure of its intellectuality."[28]

Hunt had made studies of the autopsies performed during the Civil War at Benton Barracks, Missouri, Wilson Hospital, Nashville, Tennessee, and L'Ouverture Hospital, Alexandria, Virginia. He drew up statistics derived from 405 autopsies of white and Negro soldiers made under the direction of surgeon Ira Russell of the 11th Massachusetts Volunteers. Twenty-four of the autopsies were performed on white soldiers, while 381 were black. Hunt concluded from brain-weight analysis that the full-blooded Negro brain weighed five ounces less than the white, that "slight intermixtures" of white blood in the Negro "diminish the negro brain from its normal standard," while large infusion of white blood, such as in the mulatto, "determines a positive increase in the negro brain, which in the quadroon is only three ounces below the white standard." Though the statistics of the Sanitary Commission autopsies showed a positive increase in brain weight for the mulatto, their accumulated evidence of a corresponding inferior physical development in other respects negated the benefits of miscegenation to race progress.[29]

Hunt felt that brain-weight analysis by means of autopsies confirmed the earlier pre-Civil War measurements of Samuel Morton, who measured the internal capacity of the skull in cubic inches. Since Morton's capacity in the Teutonic skull was 92 cubic inches and the Negro 82 cubic inches, the ratio of brain weights made during the Civil War, 52 ounces in the white compared to 46.40 in the Negro, confirmed Morton's earlier ratio. This meant, furthermore, that the average white had a competitive advantage over the Negro of between 5.5 and 9.5 per cent.[30]

Hunt concluded that though the autopsy statistics were crucial, they could not determine "the ultimate capacity of the negro from that which he has thus far manifested." It meant, moreover, that autopsies of the Negro needed to be

---

28. *Ibid.*, pp. 49–50.
29. *Ibid.*, p. 52; Hunt, "The Negro as a Soldier," *Quarterly Journal of Psychological Medicine*, I (Oct., 1867), p. 175.
30. Hunt, *Anthropological Review*, VII (Jan., 1869), p. 52.

taken at intervals in the future, in order to determine if the effect of freedom and education led to corresponding changes in the Negro brain. Such autopsies, he felt, would resolve the controversy that existed between the environmentalists and the hereditarians.

> As between the two races, the problem is: Does the large brain by its own impulses create education, civilization and refinement, or do education, civilization and refinement create the large brain? This problem might be solved by a series of researches in the weight of brain of the poor whites of the south, known as "sand hillers," "low-down people," or "crackers." With them civilization has retrograded. They came of a good stock originally, but have degenerated into an idle, ignorant and physically and mentally degraded people. Their general aspect would indicate small brains. If they are small, it is due to the absence of educational influences.[31]

Anthropometrists did not follow up on Hunt's suggestions in the postwar years. Indeed, large scale anthropometric investigations were not begun until the World's Columbian Exposition held in Chicago in 1893. In lieu of continued large scale anthropometric study, the burden of this investigation fell upon the physician. Ironically, however, it was the southern physician who generally carried out studies on the Negro, and his conclusions reflected not only the South's appeal for a reappraisal of Reconstruction politics, but also mirrored the race-ideology of the prewar years.

American physicians in the postwar years accumulated a body of evidence which suggested that the Negro race was not only physiologically inferior to the Caucasian, but that emancipation had precipitated the incidence of high mortality in the race. Throughout the postwar decades, doctors speculated as to the physical vigor of the race in light of national and state census reports that seemed to show that Negro mortality was climbing at a dangerous rate. The medical and surgical history of the war, published by the Surgeon-General's Office between 1870 and 1888, state studies after the war, and reports published by Johns Hopkins Hospital on Negro mortality between 1893 and 1902, corroborated the belief in the increased death rate. Charleston, South Carolina, for example, gave evidence that while in 1860 the white and black man had a mortality rate exactly the same

---

31. *Ibid.*, p. 53.

(12 per 1,000), by 1895, the Negro mortality rate had increased to 29.1 per 1,000, while the white death rate had increased to 18.7 per 1,000.[32]

Census statistics were the basis of much of the speculation. The Ninth Census (1870) had showed that the white population during the years from 1860 to 1870 had increased 34.76 per cent, while the blacks had increased a mere 9.86 per cent. This news came as a surprise, since the previous rates of increase for the blacks in America had averaged 29.98 per cent in the census reports from 1790 to 1850. The results of these new statistics caused immediate concern and speculation as to the future of the Negro race. The Ninth Census report was offset by the Tenth Census report which showed the comparative rate of increase from 1870 to 1880 as being 29.22 per cent for the Caucasian and 34.85 per cent for the Negro. However, the Eleventh Census again reversed the black increase. From 1880 to 1890, the whites increased 26.68 per cent while the blacks increased only 13.51 per cent. The census officers, looking back on the one hundred years of census statistics, remarked that "the whites increased from 80.83 to 87.80, while the colored element today is two-thirds less than it was a hundred years ago."[33] Missouri, Texas, Alabama, Maryland, Georgia, North Carolina, South Carolina, Louisiana, Tennessee, Virginia and the District of Columbia gave evidence that although with emancipation began the Negro's "career as a freedman and the struggle for elevation," that in fact, it also led to his "physical decline."[34] The physician Van Evrie suggested that the Negro's tendency toward race extinction was "accelerated or diminished in exact proportion as 'impartial freedom' [was] thrust upon him." As the Negro began to enjoy equality as a result of the "blind and cruel kindness and exterminating goodness" of the Caucasian, he succumbed to the harshness of natural race laws.[35]

---

32. U. S. Surgeon-General's Office, *The Medical and Surgical History of the War of the Rebellion* (Washington, 1870-1880). Extensive examination of comparative mortality found in Vol. I, pt. 3; "The Negro," *Atlanta Journal-Record of Medicine*, V (June, 1903), pp. 186-87; Frederick L. Hoffman, "The Statistical Experience Data of the Johns Hopkins Hospital," *Hospital Reports*, n.s. IV (1913), pp. 5, 21, 24, 33, 37, 40.

33. J. T. Walton, "The Comparative Mortality of the White and Colored Races in the South," *Charlotte Medical Journal*, X (1897), p. 292; S. S. Herrick, "Comparative Vital Movement of the White and Colored Races in the United States," *New Orleans Medical and Surgical Journal*, n.s. IX (1881-1883), p. 678.

34. Walton, *Charlotte Medical Journal*, X (1897), p. 292; A. R. Kilpatrick, "An Account of the Colored Population of Grimes County, Texas. A Comparison Between Their Present and Former Condition," *Richmond and Louisville Medical Journal*, XIV (Nov., 1872), p. 610; L. S. Joynes, "Remarks on the Comparative Mortality of the White and Colored Population of Richmond," *Virginia Medical Monthly*, II (June, 1875), p. 155.

35. John H. Van Evrie, *White Supremacy and Negro Subordination* (New York, 1868), pp. 311-12.

Statistics of still-births among blacks caused many doctors to suggest that syphilis was one of the causative factors in the mortality of the race.[36] According to some physicians, the apparent increase in black population in the immediate years after the Civil War was evidence of the promiscuity of the freed Negro. But "nature abhors promiscuous sexual intercourse," wrote Dr. Seale Harris, vice president of the Tri-State Medical Society of Georgia, "and the abuse of the organs of reproduction will certainly result in their becoming functionless."[37] The Ninth Census report seemed to confirm his suspicions of the irreparable damage done to the sex organs. "What can we expect of the negro," he wrote, "but that he will in time share the fate of the North American Indian."[38]

During the 1880's and 1890's, medical doctors initiated newer studies on the Negro in an effort to analyze the effect of freedom upon his physical, mental and moral capacity. They compared and contrasted their evidence with the medical investigations made by both the Army and the United States Sanitary Commission during the Civil War. Doctor Thomas P. Atkinson of Virginia concluded that there was a much higher death rate among black soldiers than among whites during the war and that this rate continued after the war. From the wartime evidence of Baxter's medical and anthropometrical history, and from his own statistics, Atkinson concluded that not only had the Negro deteriorated mentally, morally, and physically from his earlier condition in slavery, but that "a different mode of treatment is indicated in the management of his diseases."[39] The secretary of the Texas State Medical Association, Doctor W. J. Burt, also drew upon the Civil War medical reports to confirm his own belief in Negro inferiority. He concluded that not only did the osteological measurements made during the war

---

36. Seal Harris, "The Future of the Negro from the Standpoint of the Southern Physician," *Alabama Medical Journal*, XIV (Jan., 1902), p. 63; Hunter McGuire and G. Frank Lydston, "Sexual Crimes Among the Southern Negroes; Scientifically Considered," *Virginia Medical Monthly*, XX (May, 1893), p. 106.

37. Harris, *Alabama Medical Journal*, XIV (Jan., 1902), p. 62; Hoffman, "Vital Statistics of the Negro," *Arena*, XXIX (Apr., 1892), p. 534.

38. Harris, *Alabama Medical Journal*, XIV (Jan., 1902), p. 65.

39. Thomas P. Atkinson, "On the Anatomical, Physiological and Pathological Differences Between the White and the Black Races," Medical Society of Virginia, *Transactions* (1873), p. 67; Joseph R. Smith, "Sickness and Mortality in the Army," American Medical Association, *Transactions*, XXXIII (1882), pp. 313-14; Robert Reyburn, "Types of Disease Among the Freed People (Mixed Negro Race) of the United States," *Medical News*, Philadelphia, LXIII (Dec, 1893), pp. 624, 626; W. J. Burt, "Report on the Anatomical and Physiological Differences Between the White and Negro Races; and the Modification of their Respective Diseases and Difference in the Treatment Resulting Therefrom," Texas Medical Association, *Transactions*, VIII (1876), pp. 115-23.

place the Negro "next below man in the zoological scale," but that the Negro's physiological peculiarities made him more susceptible to disease and death.[40] Burt relied upon the post mortem examinations of Doctor A. McDowell on white and colored troops, who found differences in chest measurements, lung weight, and size of liver and spleen.[41] From these bodily differences and the fact that the Negro brain was about one-eighth less than that of the Caucasian, Burt argued that the Negro seldom endured surgical operations due to his lack of "nervous endurance and fortitude." The Negro's physiological inferiority, his poorer "mental manifestation and power," as well as his lack of "moral courage," made him unable to withstand surgical operations.[42]

From the wartime statistics of Doctors George A. Otis and Joseph J. Woodward on Negro mortality, other physicians argued that the sudden susceptibility of the emancipated Negro to disease demonstrated the consequences of breaking the natural race pathology of the Negro which existed within the framework of the institution of slavery.

> Surely there must be something more than mere chance in this sudden reversion of settled facts. Was there not something in the rigid regime under which the slave lived that rendered his system a barren soil to the germs of tuberculosis? ... and this change has come, in my opinion, as the result of the violent striking of the shackles from the hands of a people who, for generations, had lived as slaves; the sudden lifting of all restraint, the violent swing of the pendulum from a simple life of toil and bondage to one of liberty, license, and all that inevitable brood of disasters that follows surely and swiftly upon the heels of outraged and violated natural laws.[43]

Doctor J. F. Miller, superintendent of Eastern Hospital, Goldsboro, North Carolina, published a study in the *North Carolina Medical Record* for 1896, which

---

40. Burt, "On the Anatomical and Physiological Differences Between the White and Negro Races, and the Modification of Disease Resulting Therefrom," *St. Louis Courier of Medicine*, VIII (Nov., 1882), p. 419.

41. *Ibid.*, p. 420.

42. *Ibid.*, p. 421; discussion in Louis McLane Tiffany, "Comparison Between the Surgical Diseases of the White and Colored Races," American Surgical Association, *Transactions*, V (1887), p. 272.

43. F. Tipton, "The Negro Problem from a Medical Standpoint," *New York Medical Journal*, XLIII (May, 1886), p. 570; J. G. Rogers, "The Effect of Freedom Upon the Physical and Psychological Development of the Negro," American Medico-Psychological Association, *Proceedings*, VII (1900), 88-99.

attempted to judge the effects of emancipation upon the mental and physical capacities of the Negro. Using the statistics of the superintendent of the Georgia lunatic asylum, he concluded that the number of insane Negroes had increased measurably since emancipation. While in 1860 there were but forty-four insane Negroes in the state of Georgia, or one in every 10,584 of the population, the censuses of 1870, 1880, and 1890 had shown significant increases. The census of 1890 showed an increase of insane Negroes to one in every 943 of the population.[44] The untutored slave, wrote Miller, with "no thought for the morrow, wherewithal he should be fed and clothed," had no ambitions, hopes or possibilities in his future. His quiet, "humble life in his little log cabin, with his master to care for every want of self and family, in sickness and in health," had been commensurate with his physiological and mental condition.[45] The violation of those natural laws by emancipation had "left its slimy trail of sometimes ineradicable disease upon [the Negro's] physical being," and the licentiousness Miller thought evident in the freed Negro brought upon him "a beautiful harvest of mental and physical degeneration and he is now becoming a martyr to an heredity thus established."[46]

In 1896, the American Economic Association published *Race Traits and Tendencies of the American Negro*, a study by Frederick L. Hoffman (1865–1947), a statistician for the Prudential Insurance Company of America. Hoffman had published earlier studies concerning the Negro in *Arena* (1892), *Medical News* (1894), and the *Publications of the American Statistical Association* (1895). A member of the American Academy of Medicine, the American Statistical Association and the Royal Statistical Society of London, Hoffman's work on the race characteristics of the American Negro was in some ways, a summation of the century's medical and anthropometrical accumulations concerning racial relations in America. His conclusions mirrored the cumulative tendencies of a century of American studies on race. It became apparent, as Hoffman's inquiry developed through more than three hundred pages of statistics and synthesis of pre-Darwinian, evolutionist, and medical investigations, that the efforts of the "higher races" to ameliorate the condition of the Negro, or for that matter, of any of the "lower races," had the effect of exaggerating the differences between the races. After thirty years of freedom, the Negro and Caucasian were "farther apart than ever in their politi-

---

44. J. F. Miller, "The Effects of Emancipation Upon the Mental and Physical Qualifications of the Negro in the South," *North Carolina Medical Journal*, XXXVIII (Nov., 1896), p. 287; T. O. Powell, "The Increase of Insanity and Tuberculosis in the Southern Negro Since 1860, and Its Alliance and Some of the Supposed Causes," American Medical Association, *Journal*, XXVII (1896), pp. 1185–88.

45. Miller, *North Carolina Medical Journal*, XXXVIII (Nov., 1896), 289.

46. *Ibid.*, p. 290.

cal and social relations."⁴⁷ In order to determine the actual degree of difference between the white and black races, Hoffman turned to the evidences of race vitality to learn whether the Negro had undergone change from the time of his servitude to that of a freedman. His effort to ascertain such change developed out of the seemingly "indisputable evidence" of physicians and statisticians in the 1880's and 1890's that the Negro showed "the least power of resistance in the struggle for life."⁴⁸ Though he argued that the Negro race had an excessive mortality rate, he discounted all arguments that placed blame or causation on the low social and economic conditions of the people. It was impossible to accept the argument that "given the same social, economic and sanitary conditions of life, the colored race would enjoy the same health and favorable death rate as the white population."⁴⁹ He drew upon the evidence of Dr. John Moore, Surgeon-General of the United States Army, and Dr. R. M. Cunningham of the Alabama Penitentiary, who argued that "even under the same conditions . . . the negro is still subject to a higher death rate."⁵⁰

Hoffman, agreeing with physicians, believed that the Negro, prior to the Civil War, "enjoyed health equal if not superior to that of the white race."⁵¹ Borrowing his terminology from the Englishman, Benjamin Kidd, Hoffman argued that the new generation of Negroes in America showed the greatest loss of "social effectiveness."⁵² To substantiate his own personal findings, Hoffman delved into the Civil War Sanitary Commission anthropometrical investigations of Gould, the somatometric reports of the Provost-Marshal-General's Bureau, and the study of Dr. Sanford B. Hunt on Negro soldiers. There was abundant proof in their investigations, Hoffman argued, that the post–Civil War generation of Negroes were more liable to disease than their prewar ancestors. For Hoffman, it meant that the Negro soldier, forced for the first time to undergo as an equal the hardships and problems of the white soldier, "showed a higher mortality rate while subjected to the same, or perhaps more favorable conditions."⁵³

Again, Hoffman looked to the Civil War anthropometric statistics to demonstrate

---

47. Hoffman, "Race Traits and Tendencies of the American Negro," *Publications of the American Economic Association*, XI (Aug., 1896), p. 1. See Albert B. Hart, *The Southern South* (New York, 1910), pp. 10-11. Hart called Hoffman's statistical findings "very widely read and quoted in the South." See also N. S. Shaler, "Science and the African Problem," *Atlantic Monthly*, XLVI (July, 1890), 37, 42.
48. Hoffman, *Publications of the American Economic Association*, XI (Aug., 1896), 37.
49. *Ibid.*, 49.
50. *Ibid.*, 50.
51. *Ibid.*, 55.
52. *Ibid.*, 57.
53. *Ibid.*, 99; Hunt, *Anthropological Review*, VII (Jan., 1869), 40.

the "lower vital power" among the Negroes. Comparing the war findings with later medical and anthropological statistics on the same bodily parts, he found reason to believe that the discrepancy gave conclusive evidence of a degeneration among the Negro population.[54] Subsequent anthropometry by the medical departments of the New York Life Insurance Company in 1874 and 1895, by the Washington Life Insurance Company in 1886, the Prudential Insurance Company of America in 1895, and the statistics drawn up in 1893, 1894, and 1895 by the United States Army, showed a decline in physiological capacity since the Civil War findings.[55] The decrease in chest expansion, the decrease in the size of the thorax, the increase in consumption and respiratory diseases, the smaller weight of the Negro lung (four ounces), "the mean frequency of respiration" which was greater in the Negro than in the white, and the inferior power of vision in the Negro, "prove conclusively that there are important differences in the bodily structure of the two races, differences of far-reaching influence on the duration of life and the social and economic efficiency of the colored man."[56] Agreeing with Sir Duncan Gibb of the London Anthropological Society that "the vital energies of a people had a great deal to do with the state of the body, and that the capacity of the chest should count for something very considerable as an indication of natural power," Hoffman predicted a fateful end to Negro aspirations.[57]

> The general conclusion is that the negro is subject of a higher mortality at all ages, but especially so at the early age periods. This is largely the result of an inordinate mortality from constitutional and respiratory diseases. Moreover, the mortality from these diseases is on the increase among the colored, and on the decrease among the whites. In consequence, the natural increase in the colored population will be less from decade to decade and in the end a decrease must take place. It is sufficient to know that in the struggle for race supremacy the black race is not holding its own; and this fact once recognized, all danger from a possible numerical supremacy of the race vanishes. Its extreme liability to consumption alone would suffice to seal its fate as a race.[58]

Hoffman believed that intermarriage among races of similar culture resulted in physical and psychical advantages for both stocks, but that mixtures of Germans

---

54. Hoffman, *Publications of the American Economic Association*, XI (Aug., 1896), p. 162.
55. *Ibid.*, p. 149.
56. *Ibid.*, p. 171.
57. Hoffman quoting Gibb, *ibid.*, pp. 171–72.
58. *Ibid.*, p. 148; John B. Haycraft, *Darwinism and Race Progress* (London, 1900), pp. 52–55.

and Italians, English and Spaniards, Swedes and Turks, let alone Caucasians and Negroes, were an altogether different matter.[59] Concerned primarily with the crossing of white and black, Hoffman emphasized that the product was inferior both physically and morally to the organization of both parents. Agreeing with earlier conclusions of the polygenist Josiah Nott, he argued that the mulatto was "possessed of the least vital force" of all races.[60] To substantiate Nott's earlier prewar findings, Hoffman went to the opinions of northern physicians in J. H. Baxter's *Statistics, Medical and Anthropological of the Provost-Marshal-General's Bureau*, who, with near unanimity, agreed that the mulatto was least capable of army life and most susceptible to physical disability. Despite the mulatto's undoubtedly superior intellectual capacity over the pure black, a situation verified from Sanford Hunt's investigations of brain weight after autopsy, the increasing intellectuality in no way compensated for the overburdening deterioration in physical and moral capacity. On the strength of such experiments, Hoffman concluded that miscegenation was detrimental to the true progress of both white and black and resulted in an "inferior social efficiency and diminishing power as a force in American national life."[61]

> Hence the conclusion is unavoidable that the amalgamation of the two races through the channels of prostitution and concubinage, as well through the intermarrying of the lower types of both races, is contrary to the interest of the colored race, a positive hindrance to its social, mental and moral development. But aside from these considerations, important as they are, the physiological consequences alone demand race purity and a stern reprobation of any infusion of white blood. Whatever the race may have gained in an intellectual way, which is a matter of speculation, it has been losing its greatest resources in the struggle for life, a sound physical organism and power of rapid reproduction.[62]

---

59. Hoffman, *Publications of the American Economic Association*, XI (Aug., 1896), pp. 179-180; Alfred H. Stone, "The Mulatto Factor in the Race Problem," *Atlantic Monthly*, LXI (May, 1903), pp. 658-62; Richard Mayo-Smith, "Theories of Races and Nationalities," *Yale Review*, III (1894), pp. 166-85.
60. Hoffman, *Publications of the American Economic Association*, XI (Aug., 1896), p. 182; Jabez Lamar M. Curry, "The Negro Question," *Popular Science Monthly*, LV (June, 1899), p. 178. Curry was general agent of the Peabody Education Fund and of the John F. Slater Education Fund.
61. Hoffman, *Publication of the American Economic Association*, XI (Aug., 1896), pp. 187-88; Van Evrie, *White Supremacy and Negro Subordination*, p. 148.
62. Hoffman, *Publication of the American Economic Association*, XI (Aug., 1896), pp. 206-207.

As late as 1910, Hoffman accepted the substance of his earlier investigations. In a book written by Edward Eggleston, Hoffman was quoted as still believing that the Negro race was of a basically inferior constitution. Medical science had removed the possibility of the race's ultimate extinction, yet his correspondence with southern physicians, as well as his own investigations, convinced him that, at most, the Negro race would become like the Gypsy of Europe, an anachronism of modern civilization, existing on the fringe of society, and neither contributing to nor detracting from civilization's progressive development.[63]

With the use of the comparative method, "the great talisman" of the nineteenth century as John Fiske once called it, and the statistical methodology of Quetelet, anthropometry and medical science ripened, bringing meaning to the vast amounts of data accumulated during the Civil War. Medicine and anthropometry became a funding source for both military and public investigations on the varieties of man, and the Negro in particular. One of the more immediate effects was to provide the statistical justification for both the Prudential and Metropolitan insurance companies for discontinuing life policies on blacks. As statistician for Prudential, Hoffman's investigations became the basis of the company's discriminatory policy.[64] Another result of the wartime anthropometry and post war medical examinations was to provide data for the belief in the Negro's extinction, which became one of the most pervasive ideas in American medical and anthropological thought during the late nineteenth century. The "scientific" and racialist environment out of which these ideas grew was also a fitting culmination to the concept of racial inferiority in American life. No longer would attitudes of racial inferiority have to employ those prewar measurements and conclusions which had been tainted with the proslavery arguments. Now, conclusions could appear "scientific" and, indeed, "proved" on the basis of the Civil War investigations. Perhaps the greatest irony of the Civil War was that its anthropometric investigations were used in the late nineteenth century to support institutional racism. It acted as a "carrier" for those racial attitudes that were part of the prewar period.

---

63. Letter from Hoffman to Eggleston, Aug. 5, 1910, in Edward Eggleston, *The Ultimate Solution of the American Negro Problem* (Boston, 1913), pp. 272-73.

64. Hoffman, *History of the Prudential Insurance Company of America* (New Jersey, 1900), pp. 210-211, 137; Raymond V. Carpenter, *An Epoch in Life Insurance* (New York, 1924), p. 9; W. J. Trent, Jr., *Development of Negro Life Insurance Enterprises* (Philadelphia, 1932), p. 15; Winfred O. Bryson, Jr., *Negro Life Insurance Companies, a Comparative Analysis of the Operating and Financial Experience of Negro Legal Reserve Life Insurance Companies* (Philadelphia, 1948), p. 8.

Communities at War

Sons and Soldiers

Deerfield, Massachusetts, and the Civil War

EMILY J. HARRIS

The Civil War monument in the town of Deerfield, Massachusetts is inscribed as a memorial to the 42 "lamented sons and soldiers who for their country and for Freedom laid down their lives in the war of the Great Rebellion." These 42 were among the 303 individuals credited to Deerfield in the Union's war records, 167, or 55 percent, of whom were Deerfield's "sons"—men who resided in the town—and 136 of whom were "soldiers"—recruits hired from near and far to fill the town's quotas (see Table 1). The story of how these troops were raised, and of who they were, provides an instructive case study of one northern community's war experience. It is essentially a record of how the community accommodated its behavior to constant national demands. At the outset of the war, Deerfield accepted responsibility for inspiring self-sacrifice among its citizens. By the end, the town expressed its commitment to the Union by assuming a collective financial burden. For the most part, Deerfield's "sons" who went to war left home in 1861 and 1862. Starting in 1863, the town answered the Union's calls primarily with "soldiers" who were not Deerfield natives, but this shift occurred within the context of constant local patriotism.[1]

The author acknowledges the assistance of the Elizabeth Fuller Fellowship, Historic Deerfield.

1. Few historians have approached the Civil War from the point of view of a northern town's community experience. One exceptionally good model for this approach is Michael Frisch, *Town into City: Springfield, Massachusetts, and the Meaning of Community 1840-1880* (Cambridge: Harvard

Table 1
Deerfield "Sons" and "Soldiers" by Year of Enlistment

Year	SONS			SOLDIERS			TOTAL SONS AND SOLDIERS	
	No.	% of Total Enlistees for Year	% of Total Sons	No.	% of Total Enlistees for Year	% of Total Soldiers	No.	% of Total Who Served for Deerfield
1861	49	65	29	26	35	19	75	25
1862	80	82	48	18	18	13	98	32
1863	17	50**	10	17*	50	13*	34*	11
1864	13	30**	8	29*	70*	21*	42*	14
1865	8	23**	5	26*	77*	15*	34*	11
Unknown				20*		19	20*	7
Total	167	55		136	45		303	

*The totals and percentages of "soldiers" for 1863–65 are low because enlistment dates for these men could not be substantiated.
**These percentages are high because of the group of "soldiers" for whom enlistment year is unknown.

When the "Great Rebellion" began in 1861, Deerfield's population was approximately 3,073, an increase of 27 percent over 1850. Roughly 17 percent, or 510, of Deerfield's residents were men between the ages of twenty and forty-five, and therefore potentially eligible to serve in the Union army. Much of the population growth in this New England farming village resulted from the influx of native and immigrant laborers who came to work in the cutlery in Cheapside (the town's northern section), on the railroads, or in smaller industries such as wallet making in South Deerfield. In this essay Deerfield refers to the area covered by Old Deerfield, South Deerfield, and Cheapside, all of which shared one town government.[2]

University Press, 1972). Chapter 3 addresses the local response to the war and its impact on the changing definition of community. "The Civil War," chapter 8 of Paul Jenkins's *The Conservative Rebel: A Social History of Greenfield, Massachusetts* (Greenfield: 1982), suggests a transition from enthusiasm to a mood that was "subdued," but does not offer any details of the town's response after 1863. Studies which provide insight into the later response are Richard H. Abbott, "Massachusetts and the Recruitment of Southern Negroes, 1863-65," *Civil War History*, 16 (September 1968): 197-210; Adrian Cook, *The Armies of the Streets: The New York City Draft Riots of 1863* (Lexington: University Press of Kentucky, 1974); Hugh G. Earnhart, "Commutation: Democratic or Undemocratic?" *Civil War History* 12 (June 1966): 132-42; Peter Levine, "Draft Evasion in the North during the Civil War, 1863-1865," *Journal of American History* 67 (March 1981): 816-34; Eugene C. Murdock, *One Million Men: The Civil War Draft in the North* (Madison: State Historical Society of Wisconsin, 1971); Arnold M. Shankman, *The Pennsylvania Anti-War Movement* (Cranby, New Jersey: Associated Press, Inc., 1974); Judith Lee Hallock, "The Role of Community in Civil War Desertion," *Civil War History* 29 (June 1983): 123-34.

2. General information on Deerfield is compiled from George Sheldon, *A History of Deerfield, Massachusetts* (Greenfield, Massachusetts: E. A. Hall, 1896), and the excellent resources of the Historic Deerfield Library, Deerfield, Massachusetts. These include Historic Deerfield Summer Fellowship papers; of particular note for information on population are Stacey Flaherty, "Cheapside's Story" (1978), and Stacy Pomeroy, "A Fragile Community: The Irish in Deerfield, Massachusetts, 1850-80." Statistics and information on individuals referred to in this essay are compiled from *Finance Reports of the Town of Deerfield for 1862-63; 1863-64* (Greenfield: 1864, Manuscript Collections of the Pocumtuck Valley Memorial Association Deerfield, Massachusetts, hereafter, PVMA); *Greenfield Gazette and Courier;* "Rebellion Record: Complete Record of the Names of All the Soldiers and Officers in the Military Service and of All the Seamen and Officers in the Naval Service of the United States from the Town of Deerfield, Franklin County, Massachusetts, during the Rebellion Begun in 1861" (Town Office, South Deerfield, Massachusetts). The Records of the Provost Marshall General's Bureau (Civil War) (Record Group 10), National Archives, Washington, D.C., were an invaluable source. They include "Consolidated Lists of All Persons of Class I Subject to do Military Duty in the Ninth Congressional District, Counties of Franklin, Hampshire and Worcester, Massachusetts," June 1863, also Class II and Class III (hereafter referred to as enrollment lists); "Descriptive Books of Drafted Men and Substitutes," June to September 1863 and May 1864; "Record of Drafted Men Who Paid Commutation Money, July 1863 to June 1865"; "Record and Descriptive List of Volunteer Recruits Enlisted and Mustered into Service." Other sources are "Town Records," Deerfield, Massachusetts, 1847-1868 (microfilm Reel #3, Henry N. Flynt Memorial Library, Historic Deerfield, Deerfield, Massachusetts, hereafter cited as "Town Records"); U.S. Census Bureau, "Eighth Census of the U.S., Franklin County, Massachusetts, 1860."

Deerfield's first response to the war was enthusiastic. The *Greenfield Gazette and Courier* reported that patriotism in Deerfield was "universal and genuine." In April 1861, citizens burned an effigy of Jefferson Davis on the common and a thirty-four-gun salute was fired as the crowd cheered the Union. The month of May 1861 brought further public ceremonies and an agreement in a town meeting to spend $1,600 for a militia company, $1,200 for the support of volunteers, $20 per man who enlisted, and $10 per month for each volunteer in addition to his government pay. The total represented well over 10 percent of the town's expenditures for the year. While recruiting papers circulated, citizens raised a war banner in the center of town.[3]

In June, three Deerfield residents left with the Greenfield and Shelburne Falls Company. In July, after the Battle of Bull Run had dispelled hopes of a quick Union victory, thirteen Deerfield "sons" left with the Tenth Regiment Massachusetts Volunteers. Among them were Dwight C. Pervere, a twenty-eight-year-old farmer with two children, and his brother, Horace Pervere, a thirty-seven-year-old married farmer. In September, twenty-year-old Rufus and twenty-two-year-old Russell Pervere enlisted in the same company with their older brothers, leaving only one son on the family farm. The departure of an entire family in one regiment illustrates the fervoured and self-sacrificing response of Deerfield's citizens to early calls to arms.[4] The extension of family and community into the battlefield became a common experience throughout the Union, as each town raised its own companies. Deerfield would follow suit in 1862.[5]

---

3. *Greenfield Gazette and Courier*, vol. 24, no. 8, May 11, 1861, p. 3; vol. 24, no. 9, May 16, 1861, p. 2, hereafter referred to as *Gazette and Courier*. All volume and number references are to *Courier* numbers. Citations with no page number or title are to the weekly columns entitled "The News from Home." George Sheldon, "Diary" (PVMA), April 20, 1860 to July 12, 1867. Entries on April 13, May 25, 1861.

4. Other brothers and cousins who enlisted were brothers Arthur and Francis Ball and their cousin Charles M. (all Fifty-second Regiment, Company D, 1862); Calvin S. and William H. Clapp and cousins Alfred D. and Rollin N. Clapp (all Fifty-second Regiment Companies D and F); brothers Charles, George, Henry, and Lorenzo Hastings, all of whom enlisted in 1861, all sons of Alvah, all workers in cutlery; brothers George and Isaac Rice (Twenty-seventh Massachusetts Company C, 1862) and possible relative, Luther (Tenth Massachusetts Company A, 1861); half brothers Orrin D. and William P. Saxton (different regiments); brothers Henry M. and Erastus C. Smith (different regiments); father, Hiram M., and Son, Hiram B. Stearns (different regiments); brothers Albion L., Bushrod Washington, and Wellington H. Stebbins and their cousins, James T. and William H. H. Stebbins (also brothers, various regiments); brothers Charles, Cyrus O., and Myron E. Stowell (different regiments); Asa E., David E., and William H. Todd (different regiments).

5. Numerous regimental histories attest to this pattern. In addition, see Marvin R. Cain, "A 'Face of Battle' Needed: An Assessment of Motives and Men in Civil War Historiography," *Civil War History* 27 (March 1982): 15; J. G. Randall and David Donald, *The Divided Union* (Boston: Little Brown & Company, 1961), ch. 17.

Citizens of Deerfield viewed participation in the war as an opportunity to establish continuity with the town's Revolutionary War heritage. A community resolution at an 1862 mass meeting exemplifies local rhetoric: "Remembering the ancient patriotism of our stock and desiring to secure for our posterity the blessing of a country free, Christian and respected among nations, we will come forward like sons of brave and loyal men, and if need be like our fathers in behalf of our country, pledge our lives, our fortunes and our sacred honor."[6]

In accordance with this spirit, the community celebrated each departure of troops. Even soldiers passing through from other towns and states were recognized, such as the three Vermont regiments who were cheered at the Deerfield Depot by a crowd and canon fire in July 1861.[7]

By the close of 1861, seventy-five enlisted men, forty-nine of whom lived in Deerfield, were credited to the town. In the summer of 1862, an additional eighty of the town's "sons" left for war. While enlistments dwindled during the winter and spring, the president's call for 300,000 "three years men" in July 1862 stimulated renewed community recruitment efforts.[8] At a patriotic mass meeting on Saturday, July 12, Deerfield citizens resolved to ignore differences of opinion over the conduct of the war and promised "more whole-hearted sacrifice of ourselves and all that we have." In their statement of purpose they declared: "conviction in the justice of our cause and ... confidence in the integrity of the present administration, and recognizing the overwhelming embarrassments of the situation, burying all minor differences, we regard as our first duty the suppression of the rebellion and are not disposed to judge too cautiously the conduct of affairs."[9] These citizens viewed the war as a threat to American democracy, and the preservation of democratic institutions was, they believed, the "Cause of God and humanity."[10]

Soon after this meeting, Elisha Wells, chairman of the Board of Selectmen, was authorized to enlist men at the railroad depot in Old Deerfield. The town voted to raise $3,400 to go toward paying a bounty of $100 to every volunteer counted towards the local quota, which was filled by August 14.[11]

Even before this quota was filled, the president issued a call for 300,000 "nine

---

6. *Gazette and Courier*, vol. 25, no. 19, July 14, 1862, p. 3. Frisch, *Town into City*, pp. 53–66, notes similarly that war rhetoric in Springfield constantly evoked "The Spirit of '76."

7. For examples, see *Gazette and Courier*, vol. 24, no. 20, July 22, 1861, p. 2; Sheldon, "Diary," July 24, 1861.

8. "Town Records," Warrant for July 23, 1862, p. 646.

9. *Gazette and Courier*, vol. 25, no. 19, July 14, 1862, p. 3.

10. Ibid.

11. *Gazette and Courier*, vol. 25, no. 20, July 21, 1862, p. 3; vol. 25, no. 24, August 18, 1862, p. 3; "Town Records," Meeting of July 23, 1862, p. 646.

months' men" on August 4, 1862. On August 27, 1862, the town voted to raise a bounty of $125 for each man. This was subsequently reduced to $100, possibly because the extra financial incentive was not necessary to stimulate enlistments. Deerfield met its quota of forty-seven by November 1862. Forty-five of the new recruits mustered into the Fifty-second Regiment, Company D, known as "The Franklin County Nine Months' Volunteers." At least thirty-five men in Company D lived in Deerfield, while the remainder were from the neighboring towns of Conway and Whately. Like towns throughout the Union, Deerfield now had its own company in the Union army.[12]

Recruiting to fill this quota culminated on September 3 and 4, 1862. In war meetings in Old and South Deerfield, prominent citizens and outside speakers addressed assembled crowds. In South Deerfield, stores were closed and a procession formed, including bands from Conway and Greenfield, twenty men on horseback, citizens, and town officers. After a thirty-four-gun salute, the crowd marched to the church as the bells tolled.[13]

The meetings and processions mixed celebrations of the Union cause with poignant and difficult decisions. For example, eighteen-year-old Cyrus O. Stowell sat at a war meeting with his father, who had already sent his two older sons, Myron and Charles, off to the war. According to a later account, a call for volunteers at the close of the meeting produced only two or three responses followed by a "painful" pause until:

> Cyrus Stowell rose, his eyes kindling with great purpose. . . . He was next seen whispering in his father's ear. Then that father rose, and with tears and choking emotion said, "I have felt that I could not spare my only remaining son—that the time had not come that required of me such a sacrifice—but I do not know but that the time has come now. All I can say is that he is at liberty to go if he choose!" No sooner had he finished that Cyrus sprang across the platform, his face wreathed with smiles, and wrote his name. The effect was electric. Cheers filled the house, bouquets were showered upon the young volunteer, while sobs and tears witnessed to the deep sympathy of the crowd.[14]

12. *Gazette and Courier*, vol. 25, no. 31, October 6, 1862, p. 3; vol. 25, no. 27, September 8, 1862, p. 3; vol. 25, no. 38, November 24, 1862; John F. Moors, *History of the Fifty Second Regiment* (Boston, 1893); see note 4 above.

13. *Gazette and Courier*, vol. 25, no. 27, September 8, 1862, p. 3.

14. Rev. Perkins K. Clark, *Sacrifices for our Country: A Discourse Delivered July 17, 1864, in The First Church, South Deerfield, Massachusetts at Funeral Services for James T. Stebbins and Myron E. Stowell Who Were Killed in the Armies of the Union*. With an Appendix containing sketches of other deceased soldiers from the same place (Greenfield: S. S. Eastman & Co., 1864), pp. 32–33.

The formation of Company D illustrated the broad base of local support for the Union cause and provided the community with a forceful link to the battlefield. Young, single men were joined by at least five who had children and nine who were married. Brothers and cousins were comrades-in-arms with neighbors who were new arrivals in town. The Reverend James K. Hosmer marched with Irish-born farm laborer Richard Costello, whose wife had done the minister's washing.[15]

From October 11 to November 20, 1862, Company D was stationed at Camp Miller in neighboring Greenfield, which became an extension of the community. Prominent citizens visited the troops daily and special trains were advertised.[16] Crowds attended a farewell meeting in November. Hosmer described the regiment's poignant departure in his war journal, which was sent back to town in installments and later published:

> It rains harder and harder, but Greenfield streets were full of people and the nearer we came to the Depot, the thicker the crowd. Now came the last partings and hand shakings, eyes were full and lips in a tremble. I had my cry the night before.... The heart came out grandly in some of these fellows. There was Dodge, the cook, heavy and rough, who pulled his little girl up from the platform into the car window to kiss her through his tears. Stout George Wells, too, as the train went off had his head on the window sill, and little Ed Hoyt whimpered as he did when a baby. We swept through Deerfield, the white spire, the strict and familiar houses going behind, seen through that pouring rain perhaps for the last time. Now forward.[17]

As citizens of Deerfield bade their enlisted neighbors and relatives farewell, they probably expected a rapid end to the national crisis. By the time these enthusiastic recruits returned home in August 1863, however, it was clear that their optimism was naïve. Expectations about the war and solutions to meeting its demands changed as the town faced the reality of extended conflict.

On both national and local levels, 1863 marked a break with tradition. In Deerfield, the search for new solutions to the problem of meeting quotas had three basic characteristics. First, it continued to rely heavily on patriotic rhetoric

---

15. See note 2 above; James K. Hosmer, manuscript of "Civil War Diary," PVMA, Box 8H, p. 8 (Later published as *The Color Guard*, without names of men).
16. *Gazette and Courier*, vol. 25, no. 33, October 27, 1862, p. 3, Adv.; Sheldon, "Diary," 1862, especially entries for September 21, October 20, October 21; Elisha Wells, Letterbook, 1863 (PVMA "Deerfield Town Records," Box 5-40).
17. *Gazette and Courier*, vol. 25, no. 36, November 11, 1862, p. 2. Hosmer, "Civil War Diary."

and sentiment. Second, the search reflected local class and ethnic differences. Finally, it made use of "corporate" tools, which shifted the burden from individual self-sacrifice through enlistment to collective financial expenditures.

In 1863, the Union made its first attempts at conscription. These symbolized the magnitude and complexity of the national crisis. Voluntarism and community recruiting were no longer sufficient sources of manpower. Across the Union, citizens found conscription a distasteful concept because, as historian Eugene C. Murdock explains in his 1971 study of the draft: "There was something un-American about it; it was coercive; it was almost unpatriotic to allow one's community to be drafted; the draft simply had no place in a free society."[18] Despite public opinion, the draft was finally implemented as a necessary evil.

Deerfield first experienced conscription on January 19, 1863, when eleven men were drafted. Three days later, in a town meeting, the selectmen were directed "to obtain substitutes in cases where the originals do not enlist at as reasonable a rate as possible." To meet the cost, the town voted to raise $100 per drafted man. Eleven substitutes were hired from the town of Lowell, Massachusetts, probably with the assistance of the Greenfield recruiting office, which advertised its ability to help towns locate substitutes. Each received $75 from Deerfield's coffers.[19]

After this first experiment, the Enrollment Act of March 1863 was enacted to establish formal drafting mechanisms. It allowed those who paid $300 commutation or furnished a substitute to remain at home.[20]

The draft of eleven men in January 1863 was only a hint of what was to come. On July 14, 1863, under the new Enrollment Act, eighty-three men were drafted from Deerfield. This time the town took no official action to hire substitutes or raise funds, perhaps not believing that a draft of so many men could be legitimate. The *Gazette and Courier* attempted to reassure its readers by informing them of the draft's inaccuracies: "A cripple has been drafted in Ashfield . . . a deaf and dumb man in Deerfield . . . in South Deerfield, several of its leading citizens and businessmen."[21] For the first time in response to a call for troops,

18. Murdock, p. 4.
19. *Gazette and Courier*, vol. 25, no. 46, January 19, 1863, p. 2; *Finance Report, 1862-63;* "Town Records," Meeting of January 22, 1863, Articles 2 and 3, p. 667.
20. Murdock, ch. 1.
21. *Gazette and Courier*, vol. 26, no. 20, July 20, 1863, p. 3; "Proceedings of the Board of Enrollment, May 1863 to June 1865," in Records of the Provost Marshall General's Bureau (Civil War) (Record Group 10), National Archives, Entry 961, also, "Consolidated Lists of Class I, II and III," and "Descriptive Book of Drafted Men."

Deerfield's patriotic citizens seemed mute. The town focused its attention on the two other events, both related to the draft. First, on July 18, 1863, an incident in Cheapside, where most of Deerfield's immigrant population resided, prompted speculation that the sentiment expressed by antidraft rioters in New York, Boston, and elsewhere was not absent from Deerfield. That night the Connecticut River Railroad Bridge over the Deerfield River was burned. The *Gazette and Courier* reported that this was the act of "secession incendiaries" and linked it to the Irish community. A week later the paper reported:

> A reward of $1,000 has been offered for the incendiaries. The Republican thinks the burning of the bridge had nothing to do with the draft. People here think different. If it had not been for the draft and the riots elsewhere, the bridge would not have been burned. They are all connected and more damage was intended to the property of loyal people.[22]

While citizens' committees were formed in neighboring Greenfield in response to this perceived threat, no record of formal action exists in Deerfield. Nevertheless, the incident focused local patriotic sentiment on a local enemy. It accurately reflected class and ethnic tensions within Deerfield. During the first two years of the war, local rhetoric painted a picture of unity, highlighting such incidents as the Reverend Mr. Hosmer's departure as a fellow soldier with the husband of his Irish washerwoman. In contrast, the bridge-burning incident emphasized the socioeconomic divisions in the town, which would also be reflected in enlistment patterns from 1863 to 1865.

The second event coinciding with the July 1863 draft was the return of the Fifty-second Regiment on August 3, 1863. They were welcomed at the Greenfield Depot by a crowd, a band, and the engine company, and carried with cheers to the Greenfield Town Hall. Fifteen of Company D were dead. Among them was Cyrus O. Stowell, the eighteen-year-old recruit who had enlisted with such ceremony just nine months earlier. The moving memorial sermon preached on August 23 by South Deerfield's Rev. Perkins Clark, as well as those by other ministers for other volunteers, replaced mass war meetings as the dominant collective activity in Deerfield during this call for troops.[23]

With this sad homecoming the town was poignantly reminded of the grim

---

22. *Gazette and Courier*, vol. 26, no. 21, July 27, 1863, p. 3; Jenkins, pp. 123–25.
23. Clark, "Sacrifices for our Country"; Hosmer, "Diary"; Moors, *History of the Fifty-Second*.

reality of war. Men who were called in the July 1863 draft were confronted face-to-face with relatives and friends, many sick, who had just returned from the front. For instance, twenty-nine-year-old Alden Sprout, a married wagonmaker, was among the drafted. When he went for his medical examination, his twenty-four-year-old brother, Dana, who had just returned with the Fifty-second, lay dying at home. The day after Alden Sprout's examiners found him physically fit for service, he paid the $300 commutation fee; six weeks later, his brother died.[24]

Alden Sprout was not alone in his decision to avoid the draft. Of the 83 men drafted from Deerfield, one was in service, 49 percent (40) were found to be exempt for medical reasons, 20 percent (16) were aliens, and 7 percent (6) were exempt for other reasons. Twenty men (24 percent) were found eligible for the army. Seventeen of these paid the $300 commutation fee required to avoid service, and two furnished substitutes. One, Lorenzo Brizee, a twenty-seven-year-old married farm laborer with one child, enlisted.[25]

Less than half (9 or 47 percent) of the 19 drafted men who paid commutation or furnished substitutes were, like Sprout, between the ages of twenty and twenty-nine. Over half (5 or 56 percent) of this younger group were married. Of the remaining 10 men between the ages of thirty and forty-five, 70 percent (7) were married.[26] The men who were drafted and found eligible were those who had already decided, during previous calls, not to go. Perhaps the return of the Fifty-second Regiment further contributed to their antipathy. Given their financial ability to avoid the draft, apparently without town assistance, it was unlikely that any would enlist.

The payment of commutation was socially acceptable, and among those who paid were such prominent citizens as William Wells, brother of the chairman of the Board of Selectmen, and the wealthy South Deerfield manufacturer and merchant, Benjamin R. Hamilton. Henry C. Haskell, who would serve as a selectman in later years, hired a substitute. While the draft may have been a greater burden for the ethnic poor, draft avoidance was not purely the province of the

---

24. See note 2 above, also Deerfield Monument; Grand Army of the Republic, "Personal War Sketches Presented to the Myron E. Stowell Post No. 84, S. Deerfield," 1895, PVMA, Sketch on Dana Sprout.

25. See note 2 above.

26. Of the married men who enlisted in 1861–62, 19 were between the ages of twenty and twenty-nine and 16 were between thirty and thirty-nine; married men comprised 50 percent of the thirty to thirty-nine-year-old age group, demonstrating a strong willingness to sacrifice during the early years.

native born, for Gottlieb Decker, German-born farmer, and Frederick Kiplinger, a mechanic originally from Prussia, were among those able to pay commutation.[27]

In Deerfield, the draft, the bridge burning, and the solemn return of the Fifty-second Regiment were symbols of the second half of the Civil War, as mass meetings, effigies of Jefferson Davis and processions had been symbols of the conflict's first two years. There is no evidence that the town's commitment to the Union cause diminished in 1863, but its capacity to contribute did change fundamentally. On the national level, the Enrollment Act of 1863 addressed the same problem which faced Deerfield: how to raise the army needed to win the war after two years of recruiting volunteers. Comparison of the men drafted in 1863, a study of enrollment lists for the town, and an analysis of the men who were counted as part of Deerfield's quotas between 1861 and 1865 underscore the message implied by the almost mute response to the July 1863 draft. Local volunteers were no longer available to meet the demands of the Union army. Deerfield's capacity to sacrifice her "sons" was exhausted.

The combined total of men on Deerfield's enrollment and enlistment lists indicates that approximately 510 of Deerfield's male inhabitants were between the ages of twenty and forty-five between 1861 and 1865, and were thus eligible to be enrolled as candidates for the Union army. If the draft of 1863 is an accurate random sample of men of eligible ages, 75 percent of the total were actually exempt from serving for medical reasons, alienage, or unusual family circumstances. This suggests that only 25 percent of the men on the enrollment lists, or 128 men, could actually be expected to serve in the Union army.

By the end of 1862, 129 residents of Deerfield had enlisted, that is, the total number of men between the ages of twenty and forty-five who were qualified for service. The town, then, had sent all the men it could be expected to in the first two years of the war. As a further measure of the town's patriotism, by the end of the war an additional 38 "sons" of Deerfield had enlisted. There is probably no coincidence that the number of additional recruits matches the number of enlistees under the age of twenty.

Regardless of the demographic realities, the Union continued to call upon Deerfield for troops. The solution, in addition to continuing the search for recruits among the town's male residents, was to seek "soldiers" elsewhere. Although recruiting from outside Deerfield's town limits was not new in 1863, of

---

27. "Descriptive Book of Drafted Men and Substitutes, June-September 1863" (Record Group 10); Sheldon, *History*, for miscellaneous personal information.

the 171 troops counted towards Deerfield's quotas in 1861 and 1862, 129, or 75 percent, lived in Deerfield. Of the 44 others, 18, or 41 percent, lived in neighboring towns or had family ties to Deerfield. In contrast, during 1863, 1864, and 1865, of the total of 130 enlisted men counted for Deerfield's quotas, only 29 percent were Deerfield's "sons." The remaining 71 percent or 92 "soldiers" were recruited as volunteers from other towns or hired as substitutes. Only 4 of these "soldiers" were neighbors or relatives of Deerfield. The remaining 88 had more tenuous connections (see Table 2).[28]

Table 2
Deerfield "Soldiers" by Place of Origin

Year	NEIGHBORS* No.	% of Soldiers for Year	OTHERS No.	% of Soldiers for Year	TOTAL No.	% of All Soldiers for Four Years
1861	8	31	18	69	26	19
1862	10	56	8	44	18	13
1863	0		17	100	17	13
1864	4	14	25	86	29	21
1865	0		26	100	26	15
Unknown 1863–65	0		20		20	19
Total	22		114		136	100

*Men positively identified as residents of neighboring towns in the vicinity of Deerfield (e.g., Conway, Whately, Greenfield) or with family ties to Deerfield.

Despite the increased reliance on recruited "soldiers," the town's actions to meet quotas from 1863 to 1865 continued to demonstrate its firm patriotic commitment. In fact, when a call for troops came on November 2, 1863, and Deerfield was given until January 5, 1864 to fill its quota, the town turned back to its traditional recruiting method. In December 1863, Deerfield held its last war meeting.

The dominant message at this meeting was that despite its record of sacrifice, the town must continue to contribute its "sons." Deacon Stowell was president of the day, a symbol to the town that a man, who had sent three sons to the war and lost his youngest, still believed in the Union cause. Edgar P. Squires, a veteran of the Fifty-second Regiment, Company D, announced in an impassioned speech that he had reenlisted three days earlier and urged others to join him again.[29]

28. See note 2 above.
29. *Gazette and Courier*, vol. 26, no. 42, December 7, 1863, p. 2.

Apparently, the selectmen's recruitment efforts following this meeting were successful, for there was no draft in Deerfield in January 1864. It is not clear from the available records, however, who filled this quota. Given the aggregate statistics for the men who mustered into service in 1863 and 1864, probably the majority of the 41 men who met this quota were not from Deerfield. The *Gazette and Courier* reported in December that towns were enlisting men wherever they could be found and warned that this might affect quota counts. Although the town still relied outwardly on such customary recruitment channels as war meetings, the audience it reached was fundamentally different, primarily made up of recruits from outside the town limits.[30]

The character of Deerfield's "sons" who did enlist in 1863, 1864, and 1865 also changed. These few "sons" were generally younger than those who had enlisted in the first two years of the war and were more often single. The percentage of enlistees over thirty dropped dramatically from 22 percent of the total "sons" who enlisted in 1861 and 1862 to 2 percent in the last three war years. Many of those who enlisted after 1863 had just come of age, and a high percentage, particularly in 1865, were under twenty when they enlisted. The "sons" of Deerfield likely in service at the end of the war were those who had perhaps jealously watched older relatives depart earlier and had fewer responsibilities on the homefront (Table 3).

Table 3
Deerfield "Sons" by Age and Marital Status

Year	Total "Sons" Enlisted	19 or Under No.	%	20–29 No.	%	30 or Over No.	%	Married No.	%	Single No.	%
1861	49	13	27	27	55	9	18	14	29	35	71
1862	80	12	15	48	60	20	25	30	38	50	62
1863	17	5	29	11	65	1	6	3	18	14	82
1864	13	2	15	10	77	1	8	6	46	7	54
1865	8	6	75	2	25	0	-	0	-	8	100
Total	167	38	23	98	59	31	18	53	32	114	68

Furthermore, after 1862, the immigrant community sacrificed its "sons" in much greater proportion, suggesting that those most likely to enlist were those who had less power or financial ability. Of the 129 residents of Deerfield who served in 1861 and 1862, 9, or 7 percent, are known to have been foreign born. In contrast, the 38 Deerfield residents who enlisted between 1863 and 1865 included

30. Ibid.

14, or 37 percent, who were born abroad. Occupational statistics also suggest that the "sons" who served for Deerfield at the end of the war came in greater proportion from the industrial working-class community. In 1861 and 1862, 66 percent of those who served were in farm-related occupations and 16 percent were professionals or craftsmen, while 17 percent were cutlers or mechanics. In 1863, only 11 percent of those Deerfield residents who enlisted were cutlers or mechanics, but in 1864 this group composed 77 percent of the 13 "sons" who enlisted and, in 1865, 2 of the 4 Deerfield citizens who enlisted were cutlers.[31]

The majority of the men who met Deerfield's quotas between 1863 and 1865 lived outside the town, but the most dramatic change in recruiting activities came in May 1864, after 26 men were drafted. Following medical examinations, 17 of these men were found eligible for service. On May 24, 1864, the day after the examinations, Deerfield's citizens voted in a town meeting to raise $300 for each drafted man. The selectmen were directed to procure substitutes with this sum "provided that 8/10 of the taxpayers representing 8/10 of the property will pledge themselves to pay the amount necessary to raise a sum sufficient to raise $300 for each drafted man."[32] This unprecedented financial burden on the town received the consent of the taxpayers. Their action would prevent those who paid commutation from being counted towards future quotas.

Eleven of the men drafted in May 1864 paid commutation. Five of them furnished substitutes, and one apparently went to war. Like the men drafted in 1863, most of these 17 men were over thirty and married. Only 24 percent (4) were under twenty-nine, and of the 13 over thirty, all but one were married. Single men between ages twenty and twenty-nine who were eligible for service simply did not remain in Deerfield. To replace these men and help fill the quota set in this draft, the town's own "Rebellion Record" lists 13 men "Bot [bought] in Washington, D.C. at $325 each and accepted 26, July 1864" and an additional man hired for $325 to enlist in June.[33] The town in 1864 met its quotas through a combination of individual and community willingness to bear the financial responsibility of seeking and purchasing substitutes.

Even while the town was securing men to fill the May draft, its requirement to supply manpower was growing. In a July call for troops Deerfield's quota was 41 men. The citizens of Deerfield did not turn again to town government to

31. See note 2 above.

32. "Descriptive Book of Drafted Men, May 13, 1864"; "Town Records," Meeting of May 24, 1864, pp. 738–39.

33. "Descriptive Book of Drafted Men and Substitutes, May 13, 1864"; "Rebellion Record," page directly after list of men who furnished substitutes and paid commutation.

meet this quota but called a public meeting, which was not recorded in the town records. At this meeting, the decision was reached to circulate a subscription paper raising money to hire substitutes as necessary. By August 1, the townsmen reported having obtained 22 men out of its quota.[34] Even if the established channels of town government were overburdened by the requirements of the draft, the community rallied to fulfill its responsibilities.

The frenzied and expensive efforts to fill quotas by outside recruiting and hiring substitutes ended in March 1865 when a new procedure drafted men from the state at large and assigned them to the towns.[35] Finally, the state government recognized what was apparent in Deerfield by 1863: the town had furnished all the native manpower it had to give. While the financial burden continued, recruitment responsibilities were over.

The ramifications of the financial burden extended into Deerfield's governing structure. The town's budget increased by 61 percent between 1861 and 1863, and more than doubled between 1863 and 1864. Even accounting for Civil War inflation, the increase in town expenditures from $11,874 in 1861 to $19,150 in 1863, to $41,596 in 1864, and $44,563 in 1865, was far greater than the incremental growth of previous years. This increase suggests a dramatic shift in local fiscal responsibility and sophistication. The budget stayed in the $40,000 range after the war and did not change substantially until new accounting and taxation procedures were implemented in the 1870s.[36]

By its end in 1865, the Civil War had left Deerfield a number of legacies. One was the collective experience of raising troops, an effort which shifted from mass meetings directed toward inspiring enlistment to the circulation of subscription papers, the enactment of new levies, and the far-reaching recruitment of substitutes. A second legacy was an expanded budget, which included new levels of debt to Greenfield banks and wealthy citizens. Finally, the town had celebrated the return of approximately 133 "sons" home from the front and shared the loss of 34 "sons" who gave their lives for the Union.

The town's Civil War monument symbolized these legacies for Deerfield's

---

34. *Gazette and Courier*, vol. 27, no. 21, August 1, 1864.

35. *Gazette and Courier*, vol. 28, no. 3, March 20, 1865, p. 3. Law passed March 8, 1865. "Rebellion Record," p. 90, lists 22 soldiers furnished by the state at large and assigned to Deerfield.

36. Town Expenditures compiled from yearly "Recapitulation of Money paid from the Treasury," in *Finance Reports*, first published for the year ending February 25, 1858, PVMA. Accounting techniques vary, and payments rather than totals are used here because they are comparable on an annual basis. The reports also indicate a dramatic increase in municipal indebtedness during the war years. Frisch, *Town into City*, suggests a similar change in Springfield.

citizens when they gathered to dedicate it in 1866. Cyrus and Myron Stowell, Dana Sprout, and Edgar Squires, who spoke at Deerfield's last war meeting in 1863, are among the 42 names engraved on the monument. With them are Michael Glasset, an Irish-born worker in Cheapside's cutlery who enlisted in 1864; Edward J. Hosmer, not a "son" of Deerfield, but a "soldier" from Buffalo, New York, who served for the town because of his connection through his brother, the Rev. James K. Hosmer; and Leonard A. Barnes, about whom no information survives. In total, the monument lists 34 "sons" and 8 "soldiers," comprising 14 percent of the 303 men who served for the town and 20 percent of its "sons" who went to war. In dedicating the monument a civic leader stated:

> The town bore cheerfully and with alacrity its full share of the burdens of the war. Its ancient prestige and ancestral renown inspired the patriotic impulses of its inhabitants and clothed the privations and perils of the service with a poetic charm, making the voice of duty as powerful as the command of God. She responded to every call for her young men, and she parted with her substance that they might be sustained without a murmur.

Buried in the cornerstone of the monument were documents including lists of enrolled men, town finance reports showing the expanded budget, and newspapers which told the story of the war in greater detail.[37]

This monument commemorated individuals and Deerfield's shifting community response to the national crisis. The third year of war brought home the war's tragic realities and the recognition that the town had a finite number of "sons" to contribute. The collective response to the second half of the war, no less patriotic than the first, shifted the burden of fighting from individuals to the community as a whole. When the state finally took over recruiting responsibilities in the final year of the war, it recognized that the ability of local communities to meet national responsibilities was exhausted, despite the growing sophistication of towns like Deerfield as they turned to a variety of governing mechanisms to provide troops. Deerfield truly responded to the Union's calls with a willingness to "part with her substance." The monument to her "sons and soldiers" memorialized the range of activities which that willingness implied.

---

37. "Dedication," *Gazette and Courier*, vol. 30, no. 28, September 9, 1867, p. 2; "War Memorial Papers," 1866-1867 (PVMA "Deerfield Town Records," Box 540); "Contents of Cornerstone" and "Statement of Nathaniel Hitchcock."

Introduction to War

The Civilians of Culpeper County, Virginia

Daniel E. Sutherland

Consider the numbers: 3.5 million versus 28 million. Consider that historians most often write about the 3.5 million Union and Confederate soldiers who participated in the Civil War, while the 28 million civilians of the North and South remain the forgotten majority. We still do not know much about these people, and the framework of community life within which most of them witnessed the war. In the case of Southern civilians (9 million of the 28 million), a few writers have described their plight in towns under siege or in areas occupied by Union troops, but such studies tend to dwell more on military affairs than on the populace. And while some scholars are beginning to analyze the effects of war on individual counties, the most representative form of Southern community, even these studies tend to dwell on long-range social and economic changes. Little time is spent describing the initial exposure of a community to war, the response of its farmers and merchants as rival armies jockeyed for control of farms and towns, the shock of the first battle.[1] Yet some appreciation of this first

---

1. Among the most balanced studies of Southern communities during the war are: Stephen V. Ash, *Middle Tennessee Society Transformed 1860-1870: War and Peace in the Upper South* (Baton Rouge: Louisiana State Univ. Press, 1988); Gerald M. Capers, *Occupied City: New Orleans under the Federals, 1862-1865* (Lexington: Univ. of Kentucky Press, 1965); James T. Currie, *Enclave: Vicksburg and Her Plantations, 1863-70* (Jackson: Univ. of Mississippi Press, 1980); Wayne K. Durrill, *War of Another Kind: A Southern Community in the Great Rebellion* (New York: Oxford Univ. Press, 1990); Peter Maslowski,

Civil War History, Vol. XXXVII No. 2 © 1991 by The Kent State University Press

response to the cross-currents of war would seem essential for understanding the Southern homefront. As an example of the sort of inquiry being suggested, consider how the residents of one Virginia county, Culpeper County, weathered their shocking introduction to war.

The people of Culpeper had no reason to think the summer of 1862 would differ very much from that of the previous year. The summer of 1861 had been good to them, even invigorating. When Virginia seceded, most of Culpeper's free citizens supported the Confederacy. Young men rushed to join one of six county-sponsored infantry and cavalry companies. Women sewed flags and uniforms and raised money for families who might be financially strapped when their men set out to repel the Yankees. Merchants had difficulty stocking items like powder, ball, knives, and boots, as patriotic citizens prepared for war. Excitement intensified when Colonel Philip St. George Cocke arrived to recruit troops in Culpeper and surrounding counties, and to establish a training camp, Camp Henry, on the outskirts of Culpeper Courthouse, the county seat. The camp gave everyone a sense of security. Local merchants and farmers prospered by filling the camp's demands for food, firewood, and equipment. Culpeper seemed destined to help lead a glorious crusade against northern aggression. People spoke of it as a "good war," a just war, and a war that would doubtless be brief.[2]

Culpeper seemed safe, too. The county had experienced the war vicariously when it received hundreds of wounded and dying men from the battlefield of First Manassas, just twenty-five miles to the northeast; but residents did not feel personally threatened until early 1862, when Yankee patrols began to appear along the Rappahannock River, the county's northeastern boundary. One rebel soldier reported in March, "People in this region . . . a good deal scared. Not a few breaking up & going southward." General Richard S. Ewell drew a similar

---

Treason Must Be Made Odious: Military Occupation and Wartime Reconstruction in Nashville, Tennessee, 1862-65 (Millwood, N.Y.: KTO Press, 1978); Emory M. Thomas, *The Confederate State of Richmond: A Biography of the Capital* (Austin: Univ. of Texas Press, 1971); and Peter F. Walker, *Vicksburg: A People at War, 1860-1865* (Chapel Hill: Univ. of North Carolina Press, 1960). Another excellent work, but with a broader concept of community, is Michael Fellman, *Inside War: The Guerrilla Conflict in Missouri during the American Civil War* (New York: Oxford Univ. Press, 1989). For a more detailed discussion of new directions in the study of Civil War communities, see Daniel E. Sutherland, "Getting the 'Real War' into the Books," *Virginia Magazine of History and Biography* 98 (Apr. 1990).

2. Eugene M. Scheel, *Culpeper: A Virginia County's History Through 1920* (Culpeper: Culpeper Historical Society, 1982), 172-77; G. F. Carter Account Books, Univ. of Virginia Library, Charlottesville; *Camp Henry Account Book, 1861-62*, Eleanor S. Brockenbrough Library, Museum of the Confederacy, Richmond.

conclusion. Ewell selected the abandoned residence of Richard H. Cunningham, about two miles from Rappahannock Station, to serve as his headquarters in Culpeper. "He has left his home and most of his furniture with orders to his overseer to apply the torch when the Yanks come," said Ewell of Cunningham, a sixty-two-year-old planter worth over one hundred forty thousand dollars and the owner of sixty slaves. What was more, added Ewell, the early enthusiasm of Culpeper's men to fight Yankees had waned noticeably. The "chivalry" of the county seemed "to be pretty generally played out. Very few reenlisting—none to all intents and purposes." Even the county newspaper felt compelled to remind young men that the war had yet to be won. "A great crisis is upon us," warned the *Culpeper Observer,* "and we cannot disguise the fact, nor hide it from our eyes, that we are in imminent peril. Numerous and well appointed armies and navies, flushed with recent triumphs, are bearing down upon us."[3]

The county's slaves had begun to make trouble, too. People had been shocked in September 1861 when a woman living in the village of Waterloo, on the upper Rappahannock, had been murdered by a sixteen-year-old female servant. The girl, who had taken exception to being reprimanded by her mistress, had clubbed her victim with a piece of fence rail and then choked her to death. A shiver ran through the county, where, despite a majority black population (7,104 blacks to 4,959 whites), violence by slaves, indeed serious trouble of any kind, had been rare. Some people, like Mr. Cunningham, began moving their slaves further south. More resolute people decided to stay put, but remained alert to the possibility of retreat should an actual Yankee "invasion" require it.[4]

And the likelihood of invasion seemed to be growing. An infantry skirmish and artillery duel at Rappahannock Station in late March had ended with Confederate forces blowing up one of three stone pillars supporting the railroad bridge and burning the bridge's wooden trestles. Yankee cavalry patrols began to skirt the borders of Culpeper in April, and many civilians, particularly isolated women whose men had joined the army, felt increasingly vulnerable. "You can form no idea how lonely it is here," Martha Coons informed a married sister from the family plantation, Northcliff. With her father dead and three older brothers

---

3. William N. Pendleton to Anzolette E. Pendleton, March 13, 1862, William Nelson Pendleton Papers, Southern Historical Collection, Univ. of North Carolina at Chapel Hill; Richard S. Ewell to Rebecca L. Ewell, [Apr.] 23, 1862, in *The Making of a Soldier: Letters of General R. S. Ewell,* ed. Percy Gatling Hamlin (Richmond: Whittet & Shepperson, 1935), 109; *Culpeper Observer,* Feb. 21, 1862.

4. *Lynchburg Daily Virginian,* Sept. 23, 1861; James M. Farish to Tom Brown, Mar. 23, 1862, Morton-Halsey Papers, Univ. of Virginia Library.

in the army, Martha resided with her stepmother, two younger brothers, and an overseer. "I understand the Yankees are treating the people generally very bad [in adjoining counties]; but we hear so many rumors that it is impossible to get the truth.... We are in a very helpless condition." The appearance of Yankee cavalry patrols forced some churches to suspend worship services. As inhabitants came to regard travel over even relatively short distances an unnecessary hazard, the pastor of the Baptist church at Criglersville announced that "in consequence of the presence of the publick enemy and the excitement incident thereto" he would hold services "whenever he could."[5]

Then it happened. The defilement was brief, only eighteen hours, but on Monday, May 5, 1862, the Yankee hordes arrived in force. Federal artillery batteries had begun lobbing shells across the Rappahannock in mid-April. Ewell had not been impressed. In fact, as enlistments increased his division to over eight thousand men, he had contemplated launching his own attack across the river. But General Thomas J. Jackson needed his help in the Shenandoah Valley, so on April 19, Ewell led most of his men out of Culpeper. With only a couple of hundred cavalrymen left to occupy Culpeper Courthouse, the way was clear for Major D. Porter Stowell to ford the Rappahannock with a battalion of the 1st Maine Cavalry at about midnight on May 4. Ironically, the first residence he encountered was that of Richard Cunningham. Stowell woke John Wilcher, a local miller serving as Cunningham's overseer, and demanded entrance to the house. Stowell's men enjoyed a three-hour rest as they lounged "promiscuously" on the comfortable beds, sofas, and easy chairs of the "well-furnished mansion," although Stowell later stressed in his report that "not a dollar's worth of property was destroyed." After feeding their horses, the detachment, with Wilcher serving as guide, advanced toward Brandy Station. From Brandy they pushed on toward the courthouse, a distance of about ten miles from the river. The outnumbered Confederate troops offered no resistance and steadily withdrew before the Yanks. Stowell remained at the courthouse only forty-five minutes before retracing his route and recrossing the river at about 6 P.M.[6]

---

5. *The War of the Rebellion: A Compilation of the Official Records of the Union and Confederate Armies*, 53 vols., in 127 parts (Washington, D.C.: GPO, 1880–1901), ser. 1, vol. 12, pt. 1:412–17 (hereafter cited as *OR*); Martha E. Coons to Mollie D. Corbin, Apr. 22, 1862, Coons Family Papers, Virginia Historical Society; Minutes of the Baptist Church of Christ, Criglersville, Culpeper County, Apr. 1862, Univ. of Virginia Library.

6. *OR*, vol. 12, pt. 1:451–55, pt. 3:850–57; Torlief S. Holmes, *Horse Soldiers in Blue* (Gaithersburg, Md.: Butternut Press, 1985), 28–29; Daniel Amon Grimsley, *Battles in Culpeper County, Virginia, 1861–1865* (Culpeper: Exponent Printing Office, 1900), 4–5.

Two results of the raid are worth mentioning. First, Stowell became impressed, even on so hurried an expedition, by the prosperity of Culpeper. "The general appearance of the country," he stressed in his report, "is very favorable, gently rolling, open, highly cultivated, and fruitful, rich plantations, with an abundance of forage and subsistence." Then came a fateful observation: "The planters on our route, as near as I could judge, are nearly all secesh, and a little bleeding would reduce their fever a little and do them good." Two months later, motivated at least partly by Stowell's report, Federal forces would try to do exactly that. The second result of Stowell's expedition caused more immediate concern in the county, for as his men withdrew from Culpeper Courthouse, they seized eight citizens as hostages. The only four who can be identified with certainty were the proprietor of the Piedmont Hotel, a forty-two-year-old railroad depot agent (and father of five children), a forty-seven-year-old judge, and an elderly "colonel." Stowell released them all within a few days except for the landlord of the Piedmont, Thomas Lewis, who had been armed at the time of his capture and had apparently resisted arrest; but the fact that four respected citizens could be so abruptly kidnapped visibly affected the community. When a company of Confederate cavalry rode back into Culpeper Courthouse, one elderly citizen, known to be "a very quiet, passive, undemonstrative man," watched "tenderly and earnestly ... with the tears rolling down his furrowed cheeks" as the column passed through town.[7]

Civilian spirits rallied over the next few weeks. The Federals seemed to be uninterested in returning to Culpeper, and residents grew less concerned about occasional sightings of Union patrols at the river crossings. Susan Coons, stepmother of Martha, felt safe enough by late June to visit neighbors "without any danger of being molested by the Yankees." She was thankful that she had resisted an earlier impulse to flee the county. "Here we have all the comforts of life," she explained, "go where we please, come when we please." She looked forward to harvesting the summer wheat soon. She harvested her wheat, but Yankees would be the beneficiaries.[8]

On July 12, 1862, advance units of General John Pope's newly-formed Army of Virginia carried the full fury of war into Culpeper. After routing a handful of Confederate cavalry in the streets of Culpeper Courthouse, Pope's army claimed the county as Union territory. Within two weeks, ten thousand men had settled into camp, although Pope did not make a personal appearance until August 8.

7. *OR*, vol. 12, pt. 1:452–55; Bettie Browning to Daniel A. Grimsley, May 11, 1862, Grimsley Family Papers, Virginia State Library; Grimsley, *Battles in Culpeper County*, 5.
8. Susan E. Coons to Mollie Corbin, June 31, 1862, Coons Family Papers.

Pope's strategic assignments were to seize control of the Orange & Alexandria, thus severing Richmond from the bountiful Shenandoah Valley, and to bleed Culpeper's rebels. To thwart him, General Robert E. Lee rushed Stonewall Jackson from the Peninsula to Gordonsville, the southeastern terminus of the railroad thirty miles from Culpeper. Jackson succeeded in protecting the railroad, but he could not halt the bleeding. "The Yanks are now in Culpeper," reported Richard Ewell, whose division was still operating under Jackson, "and I learn, are systematically destroying all the growing crops and everything the people have to live on. Sometimes they ride into the fields and swing their sabres to cut down the growing corn. They seem bent on starving out the women and children left by the war."[9]

And things got worse, for Pope was about to nudge the war in a devastatingly new direction. While still in Washington, D.C., Pope had received reports of civilian resistance, sabotage, and bushwhacking in Culpeper and surrounding counties. In response, he issued his infamous General Orders No. 5, 7, and 11. These orders authorized his troops to confiscate from local citizens whatever food, forage, animals, and other supplies they might require; to exile beyond Federal lines all male citizens who refused to swear allegiance to the United States; to execute all persons who fired upon Federal soldiers; to destroy the property of all such persons; and to force local residents to repair any railroads, wagon roads, or telegraphs destroyed in their neighborhoods. The orders applied to the entire region of northern Virginia under Pope's command, but Culpeper, which was to serve as Pope's headquarters and where the bulk of his troops were concentrated, was hit especially hard. Abraham Lincoln had quite likely approved the orders, too. Indeed, Lincoln, who had become alarmed by the recent spread of Confederate guerrilla activity, recommended that Pope's orders be applied to other Union-occupied regions as a means of curbing such actions. The Pope-Lincoln policy of making war on civilians as well as soldiers would become the hallmark of the army's strategy of exhaustion in the final year of the war, but official endorsement of such a policy of total war was unheard of in mid-1862. Robert E. Lee was so outraged by what he regarded as Pope's immoral methods that he ordered Stonewall Jackson not just to defeat Pope but to "destroy him." Lee wanted the "miscreant" Pope "suppressed."[10]

---

9. Richard S. Ewell to Elizabeth Ewell, July 30, 1862, in *Making of a Soldier*, ed. Hamlin, 113.
10. *OR*, vol. 12, pt. 2:50–52; Abraham Lincoln to Edwin M. Stanton, July 26, 1862, in *The Collected Works of Abraham Lincoln*, ed. Roy P. Basier, 8 vols. (New Brunswick, N.J.: Rutgers Univ. Press, 1953), 5:344; Douglas Southall Freeman, *R. E. Lee: A Biography*, 4 vols. (New York: Charles

Culpeper citizens who owned anything that could be of use to the Union army, regardless of race, wealth, or loyalties, suffered confiscation and, in some instances, wanton destruction. Federal officers were supposed to supervise confiscation and issue vouchers specifying the type, amount, and value of goods requisitioned; but many soldiers, sensing a license in Pope's orders that probably had not been intended, seized whatever took their fancy. A private in the 21st Massachusetts Infantry admitted that he and his mates "immediately proceeded to take advantage" of Pope's confiscation order. Some members of his company liberated a beehive and another man captured a sheep, all without the formalities of vouchers or payment. "We had plenty of pork and bread," he boasted, "and with mutton and honey added, we lived very well." Some officers expressed abhorrence. "Straggling soldiers have been known to rob the farm houses and even small cottages, the homes of the poor, of every ounce of food or forage found in them," swore a commissary lieutenant. "Families have been left without the means of preparing a meal of victuals." What was more, he added bitterly, "The villains urge as authority, 'General Pope's order.'" A few officers took steps to soften the harshest applications of the orders. Lieutenant Colonel Joseph Karge, of the 1st New Jersey Cavalry, went so far as to issue a regimental order warning that any officer or enlisted man caught "committing depredations or appropriating things of citizens without authority" would be court-martialed "as a marauder."[11]

The most confused, and perhaps abused, portion of Culpeper's population may have been its black residents, slave and free. Pope's occupation gave Culpeper slaves their first good opportunity to escape bondage. Some did so with a vengeance, as they liberated not only themselves but a few of their masters' possessions, especially clothes and jewelry. The vast majority of Culpeper's slaves would

---

Scribner's Sons, 1934–35), 2:264; Robert E. Lee to Thomas J. Jackson, July 27, 1862, in *The Wartime Papers of R. E. Lee*, ed. Clifford Dowdey and Louis H. Manarin (Boston: Little, Brown, 1961), 239; *OR*, vol. 11, pt. 2:936. Pope tried to eliminate the worst abuses of his orders, even to disavow them; but his actions did not come until mid-August, by which time Lee was about to expel him from Culpeper. Also, by that time the U.S. War Department had issued General Order No. 107 as a means of amending Pope's earlier orders. See *OR*, vol. 12, pt. 3:573, 577; John Esten Cooke, *Stonewall Jackson* (New York: D. Appleton, 1866), 254. Pope's biographers seek to justify his actions; see Wallace J. Schutz and Walter N. Trenerry, *Abandoned by Lincoln: A Military Biography of General John Pope* (Urbana: University of Illinois, 1990), 104–5.

11. James Madison Stone, *Personal Recollections of the Civil War* (Boston: n.p., 1918), 57; Edward J. Stackpole, *From Cedar Mountain to Antietam* (Harrisburg, Pa.: Stackpole, 1959), 25; Henry R. Pyne, *History of the First New Jersey Cavalry* (1871; reprint, New Brunswick, N.J.: Rutgers Univ. Press, 1961), 49–50; *Regimental Order Book*, First New Jersey Cavalry, Order No. 164, Aug. 6, 1862, Records of Adjutant General's Office, RG 94, National Archives.

find sanctuary behind Union lines during the next two years, but not all blacks received kind treatment. Acts of the "most beastly and infamous character" were reported to have been perpetrated by Union soldiers against slave women, and the confiscation order applied to everyone, regardless of color. Willis Madden, one of the county's most prosperous free blacks, watched Union soldiers march away from his 281 acre farm with two horses, a cart, forty fowls, forty bushels of corn, two hundred pounds of bacon, and eight thousand pounds of wheat, the whole worth nearly three hundred dollars. Ira Field, a barber at Culpeper Courthouse, surrendered a horse worth two hundred dollars. Even Alexander Jackson, a slave belonging to William Day, lost property to confiscation. Day had permitted Jackson, a skilled saddler and harnessmaker, to hire out his own free time. Over the years, Jackson had accumulated his own leather-working tools and stock. On July 28, he lost ten dollars worth of leather, his saddle bench, and some tools, worth another ten dollars, to Pope's army. No one was immune from Pope's concept of total war. As one woman insisted, "Civilians, women, children, and slaves feared Pope."[12]

The effects were visually apparent. Almost without exception, new arrivals in Culpeper, like Major Stowell four months earlier, had praised the natural beauty of its land and the trimness of its villages. "Culpeper is quite a neat and pretty little town of about 800 inhabitants," noted a Pennsylvania soldier in mid-July, before the impact of impending occupation could be felt, "and by appearance in time of peace must be quite a business place." Later, a correspondent tracking Pope's army for the *New York Herald* described Culpeper Courthouse as "a trim little village, lying in the hollow of several hills. A couple of steeples added to its picturesqueness." However, upon closer inspection, the journalist sensed a queer atmosphere: "It looked like Sunday when I rode through the principal street. The shutters were closed in the shop windows, the dwellings seemed tenantless, no citizens were abroad." He found William Payne, the proprietor of the Virginia Hotel, in such a state of shock and distress as to be "somewhat out of his head." The citizens of the town, this journalist learned, had already suffered more than their rural neighbors because of inflated prices for food. The shock of the Federal invasion, with soldiers fighting in the town's streets, was more than older people, like Payne, could bear.[13]

12. *Richmond Enquirer*, Aug. 5, 8, 1862; Willis Madden (No. 128), Ira Field (No. 3003), Alexander Jackson (No. 3008), *Southern Claims Commission Case Files (Allowed), 1877-83*, Records of Government Accounting Office, Records of Third Auditor's Office, RG217, National Archives; Myrta Lockett Avary, *A Virginia Girl in the Civil War* (New York: D. Appleton, 1903), 49.

13. *William P. Lloyd Diary*, July 21, 1862, Southern Historical Collection, Univ. of North Caro-

The countryside fared no better, perhaps worse. "In every direction there appeared a frightful scene of devastation," confirmed a Union cavalryman, as he surveyed the work of his predecessors. "Furniture, valuable in itself and utterly useless to them, was mutilated and defaced; beds were defiled and cut to pieces; pictures and mirrors were slashed with sabres or perforated by bullets; windows were broken, doors torn from their hinges, houses and barns burned down." Witnesses to the scene were hard-pressed to describe it. "The owner of [a farm] . . . gave us some heartrending accounts of the savage and barbarous treatment he and his family had received from Lincoln's bandits," revealed a horrified Confederate chaplain after Pope's withdrawal. "They plundered him of all he had, his corn, wheat, and pork, killed his hogs, drove off his beef cattle and even his milch cows. . . . They even threatened to shoot this gentleman for having a loaded musket in the house." "The people all have the same tales to tell," reported a member of the Richmond Howitzers. "They [the Yankees] took everything they could lay their hands on & not content with that would break up costly furniture, tear down banisters, kick the panels out of doors, etc." At Berry Hill plantation, Lucy Thorn had all of her clothes stolen by Yankee soldiers and watched helplessly as they carried her melodeon to the slave quarters. The family's horses were also confiscated and its corn destroyed. Soldiers ransacked the house of Episcopal minister Philip Slaughter and then proceeded to wreck his church on orders of their officers. Likewise, they seized twenty-eight slaves from the farm of Captain John Taylor, of the Confederate army, burned his house and outbuildings, confiscated his livestock, and "laid waste his entire farm."[14]

Worse even than this material destruction was the physical abuse of civilians. Blacks and whites, adults and children, had food "wantonly snatched from their mouths and wasted by brutal men." Nor, recounted one witness, were inhabitants "secure from evils worse than these: for insult and outrage ever walk hand-

---

lina at Chapel Hill; George Alfred Townsend, *Campaigns of a Non-Combatant* (New York: Blelock & Company, 1866), 239-40. Townsend claims that the residents of Culpeper Courthouse were "almost starving" because of the way in which the *Confederate* army had "swept the county like famine," but he is the only person to make such an accusation.

14. Pyne, *Ride to War*, 50; James B. Sheeran, *Confederate Chaplain: A War Journal of Rev. James B. Sheeran*, ed. Joseph T. Durkin (Milwaukee: Bruce, 1960), Aug. 8, 1862, pp. 2-3; William H. Tatum to Louisiana Tatum, Oct. 9, 1862, William Henry Tatum Papers, Virginia Historical Society; W. A. Thorn to Pembroke Thorn, Sept. 16, 1862, in *"My Dear Brother": A Confederate Chronicle*, comp. Catherine Thorn Bartlett (Richmond: Dietz, 1952), 67; "Philip Slaughter," ms. in Jane C. Slaughter Papers, Univ. of Virginia Library; *Richmond Enquirer*, Aug. 5, 1862. Cecil E. Eby, Jr., ed., A *Virginia Yankee in the Civil War: The Diaries of David Hunter Strother* (Chapel Hill: Univ. of North Carolina Press, 1961), 81, claims that Confederate soldiers destroyed the Slaughter house, but that was not how the family remembered it.

in-hand with plunder." "Instances are reported," lamented another source, "of deeds of violence perpetrated upon respectable ladies ... which are without a parallel, save in the annals of the infamous Yankee race." One man could not bear to describe "the disagreeable and repulsive details of these excesses of the troops," but a British journalist confirmed that the war in Culpeper was being waged "in a way that cast mankind two centuries back toward barbarism." A Northerner agreed, admitting that Pope's orders had "produced a decided revolution in the feelings and practices of the soldiery." "Men who at home would have shuddered at the suggestion of touching another's property," he explained, "now appropriate whatever comes in their reach."[15]

Pope did not execute or banish anyone during the occupation, and he very likely never intended to do so; but he did arrest a good many civilians. Federal troops incarcerated Miss Ella S. Stringfellow "for resenting with becoming spine" the brutal insults of one soldier. Similarly, Miss Ella Slaughter, "a young and lovely lady and one of the most accomplished in Culpeper," was thrown into jail when she drew a pistol against a soldier who had entered her house and "grossly and brutaly insulted" her. Yankee soldiers dragged John Cole, an elderly Episcopal minister, from his church and sent him to Washington, D.C., when he led his congregation in a prayer "for the welfare of the Southern Confederacy and the success of its arms." Evidently Cole was not alone in being singled out for interrogation in the Yankee capital. "Citizens of the county are constantly being arrested and sent to Washington," reported the *Richmond Enquirer,* "there to be immured in a dungeon." Such threats had an effect on many people, who rushed to take the "exorable oath" in order to save self and property. Slightly bolder citizens still refused to swear allegiance to the United States, but did promise not to interfere with Federal troops while they occupied the county.[16]

Pope's invasion also tested neighborly feelings by releasing a hitherto repressed current of unionist sentiment in the county. Many residents had never supported the war, but most of these people had been too timid to denounce it. County voters had approved Virginia's ordinance of secession unanimously with 1,051 votes in April 1861, but many people had been dissuaded by popu-

---

15. *Richmond Enquirer,* Aug. 5, 1862; Cooke, *Stonewall Jackson,* 251-54. It is worth noting that the Northerner quoted in Cooke was not so much concerned with the South as he was with the consequences of the army's lack of discipline for the North. He feared that "when the enlistments have expired we shall let loose a den of thieves upon the country" (254).

16. George M. Williams to Gertrude Williams, Aug. 5, 1862, quoted in Scheel, *Culpeper,* 189; *Richmond Dispatch,* Aug. 23, 1862; *Richmond Enquirer,* Aug. 5, 1862.

lar opinion or the threat of retaliation from voicing their opposition, either in public debate or at the ballot box. Such people now began to make mischief. With Pope's juggernaut apparently ready to liberate them, previously cautious unionists stepped smartly forward to aid the Federals. Free blacks, like Ryburn Bundy, now felt bold enough to supply U.S. troops with food and "information of the rebel movements." George Mars boasted, "I have often fed the picket posts & always gave them all the information I had of the roads & the rebel forces." So did Culpeper's white unionists. Archibald Shaw, who escaped Confederate conscription because of partial deafness, suffered no disability that prevented him from feeding Union soldiers and providing them with information "as to roads, fords, & the position of the enemy." "The officers were as kind to me as they could be," reported widow Matilda Hudson of her Union guests. "I told them to use my place for their convenience, and they did so." Mrs. Hudson provided Pope's army with nearly one thousand dollars worth of food, fodder, and livestock, including eight cattle and fatted calves. "They did the butchering," explained Mrs. Hudson of the arrangements for the cattle, "and when they moved away gave me a number of hides and the tallow from 9 beeves."[17]

But if Pope thought he had cowed all of Culpeper's civilians, he was wrong. "Secession is more rabid and bitter here than in any other place we have been in Virginia," swore a trooper in the 1st Pennsylvania Reserve Cavalry. "The men generally retain a sullen silence while the women wear a contemptuous and disdainful sneer." If Mr. Payne, landlord of the Virginia Hotel, had been emotionally paralyzed by the invasion, the same could not be said of his four tempestuous daughters. "They were very bad-mannered and always sat apart at one end of the cloth [when dining], talking against the 'Yankees,'" reported the *Herald* correspondent. They assumed this manner, he emphasized, with "no direct provocation" by the occupation forces. Every afternoon they promenaded the town's streets dressed in their finest crinoline. They never condescended to speak to, or even acknowledge, any Yankee during these tours, but they relished every opportunity to scorn with a "pert flourish" any symbol of Federal authority, particularly the national flag. The journalist attributed their actions to "patriotism run mad." Physical attacks on Union troops continued, too. "A man was shot a few minutes [ago] down to the creek bathing by some bushwhacker," a Union

---

17. Scheel, *Culpeper,* 177; William A. Soutter (No. 17,756), Ryburn Bundy (No. 19,818), George Mars (No. 12,707), Archibald Shaw (No. 14,135), Simeon B. Shaw (No. 14,136), and Maltilda G. Hudson (No. 15,194), *Southern Claims*.

soldier informed his wife well into August. Even as he wrote, he continued, an officer had been dispatched to arrest several suspected bushwhackers.[18]

People showed their defiance in different ways. At one extreme, they openly proclaimed their Confederate sympathies. However, unlike Mr. Payne's daughters, many civilians cloaked their passion in a mantle of politeness. A New Jersey cavalryman reported taking supper with a family, neither poor nor particularly well-to-do, that maintained a civil air with him but left no question as to their loyalties. "None of the family doubted for a moment that we were only there until General Jackson strove to drive us back," he testified. Their "firm conviction of their superiority, their assured faith in the military supremacy of the South," he concluded, "were not obtruded as points to be proved or disputed, but were quietly assumed as principles from which to draw conclusions." He dismissed the family as "amusing." At the other extreme, he encountered a barefoot, dirty, ragged, and hungry family of *"poor white trash."* The mother of this family seemed "reconciled to the kindred sordidness of her life," while both she and her husband apparently "lived in the labors of the day, caring for little outside their farm and homestead, letting the war pass on with no interest beyond that of the safety of their little [live]stock." When even their stock was snatched from them by Union troops, "they looked on with an apathy which almost resembled indifference." However, the soldier's undisguised contempt for these herders may have led to his own deception, as Major Stowell had almost certainly been deceived by some of the "loyal" citizens he encountered in May. Some people used apathy, or an apparent willingness to cooperate with the Federals, as a pose. It was just such people who, under cover of darkness or the terrain, could become deadly bushwhackers and sabatours.[19]

The final and most terrifying phase of the Federal occupation now occurred. On August 9, Stonewall Jackson came to Culpeper's rescue, but in doing so he initiated the Battle of Cedar [or Slaughter's] Mountain. This bloodiest of all battles fought on Culpeper soil produced 3,821 casualties, nearly two-thirds of them Yankees. Jackson withdrew to Gordonsville two days later, but when Lee arrived a week after that, their combined forces drove Pope back across the Rappahannock and out of Culpeper. Thus began the Second Manassas campaign, which would

---

18. *Lloyd Diary*, July 21, 1862; Townsend, *Campaigns of a Non-Combatant*, 211; Mark to wife, Aug. 7, 1862, Federal Soldiers Letters, Southern Historical Collection, Univ. of North Carolina at Chapel Hill.

19. Pyne, *Ride to War*, 42–46. For a discussion of the possibility of false information being given to Stowell see Grimsley, *Battles in Culpeper County*, 4–5.

end with Pope's humiliation in September. Culpeper's citizens would relish that moment, but meanwhile, their introduction to war held immediate perils.[20]

The battle itself was terrifying. Random patrols, martial law, and confiscation were nothing compared to the pounding of artillery, screams of wounded men, and chaos of advancing armies. The suddenness with which it all began, the shock of having the mid-afternoon peace shattered by booming guns and swiftly assembled forces, set the tone. At the Virginia Hotel, Mr. Payne's daughters had been playing a spirited version of "The Bonnie Blue Flag" on the parlor piano when the thunder began to roll. It began with "a cannon peal, so close that it shook the houses," reported the *Herald* correspondent, who had been at the hotel. "Cannon upon cannon exploded; the young ladies ceased their mirth; the landlord staggered with white lips into the air, and after a couple of hours, I heard the signal that I knew so well—a volley of musketry." Afterwards, Mrs. Payne could only recall being so terrified by events that she could not easily describe her emotions. "I was in such a state of excitement," she explained, "that I don't know how I felt." As a member of Pope's staff dashed out of town and toward the battlefield, six miles to the southwest, he noticed that "the windows and porches were clouded with pale, anxious faces of women, children, and grandsires."[21]

Most of the people in Culpeper Courthouse laid low during the battle, which raged until after dark; but farmers living on the slopes of Cedar Mountain, or on the plain at its base, found the situation more urgent. The most rational course was flight, and by the end of the day, many civilians had found their way to the homes of neighbors and friends outside the range of the guns. Other refugees staggered into Culpeper Courthouse. Yet even flight could be dangerous. George Curtis, fearful that his wood frame cottage could not survive the whistling shells, sought shelter in the sturdy brick house of a neighbor. Alas, while waiting out the bombardment in his neighbor's basement, Curtis was killed by a shell that smashed through the roof and the floor above him.[22]

More stubborn or adventurous folk refused to leave their homesteads. A Mr. Hudson, whose house was seized by Pope for his headquarters during the battle, refused to leave his property in Union hands. Miraculously, neither he nor his

---

20. The best analysis of the Battle of Cedar Mountain may be found in Robert K. Krick, *Stonewall Jackson at Cedar Mountain* (Chapel Hill: Univ. of North Carolina Press, 1990).

21. Townsend, *Campaigns of a Non-Combatant*, 254-55; Mary L. Payne (No. 22, 128), *Southern Claims;* Eby, ed., *A Virginia Yankee in the Civil War,* 76.

22. Townsend, *Campaigns of a Non-Combatant*, 264-65; Mrs. Berkeley G. Calfee, *Confederate History of Culpeper County in the War Between the States* (Culpeper: n.p., 1948), 3.

house suffered serious damage during the fight, even though a Union artillery battery less than twenty yards from his doorstep attracted Confederate fire all day. On the Confederate side of the field, Mrs. Catherine Crittenden and her daughter Annie refused the repeated urgings of Confederate officers either to leave their house or find shelter in the cellar. The two women insisted that they must prepare food and bandages for the many Confederate boys who were sure to be wounded in the fight. When artillery shells came crashing through the roof, Mrs. Crittenden reluctantly moved below ground, but the spunky Annie remained at her post and began nursing the wounded as they arrived at her door. Equally oblivious to danger was a "passle" of slaves, including twelve-year-old William Yager, who watched the spectacle from the roof of a shed near the battlefield.[23]

Still worse shocks to civilian morale and sensibilities came after the battle. As Union officers casually posed for photographs on the battlefield after Jackson's departure, Culpeper's civilians stood stupified. They had read descriptions of battles in newspapers and in letters sent home by local heroes; they had heard blood-chilling accounts of combat from Northern and Southern soldiers stationed in Culpeper. But none of that had prepared them for what they now saw. Unharvested wheat and corn fields had been leveled, their surfaces littered with the carcasses of man and beast, destroyed or disabled cannons and wagons, splintered gun carriages and limbers, and an indescribable array of personal effects and military equipment, including uniforms, shoes, haversacks, canteens, cartridge boxes, bayonets, knives, blankets, and rifles. Pools of blood lay thick, and the early stages of rigor mortis lent dead men and animals a grotesque and horrifying appearance. "For nearly a mile," estimated a witness, "the dead lay scattered or in heaps, many disembowelled, decapitated and mangled by shells." Fences girding fields had been torn asunder, either knocked down by advancing troops or shredded into "kindling-wood" by cannon and rifle fire. Wooded areas bore the same identifying marks. "All the tree boles were pierced and perforated," confirmed one witness, "and boughs had been severed so that they littered the way." More grimly, the same men reported this scene: "Looking down one of

---

23. William H. Tatum to Louisiana Tatum, Oct. 9, 1862, Tatum Papers; Susan Leigh Blackford, *Letters from Lee's Army, or Memoir of Life In and Out of the Army in Virginia During the War Between the States* (1947; reprint, New York: A. S. Barnes, 1962), 103; *New York Herald*, Aug. 13, 1862; J. P. Thompson, "Byrd Eastham Place—'Cloverdale,'" No. 388, Works Progress Administration of Virginia, *Historical Inventory for Culpeper County, Virginia* (typescript, 1936-39), Culpeper Town and County Library; Charles L. Perdue, Jr., et al., eds., *Weevils in the Wheat: Interviews with Virginia Ex-Slaves* (Charlottesville: Univ. of Virginia Press, 1976), 335.

the rows of corn, I saw the first corpse—the hands flung stiffly back, the feet set stubbornly, the chin pointing upward, the features losing their sharpness, the skin blackening, the eyes great and white." Symbolic of the disruption of ordinary life for Culpeper's civilians, an old plow left standing on the battlefield had been broken in half by a cannonball.[24]

Both soldiers and civilians rushed to bury the dead, partly from humane impulse, partly because of the horrible smell. The hot August sun had accelerated the process of decomposition of men and animals, and the stench of rotting flesh would infect the air for many days. Dead horses and mules, being too large to bury, were generally burned. Yet burial did not alway erase memories of the slaughter. During the following days and weeks, even corpses that had been buried were sometimes uncovered by animals, and other graves—most of them common pits or trenches—had been dug so hastily that, as the earth settled, hands, feet, shoulders, even faces soon protruded from the ground.[25]

Equally pressing was the need to attend wounded survivors, whose pitiful cries echoed across the battlefield. William Yager, the slave boy who had watched the battle from a shed roof, discovered a prostrate Yankee apparently so badly wounded that he could not even call for help. "He wuz alayin' there, the sun broilin' down in his face, his arms jus' agoin' it," reported Yager. "But he couldn't talk none. His throat seemed like wuz wounded." Yager tenderly helped the stricken fellow take a drink from a canteen. Suddenly, the man jumped up, looked around, and without saying a word simply walked away. "It nearly skeered me to death," asserted Yager. "I guess he died after that but I never went back no mo."[26]

Most Culpeper residents did not have to go in search of the wounded; the wounded were brought to them. Ambulances, wagons, litters, whatever means could be procured were used to transfer men from the field of death. Likewise, every conceivable sort of building, be it plantation house or cabin, church or tavern, served as a hospital for Yankee and rebel alike. "The shady little town was sort of a Golgotha now," observed the *Herald* correspondent of Culpeper Courthouse. "Feverish eyes began to burn into one's heart, as he passed along the sidewalks.

---

24. Eby, ed., *A Virginia Yankee in the Civil War*, 80–81; Townsend, *Campaigns of a Non-Combatant*, 271–73; *New York Herald*, Aug. 13, 15, 1862.

25. Lewis M. Haupt to wife, Aug. 19, 1862, Lewis Muhlenberg Haupt Papers, Library of Congress; Constant C. Hanks to sister, Sept. 26, 1862, Constant C. Hanks Papers, Perkins Library, Duke Univ., Durham, N.C.; Cornelius M. Buckley, trans., *A Frenchman, a Chaplain, a Rebel: The War Letters of Pere Louis-Hippolyte Gache* (Chicago: Loyola Univ. Press, 1981), 130.

26. Perdue et al., eds., *Weevils in the Wheat*, 335.

Red hospital flags hung like regalia from half the houses." The eighteen rooms of the Virginia House were stripped of all mattresses and beds, anything that could be used as a litter or a cushion for wounded men. As he surveyed the rows of bloodied men on the floor of his hotel, Mr. Payne, a tear in his eye, cried out to the journalist, "'My good Lord, sir! Who is responsible for this?'" The journalist knew the old man did not expect an answer. He had only expressed the pain of "a human heart pitying its brotherhood." Local doctors joined army surgeons in trying to save lives, and the county's women again turned out to administer care. Mrs. Crittenden and Annie "begged" Confederate surgeon Hunter McGuire to use their house as a hospital. Dr. McGuire tried to convince the ladies that they would find a home filled with wounded and dying men "very disagreeable," but he could not dissuade them. "They replied that they had no higher ambition than to do what they could to give aid and comfort to our men; that they had been subjected to insults by yankee soldiers and would glory in the opportunity of nursing our sick and wounded." Eventually, they nursed the men of both armies.[27]

Unionist Thomas B. Nalle, a retired U.S. Navy officer, offered his fine brick mansion to Pope's surgeons. The grounds quickly filled with the wounded, the dying, and the dead. Surgeons hastily dragged kitchen tables outside to the garden, where they erected a makeshift operating room beneath a stand of locust trees. A growing pile of severed arms and legs measured the furious pace of their work. Yet not a few men, arranged on blood-soaked stretchers and mattresses, died before they received attention. "Blood, carnage, and death among the sweet shrubbery and roses," was one blunt assessment of the scene. No one attempted to describe the moans and cries of shattered men. Meanwhile, another team of doctors at work in the parlor soon transformed that room into a butcher's shop. "Beside the piano stood the operating table," testified one witness. "Rich carpets hurriedly bundled into the corners were replaced by bloody blankets and sheets. The furniture not removed was dabbed with blood and cases of amputating instruments lay upon the table and mantlepieces lately dedicated to elegant books and flowers." Captain Nalle's wife and daughters, working as feverishly as did the Crittenden women, tore sheets and garments into bandages and ministered to the men. The lasting impression these scenes made on the youngest Nalle children, aged four through twelve, may be imagined.[28]

---

27. Townsend, *Campaigns of a Non-Combatant*, 270; Mary L. Payne, *Southern Claims;* Blackford, *Letters from Lee's Army*, 110; Thompson, "Byrd Eastham Place—'Cloverdale,'" Works Progress Administration.

28. Eby, ed., *A Virginia Yankee in the Civil War*, 79; Calfee, *Confederate History of Culpeper County*, 3.

But the battered populace would undergo one more shock when Pope began his withdraw, for the exodus inspired a final wave of confiscation and pillaging, as the Federals sought to deprive rebel soldiers and civilians of as much food, supplies, and "contraband" as possible. Slaveowners suffered in silence as "a great many negroes," mistaking the Rappahannock for the Jordan, swarmed northward into the promised land. Railroad cars filled with wounded men and stuffed with as much food, forage, and equipment as they could hold, crept out of Culpeper Courthouse toward the rebuilt Rappahannock bridge. As the *Herald* reporter joined the dash for the river, he looked back to see "the depot ... stripped of everything and the town left to barrenness and desolation." Similarly, as Union infantry and cavalry moved across country toward the river crossings, they paid farewell calls at houses along their routes. Albert Gallatin Simms, a venerable and idiosyncratic Latin teacher who had operated a school for boys before the war, received a visit from a gang of marauders bent on ransacking his house and satisfying their lust for his two daughters. While Simms stalled the men, his daughters escaped through a rear window. After spending the night shivering in a cornfield, they returned the next morning to find their house plundered, the stock driven off, and their aged father bruised and bloodied.[29]

One can imagine the joy with which the majority of Culpeper's civilians greeted the arrival of grey-clad troops in pursuit of Pope. "God preserve you, my boys!" shouted a grateful gentleman as the 30th North Carolina Infantry marched past his gate. "Men, women, and children came running out of all the houses towards us with long exclamations of delight," attested a Confederate officer, "many thanking God on their knees for their deliverance from the enemy.... The enthusiasm was so great that old men and boys, all that were able to carry a gun, in spite of our earnest remonstrance, followed our column to join in the fight with the detested Yankee." On Main Street in Culpeper Courthouse, Joseph B. Gorrell, the town druggist, prepared a large tub of lemonade to distribute to parched Confederates passing through town. "Just think of it!" exclaimed one of his beneficiaries. "Ice cold lemonade, with plenty of lemon in it to make it sour, and plenty of sugar to make it sweet, and ice to make it cold, to a tired, weary, dirty, dusty Confederate soldier, on a hot day in August."[30]

29. Theodore B. Gates, *The "Ulster Guard" and the War of the Rebellion* (New York: B. H. Tyrrel, 1879), 241; *New York Herald*, Aug. 26, 1862; Scheel, *Culpeper*, 71; Calfee, *Confederate History of Culpeper County*, 4–5.

30. *Richmond Dispatch*, Aug. 25, 1862; Alexander D. Betts, *Experiences of a Confederate Chaplain, 1861–64* (n.p.: n.d.), 14; Heros Von Borcke, *Memoirs of the Confederate War for Independence*, 2 vols. (1866; reprint, New York: Peter Smith, 1938), 1:110–11; Grimsley, *Battles in Culpeper County*, 4.

Pope held Lee at bay on the Culpeper side of the Rappahannock for a few days before both armies tumbled toward their rendezvous at Manassas. As the Confederates passed out of the county, Culpeper's civilians were left alone to survey the damage and reflect on the events of the previous six weeks. The silence, after so many days of clamorous activity, was eerie. It seemed as though a tornado, with its roaring, swirling winds, had touched down and left everything in utter confusion. Now, as the tornado sped away over the hills, the last swirls of dust and chaff settled once again to earth and stillness prevailed. Standing silent vigil, the Confederate cemetery, erected a year earlier to hold the victims of First Manassas, now contained 311 graves. Few people would deny that the future looked grim. "A melancholy picture of desolation and devastation" stared at them from all sides. The "unbridled license" of Pope's soldiers had left the county "almost a desert." A conservative estimate of the value of property *officially* confiscated by the Union army exceeds forty-five thousand dollars. "Unoffending citizens have been impoverished in a day," reported a Richmond newspaper to shocked readers, "their fencing destroyed, their sheep and hogs and cattle butchered, their grain entirely consumed, their horses all stolen. . . . Many a family has been left in a condition verging upon absolute want and starvation." Nor, in truth, had the passage of Lee's army helped matters. While not deliberately destructive, the sheer numbers of Confederate troops rolling over the countryside produced additional damage. The boys in grey found it particularly difficult to resist apple orchards and still-standing corn fields. Lee's provost marshal tried to limit the thefts, and Confederate soldiers were more likely to pay for their meals than the Federals had been, but the results were much the same.[31]

Still, as they contemplated their scars, Culpeper's civilians saw hope in the fact that they had, after all, survived. Few people had actually perished; houses could be repaired and crops could be replanted. Some families had been far enough removed from the center of Pope's army to be only partially stung by confiscation. Other people had cleverly concealed many valuables or caches of food. A few had preserved their property by spunk. Mrs. Mary Mason, for instance, may have been the only resident to save the contents of her smokehouse. Learning of

---

31. Constant C. Hanks to sister, Sept. 26, 1862, Hanks Papers; Andrew J. Gillespie to Susan Gillespie, Nov. 13, 1862, Randall Family Papers, Univ. of Virginia Library; *Richmond Dispatch*, Aug. 25, 1862; Shephard Pryor to wife, Aug. 18, 1862, in *"Dear Mother: Don't Grieve About Me" . . . Letters from Georgia Soldiers in the Civil War*, ed. Mills Lane (Savannah: Beehive, 1977), 181; Spencer Glasgow Welch, *A Confederate Surgeon's Letters to His Wife* (New York: Neale, 1911), 20. The total of confiscated property is calculated from surviving petitions in the records of the Southern Claims Commission.

the approach of a Yankee raiding party, she ordered all of her hams and bacon thrown into the vegetable garden. When the Yankees galloped up, she pointed at the meat and shouted to them, "There it is; take it!" The soldiers, being suspicious that Mrs. Mason had poisoned the meat, left it untouched, although they retaliated by severing the heads of her geese. "Things are never so bad as they seem," reflected one person, who estimated that most of his family's grain and livestock had survived the onslaught. Most of the slaves had fled, but a few loyal ones remained. The fences in front of the house and along the road had been leveled, but a portion still enclosed surviving crops. Perhaps, the worst was over. Perhaps Lee would overtake Pope and smash him. Perhaps such a victory would demoralize the North and the war would end. Perhaps the South's military fortunes in the West could be reversed, and perhaps England would finally intervene.[32]

Luckily, the people of Culpeper could not see into the future. They would have shuddered to know that the war had only just arrived at their doorsteps. Both armies would take turns occupying their county in the long months to come. The Federals, under Ulysses S. Grant and George Gordon Meade, would linger for a particularly long time in the winter of 1863–1864. The sights and sounds of combat would be repeated in nearly a hundred more battles and skirmishes. The Confederate cemetery would eventually hold 568 bodies, and no one would ever know how many other men lay buried in trenches and single graves scattered throughout the countryside. But at least when the armies returned, Culpeper would know what to expect. Culpeper's civilians had received a very practical education in the preceding six months, a thorough, if sometimes brutal, introduction to war.[33]

---

32. Calfee, *Confederate History of Culpeper County*, 4; W. A. Thorn to Pembroke Thorn, Sept. 16, 1862, in *"My Dear Brother"*, comp. Bartlett, 66–67.

33. Scheel, Culpeper, 371–74; Robert A. Hodge, comp., *A Death Roster of the Confederate Hospital at Culpeper*, Virginia (Fredericksburg, Va.: n.p., 1977), 6.

Filling the Ranks

Was It a "Poor Man's Fight"?

EUGENE C. MURDOCK

The most controversial feature of the Enrollment Act of March 3, 1863—Section Thirteen—permitted commutation payments of $300 by anyone wishing to avoid military service if drafted. Commutation was defended on two grounds: (1) it kept the price of substitutes down, since no one would pay more than $300 for a substitute if he could "commute" for that amount; and (2) it raised a reservoir of funds, which might be used for federal bounties. Commutation was also denounced on two grounds: (1) it raised money, but not troops; and (2) it favored the rich and penalized the poor. Since $300 might be equivalent to a workingman's annual wage in those days, it would be almost impossible for him to commute, whereas a rich man could commute without feeling a financial loss. For this reason the protest that it was "a rich man's war, but a poor man's fight," became widespread with reference to the commutation clause. So loud did this cry become that the clause was finally repealed in July, 1864.

Until now no study has ever sought to learn if there really was a positive correlation of wealth with commutation, as well as with other aspects of conscription, such as substitution and the draft. But a preliminary examination of the situation in New York state suggests that no such relationship existed. In other words, there was just as much paying of commutation money to avoid the draft

Civil War History, Vol. X No. 3 © 1964 by The Kent State University Press

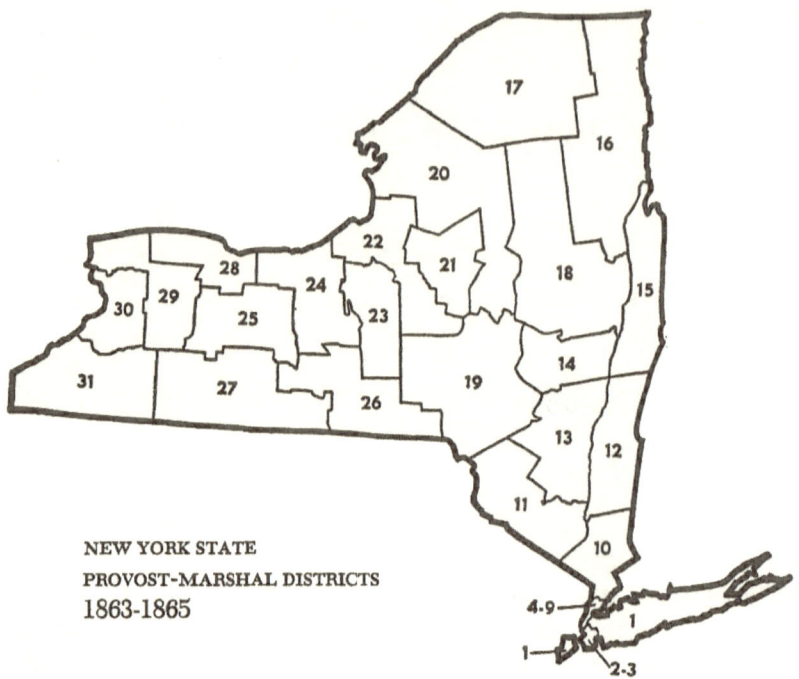

NEW YORK STATE
PROVOST-MARSHAL DISTRICTS
1863-1865

in poor districts as there was in wealthy districts. Before analyzing the evidence, let us set forth a few guidelines used in making this inquiry.[1]

First, in determining the wealth of a provost-marshal district[2] I have taken the total personal and real property valuation for each county in each district as of 1858, added these figures together, and then divided by the 1860 population of the district. This has given me a "per capita valuation" for each district, which

---

1. This present article is but a small part of a much broader examination of New York's Civil War bounty system. This larger study will be particularly concerned with the human, as well as the statistical, factors of bounties, bounty-jumpers, and bounty-brokers. It will be based chiefly upon the *Official Records*, Provost Marshal General James B. Fry's *Final Report*, national and state government documents, and contemporary newspapers. The present article is prepared from statistics found in U.S. Census Office, *Population of the United States in 1860, Compiled from the Original Returns of the Eighth Census* (Washington, 1864), pp. 322–347; *Final Report of the Provost Marshal General to the Secretary of War* (House Exec. Doc. No. 1, pt. 2, 39 Cong., 1 sess.), IV, pt. 1, 165–213; *Historical and Statistical Gazetteer of New York State* (Syracuse, 1860). Since the tables have been especially prepared for this study from all of these sources, no attempt has been made to provide particular citations.

2. For the purposes of the draft, each state was divided into districts, coincidental with congressional districts, but labeled provost-marshal districts. Each district had an enrollment board, headed by a provost marshal operating directly under Provost Marshal General Fry. All the drafting was administered through these district offices. New York contained thirty-one such districts.

provides a yardstick for determining rich, poor, and intermediate districts. Admittedly, there are other means of determining wealth in a district, and this method may not be the most accurate. But all things considered, it does give us a rough approximation of a district's wealth and seems adequate enough to allow some comparisons on the questions of commutation, substitution, and the draft.

Secondly, the two Brooklyn districts (numbers 2 and 3 on the map), and the six New York City districts (numbers 4, 5, 6, 7, 8, and 9) have no per capita valuation because the property valuations of the individual wards of the two cities are not readily available. Furthermore, so many abnormal factors operated in New York and Brooklyn that a normal rich-poor pattern would not prove too meaningful. I will refer to this again in a moment.

Of the twenty-three districts for which property valuation data are available, ten have a per capita valuation of over $300, ten more have a per capita valuation of from $200 to $300, and only three fall below $200. The ten $300-plus districts are concentrated in two areas, one along the Hudson River valley just north of New York City, and the other in the northwestern part of the state from Lake Cayuga to Buffalo. The ten $200-$300 districts are located along the Pennsylvania border and in the central upstate region. The three sub-$200 districts are along the Canadian border, down Lake Champlain, and in Oneida County (Utica).

The highest percentage of commutation among those held to service[3] is found in the Twentieth District, a rural upstate area, comprising Herkimer, Lewis, and Jefferson counties (see Table 1). In this district, where the per capita valuation was $221, 88 per cent of those held to service commuted. Close behind the Twentieth was the Nineteenth District (Otsego, Chenango, and Delaware counties) with a per capita valuation of $239, where 87 per cent of those held to service commuted. Next was the Twenty-third District (Onandaga and Cortland counties) with a per capita valuation of $290, where 85 per cent commuted. And most astonishing, the fourth highest commuting district was the Twenty-first (Oneida County), one of the three sub-$200 districts. In fact, not until we move on to fifth place do we finally reach a $300-plus district, the Fifteenth (Rensselaer and Washington counties), located along the upper Hudson.

At the lower end of the list, not counting the New York and Brooklyn districts,

---

3. The phrase "held to service" refers to all those who were examined under the terms of the Enrollment Act and not exempted. One held to service could either pay commutation or furnish a substitute, and if unable to do either of these he would be drafted. In the following tables, if one adds up all the persons in a district who commuted, furnished substitutes, or were drafted, the total should equal the number "held to service."

Table 1			Table 2			Table 3		
Dist. No.	Per cap. valuation	Per cent* commuting	Dist. No.	Per cap. valuation	Per cent* substitution	Dist. No.	Per cap. valuation	Per cent* drafted
20	$221	88.0	9	—	94.5	27	$207	25.0
19	239	87.0	5	—	93.5	24	331	22.0
23	290	85.0	7	—	92.7	26	222	19.9
21	158	82.5	2	—	80.8	16	141	19.4
15	323	82.0	6	—	78.5	18	223	16.5
12	387	81.0	8	—	78.0	31	214	16.5
25	385	77.8	4	—	78.0	11	317	15.8
18	223	76.0	3	—	72.7	29	309	11.2
26	222	72.7	13	$211	71.3	17	187	10.6
22	223	71.3	30	354	64.3	25	385	10.1
14	309	69.4	10	375	62.0	30	354	9.0
17	187	66.8	31	214	43.5	22	223	8.5
24	331	60.0	28	304	43.5	28	304	8.0
27	207	58.0	29	309	37.6	1	296	8.0
16	141	56.0	1	296	37.5	19	239	7.3
1	296	54.5	11	317	30.7	21	158	6.8
11	317	53.5	14	309	27.7	2	—	6.6
29	309	51.0	16	141	24.6	23	290	6.4
28	304	48.5	17	187	22.6	12	387	5.5
31	214	40.0	22	223	20.2	20	221	5.3
10	375	33.0	24	331	18.0	13	211	4.4
30	354	26.7	27	207	17.0	10	375	4.1
13	211	24.3	15	323	16.5	3	—	3.7
3	—	23.6	12	387	13.5	14	309	2.9
4	—	21.5	25	385	12.1	5	—	2.2
8	—	20.5	21	158	10.7	15	323	1.5
6	—	20.1	23	290	8.6	8	—	1.5
2	—	12.6	26	222	7.4	6	—	1.4
7	—	7.0	18	223	6.8	9	—	0.8
9	—	4.7	20	221	6.7	4	—	0.5
5	—	4.3	19	239	5.7	7	—	0.3

*Percentages are of all those held to service.

a relatively poor district, the Thirteenth (Greene and Ulster counties), with a $211 per capita valuation, had a commutation percentage of 24.3 per cent. And of the six districts just above the Thirteenth in lowest percentage of commutation rates, five of them had a $300-plus per capita valuation. Obviously, from this table one can find little to sustain the argument that the rich districts commuted more than poor districts. There seems to be no pattern at all, with some poor and some rich districts commuting at a high rate, and some rich and some poor districts commuting at a low rate. Whatever factors explain commutation, wealth does not appear to be one of them.

While it might also be assumed that districts which furnished the most substitutes[4] would be the wealthier districts, the statistics refute this assumption, too (see Table 2). It is true that there is a closer correlation between wealth and substitution than between wealth and commutation, but still many discrepancies occur. Of the twenty-three districts for which data are available, the Thirteenth, with a $211 per capita valuation, led the state, 71.3 per cent of those held to service furnishing substitutes. Of the next eight districts, six are $300-plus, one high in the $200-plus category, and one low in the $200-plus bracket. The poorest district in the state, the Sixteenth (Clinton, Essex, and Warren counties), located along Lake Champlain, was tenth in the list, 37.5 per cent furnishing substitutes. At the bottom of the list are $100-plus and $200-plus districts, but not too far from the bottom also may be found several $300-plus districts, including the two wealthiest in the state, the Twelfth and the Twenty-fifth.

In considering the percentages of people actually drafted, it has always been assumed that the poorest districts had the highest draft rates. This would follow logically since poor people would be unable to commute or furnish substitutes, and had no choice but to be drafted. Yet here again the pattern is unclear, with both poor and rich districts scattered throughout the whole list in confusing fashion (see Table 3). Hence in none of the three matters—commutation, substitution, and the actual draft—is there any correlation with the wealth of the particular district.

New York City and Brooklyn constitute a special case, in which more research will have to be done. From the tables we can see that those metropolitan districts were at the bottom of the commutation and the draft lists, while at the top of the substitution list. It might also be noted that these districts led the field in the percentages of persons whose names were drawn but who did not report. All of this is tied in with the draft riots, the widespread recruiting frauds in the military and naval service in New York City, revised and rigged enrollment lists, and so many other matters that it will not be easy to piece together the full story. Then there will be the further problem of trying to collate this data with per capita valuation. Still the figures on upstate New York are illuminating, and we may have to rethink our traditional concept about wealth, commutation, substitution, and the draft.

---

4. The phrase "to furnish a substitute" was commonly used to describe the practice whereby a draftee who did not wish to commute, but also did not wish to serve, would pay someone else to serve for him. Generally, no one who was himself eligible for the draft could be a substitute, but this rule varied from time to time. Some of the worst frauds in the whole recruiting business were tied in with substitution where brokers and jumpers posing as substitutes, robbed principals of large sums of money, and deprived the government of needed troops.

Confederate Volunteering and Enlistment in Ashe County, North Carolina, 1861–1862

Martin Crawford

Alfred Blevins was twenty-seven years old when the Civil War began. A tenant farmer, he lived with his young wife, Margary, and their infant daughter in the Southeastern district of Ashe County, North Carolina. The Blevins's economic resources were meagre: aside from their own labor, the 1860 census revealed no land ownership and personal property valued at only fifty dollars. Much of this was in the shape of livestock, including a milk cow, five sheep, and nine pigs. The Blevins owned no slaves, nor did any of their immediate kinfolk.[1] After North Carolina's secession in May 1861, Alfred Blevins declined to respond to the governor's call for military volunteers. Although nothing is known of his political affiliations nor of his views on the disunion crisis, Blevins's decision was probably not based on any principled opposition to the Southern cause. At least two of his unmarried brothers, Felix and Horton, who were still living with

---

An earlier version of this chapter was delivered to the Organization of American Historians Annual Meeting, St. Louis, 1989. I am grateful to session commentators Eric Foner and Lawrence N. Powell, and also to Richard Blackett, John C. Inscoe, and Gordon B. McKinney, for helpful criticism and advice.

    1. Information on the Blevins family is derived from the following sources: U.S. Census, Ashe County, North Carolina, 1860, Population, Agricultural, and Slave Schedules; Ruth W. Shepherd, ed., *The Heritage of Ashe County, North Carolina* . . . (Winston-Salem, N.C: Hunter Publishing Co., 1984), 168; Wade Edward Eller, "Collection of History and Geneology of Ashe County," North Carolina Division of Archives and History, Raleigh.

Civil War History, Vol. XXXVII No. 1 © 1991 by The Kent State University Press

their parents, joined the first wave of North Carolina Confederate recruits in the spring of 1861, while his sister Easther's husband, Reuben Sexton, enlisted in August. A third brother, Albert, volunteered in the following spring.[2]

In August 1862, however, well over a year after the commencement of the war, Alfred Blevins, together with several of his relations, journeyed to Iredell County where they enlisted in Company K (the "Alleghany Tigers") of the 37th North Carolina Regiment. As part of General Robert E. Lee's Army of Northern Virginia, Blevins participated in many of the major battles of the conflict, including Antietam, Fredericksburg, Chancellorsville, Gettysburg, and Spotsylvania Court House. Promoted to a sergeant in November 1862, he was reduced to the ranks the following summer "for disobeying orders." Blevins sustained two incapacitating injuries, both of which necessitated convalescent leave. The first wound, in his right thigh, occurred at Gettysburg, where all three of his brothers were also seriously injured, and the second, in his left hand, at Jericho Mills, Virginia, in 1864. Unlike many of his fellow recruits who used the opportunity of leave to desert, Private Blevins rejoined his regiment on both of these occasions. On April 9, 1865, in company with twenty-five thousand other veterans of Lee's campaigns, he surrendered to Federal forces at Appomattox Court House and returned home.[3]

Alfred Blevins's military record, which mirrored that of thousands of other Confederate soldiers of similar class and circumstance, provides some evidence of the Civil War's impact on the individual, his family, and their community. In a remarkable letter home from his winter quarters near Petersburg, Virginia, on New Year's Eve, 1864, Blevins offered a tantalizing glimpse of the psychological and material deprivation that the military conflict engendered in its individual participants. The immediate cause of Blevins's reflections was hunger. "Men can't stay here and fight and work and not eat," he told his Uncle James Blevins. "I tell you they can't and won't." But beyond this provocation, Blevins had clearly become disillusioned both with the Confederate cause ("a Nationality which was not intended for us") and also with the very idea of war itself, which he

---

2. Louis H. Manarin and Weymouth T. Jordan, comps. and eds., *North Carolina Troops, 1861–1865: A Roster*, 12 vols. (Raleigh: North Carolina Division of Archives and History, 1966–), vol. 7, *Infantry*: 469–70; vol. 9, *Infantry*: 482. Two other brothers, Daniel and Calvin, also probably served in North Carolina regiments.

3. Manarin and Jordan, comps. and eds., *North Carolina Troops*, 9:463–68, 591, 593. For Ashe County Confederate fears that home leave would be exploited, see Private Thornton Sexton to his parents, Mar. 11, 1862, Thornton Sexton Papers, William R. Perkins Library, Duke University.

contrasted to the tranquil republican domesticity that he had been forced to abandon over two years earlier. "I have tried war," he explained, "and use to enjoy peace and plenty and I can assure you that I do greatly prefer peace and plenty as I once enjoyed it to the awful realities of this Horrible war. Why sir it is the most cherished idea of which human capacity can conceive. The idea of enjoying peace with the pleasure of being with our friends is one of the most glorious attributes of the goddess of Liberty."[4]

Throughout 1861 and 1862 thousands of young American men like Alfred Blevins and his brothers enlisted in the Union and Confederate armies. Their purpose, individually and collectively, was to defend their respective societies, and the values around which they were organized, against external attack. Though unprecedented in its dimensions, the process of civilian volunteering was fully in accordance with the American military tradition.[5] Disenchantment eventually set in on both sides; but during the early phases of the war the doubts expressed by Alfred Blevins were little in evidence, and popular enthusiasm for the struggle appeared both widespread and infectious. In his celebrated analysis of American society published a generation earlier, the French aristocrat, Alexis de Tocqueville, seems seriously to have underestimated the martial capacity of American democratic society, although he did acknowledge that the longer a conflict lasted the more likely it was that popular commitment would be sustained. "Men living in democracies have not naturally the military spirit," he argued; "they sometimes acquire it when they have been dragged by compulsion to the field, but to rise in a body and voluntarily to expose themselves to the horrors of war, and especially of civil war, is a course that the men of democracies are not apt to adopt."[6]

If nothing else, Tocqueville's comments should alert us to a serious deficiency in historians' understanding of the Civil War experience. Despite the enormous volume of research devoted to the sectional struggle, surprisingly little attention has been paid to volunteering and enlistment activity, indicative of the larger

---

4. Alfred Blevins to Uncle James Blevins, Dec. 31, 1864, Ashe County Civil War Letters collection (copy), Ashe County Public Library, West Jefferson.

5. Civil War mobilization is concisely described in Allan R. Millett and Peter Maslowski, *For the Common Defense: A Military History of the United States* (New York and London: Free Press, 1984), 165–66; and in James M. McPherson, *Battle Cry of Freedom: The Civil War Era* (New York: Oxford Univ. Press, 1988), 308–38. For the contradictory tendencies in the American military tradition before the Civil War, see Marcus Cunliffe, *Soldiers and Civilians: The Martial Spirit in America, 1775–1865* (London: Eyre and Spottiswoode, 1968).

6. Alexis de Tocqueville, *Democracy in America*, 2 vols. (1835, 1840; reprint, New York: Vintage Books, 1945), 2: 301. See also 2: 292.

neglect of the war as a social process.[7] Yet the act of volunteering, as Tocqueville recognized, was a significant one, a crucial demonstration of the individual citizen's relationship with, and loyalty to, the wider society. It was also a vital test of private duty and of personal character. For Southerners in particular, invasion from the North not only challenged the independence of the new Confederate nation; but it simultaneously threatened the security of the local community and the homes and families of its individual members. It is in the context of this dual responsibility, therefore, that volunteering and enlistment during the Civil War can most appropriately be examined.

Nowhere was the relationship between public and private duty more thoroughly tested than in those areas of the Southern states outside the dominant plantation society. For the majority of communities in the upland South, where sectional loyalties were refracted through a variety of countervailing political, economic, and geographic influences, Abraham Lincoln's election in November 1860 had proved an insufficient threat to local security. However, after Fort Sumter and the call for seventy-five thousand federal volunteers, the situation rapidly altered. Although many upland areas continued to support the Union after April 1861, others, including western North Carolina, quickly succumbed to the secessionist appeal.[8] This essay will examine the Confederate volunteering and enlistment process in one Southern mountain community, Ashe County, North Carolina, during 1861 and 1862. Its wider purpose is to help illuminate the social foundations of popular loyalty to the Southern cause and to provide the basis for further examination of the Civil War's impact on the individual community.

---

7. The larger neglect is forcefully highlighted in the recent essay, Maris A. Vinovskis, "Have Social Historians Lost the Civil War? Some Preliminary Demographic Speculations," *Journal of American History* 76 (June 1989): 34–58. However, a number of new studies indicate that a fundamental reevaluation of the military conflict as a social and cultural experience has already begun. See Gerald F. Linderman, *Embattled Courage: The Experience of Combat in the American Civil War* (New York: Free Press, 1987); Randall C. Jimerson, *The Private Civil War: Popular Thought During the Sectional Conflict* (Baton Rouge: Louisiana State Univ. Press, 1987); Reid Mitchell, *Civil War Soldiers* (New York: Viking, 1988); and James I. Robertson, Jr., *Soldiers Blue and Gray* (Columbia: Univ. of South Carolina Press, 1988); Michael Fellman, *Inside War: The Guerilla Conflict in Missouri During the American Civil War* (New York: Oxford Univ. Press, 1989); and Wayne K. Durrill, *War of Another Kind: A Southern Community in the Great Rebellion* (New York: Oxford Univ. Press, 1990).

8. There is no separate study of the secessionist movement in the Southern mountain region, but for the Upper South as a whole see Daniel W. Crofts, *Reluctant Confederates: Upper South Unionists in the Secession Crisis* (Chapel Hill: Univ. of North Carolina Press, 1989). On western North Carolina, see Marc W. Kruman, *Parties and Politics in North Carolina, 1836–1865* (Baton Rouge: Louisiana State Univ. Press, 1983), 180–221; and in particular, John C. Inscoe, *Mountain Masters, Slavery and the Sectional Crisis in Western North Carolina* (Knoxville: Univ. of Tennessee Press, 1989), 211–57.

Perched high up in the Blue Ridge region of North Carolina at the junction of Virginia and Tennessee, Ashe County was, in most important respects, typical of other Southern mountain communities in the mid-nineteenth century. Despite the county's inaccessibility and, at points, extreme elevation, an abundance of well-watered agricultural land helped sustain a vigorous and largely self-sufficient small-farm economy, the basic characteristics of which were replicated throughout the western North Carolina mountain region. By the time of the Civil War, Ashe County's population had reached nearly eight thousand, including over five hundred slaves and free blacks. Although the majority of the county's yeoman farmers were independent proprietors, with holdings that ranged from only a few to a thousand acres of improved land, more than a quarter (26.8 percent) reported no landownership in the 1860 agricultural census.[9]

At the top of the socioeconomic pyramid were the prosperous slave-holding farmers whose authority in large part derived from early family exploitation of the fertile bottom lands of the North and South Forks of the New River. As the Dun Credit Ledgers reveal, many of the county's wealthiest farmers were also engaged in merchandising and other commercial activities on the eve of the Civil War, thus implicating the region, albeit imperfectly, in the complex trading networks of an expanding market economy.[10] Ashe County's slaveholders, in fact, who comprised a mere 6.6 percent of the farm population in 1860, owned a disproportionate 49.8 percent of its total real and personal wealth. Moreover, despite the limited and potentially more benign character of mountain slavery, it is possible that fears for the security of the system were as prevalent there as in many other parts of the South. There were at least two major incidents of slave violence in and around Ashe County during the 1850s; and with the onset of secession, the white community's apprehensions increased. In October 1861 the county's wealthiest slave-holder and most respected Democratic leader, George

---

9. U.S. Census, Ashe County, North Carolina, 1860, Agricultural Schedule. The southern mountain farm economy before the Civil War is discussed in Ronald D. Eller, "Land and Family: An Historical View of Preindustrial Appalachia," *Appalachian Journal* 6 (Winter 1979): 83-110; and in Inscoe, *Mountain Masters, Slavery and the Sectional Crisis*, 11-58; for the history of Ashe County, see Arthur L. Fletcher, *Ashe County: A History* (Jefferson, N.C.: Ashe County Research Assoc., 1963); John Preston Arthur, *Western North Carolina; A History (From 1713 to 1913)*, (Raleigh, N.C.: Edward & Broughton, 1914), 159-66; and Thomas J. Schoenbaum, *The New River Controversy* (Winston-Salem, N.C.: John F. Blair, 1979), 3-46.

10. R. G. Dun and Company, Credit Reporting Ledgers, North Carolina, vol. 1, 20-21; vol. 2, 1-7, 25D-36, Baker Library, Harvard University. Commercial activity in western North Carolina as a whole is sensitively explored in Inscoe, *Mountain Masters, Slavery and the Sectional Crisis*, 25-58.

Bower, was drowned pursuing a runaway slave across the Yadkin River, while in adjacent Wilkes County a free black was lynched after shooting a white man who had been attempting to impress him as a servant into the army.[11]

Although deeply committed to defending Southern interests, throughout the secession winter the citizens of Ashe County revealed little inclination to join the disunion movement. Situated in the extreme northwest corner of the state, Ashe County's commercial ties with the lower South were probably not as extensive as those of other western North Carolina counties, where enthusiasm for the secessionist cause was more evident. Two years earlier the county's partisan balance had been undermined by the loss of its strongly Democratic eastern section to the newly created Alleghany County; and in the presidential election in November 1860, voters gave a large majority to the Constitutional Union ticket of John Bell and Edward Everett. The following February, secessionist blandishments were decisively rejected in the referendum on a state convention.[12] Speaking to the North Carolina House of Commons on January 10, the county's elected representative, Thomas N. Crumpler, argued passionately against disunion. In 1775, he said, North Carolina, "a modest and conservative State," had laid the cornerstone for the new republic and it should now take the initiative in the movement for its preservation. "Let us labor for this result," Crumpler concluded, "and even if we do fail, and in civil war we are called on to die upon some gory field far from home and kindred, it will not be unpleasant to reflect in the last hour, that we strove to avert the ruin of our country."[13]

Direct testimony concerning the mobilization process in Ashe County is limited, but the evidence suggests that the underlying nature of the community's response was similar, if not identical, to that in other areas of the Upper South. As John Inscoe has recently described, the popular outrage engendered by President Lincoln's call for seventy-five thousand troops following the attack on Fort

---

11. See *Raleigh Register and North Carolina Gazette*, Sept. 3, Oct. 1, 8, 1851, Oct. 16, 1861; *Charlotte Western Democrat*, Mar. 31, 1854; *Raleigh North Carolina Standard*, Oct. 18, 1861; Arthur, *Western North Carolina: A History*, 165. For a fuller discussion of Ashe County slaveholding and its relationship to economic and political authority, see Martin Crawford, "Political Society in a Southern Mountain Community: Ashe County, North Carolina, 1850-1861," *Journal of Southern History* 55 (Aug. 1989): 373-90. For a pioneering study of mountain slaveholding, see John C. Inscoe, "Mountain Masters: Slaveholding in Western North Carolina," *North Carolina Historical Review* 61 (Apr. 1984): 143-73.

12. Inscoe, *Mountain Masters, Slavery and the Sectional Crisis*, 246-47; Crawford, "Political Society in a Southern Mountain Community," 383-88.

13. *Speech of T. N. Crumpler of Ashe on Federal Relations Delivered in The House of Commons*, Jan. 10, 1861 (Raleigh, N.C: Printed at office of *Raleigh Register*, 1861), 16.

Sumter transformed political sentiment throughout the western North Carolina mountain region.[14] Even before North Carolina's secession on May 20, 1861, organization of Ashe County's Confederate volunteers was well under way. In a letter to his father-in-law in Tennessee, James M. Gentry, a local merchant and innkeeper, described the "intense excitement" in the county. By the middle of May, Gentry claimed, at least two hundred volunteers would have responded to the state's call to arms. "We are all now for an independent southern Confederacy for nothing short of extermination will ever conquer the southern people," he wrote. "We watch and wait men are out now. We have greater reasons to fall out with Lincoln than you cecessionest. While we were watching & waiting he was undermining for our subjugation, but now we are for separation and against all sorts of compromise. Death or victory is our motto."[15]

In a widely acclaimed study, Gerald Linderman has highlighted the moral imperatives that encouraged popular participation in the Civil War and there seems no reason to doubt that the values he defines for the broader American experience prevailed in Ashe and other mountain communities.[16] Linderman's central focus upon courage as a sustaining impulse is confirmed by the testimony of William M. Norman, a twenty-seven-year-old teacher from nearby Surry County, who volunteered in the first wave of enthusiasm on May 4, 1861. Norman's doubts about leaving his wife, Letitia, were quickly dispelled as he recognized the consequences of failing to respond to the Confederate call to arms. "A great many young men who had nothing to hinder them from volunteering failed to act the part of a soldier," he later recalled. "Their cowardice began to be discussed freely. Some who had already volunteered began to back out, and their cowardice and toryish principles, talked of in every crowd, caused Letitia to reconsider and begin to think that, if I was to get a substitute or back out, it would affect my standing as well as hers, for she knew that a great many would accuse her of proving recreant to my duty."[17]

Letitia Norman's change of heart, which was instrumental in persuading her husband to enlist, demonstrates the pivotal role of women in the volunteering process. Politically proscribed, Southern women nonetheless showed a keen

---

14. Inscoe, *Mountain Masters, Slavery and the Sectional Crisis*, 250-57.

15. James M. Gentry to Jonathan Faw, May 6, 1861, Walter Wager Faw Papers, Tennessee State Archives, Nashville.

16. Linderman, *Embattled Courage*.

17. William M. Norman, *A Portion of My Life: Being a Short and Imperfect History written while a prisoner of war on Johnson's Island, 1864* (Winston-Salem, N.C: John F. Blair, 1959), 117-18.

interest in the secession crisis and its aftermath. At a well-attended Unionist rally in Ashe County in November 1860, for example, women were specifically requested by former Whig congressman Nathaniel Boyden to register their opposition to disunion.[18] Over the next few months their practical and emotional support was of crucial importance in the community's transformation from peaceful to martial pursuits. As George C. Rable has recently described, the onset of war in the spring of 1861 provoked a "family crisis" of unprecedented dimensions in the South, and the decision to volunteer, however patriotically inspired, was bound to conceal complex and possibly unresolved tensions within the individual household. The situation was likely to be particularly critical in the overwhelmingly yeoman farm society of the mountain region, where the loss of one or more males to military service would place an inordinate burden on the female members. Although yeoman women, as Elizabeth Fox-Genovese has recently acknowledged, engaged in a far wider range of household and farm tasks than did the majority of their plantation counterparts, they were also forced to work harder, thus offsetting any advantage that might be gained by easier adaptability to wartime exigencies.[19]

Yet whatever their private reservations, in public, at least, women both encouraged and legitimized the enlistment act by reminding their menfolk of their dual responsibility as defenders of Southern and domestic liberty. For many communities, including Ashe County, this involved the ritualistic raising or presentation of a Southern flag, invariably made by the local women themselves. Ashe County's flag, which James M. Gentry proudly reported as "one of the largest and finest" that he had ever seen, was raised forty-five feet above the county seat of Jefferson.[20] As the emblem of freedom, the flag served not only as a reminder of the community's determination to resist tyranny but also of the clear relationship between public and private duty in the disunion crisis. As the women of another mountain community, Yadkin County, would emphasize on presenting their flag to the newly organized "Yadkin Grey Eagles" in June 1861, male hesitation in the face of such preeminent danger was unthinkable.

---

18. *Raleigh North Carolina Standard*, Feb. 6, 1861. Southern women's determination not to remain passive spectators of the disunion struggle is revealed in the address reprinted in Samuel Proctor, ed., "The Call to Arms: Secession from a Feminine Point of View," *Florida Historical Quarterly* 35 (Jan. 1957): 266-70.

19. George C. Rable, *Civil Wars: Women and the Crisis of Southern Nationalism* (Urbana: Univ. of Illinois Press, 1989), 50-72; Elizabeth Fox-Genovese, *Within the Plantation Household: Black and White Women in the Old South* (Chapel Hill: Univ. of North Carolina Press, 1988), 165-66.

20. Gentry to Jonathan Faw, May 6, 1861, Faw Papers.

"Your mothers, wives, & sisters all bid you go, trusting to the God of Liberty & your own brave deeds to bring you off conquerors in the conflict," the delegation urged.[21] A few days after their arrival in Asheville, a volunteer company from Watauga County, which bordered on Ashe County, was visited by a group of town women who serenaded them with "Dixie." It was the first time, according to one member, that they had heard the song. In a resoundingly ambivalent gesture, the orderly sergeant put the women through their drill paces. This greatly amused the volunteers, whose commitment was reinforced a short time later by the presentation of a company flag. Although female participation in such rituals was usually dominated by members of the social elite, including the wives and sisters of company officers, their significance in establishing a standard for all classes within the community cannot be overlooked.[22]

By the end of August 1861, a little over four months after the attack on Fort Sumter, four full companies of Ashe County volunteers had been organized involving a total of 328 residents, just under a quarter of its fifteen- to thirty-nine-year-old male population. By the end of the following year two more companies had been raised, both composed predominantly of Ashe residents, who also joined several other units in neighboring Alleghany and Watauga counties. An estimated 750 to 800 Ashe County residents enlisted in the North Carolina Confederate forces during 1861 and 1862, representing well over half of its appropriate age cohorts. By using the published troop rosters in conjunction with local geneological and other data, it has been possible to provide positive identification for 493 of Ashe County's Confederate volunteers in the 1860 population census. This sample forms the basis of the analysis presented here.[23]

21. *Salem People's Press*, June 21, 1861.
22. Francis B. Dedmond, "Harvey Davis's Unpublished Civil War 'Diary' and the Story of Company D of the First North Carolina Cavalry," *Appalachian Journal* 13 (Summer 1986): 382. For further discussion, see Linderman, *Embattled Courage*, 87–89; Mitchell, *Civil War Soldiers*, 18–23; J. William Harris, *Plain Folk and Gentry in a Slave Society: White Liberty and Black Slavery in Augusta's Hinterlands* (Middletown, Conn.: Wesleyan Univ. Press, 1985), 141–42; and Bell Irvin Wiley, *The Life of Johnny Reb: The Common Soldier of the Confederacy* (1943; reprint. Baton Rouge: Louisiana State Univ. Press, 1971), 21–22.
23. The sources for the identification of Ashe County soldiers in 1861 and 1862 are: Jordan and Manarin, comps. and eds., *North Carolina Troops;* John W. Moore, ed., *Register of North Carolina Troops in the War between the States*, 4 vols. (Raleigh, N.C: Ashe Publishing Co., 1882); U.S. Census, Ashe County, North Carolina, 1860, Population and Agricultural Schedules; Eller, "Collection of History and Geneology of Ashe County"; Shepherd, ed., *Heritage of Ashe County; Alleghany County Heritage 1983* (Winston-Salem, N.C.: Hunter Publishing Co., 1983); Dr. A. B. Cox, *Footprints on the Sands of Time: A History of South-western Virginia and North-western North Carolina* (Sparta, N.C.: Star Publishing Co., 1900); Fletcher, Ashe County: A History.

Detailed investigation of residential patterns in the Ashe County enlistment process confirms the local neighborhood basis of volunteer company organization. Not unexpectedly, the company with the highest proportion of volunteers from a single district, Company A, 34th Regiment was also the only company to incorporate its neighborhood identity into its popular name, the "Laurel Springs Guards." Other company names in 1861 more obviously reflected the community's determination to identify itself with the emergent symbols of Confederate independence. Company A, 26th Regiment, for example, which recruited predominantly from the Southeastern and Town districts, proclaimed itself the "Jeff Davis Mountain Rifles" or "Mountaineers," while Company A, 37th Regiment chose another newly canonized figure for its rallying cry, becoming the "Ashe Beauregard Rifles."[24] For the majority of Ashe County volunteers, in fact, neighborhood loyalties intersected with kinship loyalties in the enlistment process, with high family concentrations in individual companies. As the war progressed, such loyalties became increasingly difficult to sustain, but they were certainly not dispensed with, as the second-year enlistment patterns for Company A the 26th and Company D of the Fifth Battalion demonstrate. The importance of residency and kinship is further underlined by the numerous examples of soldiers who changed companies during the war. In June 1863, for example, six volunteers from Company A, 1st North Carolina Cavalry—including members of the Ray, Hardin, and Latham families—transferred to Company D, Fifth Battalion, North Carolina Cavalry, where numerous close relations were already serving. Their decision to transfer was also possibly influenced by the fact that the Fifth Battalion was currently stationed in East Tennessee, thus placing them closer to their homes in northwest North Carolina.[25]

As Robert Kenzer has argued in his study of Orange County, North Carolina, this pattern of neighborhood enlistment probably reflected the existing militia

---

24. Principal district origins for five Ashe County companies were as follows:
9TH REGT. (1ST CAVALRY), COMPANY A: 1861 (total sample 45) Southeastern 13 (28.9%); Old Fields 12 (26.7%); Town 11 (24.4%). 1862 (total sample 11) Southeastern 4 (36.4Vo).
26TH REGT., COMPANY A: 1861 (total sample 57) Southeastern 30 (52.6%). 1862 (total sample 37) Southeastern 17 (45.9%).
34TH REGT., COMPANY A: 1861 (total sample 42) Southeastern 35 (83.3%). No recruitment 1862.
37TH REGT., COMPANY A: 1861 (total sample 61) Old Fields 21 (34.4%); Southeastern 17 (27.9%); Town 14 (22.9%). 1862 (total sample 57) Southeastern 21 (36.8%); Town 14 (24.6%); Northeastern 12 (21.1%).
5TH BATTALION, COMPANY D: 1862 (total sample 73) Old Fields 37 (50.7%).

25. Jordan and Manarin, comps. and eds., *North Carolina Troops*, vol. 2, *Cavalry*, 337.

organization within the community; but, as he further observes, it also suggests the volunteers' determination to reproduce existing local loyalties as a means of accommodating themselves to the uncertain experience ahead.[26] Historians have long recognized the weakness of the antebellum militia system. Although a volunteer company was raised in Ashe County following John Brown's raid in October 1859, in general there appeared to be little community enthusiasm for fulfilling state militia requirements before the Civil War, reflective of the apathy of the society at large. In May 1855, the leader of one Ashe County militia company had been forced to request from Governor Thomas Bragg copies of the state's laws and tactics which, he complained, they "had never been furnished with."[27]

In a very real sense, therefore, the volunteer companies, with their closely woven kinship and neighborhood fabric, were direct extensions of the community itself, communities away from home. One consequence of this was the recreation of local allegiances, both formal and informal, through the jealously guarded prerogative of choosing company officers and, in many cases, other noncommissioned posts. The moving spirit and first captain of the "Jeff Davis Mountain Rifles" was Aras B. Cox, a wealthy slaveholding doctor, farmer, and church leader and former clerk of the Ashe County Superior Court.[28] Company A of the 37th Regiment was raised by John Hartzog, one of the wealthiest slaveholding farmers in the county with real property valued at ten thousand dollars in 1860. In June 1862 Joseph Hardin, a twenty-eight-year-old slaveholding farmer from the Town district, organized Company D of the Fifth Battalion, North Carolina Cavalry. His father, James Welborn Hardin, who farmed over 1,500 acres of land in the same district, was the third largest slaveholder in Ashe County on the eve of the Civil War.[29]

These leadership patterns were further sustained in the choice of other company officers during 1861 and 1862. Analysis of wealth and status among the seventeen officers who were appointed to command five of the six Ashe

---

26. Robert C. Kenzer, *Kinship and Neighborhood in a Southern Community: Orange County, North Carolina, 1849–1881* (Knoxville: Univ. of Tennessee Press, 1987), 71–74.

27. Colonel T. Edwards to Governor Thomas Bragg, May 24, 1855, Governor's Letter Books 1855–1856, vol. 43, 177, North Carolina Division of Archives and History. On the weakness of the antebellum militia, see Cunliffe, *Soldiers and Civilians*, 201–12.

28. For a profile of Cox, see Shepherd, ed., *Heritage of Ashe County*, 203–4. See also Cox's own biographical account in *Footprints on the Sands of Time*, 151–62.

29. Before the war Hardin had served in Ashe County as Captain of the 97th N.C. Militia. See Weymouth T. Jordan, comp., *North Carolina Troops: Volume Two Addenda* (Raleigh: North Carolina Division of Archives and History, 1988), 805.

County companies reveal property holdings far in excess of the community average. Seven of the seventeen owned slaves or lived in slaveowning families, whereas slaveholders constituted less than 7 percent of Ashe County farmers at the beginning of the Civil War. Later, as more officers were promoted from the ranks, the emphasis upon wealth as a prerequisite for leadership appears to have declined, but the insistence upon familiar authority was not completely abandoned. Among the thirteen men who were subsequently advanced to officer rank, for example, at least three were engaged in professional occupations, including teaching, while a fourth, Samuel P. Wagg, who died at Gettysburg, was the son of a prominent Ashe County physician and Methodist minister.[30]

On May 21, 1861, the nineteen-year-old son of an aristocratic eastern North Carolina family, Henry King Burgwyn, Jr., arrived in Ashe County on a recruiting drive. His mission, which was a spectacular failure, highlights the community priorities in the volunteering and enlistment experience. Initially, the majority of North Carolina recruits, including three of the four 1861 Ashe County companies, were mustered into state and, subsequently, Confederate service for a twelve-month period only; but in the State Troops Act passed on May 8, the legislature further authorized the enlistment of ten thousand volunteers who would serve for the duration of the war.[31] It was under this authority that Henry King Burgwyn hoped to recruit a company of regular soldiers in Ashe County through which, he believed, his boundless ambition for military glory would be realized.

On his arrival in Jefferson, Burgwyn—who had only a few weeks earlier graduated from the Virginia Military Institute—seemed highly optimistic as to his ability to organize a regular company. He judged the local inhabitants, although lacking in energy and apparently in dread of the low country, to be "good natured easy people ... rather disposed to take the world as it is." They were also "the best rifle shots in the state."[32] Within a few days, however, the young man's enthusiasm was seriously deflated, and in a letter to his sister Burgwyn complained bitterly of his lack of success. This he ascribed not to his own deficiencies, but rather to the unwillingness of Ashe County citizens to join a regular company as opposed to a

---

30. Cox, *Footprints on the Sands of Time*, 113–14.
31. John G. Barrett, *The Civil War in North Carolina* (Chapel Hill: Univ. of North Carolina Press, 1963), 14–15.
32. Henry King Burgwyn, Jr., to his mother. May 21, 1861, Burgwyn Family Papers, Southern Historical Collection, University of North Carolina, Chapel Hill. See Archie K. Davis, *Boy Colonel of the Confederacy: The Life and Times of Henry King Burgwyn, Jr.* (Chapel Hill: Univ. of North Carolina Press, 1985), 71–74, for the biographical context of his visit to the mountains.

twelve-month volunteer unit.[33] By the following week the sum total of Burgwyn's recruiting efforts, which involved an intense round of public and private meetings, was two Virginians, and, as he reported to his mother, even they were undecided as to whether they wished to enlist or not. "I hope I am not easily discouraged and hope that my patriotism is far from being exhausted," he wrote, "but a reflecting mind must institute sooner or later the inquiry, if it takes two weeks time & great trouble to secure 2 uncertain men how long will it take to get 64."[34]

Particularly galling to Burgwyn was the fact that his failure was in stark contrast to the achievement of another young man on the make, Thomas Newton Crumpler, who had recently returned from Raleigh after resigning from the state legislature. Crumpler, who Burgwyn dismissed as possessing no military knowledge or experience, had just been appointed a captain in the regular cavalry, and was in the process of successfully organizing an Ashe County company under the terms of the State Troops Act. The crucial difference, which completely eluded the immature Burgwyn, was not the duration of service but the volunteers' insistence on maintaining local leadership in the extended community. Despite his military innocence, the twenty-six-year-old Crumpler was a familiar and respected figure in Ashe County whose abilities had already been endorsed in his legal and commercial dealings and, most indicatively, at the ballot box. Henry King Burgwyn, on the other hand, offered no such security; at the same time, his military credentials were not entirely disregarded by the local community. After his failure to recruit a regular company, Burgwyn remained in Ashe County to assist in the training of the "Jeff Davis Mountain Rifles." Their gratitude was publicly expressed at a meeting on June 10.[35] On July 1, 1863, Burgwyn, the "boy colonel" of the Confederacy, was killed leading the 26th North Carolina regiment in a desperate and costly assault at Gettysburg. Among the numerous casualties that day were several members of Company A, the "Jeff Davis Mountain Rifles," whom Burgwyn had helped initiate into war two years earlier.[36]

If the defense of community and community values lay at the heart of the volunteering and enlistment experience, the complex public and private dilemmas implied in that commitment also became apparent. Despite initial enthusiasm for the war in western North Carolina ("The mountains are pouring forth their brave

---

33. Burgwyn to his sister, May 27, 1861, Burgwyn Family Papers.
34. Burgwyn to his mother, June 2, 1861, Burgwyn Family Papers.
35. *Raleigh Register and North Carolina Gazette*, July 3, 1861.
36. Davis, *Boy Colonel of the Confederacy*, 292–339; Manarin and Jordan, comps. and eds., *North Carolina Troops*, 7:466–81.

sons in large numbers, and still they come"),[37] only a minority of Ashe County's young male residents responded to the Confederate call to arms during the first year of the Civil War. At this stage, the precise extent and character of the county's overall response to the war cannot be determined. It is possible, for example, that some Ashe citizens moved across the state line to join kinfolk in Virginia regiments. More seriously, an unknown but potentially large number actively opposed the Confederate cause by enlisting in the Federal army, an action facilitated by the county's close proximity to the Unionist stronghold of East Tennessee.[38] During the later stages of the conflict, western North Carolina also suffered badly from the depredations of bushwackers and deserters, whose activities helped aggravate existing social and political antagonisms within the mountain region.[39]

After North Carolina's secession in May 1861, Ashe County residents were faced with a complex amalgam of individual, family, and civic concerns, the collective resolution of which would determine the community's overall commitment to the Confederate cause. Clearly, for a minority of residents, whether for ideological or material reasons, the Southern call to arms proved deeply offensive. By actively supporting the Federal cause, even to the point of enlisting in its armed forces, Ashe County Unionists demonstrated the potentially fragile nature of community cohesion in the Southern highlands. But even for the majority, who were initially supportive of the Southern cause, the decision as to whether to enlist or not invited deep and often painful deliberation, which the changing demands of the Confederate war effort could only intensify.

Even before Ashe County troops were actively engaged on the battlefield, the war's effects were already being felt in the remote mountain community. At least nine Ashe County Confederate volunteers had died from disease before the end of 1861, including four from Thomas Crumpler's cavalry company. An even larger number died during the following year. In a letter to his father-in-law in October 1861, James M. Gentry poignantly described the return to Ashe County of the body of one such victim, Private Jacob Latham, a twenty-five-year-old unmarried farmer

37. *Raleigh Register and North Carolina Gazette,* July 9, 1861.
38. Fletcher, *Ashe County,* 140.
39. There is no adequate modern history of western North Carolina during the Civil War, but see Ora Blackmun, *Western North Carolina: Its Mountains and its People to 1880* (Boone, N.C.: Appalachian Consortium Press, 1977), 328–55; William R. Trotter, *Bushwackers/The Civil War in North Carolina: The Mountains* (Greensboro, N.C.: Piedmont Impressions, 1988); and in particular, Philip Shaw Paludan, *Victims: A True Story of the Civil War* (Knoxville: Univ. of Tennessee Press, 1981), and Gordon B. McKinney, "Subsistence Economy and Community in Western North Carolina, 1860–1865" (Reno, Nev.: unpublished paper, Organization of American Historians Annual Meeting, 1988).

from the Town district. Ashe County itself was suffering the ravages of disease, notably diphtheria, and the news of widespread sickness in the military camps left Gentry profoundly depressed, although by no means defeated.[40] By the early summer of 1862, Ashe recruits had also begun to appear on the lists of military casualties, and in July the county's most dynamic young leader, Major Thomas Crumpler, was killed in action at Willis' Church, Virginia.[41]

The precise impact of these developments upon Ashe County volunteering patterns remains difficult if not impossible to evaluate, at least in the short term. In April 1862, however, the Confederacy's manpower problems dictated the first national conscription law in American history. Despite its manifest deficiencies, not the least of which was the impossibility of proper enforcement, the conscription act's passage effectively guaranteed the South's continuing military participation in the war. Demands for conscription had been growing for some months prior to the congressional action. In December 1861, a misguided furlough and bounty act had been passed which served only to intensify the Confederacy's recruitment difficulties. According to published troops rosters, no Ashe County residents were forcibly conscripted into the Confederate army before the end of 1862 as a result of the April act. During the spring and summer of that year, however, under the coercive shadow of conscription, several hundred citizens from the community, including Alfred Blevins, "voluntarily" enlisted in North Carolina regiments.[42] These included 280 or 56.8 percent of the sample group identified through the population census. While individual motives must remain a matter of conjecture, comparative analysis of first- and second-year volunteers reveals significant socio-economic and family differences within the sample group.

The first pronounced difference between the 1861 and 1862 enlistment groups involved marital status, which has been determined from the 1860 population

40. Gentry to Jonathan Faw, Oct. 6, 1861, Faw Papers.
41. Crumpler's wounding and death are reported in *Asheville News*, July 24, 31, 1862; *Raleigh North Carolina Standard*, July 30, 1862. Earlier in the year he had returned to Ashe County on a recruiting drive. See *Raleigh North Carolina Standard*, Feb. 19, 1862. The action at Willis' Church is reported in *The War of the Rebellion: A Compilation of the Official Records of the Union and Confederate Armies*, 128 vols. (Washington, D.C.: GPO, 1880-1901), ser. I, vol. 11, pt. 2: 525-26.
42. See Albert Burton Moore, *Conscription and Conflict in the Confederacy* (1924; reprint, New York: Hillary House, 1963), 1-26. On the deficiencies of conscription and its role as a spur to volunteering, see E. Merton Coulter, *The Confederate States of America, 1861-1865* (Baton Rouge: Louisiana State Univ. Press, 1950), 314-28. "There seems to be a general expression amongst the men that they will volunteer rather than be subjected to a draught," noted one northwestern North Carolina observer. James Calloway to Henry T. Clark, Mar. 3, 1862, Governor's Papers (Clark), North Carolina Division of Archives and History, Raleigh.

Table 1
Marital Status by District, 1861-1862

District	1861 Married	1861 Unmarried	1862 Married	1862 Unmarried
Northeastern	5	13	26	17
North Fork	3	6	19	18
Old Fields	6	29	19	25
Southeastern	43	58	60	48
Town	8	34	21	19
Village	0	3	0	4
Unknown	1	4	1	3
Total	66	147	146	134
	(31.0%)	(69.0%)	(52.2%)	(47.8%)

census and county geneological data.[43] (At least twelve Ashe County volunteers from the sample group married between the census date and their enlistment in the Confederate army.) Among the sample group, only 31 percent who enlisted during the first year of the war were married. This compares to just over 52 percent in 1862, where the ratio of married to unmarried recruits was more evenly balanced (see Table 1).[44] Within the married group, the overwhelming majority lived in independent households, although a small number of families were boarding out, mostly with relatives. The vast majority of unmarried recruits were still living in the parental home, but a small percentage were boarders, including several identified in the 1860 census as day laborers and clerks. Although the numbers involved are small, it is perhaps worth noting that the percentage of boarders among first year unmarried volunteers was nearly three times higher than that for the second year (see Table 2). None of these unmarried boarders had yet acquired any real or personal wealth, and it is conceivable that the Confederate call to arms in 1861 provided an opportune escape route for those individuals who had failed to establish themselves economically, and who, moreover, had also become disengaged from the family household. By the spring of 1862, on the other hand, when volunteering activity recommenced, war was no longer regarded

---

43. The 1860 population census provides no specific indication of marital status. Where possible, household family relations in the Ashe County census have been verified in local genealogical data. Methodological insights into the problem have been gained from two important community studies: *Kenzer, Kinship and Neighborhood in a Southern Community;* and Orville Vernon Burton, *In My Father's House Are Many Mansions: Family and Community in Edgefield, South Carolina* (Chapel Hill: Univ. of North Carolina Press, 1985), 104-47, 326-29.

44. See Emily J. Harris, "Sons and Soldiers: Deerfield, Massachusetts and the Civil War," *Civil War History* 30 (June 1984): 168, for comparable statistics on volunteer marital status in a Northern town.

Table 2
Household Status by Enlistment Year

Household status	1861	1862
Married, own home	61 (92.5%)	132 (90.4%)
Married, boarders	1 (1.5%)	6 (4.1%)
Married between census and enlistment	4 (6.0%)	8 (5.5%)
Total	66 (100.0%)	146 (100.0%)
Unmarried, own home	9 (6.1%)	3 (2.2%)
Unmarried, parental home	120 (81.6%)	125 (93.3%)
Unmarried, boarders	18 (12.3%)	6 (4.5%)
Total	147 (100.0%)	134 (100.0%)

in such a glamorous or heroic light, and this had predictable consequences for recruitment across the whole range of occupations and social classes.[45]

The lack of enthusiasm for military service shown by Ashe County's young married citizens is further confirmed through detailed examination of wealth and age patterns among the 1861 and 1862 volunteers. Although there were many individual cases in which the opposite behavior pattern prevailed, as a group, Ashe County's married recruits during the second year of the Civil War were younger and less prosperous than their first year counterparts.[46] Seemingly, it was the relatively older, more established households, with their greater economic and domestic resources, who were better able to respond to the Confederate call in 1861. The evidence for unmarried wealth holdings, where the age differential between the two enlistment groups was minimal, also provides some support for J. William Harris's conclusion—based on an analysis of three Georgia counties—that Confederate recruits derived from progressively poorer families as the war continued into and beyond its second year.[47] In Ashe County, average family wealth for unmarried 1862 volunteers still residing in the parental home

---

45. For a parallel argument, see William S. McFeely, *Grant: A Biography* (New York: W. W. Norton, 1981), xii, 67-68. "Escaping from the ordinary" is McFeely's highly apt description of the war's appeal for the future Union commander. See also W. J. Rorabaugh, "Who Fought for the North in the Civil War? Concord, Massachusetts, Enlistments," *Journal of American History* 73 (Dec. 1986): 695-701, which probes suggestively into the socioeconomic and occupational bases of Northern urban volunteering activity.

46. Average real and personal property for married volunteers (dollars) in 1861: 878.48; in 1862: 652.11. This includes all married volunteers with the exception of the small number who married between the census and enlistment in the army, where no wealth data is available. Average age of married volunteers in 1861: 30.6; in 1862: 28.8. This includes all married volunteers.

47. Harris, *Plain Folk and Gentry in a Slave Society*, 152-53.

was nearly 15 percent less than for those who enlisted during the first year of the war. Here again the evidence suggests that support for the Confederate cause was most active among those households with sufficient resources to sustain the loss of one or more male members to military service.[48]

If the factors of age, wealth, and family circumstance helped determine the volunteering response in Ashe County, so did residential location. As the analysis of individual companies has already indicated, initial enthusiasm for the war appeared strongest in the Southeastern, Town, and Old Fields districts of Ashe County. Of a total sample of 213 volunteers for 1861, 179, or just over 84 percent, came from those three districts which embraced just 65.7% of Ashe County households. There were three recruits from the tiny Village of Jefferson district, including Thomas Crumpler, as well as five more whose residential location remains unidentified. Only twenty-seven volunteers, or just over one-eighth of the 1861 sample, came from the two remaining districts, the Northeastern and the North Fork. More revealing is the ratio of first- to second-year volunteers in the individual districts. In the Southeastern, Town, and Old Fields districts, between 44 percent and 52 percent of the sample group enlisted during the first year of the war, whereas in the Northeastern and North Fork areas the figure was only 29.5 percent and 19.6 percent, respectively.

The significance of this data soon becomes apparent when we examine the relative prosperity of individual districts. Leaving aside the Village of Jefferson, which contained only twenty-six households, there appears to be some positive correlation between district wealth and the timing of enlistment in the Confederate army. Of the five large districts in the county, the Town district, with the highest per household wealth valuation, produced the highest ratio of first- to second-year volunteers. Conversely, the Northeastern and North Fork districts, where enlistment was markedly more delayed, were among the two poorest in the county with average household wealth just over half that of the Town district. Together with the large and diverse Southeastern district, the North Fork and Northeastern also exhibited the lowest incidence of slaveowning households in Ashe County (see Table 3). Finally, the North Fork and Northeastern districts were also those which contained some of the least productive soils in the county.[49]

48. Average real and personal property for unmarried volunteers still residing in parental home (dollars) in 1861: 2259.06; in 1862: 1928.90. Average age of unmarried volunteers in 1861: 21.0; in 1862: 21.3.

49. R. B. Hardison, *Soil Survey of Ashe County, North Carolina* (Washington, D.C.: U.S. Department of Agriculture, 1914).

Equally important in explaining the greater reluctance of the North Fork and Northeastern districts to volunteer was their geopolitical relationship with contiguous communities in northeastern Tennessee and southwestern Virginia, respectively. The North Fork, in particular, where the ratio of first- to second-year volunteering was the lowest in the county, was known to be an area of considerable Unionist sympathies during the war. Already by October 1861 committed Ashe County Confederates such as James M. Gentry were expressing alarm at the violent behavior of Unionist sympathizers in Johnson County, Tennessee, which bordered on the North Fork district.[50] The following month Gentry's fears were confirmed in a report to the Confederate Secretary of War from the Governor of North Carolina, Henry T. Clark.[51] It is also important to note that the North Fork's wealthiest citizen and slaveholder, David Worth, who together with his father-in-law Stephen Thomas ran a highly successful merchandising and tanning business, appears to have remained "neutral" during the war. Worth's calculated (and, in the long term, highly profitable) indifference to the sectional conflict contrasts strongly with the behavior of leading slaveholding citizens in other Ashe County districts where engagement with the Southern cause was more pronounced.[52] Unionist sympathies were also known to exist in Grayson County, Virginia, which bordered on Ashe County's Northeastern district, and where, a decade earlier, abolitionist activity had precipitated a serious slave revolt with consequent loss of both black and white lives.[53]

What conclusions can be drawn from an investigation into the Confederate volunteering and enlistment experience in Ashe County, North Carolina, during 1861 and 1862? Undoubtedly, the coming of civil war posed a unique threat to the domestic serenity of this western North Carolina mountain community. The challenge for the historian is to identify those forces—political, economic, geographic, familial—that helped shape the community's response, while at the same time remain sensitive to the complex individual motivations that at all times and in all circumstances prevailed. For some Ashe County households,

---

50. James M. Gentry to Jonathan Faw, Oct. 6, 1861, Faw Papers.

51. Henry T. Clark to Hon. J. P. Benjamin, Nov. 16, 1861, in *The War of the Rebellion*, ser. 1, vol. 52, pt. 2: 209. See also the petition of Quincy F. Neal *et. al* of Jefferson to Henry T. Clark, Jan. 14, 1862, Governor's Papers (Clark), which requests a local military appointment to help protect against "disaffected and dangerous persons on the border."

52. Shepherd, *Heritage of Ashe County*, 47–48, 511–12; R. G. Dun and Company, Credit Reporting Ledgers, 2: 25.

53. Betty-Lou Fields, comp., and ed., *Grayson County: A History in Words and Pictures* (Independence, Va.: Grayson County Historical Society, 1976), 83, 88.

Table 3
Residency, Wealth, and Slaveholding by District

	Northeastern	North Fork	Old Fields	Southeastern	Town	Village
Total households	186	228	155	585	160	26
Avg. real and personal property per household	$888.92	$977.90	$1,161.61	$879.37	$1,669.40	$9,246.73
Slaveholding households (%)	5.4%	3.1%	9.7%	3.1%	14.4%	34.6%
Number of volunteers						
1861	18 (29.5%)	9 (19.6%)	35 (44.3%)	101 (48.3%)	42 (51.2%)	3 (42.9%)
1862	43 (70.5%)	37 (80.4%)	44 (55.7%)	108 (51.7%)	40 (48.8%)	4 (57.1%)
Total	61 (100.0%)	46 (100.0%)	79 (100.0%)	209 (100.0%)	82 (100.0%)	7 (100.0%)

Sample completed by nine volunteers (5 in 1861; 4 in 1862) whose residential location was not indicated by the census taker.

the decision to enlist was evidently taken in defiance of rational economic and familial considerations. Among the first year recruits, for example, were Michael Miller, a fifty-one-year-old farmer from the Southeastern district and his fifteen-year-old son James. In August 1861 they enlisted in the "Laurel Springs Guards" leaving behind only Michael's wife, Susan, to tend the family farm. In other cases, including that of Alfred Blevins, there appears to have been a more precise calculation of the effect of enlistment upon the family and its domestic economy. A possible example of this was the Goss family, who farmed nine hundred acres near Jefferson and whose four adult sons volunteered over a period of fourteen months beginning in May 1861.

In all of these cases, however, the household is deemed to function as a discrete unit, thus potentially obscuring the intricate web of kinship and other social relationships identified by historians and anthropologists as a defining feature of mountain community life.[54] In order to understand more thoroughly the Civil War's impact, we need to develop a more sophisticated awareness of both individual and family interdependencies within the community. The Millers's decision, for example, may well have been facilitated by and, indeed dependent upon, the effectiveness of extended family and other local support networks. As Altina Waller has demonstrated, the nineteenth-century mountain "family" was "a socially constructed institution only partially based upon blood and conjugal ties."[55] Nor should we ignore the formal provision made by the community itself for the relief of soldiers' families. On May 23, 1861, Ashe County's governing body, the County Court, appropriated two thousand dollars for disbursement to volunteer families in need of financial assistance. A system of district reporting was to provide information on such households who would obtain their relief through the agencies of the local corn miller. As a final stimulus, all Confederate volunteers were also to be exempted from payment of the poll tax.[56]

If the Ashe County enlistment evidence points up the importance of the family, however broadly defined, it also suggests the significance of local economic and political cultures to Southern mountain society. Despite its broad ethnic and

---

54. See in particular, Ronald D. Eller, *Miners, Millhands and Mountaineers: Industrialization in the Appalachian South, 1880-1930* (Knoxville: Univ. of Tennessee Press, 1982), 28-38; and Patricia Duane Beaver, *Rural Community in the Appalachian South* (Lexington: Univ. Press of Kentucky, 1986), 59-63.

55. Altina L. Waller, *Feud: Hatfields, McCoys and Social Change in Appalachia, 1860-1900* (Chapel Hill: Univ. of North Carolina Press, 1988), 83.

56. Ashe County Court of Pleas and Quarter Sessions: Minute Docket, May 23, June 3, 1861. The relief money was to be raised by a 10 percent addition to the aggregate county tax and by borrowing from the Bank of Cape Fear in Salem.

cultural homogeneity, the western North Carolina region exhibited considerable internal diversity during the mid-nineteenth century, indicative for the most part of the relative degree of integration into the market economy.[57] The low enlistment rate in the North Fork and Northeastern districts, therefore, may have reflected a more durable subsistence culture among the mass of its yeoman farm population as compared to the more commercially oriented Town district, where enthusiasm for the Confederacy was more pronounced. These local variations may in turn be deployed to investigate other responses, including support for the Union and/or Confederate desertion rates. These questions, however, among many others, will establish the agenda for further research into the mobilization experience in Ashe County, North Carolina, and, by extension, into the wider socioeconomic and political bases of popular participation in the Civil War.

Finally, what became of Private Alfred Blevins? Five years after the Confederate surrender the census enumerator discovered the Blevins family still resident in Ashe County's Southeastern district. Alfred Blevins was now employed as a farm worker, indicating a decline in the family's economic and social status during the intervening decade. By 1880 and the next Federal census, however, much of the lost ground had been recovered, with the family now renting 150 acres of mixed agricultural and forest land for which they paid an agreed share of the annual farm product.[58] What had changed dramatically was the size of the Blevins family. Prior to the mid-twentieth century the Southern Appalachian region exhibited one of the highest fertility rates in the United States; and after their marriage in 1857, Alfred and Margary Blevins produced at least ten children, nine of whom were still living in the parental home in 1880.[59] For this next generation, the forces of modernization, so bravely opposed by their father at Gettysburg and elsewhere, would prove equally challenging and, in the end, equally irresistible. It is not without significance that the Blevins's eldest daughter, Elizabeth, was now married to a Tennessee-born miner, John Tolly. Over the next half century much of the Southern mountain region would be radically transformed under the hammer of largely absentee-controlled industrial capitalism. Increasingly,

---

57. See Inscoe, *Mountain Masters, Slavery and the Sectional Crisis*, 25-58. The market economy's long-term impact on the individual mountain community, in this case in East Tennessee, can also be pursued in an important recent study: Durwood Dunn, *Cades Cove: The Life and Death of a Southern Appalachian Community 1818-1937* (Knoxville: Univ. of Tennessee Press, 1988), 63-89.

58. U.S. Census, Ashe County, North Carolina, 1870, Population Schedule; 1880, Population and Agricultural Schedules.

59. Gordon F. DeJong, *Appalachian Fertility Decline: A Demographic and Sociological Analysis* (Lexington: Univ. Press of Kentucky, 1968), 31-51.

as agricultural self-sufficiency was eroded, it was to outside the traditional community, to the coal mines and the logging camps, and to the textile mills of the Carolina piedmont that the Appalachian farm population would be forced to turn, with irrevocable consequences for the region's long-term economic and demographic survival.[60]

60. The process is thoroughly documented in Eller, *Miners, Millhands and Mountaineers*, 39–242.

Which Poor Man's Fight?

Immigrants and the Federal Conscription of 1863

TYLER ANBINDER

Why was Hugh Boyle the only one? Of the more than 15,000 New Yorkers living in the teeming Five Points slum, this sandy-haired, blue-eyed, twenty-seven-year-old laborer was the only one forced into the army as a result of the Civil War draft. Anyone familiar with either the conscription law or its reputation among New York's Irish immigrants should find this fact surprising. Few Five Pointers could afford the $300 commutation fee that exempted one from the conscription. As a result, impoverished immigrants such as those who dominated Five Points thought that the onus of conscription would fall disproportionately on their shoulders. They believed that "the draft was an unfair one," reported the *New York Herald*, "inasmuch as the rich could avoid it by paying $300, while the poor man, who was without 'the greenbacks,' was compelled to go to the war."[1] But the draft rolls from New York seem to suggest a different story. Perhaps the draft did not create a "poor man's fight" after all. Only a systematic study of immigrants in the Union draft could determine if the conscription had forced many immigrants into uniform, or if, instead, immigrants had found some way to avoid service despite their relatively modest economic circumstances.

---

1. *New York Herald*, July 14, 1863. For Boyle, see Register of Drafted Men, Fourth Congressional District of New York, Entry 1589, RG 110, National Archives; Tyler Anbinder, *Five Points The Nineteenth-Century Neighborhood That Invented Tap Dance, Stole Elections, and Became the World's Most Notorious Slum* (New York: Free Press, 2001), 317–18.

One might imagine, given the voluminous historiography of the American Civil War, that the subject of immigrants in the Northern draft would have been thoroughly examined already. But in fact no satisfying study of the subject has ever been published. The few works that specifically survey the role of immigrants in the Civil War barely mention the draft, focusing instead on the heroics of foreign-born volunteers. The two book-length studies of the Northern draft, by Eugene Murdock and James W. Geary, devote very little attention to immigrants, concentrating instead on the conscription's many procedural problems and controversies.[2] Bell Wiley and James McPherson have both published careful analyses of who fought for the North, but because their figures lump draftees together with volunteers, their statistics tell us only that immigrants were not overrepresented in the army as a whole, and leave the question of the newcomers' treatment in the draft unresolved. The drama of Civil War draft rioting continues to attract interest from a wide range of scholars, but none of them has determined whether the rioters' fear that they would be disproportionately affected by the draft actually proved to be true.[3]

Lax record keeping made the undertaking difficult. Draft officials nationwide were supposed to maintain identical records, indicating the name, age, height,

---

2. Ella Lonn, *Foreigners in the Union Army and Navy* (Baton Rouge: Louisiana State Univ. Press, 1951); William L. Burton, *Melting Pot Soldiers: The Union's Ethnic Regiments* (New York: Fordham Univ. Press, 1998). The many works on Irish units likewise ignore drafted soldiers. See D. P. Conyngham, *The Irish Brigade and Its Campaigns* (New York: McSorley and Co., 1867); Paul Jones, *The Irish Brigade* (Washington, D.C.: R. B. Luce, 1969); Patrick O'Flagherty, "The History of the Sixty-Ninth Regiment of the New York State Militia, 1852–1861" (Ph.D. diss., Fordham University, 1963); Eugene C. Murdock, *One Million Men: The Civil War Draft in the North* (Madison: State Historical Society of Wisconsin, 1971); James W. Geary, *We Need Men: The Union Draft in the Civil War* (DeKalb: Northern Illinois Univ. Press, 1991).

3. Bell Wiley, *The Life of Billy Yank: The Common Soldier of the Civil War* (Indianapolis: Bobbs-Merrill, 1952), 306–15, 343–44; James M. McPherson, *Battle Cry of Freedom: The Civil War Era* (New York: Oxford Univ. Press, 1988), 600–608. For draft riots involving immigrants, see William F. Hanna, "The Boston Draft Riot," *Civil War History* 36 (1990): 262–73; Judith Ann Giesberg, "'Lawless and Unprincipled': Women In Boston's Civil War Draft Riot," in James M. O'Toole and David Quigley, eds., *Boston's Histories: Essays in Honor of Thomas H. O'Connor* (Boston: Northeastern Univ. Press, 2004), 71–91; William Marvel, "New Hampshire and the Draft, 1863," *Historical New Hampshire* 36 (1981): 58–72; Adrian Cook, *The Armies of the Streets: The New York City Draft Riots of 1863* (Lexington: Univ. Press of Kentucky, 1974); Iver Bernstein, *The New York City Draft Riots* (New York: Oxford Univ. Press, 1990); Grace Palladino, *Another Civil War: Labor, Capital, and the State in the Anthracite Regions of Pennsylvania, 1840–1868* (Urbana: Univ. of Illinois Press, 1990), 95–117; Lawrence H. Larsen, "Draft Riot in Wisconsin," *Civil War History* 7 (1961): 421–27. For the Confederate draft, which preceded the Union conscription and was the first to inspire complaints that it would bring about "a rich man's war and a poor man's fight," the most detailed study is still Albert B. Moore, *Conscription and Conflict in the Confederacy* (New York: Macmillan, 1924).

eye and hair color, occupation, and birthplace of each draftee. Provost officers were also expected to record the ultimate disposition of each conscript—whether he was exempted for medical or other reasons, paid the commutation fee, hired a substitute, or was "held to service." But most draft officers left important portions of the ledgers blank. Some recorded most of the information but failed to note nativity, the crucial variable for this study (this was the case for most of New York City, for example). Even the fairly complete draft books do not typically indicate the nativity of those who "failed to report" (the official term for those who did not appear at a draft office after their name was drawn). Because it appears that immigrants failed to report at a higher rate than natives, ledgers lacking nativity information on draft dodgers are far less valuable than those that contain this data. Finally, the army's record keeping grew worse as the war progressed. A draft officer who kept good records during the first draft (which took place in most areas in the summer of 1863) usually recorded far less information concerning those drafted in later conscriptions. Consequently, this study focuses on the conscription of 1863, although it also includes data from cities such as Chicago and Milwaukee, whose first drafts were conducted in 1864.[4]

The pattern that emerges from this data is unmistakable: immigrants were not disproportionately forced into the army as a result of the draft. In most instances, in fact, immigrants were underrepresented in the ranks of those held to service. From Maine and New Hampshire to Ohio and Illinois, immigrants in the nation's major and mid-size cities were almost always less likely than natives to serve in the army as a result of the draft. The Irish, the most economically disadvantaged of the major immigrant groups of the period, are especially underrepresented, but other immigrant groups are lacking in the ranks of the conscripted as well, though in a few places in 1864 Germans entered the army as a result of the draft at a higher rate than either the Irish or the native-born. If one considers all those forced to contribute to the war effort as a result of the draft, by combining those forced to serve with those who hired substitutes or paid the commutation fee, then immigrants lag even further behind natives

4. The draft records of thirty-nine cities were examined for this study: Albany, Bangor, Boston, Brooklyn, Buffalo, Chicago, Cincinnati, Cleveland, Columbus, Concord (N.H.), Des Moines, Detroit, Dubuque, Fort Wayne, Harrisburg, Hartford, Lancaster, Lowell (Mass.), Manchester (N.H.), Milwaukee, New Albany (Ind.), New Haven, New York, Newark, Philadelphia, Pittsburgh, Portland (Maine), Portsmouth (N.H.), Poughkeepsie, Providence, Reading, Rochester, Scranton, Springfield (Mass.), Terre Haute, Troy (N.Y.), Vincennes (Ind.), Worcester, and Youngstown (Ohio). Those cities listed but not discussed below either had draft registers that were too incomplete to be useful for comparing the army service of immigrants and natives, or they did not conduct a draft in 1863.

in their contributions. This study indicates that one group does appear to have been disproportionately forced into service as a result of the draft—native-born laborers, especially those residing in rural areas. Their outsized contribution to the Union cause has not previously been adequately recognized.

The Data

Because the data in the tables below play such an important role in this study, a brief discussion of their source is in order. In the bowels of the old National Archives building on Pennsylvania Avenue, lining hundreds of feet of shelves in the dark, low-ceilinged stacks, sit thousands of leather-bound volumes that comprise Record Group 110, the papers of the Provost Marshal General's Bureau. Although a large portion of these records are those of the bureau's main office in Washington, the majority of the collection is comprised of ledgers maintained by the bureau's district headquarters. In March 1863, the bureau established one such office in every congressional district and in the territories as well. Each district office preserved its correspondence with Washington, kept account books detailing expenditures, and recorded the enlistment of volunteers and the pursuit of deserters and bounty jumpers. In the spring of 1863, bureau officers began recording the names of every man in each provost district presumed eligible for the draft. When the draft commenced in the summer of that year, the selected names were inscribed in ledger books, along with the information about appearance, age, nativity, and occupation. Later on, once each case had been resolved, the final status of the conscript would be recorded as well. Although their ink is fading and their bindings are disintegrating, these rich records, largely ignored by historians in the 140 years since the Civil War ended, provide the data that made this study possible.

It is also necessary to explain the organization and presentation of the figures derived from these ledgers. First, the columns of each table are arranged so that as one reads from left to right: one begins with the outcome least desirable to the government ("failed to report"), moves right through ever more desirable outcomes (exempted after reporting, paid $300 to the government for commutation, hired a substitute) until at the right one reaches the most desirable outcome for the army, a draftee who agreed to serve (i.e., was "held to service"). Second, some explanation is needed for the variations in the labeling of the far-right column in the tables. In most cases, that column is labeled "number drafted," which refers to the number of persons whose names were called to serve in the army when each draft was held. But because the ledgers for some places do not list the nativity of those who were called but failed to report, the far-right columns in the tables based on those ledger books are labeled "number reporting," to indicate the exclusion of those who failed to report. The reader needs to remember that the figures in those tables should be used to compare immigrants to nonimmigrants within each locale and should not be compared directly with the other tables. Finally, because the number of immigrant and nonimmigrant draftees within a given city sometimes varied tremendously, a comparison of the raw numbers would be misleading for determining the proportion of immigrants and natives forced into the army as a result of the draft. Percentages make for a much quicker and more relevant comparison. But for those who want to know the raw numbers, it is easy to calculate. In any given row, merely multiply the percentage (converted into a decimal) by the number at the end of that row to calculate the actual number of persons who make up the percentage. In the very first row of Table 1, for example, we can determine the actual number of natives held to service in Bangor by multiplying the percentage given (6%, or .06) by the total number drafted (298) to learn that eighteen native-born Bangor residents entered the army as a result of the draft.

With this information in mind, we can begin to examine the data from the draft ledgers. The best-kept draft books contain data for every federally prescribed category, including the nativity of those who failed to report for duty. Only six of the twenty-six urban draft ledgers from 1863 consulted for this study, about 20 percent of the total, recorded every bit of the prescribed information, and the data from these records are presented in Table 1. As Table 1 shows, these ledgers suggest that immigrants were not more likely than natives to serve in the army as a result of the draft. In five of the six cities, in fact, immigrants were far less likely to be held to service than other draftees. Only in Lowell did immigrants enter the army at rates comparable to natives. It is also notable that in most instances immigrants "failed to report" significantly more often than natives, and that Irish immigrants were typically the most likely to desert rather than report when drafted. The figures do, however, corroborate the notion that immigrants were less able to hire substitutes or pay for commutation than other Americans. In most cases, immigrants were far less likely than natives to buy their way out of the draft—anywhere from two to ten times less likely. The only exception was in Harrisburg, where a large and relatively prosperous German immigrant community was either able to pay the commutation fee or hire sub-

Table 1. Draft Results in Cities with Complete Draft Ledgers, Summer 1863

City and Nativity	Failed to Report	Exempt	Paid $300	Hired Substitute	Held to Service	Number Drafted
Bangor						
Natives	4%	63%	4%	22%	6%	298
Irish Immigrants	2%	93%	4%	0%	1%	81
Other Immigrants	21%	66%	4%	6%	2%	47
Boston (Wards 1, 2, 3, 5, 6, 9)						
Natives	13%	70%	6%	8%	0.76%	1708
Irish Immigrants	24%	74%	0.48%	0.97%	0.12%	828
Other Immigrants	19%	78%	2%	1%	0%	529
Harrisburg						
Natives	18%	53%	10%	14%	5%	398
Irish Immigrants	20%	63%	13%	3%	0%	30
Other Immigrants	10%	67%	6%	17%	0%	48
Lowell, Mass.						
Natives	8%	66%	21%	.92%	5%	434
Irish Immigrants	19%	70%	4%	0%	6%	93
Other Immigrants	7%	81%	7%	0%	4%	55
New Haven						
Natives	4%	70%	1%	23%	2%	557
Irish Immigrants	15%	77%	1%	5%	0%	163
Other Immigrants	9%	87%	0%	4%	0%	97
Reading						
Natives	6%	68%	4%	18%	3%	413
Irish Immigrants	39%	52%	0%	9%	0%	23
Other Immigrants	13%	76%	4%	7%	0%	85
Nationwide (all draftees)	13%	56%	18%	9%	3%	292,441

Source: "Descriptive List of Drafted Men," 4th Maine Draft District, Entry 559, vol. 38; "Descriptive Book of Drafted Men," 4th Massachusetts Draft District, Entry 893, vol. 13; "Descriptive Book of Drafted Men," 14th Pennsylvania Draft District, Entry 3307, vol. 26; "Descriptive Register of the Names of Persons Drawn," 7th Massachusetts Draft District, Entry 934, vol. 12; "Descriptive Book of Drafted Men," 2d Connecticut Draft District, Entry 1189, vol. 35, all in RG 110, National Archives. All "Descriptive Books" (i.e., draft ledgers) cited below are from this record group in the National Archives. Nationwide draft figures are based on data published in *The War of the Rebellion: A Compilation of the Official Records of the Union and Confederate Armies*, ser. 3 (Washington, D.C.: GPO, 1900), 5:730. These "corrected" figures differ slightly from those given in *Final Report Made to the Secretary of War by the Provost Marshal General of the Operations of the Bureau of the Provost Marshal General of the United States* (Washington, D.C.: GPO, 1866), 173–74. In this and all subsequent charts, percentages greater than one have been rounded to the nearest whole number. Due to that rounding, percentages in some charts may not add up to 100.

Table 2. Draft Results in Cities Whose Draft Ledgers Do Not List Nativity for Those Who "Failed to Report," Summer 1863

City and Nativity	Exempt	Paid $300	Hired Substitute	Held to Service	Number Reporting
Albany					
Natives	53%	19%	18%	0%	659
Irish Immigrants	77%	13%	10%	0%	326
Other Immigrants	69%	14%	16%	0.42%	236
Boston (Wards 4, 7, 8, 10, 11, 12)					
Natives	72%	13%	12%	2%	1861
Irish Immigrants	97%	.4%	1%	0.29%	701
Other Immigrants	93%	3%	3%	0.81%	493
Buffalo					
Natives	72%	4%	22%	2%	689
Irish Immigrants	88%	3%	7%	2%	220
Other Immigrants	87%	4%	14%	0.96%	937
Concord, Manchester, and Portsmouth, N.H.					
Natives	66%	.90%	29%	4%	664
Irish Immigrants	79%	0%	22%	2%	81
Other Immigrants	60%	0%	36%	3%	58
Rochester					
Natives	71%	2%	24%	3%	441
Irish Immigrants	82%	0%	15%	1%	137
Other Immigrants	77%	0%	21%	2%	406
Scranton					
Natives	54%	27%	17%	0%	104
Irish Immigrants	88%	10%	1%	0%	83
Other Immigrants	79%	18%	4%	0%	112
Nationwide (all draftees)	65%	21%	10%	4%	252,566

Source: "Descriptive List of Drafted Men," 14th New York Draft District, Entry 1881, Vol. 19; "Descriptive Books of Drafted Men," 3d Massachusetts Draft District, Entry 877, vol. 17; "Descriptive Book of Drafted Men," 30th New York Draft District, Entry 2291, vol. 21; "Descriptive Books of Drafted Men," 1st New Hampshire Draft District, Entry 654, vol. 14 (Portsmouth); "Descriptive Book of Drafted Men," 2d New Hampshire Draft District, Entry 667, vol. 19 (Concord and Manchester); "Descriptive List of Men Drafted into Service," 12th Pennsylvania Draft District, Entry 3114, vol. 23. Nationwide figures from *War of the Rebellion*, ser. 3, 5:730. The Scranton draft was held in October. The figures in this chart do not include the 211 men who failed to report in Albany, the 528 who did not report in this portion of Boston, the 396 who failed to report in Buffalo, the 32 who did not report in New Hampshire's principal cities (why so few failed to report there is not clear), and the 118 who failed to report in Scranton.

stitutes at about the same rate as natives. Yet by more often claiming exemptions and failing to report, immigrants without the money to buy their way out of the draft were able to offset the disadvantage of their limited monetary resources. Consequently, immigrants in these cities were less likely than natives to serve in the army as a result of the draft.

Although draft ledgers that do not record the nativity of those who failed to report are less useful than those that include this data, such draft books do nonetheless enable us to compare the rate at which immigrants and natives were held to service. The draft records from these cities confirm the trends found in the complete registers. Immigrants were never overrepresented in the ranks of those held to service, and in most cases they were underrepresented. Only in Albany and Scranton were immigrants held to service at the same rate as natives, and that is because, in effect, nobody from those two cities was held to serve. In Albany, almost no one was held to service because the city bought substitutes for all who could not afford them. The only Albany resident forced into the army was an immigrant who had failed to report. When he was arrested a year later, he had forfeited his opportunity to have the city pay for his substitute and was forced into service. It is not clear why no one was held to service in Scranton. The high percentage of draftees who paid the $300 commutation fee suggests that such a plan might have been adopted there as well, though the only local newspaper extant from the war years does not mention one. (Note that the "nationwide" data for Table 2 differ from that for Table 1 because the figures for Table 2 exclude all those who failed to report.) In any case, either by failing to report or by claiming exemptions at a higher rate than natives, immigrants in these thirteen cities—and Irish immigrants in particular—were able to avoid service in the army even more so than native-born citizens, who could more often afford to purchase a substitute if they were not exempted.[5]

Because the majority of draftees avoided service by claiming an exemption, it is worth considering how authorities meted them out. Those whose names were selected on draft day had to appear at the local provost marshal's office for examination in the days or weeks after the draft took place. The draftee would be exempted from service if he was seventeen or younger, forty-five or older, or thirty-five or older and married. He could also claim an exemption if he was

---

5. For the Albany substitute procurement legislation, see the *Albany Evening Journal*, July 21 and 31, 1863. The *Lackawanna Register*, a Democratic organ, does not mention any government program to pay commutation fees in Scranton. For such programs created in New York City and Brooklyn, see *New York Times*, July 28 (2, 4, 5), Aug. 16 (3), Aug. 17 (4), Aug. 20 (8), and Sept. 6 (3), 1863.

the only son (and thus the only supporter) of either a widow or infirm parents, or if he was the father of motherless children. Exemptions were also available for those who already had two brothers in service and for those who had been in uniform on March 3, 1863, the date the draft law was enacted. Draftees could also secure exemptions if they had been convicted of a felony or if they were the only brother of children under the age of twelve (though out of 290,000 drafted in the summer of 1863, only about 150 men successfully claimed either of these last two exemptions).

All the exemption categories mentioned thus far accounted for just 30 percent of the exemptions. Another 14 percent, the second largest category, went to "aliens," immigrants who had not yet become citizens. Not all aliens were exempt from the draft. According to the draft law, even noncitizens had to participate in the conscription if they had previously taken an oath declaring their intention to become citizens, a legal filing that was a prerequisite to naturalization. This clause may have been included in the law because, as Lincoln later stated, the national emergency created the need for every able-bodied person with allegiances to the United States (no matter how new or tenuous) to do his part. But this portion of the law may also have originated from the fear that, in an era when virtually any court could issue a certificate of naturalization and the federal government kept no central repository of those records, immigrants who had in fact become citizens might be able to avoid service by falsely claiming that they were in fact still aliens. Other immigrants could seek this exemption and hope that draft officials would not find out that they had already filed a declaration of intent. It is impossible to determine if immigrants employed such means of deceit to escape service. Whatever the case, the "alienage" exemption clearly enabled thousands of immigrants to avoid the draft.

The final exemption category, accounting for 55 percent of all exemptions in 1863, was for "physical disability."[6] Hernias, limps, badly healed fractures, heart and lung ailments, and nearsightedness were the physical disabilities that most commonly earned draftees exemptions. But the list of additional ailments that could excuse one from service is surprisingly lengthy and diverse. In Boston, for example, several recruits received medical exemptions for "inflamed" or "diseased" testicles. Others were excused because they were considered too short or too weak (a recruit's weakness was sometimes corroborated by recording his abnormally small

6. *War of the Rebellion*, ser. 3, 5:731; Neil C. Kimmons, "Federal Draft Exemptions, 1863-1865," *Military Affairs* 15 (1951): 25-33.

chest measurements). Others were exempted because they were missing too many teeth, presumably because they could not bite open the paper on a cartridge. But the opposite problem could bring one an exemption as well: "excessive obesity" was cited in a number of exemptions. The ability to march was clearly considered a prerequisite for service, as a number of draftees were exempted for ankle and foot problems. "Crooked toes" or even a single disabled toe was enough to earn one an exemption in Boston. One recruit was even excused because he had "tender feet." Hundreds were exempted for a variety of other maladies, including varicose veins, "chronic diarrhea," odd skin growths, syphilis, swollen hemorrhoids, "brain disease," imbecility, and "excessive stammering." With so many options available, it is little wonder that about 40 percent of all draftees who reported for examination were able to procure a medical exemption. (The 55 percent figure reported at the beginning of the paragraph describes the percentage of *exemptions* that were granted on medical grounds.)[7]

By either failing to report or obtaining an exemption, eight out of ten draftees in the urban areas sampled managed to avoid army service. The remaining men had three options: pay the $300 commutation fee, hire a substitute, or enlist. If one sought to avoid service, hiring a substitute was preferable to paying commutation. The person who hired a substitute was excused from service for the length of the substitute's enrollment (three years for the 1863 draft), whereas someone paying the commutation fee was exempted only from that particular draft. That additional drafts were already being contemplated was widely known in the summer of 1863, and three more major drafts calls were subsequently issued—in March, July, and December 1864. Unless one worried about guilt feelings should one's substitute die while serving, it was clearly more advantageous to hire a substitute than to pay commutation.[8]

Why, then, did the Lincoln administration offer the option of commutation at all, since it needed men far more than greenbacks? The commutation clause was inserted in the draft law not to enable the rich to avoid the draft, but to place a cap on the price men would have to pay for substitutes. Clearly chafing at the

---

7. "Descriptive Book of Drafted Men," 4th Massachusetts Draft District, Entry 893, vol. 13, *OR*, ser. 3, 5:731.

8. Circular No. 44 of the Provost Marshal General, July 12, 1863, reprinted in *Albany Evening Journal*, July 14, 1863; Peter Levine, "Draft Evasion in the North During the Civil War, 1863–1865," *Journal of American History* 67 (1981): 819; Geary, *We Need Men*, 81. Some sources indicate that paying the $300 commutation fee relieved the draftee of all future obligations, but Circular No. 44 clearly states otherwise.

negative reaction to the $300 clause, Lincoln composed (though he never sent or published) a rebuttal to the charge that the administration had created the commutation clause to allow the wealthy to avoid military service. Lincoln noted that substitution, "an old and well known practice, ... is not objected to. There would have been great objection if that provision had been omitted." With no choice but to allow substitution, Lincoln argued, "the money provision" had to be added to the draft law in order to be sure that the price of substitutes did not become exorbitant. "Without the money provision," wrote the president, "competition among the more wealthy might, and probably would, raise the price of substitutes above three hundred dollars, thus leaving the man who could raise only three hundred dollars, no escape from personal service. . . . The money provision enlarges the class of exempts from actual service simply by admitting poorer men into it. How, then[,] can this money provision be a wrong to the poor man?"[9]

The available evidence seems to validate Lincoln's reasoning. After the commutation option was eliminated in July 1864, the proportion of draftees able to buy their way out of the army fell from 27 percent in the summer of 1863 to just 13 percent in the summer of 1864. As Lincoln had predicted, the price of substitutes, which had ranged from about $200 to $275 in the summer of 1863, rose to $500 or more by late 1864. In New York and Washington, $800 and even $1,800 payments were not unheard of. Lincoln was right; the commutation clause helped many Northerners avoid military service who could not have done so otherwise.[10]

If this were the case, then why did so many Americans greet the commutation clause with such hostility? Perhaps what Lincoln did not understand was that "the money provision," by allowing both wealthy *and* middling Americans to avoid military service, may have made the poor feel that they were the only socioeconomic group that could not avoid service. The poor may have also resented the commutation clause because it suppressed the price they could command

9. Lincoln, "Opinion on the Draft" [Sept. 1863], in Roy P. Basler, ed., *Collected Works of Abraham Lincoln* (New Brunswick: Rutgers Univ. Press, 1953-55), 6:447-48. Although Lincoln's memorandum was never published, other Republicans echoed his sentiments in public. See, for example, the *New York Times,* Dec. 25, 1863, 4. Also see Carl Sandburg, "Lincoln and Conscription," *Journal of the Illinois State Historical Society* 32 (1939): 5-19.

10. *New York Times,* Aug. 17, 1863; Geary, *We Need Men,* 145; Murdock, *One Million Men,* 266-68. Two most-often cited studies of the fairness of the commutation clause are Murdock, "Was It a 'Poor Man's Fight'?" *Civil War History* 10 (1964): 241-45, and Hugh Earnhart, "Commutation: Democratic or Undemocratic?" *Civil War History* 12 (1966): 132-42; both, however, are problematic. A more sophisticated analysis can be found in Geary, *We Need Men,* 140-50.

for their services as substitutes. We have seen that immigrants, despite their relatively limited economic means, did not have to serve in the army more often than natives as a result of the draft. In fact, they were less likely than natives to be forced into the army. But the newcomers may not have understood this before the draft commenced, which perhaps explains why the North's major draft riots all took place before the results of the first national draft were known.

While urban immigrants were not more likely than natives to have served in the army as a result of the draft, perhaps the draft placed a disproportionate burden on the urban poor in general, regardless of nativity. Unfortunately, the data needed to answer this question are rarely found in the draft registers, as few provost officials bothered to fill in the "occupation" column in their ledger books. Even in the cases where employment data do exist, the evidence is somewhat contradictory. Classifying the socioeconomic ranking of Civil War–era Americans by their occupations is a tricky business, but for this study it was sufficient to choose five popular occupational categories that could roughly translate into economic status. Merchants and lawyers populate the upper end of the spectrum, characterized as high-status "white-collar" workers. (In Boston, merchants alone were sufficient to create a statistically significant grouping, but lawyers had to be added in the remaining cities to obtain a larger, more reliable sample.) Clerks and bookkeepers represent the lower-status white-collar occupation. Artisans are represented by the full spectrum of woodworkers, ranging from shipbuilders and carriage makers to simple coopers and carpenters. The lowest end of the occupational spectrum is represented by menial day laborers.

Predictably, those toward the top of the socioeconomic ladder were more frequently able to buy their way out of the draft than those toward the bottom. More than half of the merchants in Boston and merchants and lawyers in New Haven did so, as did nearly half of the merchants and lawyers in Harrisburg and a third of that group in Springfield. Clerks were also able to buy their way out of the army far more often than manual workers, while woodworkers could do so more frequently than unskilled laborers. But these figures also display some surprising trends. In Boston, for example, though very few manual workers could afford substitutes or commutation, this fact did not force more manual workers into the army. By claiming exemptions and by failing to report, Boston's woodworkers and laborers were able to avoid the army just as readily as more prosperous men. In Rochester, too, those in lower-status occupations were not much more likely to serve as a result of the draft than those in higher-status occupations.[11] Yet the outcome of the draft differed in New Haven, Springfield, and Harrisburg. In those cities, manual workers were much more likely to be held to service than white-collar workers, even though manual workers in those very cities were much more likely than their Boston counterparts to be able to buy their way out of the army.

What explains these incongruities? In Springfield, there seems to have been a shortage of substitutes. The predominantly immigrant laborers there could

Table 3. Draft Results by Occupational Category, Summer 1863

City and Occupation	Failed to Report	Exempt	Paid $300	Hired Substitute	Held to Service	Number Drafted
Boston (Wards 1, 2, 3, 5, 6, 9)						
Merchants	0%	45%	28%	28%	0%	44
Clerks	11%	74%	5%	10%	0.59%	339
Woodworkers	17%	77%	0.51%	5%	0%	198
Laborers	24%	74%	0.51%	1%	0%	394
Harrisburg						
Merchants and Lawyers	0%	53%	21%	26%	0%	19
Clerks	5%	67%	3%	26%	0%	39
Woodworkers	19%	53%	16%	6%	6%	32
Laborers	29%	46%	5%	11%	9%	93
New Haven						
Merchants and Lawyers	0%	38%	4%	58%	0%	26
Clerks	3%	67%	2%	29%	0%	63
Woodworkers	6%	82%	0%	10%	2%	50
Laborers	20%	72%	3%	3%	2%	65
Rochester						
Merchants and Lawyers	N/A	71%	2%	24%	2%	45
Clerks	N/A	76%	1%	20%	2%	85
Woodworkers	N/A	74%	0%	24%	2%	91
Laborers	N/A	84%	0%	12%	3%	73
Springfield, Mass.						
Merchants and Lawyers	N/A	67%	20%	13%	0%	15
Clerks	N/A	63%	30%	8%	0%	40
Woodworkers	N/A	73%	20%	0%	7%	41
Laborers	N/A	94%	4%	0%	1%	72

Source: Springfield data from "Descriptive Book of Drafted Men," 10th Massachusetts Draft District, Entry 981, vol. 17; for the data from other cities, see sources cited for Tables 1 and 2.

11. In Rochester, the one "merchant" held to service was an immigrant "fish merchant," likely fish peddler. It may be that the Rochester draft official who recorded the occupations of the draftees used the term "merchant" more loosely than the recording officials in other cities.

Table 4. Draft Results by Occupational Category and Nativity, Summer 1863

City, Nativity, and Occupation	Failed to Report	Exempt	Paid $300	Hired Substitute	Held to Service	Number Drafted
Boston (Wards 1, 2, 3, 5, 6, 9)						
Native Clerks	10%	72%	5%	11%	0.67%	298
Immigrant Clerks	15%	85%	0%	0%	0%	41
Native Woodworkers	18%	75%	0%	7%	0%	110
Immigrant Woodworkers	15%	81%	1%	2%	0%	86
Native Laborers	17%	80%	0%	3%	0%	70
Immigrant Laborers	25%	74%	0.63%	0.63%	0%	316
New Haven						
Native Clerks	0%	65%	2%	33%	0%	55
Immigrant Clerks	25%	75%	0%	0%	0%	8
Native Woodworkers	5%	73%	0%	20%	3%	40
Immigrant Woodworkers	6%	88%	0%	6%	0%	17
Native Laborers	0%	60%	10%	20%	10%	10
Immigrant Laborers	24%	75%	2%	0%	0%	55
Rochester						
Native Clerks	N/A	70%	2%	25%	3%	64
Immigrant Clerks	N/A	95%	0%	5%	0%	21
Native Woodworkers	N/A	71%	0%	33%	6%	31
Immigrant Woodworkers	N/A	75%	0%	25%	0%	60
Native Laborers	N/A	60%	0%	27%	13%	15
Immigrant Laborers	N/A	90%	0%	9%	0%	58
Springfield						
Native Clerks	N/A	67%	25%	6%	2%	51
Immigrant Clerks	N/A	50%	50%	0%	0%	2
Native Woodworkers	N/A	68%	25%	3%	5%	40
Immigrant Woodworkers	N/A	100%	0%	0%	0%	7
Native Laborers	N/A	75%	17%	0%	8%	12
Immigrant Laborers	N/A	98%	2%	0%	0%	61

Source: Same as those for Tables 1, 2, and 3. There were too few immigrants in Harrisburg for inclusion of that city in this chart with a reliable degree of statistical significance.

compensate either by taking the alienage exemption or failing to report, since their ties to the community were relatively tenuous anyway. Woodworkers, who were much more likely to be native-born and thus more likely to have longer-standing ties to the community, did not always have those options and were more likely to be forced into service. In Harrisburg, in contrast, there were not many immigrants at all. A majority of its laborers were native-born, and many were African Americans. About half of the Harrisburg laborers held to service were black men who, having been previously denied the opportunity to fight, were now probably quite willing to go into the army. The relative paucity of immigrants in Harrisburg may have also driven up the wages of manual workers there, explaining why so many of the city's artisans and laborers could afford commutation or substitutes.

A comparison of the figures in Table 3, which show relatively high rates of draft-induced army service by the least prosperous urban residents, with those from Tables 1 and 2, which show a relatively low rate of draft-related army service among urban immigrants, suggests that native-born urban workers of limited means were likely the only city dwellers disproportionately forced into the army as a result of the draft. Table 4, which offers a comparison of immigrants and natives in the same occupational groups, substantiates this conclusion. The figures in this table are grouped in pairs (native clerks with immigrant clerks, native woodworkers with immigrant woodworkers, etc.) in order to draw the reader's attention to the relevant comparisons. Whether one looks at clerks, woodworkers, or laborers, natives were much more likely than their immigrant coworkers to contribute to the war effort as a result of the draft—either by serving themselves, hiring a substitute, or paying a commutation fee that could be used to pay the bounty of a volunteer. Of all these groups, however, native-born laborers were the only ones consistently held to service at a rate higher than the national average. These workers lacked the economic means to escape service and could not avail themselves of the alienage exemption, as could so many immigrant laborers. But with the exception of that one group, relatively few city dwellers were forced into the army as a result of the draft of 1863.

THE COUNTRYSIDE

Conscription played out somewhat differently in the countryside. As Table 5 illustrates, rural residents of the very draft districts cited above ended up hiring a substitute, paying the commutation fee, or serving themselves as a result of the draft significantly more often than did their urban counterparts. For example, 38 percent of the rural residents of the Second Connecticut Congressional District helped the draft effort in one of these three ways, while only 19 percent of New Haven residents did so. In some draft districts, the disparity between rural and urban contributions was less extreme. In northern Maine, 29 percent of rural draftees contributed to the war effort as a result of the draft, while a respectable 25 percent of Bangor residents did so as well. Residents of rural areas were also more likely than city folk to enter the army themselves as a result of conscription.

In four of the eight districts sampled in fact, country folk were at least twice as likely as their urban counterparts to end up in the army as a result of the draft. In Maine, rural Mainers were nearly three times as likely to be held to service as those living in Bangor, possibly because the hardscrabble farmers of Northern Maine lacked the resources to buy their way out (a shortage of substitutes there probably contributed to this outcome as well). In three of the other four districts, however, rural and urban residents entered the army at about the same rate. Only in rural Berks County were residents less likely than their urban neighbors to enlist in the army as a result of the draft, apparently because the county was so prosperous that nearly half the draftees there could either hire a substitute or pay commutation. One might argue that because the rural districts were populated overwhelmingly by the native-born, it would be more meaningful to compare the rural draftees only to native-born city dwellers (because so many urban immigrants could take the alienage exemption). But a comparison of the statistics in Table 5 with those for natives only in Table 1 indicates that the contributions of rural residents outstripped those of urban natives too, albeit by smaller margins.

One might wonder if there might be a correlation between one's political persuasion and one's propensity to enter the army as a result the draft. Information on the party affiliations of the individuals who were held to service in the districts were not examined in this study. Nor was there an attempt to determine the political leanings of each district sampled. Because the districts considered in this study were chosen because of the quality of their draft ledgers, and not as a result of a research strategy that sought to control for partisan affiliation, it did not seem worthwhile to consider the partisan proclivities of the districts surveyed. Nonetheless, the three rural districts examined in Pennsylvania do allow for a modicum of speculation on the subject. Berks County (in the east-central part of the state) was renowned for consistently returning huge Democratic majorities; Susquehanna County (in northeastern Pennsylvania) was safely Republican; while Juniata County (located in the south-central portion of the state) was just about evenly split between the two parties. Predictably perhaps, Table 5 shows that the held-to-service rate in Democratic Berks County (1 percent) was only one-sixth of that of the rural part of heavily Republican Susquehanna County (6 percent). Yet the proportion held to service in evenly split Juniata County was higher still (9 percent), a fact that calls into question the relevance of partisanship in determining draft results. Furthermore, if one considers all contributions to the war effort one could make as a result of the draft (paying commutation, hiring a substitute, and going into service), a higher percentage of the residents

Table 5. Draft Results Comparing Rural Areas to Cities Within the Same Draft District, Summer 1863

Location	Failed to Report	Exempt	Paid $300	Hired Substitute	Held to Service	Number Drafted
Second Conn. Draft District						
Rural Central Conn.	4%	59%	18%	19%	0.94%	535
New Haven	7%	74%	1%	17%	1%	841
Fourth Maine Draft District						
Rural Northern Maine	29%	42%	8%	7%	14%	847
Bangor	6%	69%	4%	16%	5%	426
First N.H. Draft District						
Rural Southeast N.H.	0.71%	64%	1%	30%	4%	423
Portsmouth	0.70%	69%	2%	26%	2%	286
Fourteenth N.Y. Draft Dist.						
Rural Albany Co., N.Y.	7%	37%	43%	14%	0%	232
Albany	15%	53%	14%	18%	0%	1442
Eighth Pa. Draft District						
Rural Berks Co., Pa.	2%	52%	20%	25%	1%	334
Reading	9%	69%	4%	16%	3%	1046
Fourteenth Pa. Draft Dist.						
Juniata Co., Pa.	9%	50%	27%	5%	9%	371
Harrisburg	17%	55%	9%	13%	4%	485
Twelfth Pa. Draft District						
Rural Susquehanna Co.	8%	48%	33%	4%	6%	510
Scranton	28%	53%	13%	6%	0%	415

Source: "Descriptive Book of Drafted Men," 2d Connecticut Draft District, Entry 1189, vol. 35, subdistricts 9, 10, 11, 14, 16, 20, 23, 25, and 30 (all communities in New Haven and Middlesex counties in which at least 50 percent of the draftees were farmers or farm workers); "Descriptive Books of Drafted Men," 4th Maine Draft District, Entry 559, vol. 38, subdistricts 32-51 (townships in modern-day Aroostook and Piscataquis counties); "Descriptive Book of Drafted Men," 1st New Hampshire Draft District, Entry 645, vol. 14, subdistricts 6-9 (a rural portion of Rockingham County); "Descriptive Book of Drafted Men," 14th New York Draft District, Entry 1881, vol. 19, subdistricts 11-13 (the Albany County towns of Coeymans, Guilderland, and Bern); "Descriptive Book of Drafted Men," 8th Pennsylvania Draft District, Entry 2999, vol. 29, subdistricts 1-9; "Descriptive Book of Drafted Men," 14th Pennsylvania Draft District, Entry 3307, vol. 26, all 1863 Juniata County pages; "Descriptive Book of Drafted Men," 12th Pennsylvania Draft District, Entry 3114, vol. 33, draftees 3200-3700.

of heavily Democratic Berks County (46 percent) contributed than did those in either Republican Susquehanna (43 percent) or evenly split Juniata (41 percent). In this case, economics seems to trump partisanship. Mountainous Juniata was far less prosperous than either Berks or Susquehanna counties. This fact probably explains why a smaller proportion of its residents could hire substitutes or pay the commutation fee, and therefore why more of its residents had to enter the army as a result of the draft.

A first assumption was that farmers were the rural residents who contributed the additional manpower and money to the war effort, but closer examination indicated that there were a lot more nonfarmers living in the countryside than one might imagine. Table 6, which divides the rural population into farmers and nonfarmers, reveals two trends. First, farmers and nonfarmers in most rural locales were held to serve in the army at about the same rate. But if one also considers the hiring of substitutes and the paying of commutation fees, farmers contributed much more to the draft than other rural residents, and much more than the average city dweller. In rural southwest Michigan, for example, 53 percent of draftee farmers paid the commutation fee, hired a substitute, or entered the army, whereas only 38 percent of nonfarming rural residents did so. Farmers in most of the other districts studied contributed to the draft effort in equally high rates. Farmers turn out to be a lot like urban merchants—they could far more readily pay to avoid service than other members of their communities. This fact has been obscured in the past because so many studies have lumped yeoman farmers and menial farm laborers together into a single category. There was apparently more variation in age and wealth among farmers than among urban merchants, however, for while only a single merchant in the five cities sampled by occupational group became a soldier as a result of the 1863 draft, a significant number of farmers (typically younger, possibly less prosperous ones) did enter the army due to conscription.[12]

In the countryside, as in urban areas, menial laborers were the ones most often forced into the army as a result of the draft (see Table 7). Whereas a laborer in a city was most often a construction or transport worker of some sort, in rural America a "laborer" might do that kind of work or might instead be a farmhand. The census and draft records rarely distinguish between the two. As Table 7 indicates, in four of five districts sampled, rural laborers in general were much

---

12. The most thorough and sophisticated study of the draft to date, by James W. Geary, asserts that farmers were the only occupational group significantly overrepresented among the ranks of those forced to serve as a result of the conscription. My findings differ from Geary's because he made the mistake of grouping farmers and farm laborers in a single category. Farm laborers occupied a vastly different socioeconomic rank than the farmers who employed them, and it was these laborers who were most likely to be forced into military service. Geary's method of categorization may have been influenced by the work of James McPherson, who also grouped farmers and farm laborers together in his analysis of army service records. See Geary, *We Need Men*, 92-102; McPherson, *Battle Cry of Freedom*, 608-14.

Table 6. Rural Draft Results Comparing Farmers and Nonfarmers, Summer 1863

Location	Failed to Report	Exempt	Paid $300	Hired Substitute	Held to Service	Number Drafted
Rural North-Central Mass.						
Farmers	1%	71%	15%	9%	3%	286
Nonfarmers	4%	70%	16%	8%	2%	399
Rural Southwest Mich.						
Farmers	N/A	47%	41%	6%	6%	401
Nonfarmers	N/A	61%	26%	7%	6%	218
Rural Southeast N.H.						
Farmers	0%	57%	1%	39%	3%	164
Nonfarmers	0%	68%	0.84%	27%	4%	237
Rural Northeast N.H.						
Farmers	0%	61%	25%	14%	0.36%	279
Nonfarmers	0%	57%	25%	18%	0.61%	163
Rural Dutchess Co., N.Y.						
Farmers	0.5%	50%	47%	3%	0.25%	400
Nonfarmers	2%	68%	27%	2%	0%	291
Rural Berks Co., Pa.						
Farmers	0%	46%	20%	35%	0%	123
Nonfarmers	3%	56%	20%	18%	2%	206
Juniata Co., Pa.						
Farmers	6%	51%	36%	5%	3%	163
Nonfarmers	12%	51%	20%	4%	12%	220
Rural Susquehanna Co.						
Farmers	8%	42%	39%	4%	6%	252
Nonfarmers	9%	54%	27%	4%	6%	249

Source: "Descriptive Book of Drafted Men," 9th Massachusetts Draft District, Entry 964, vol. 20, subdistricts 31-47; "Descriptive Book of Drafted Men," 2d Michigan Draft District, Entry 5992, vol. 27, subdistricts 1-47; "Descriptive Book of Drafted Men," 1st New Hampshire Draft District, Entry 645, vol. 14, subdistricts 6-9 (southeast), 20-24 (northeast, all of Carroll County); "Descriptive Book of Drafted Men," 12th New York Draft District, Entry 1839, vol. 16, subdistricts 2, 3, 5, 6, 8, 11, 14, 20, 22, 23, 29, 30, 33-34, 38-40 (subdistricts in which at least half the men drafted were farmers or farm workers); "Descriptive Book of Drafted Men," 8th Pennsylvania Draft District, Entry 2999, vol. 29, subdistricts 1-9; "Descriptive Book of Drafted Men," 14th Pennsylvania Draft District, Entry 3307, vol. 26, all 1863 Juniata County pages; "Descriptive Book of Men Drafted," 12th Pennsylvania Draft District, Entry 3114, vol. 33, draftees 3200-3700.

more likely than rural nonfarmers to be forced into the army as a result of the 1863 draft. In southwest Michigan, for example, while only 6 percent of rural nonfarmers were forced into the army, 11 percent of rural laborers were held to service. In most of my rural sample areas, there were not enough immigrants to allow for a statistically significant comparison of native-born and immigrant

Table 7. Rural Draft Results Comparing Laborers to All Nonfarmers, Summer 1863

Location	Failed to Report	Exempt	Paid $300	Hired Substitute	Held to Service	Number Drafted
North-central Mass.						
All Nonfarmers	4%	70%	16%	8%	2%	399
Laborers only	10%	82%	6%	0%	2%	94
Southwest Mich.						
All Nonfarmers	N/A	61%	26%	7%	6%	218
Laborers only	N/A	68%	18%	4%	11%	57
Rural Berks Co., Pa.						
All Nonfarmers	3%	56%	20%	18%	2%	206
Laborers only	7%	53%	16%	21%	4%	190
Juniata Co., Pa.						
All Nonfarmers	12%	51%	20%	4%	12%	220
Laborers only	16%	47%	13%	4%	18%	93
Rural Susquehanna Co., Pa.						
All Nonfarmers	9%	54%	27%	4%	6%	249
Laborers only	17%	47%	19%	3%	13%	93

Source: Same as Table 6, with the following exceptions. For north-central Massachusetts (9th Draft District), to ensure enough laborers to create a statistically significant sample, the sample size for laborers was increased by collecting data from subdistricts 31–63, or roughly twice as many subdistricts as were used to create the "all Nonfarmers" category here and in Table 6. For the same reason, sample size was increased when compiling data on southwest Michigan laborers by increasing the sample to include subdistricts 1–61, a sample about 50 percent larger than the one used for the other data. Likewise, the size of the sample for Berks County laborers was increased by two-thirds by expanding the sample to include subdistricts 1–15.

laborers. The one exception was north-central Massachusetts, where native-born laborers were far more likely than immigrant laborers to be held to service.[13]

To make sense of these trends, both urban and rural, one must reconstruct the mind-set of the draftee of 1863. An urban draftee of means had relatively little incentive to fail to report, because he knew he could buy his way out of the army if he failed to qualify for an exemption. This explains why so few white-collar workers dodged the draft. In addition, many of these citizens owed their prosperity to business and community ties that would be destroyed if they fled rather than fight. Manual workers, however, tended to have jobs that were less dependent

---

13. In the north-central Massachusetts sample, two (6 percent) of the thirty-two drafted native-born laborers were held to service, while none of the sixty-two immigrant laborers was forced into the army.

on such connections. This was especially the case for immigrants, whose ties to their communities might be relatively new. Urban manual workers, especially younger, unmarried ones, typically moved each year in search of better housing; those who were single and lived in boardinghouses sometimes moved even more frequently.[14] If they did not have the savings to pay for a substitute, or even if they did barely have enough, these draftees might calculate that it was worth the risk of arrest not to respond to the draft board's call. If they lived in a big city, they could pick up quickly, move to another teeming neighborhood and take another job, knowing it was very unlikely they would ever be found by a provost marshal. They could even move to another city, making the possibility of arrest more remote still. Immigrants also had the option of lying about their citizenship status. Whether foreign or native-born, the city dweller of modest means therefore had, in some senses, even more alternatives available to him than did the well-to-do city dweller, and he was able in most cases to avoid draft-induced military service. Even the impoverished urban immigrant, it turns out, was by no means powerless to prevent his conscription into the army. He had many options, and typically he employed them skillfully in order to avoid being forced into the army.

Those of limited means in the countryside, however, had far fewer options. If a small-town resident failed to report after being drafted, he was much easier to find than a city dweller. It was also far harder for a farmhand to pick up suddenly and find a new job in a new locale, as farmers rarely hired new hands until harvest time. Residents of small towns would also have more difficulty faking medical maladies too, as their ailments (or lack thereof) were more likely to be common knowledge. The native-born rural laborer was therefore the person most likely to be forced into the army as a result of the draft—his was the only group that entered the army at far above the national rate. He was typically physically robust, everyone knew where he lived, and he was not likely to have the savings to enable him to pay someone else to take his place, or even find a substitute if he did have the means. Native-born urban laborers were the other group disproportionately compelled by the draft to enter the army. The expectation that the poor would shoulder an unfair share of the burden resulting from the initial draft thus turned out to be only partially true. Immigrants, even those who dominated the ranks of the menial labor force in eastern cities, were not compelled to contribute disproportionately to the war effort as a result of the

---

14. Kenneth A. Scherzer, *The Unbounded Community: Neighborhood Life and Social Structure in New York City, 1830–1875* (Durham: Duke Univ. Press, 1992), 19–48.

Table 8. First Draft Results in Cities That Did Not Hold a Draft in the Summer of 1863

City, Nativity and Date	Failed to Report	Exempt	Paid $300	Hired Substitute	Held to Service	Number Drafted
Cincinnati, Spring 1864						
Natives	38%	40%	14%	7%	1%	824
Irish Immigrants	42%	44%	11%	2%	1%	520
Germans	29%	40%	23%	6%	1%	1522
Other Immigrants	30%	48%	16%	6%	0.81%	246
Nationwide	24%	36%	29%	8%	3%	113,446
Chicago (Wards 6, 8, 9, and 12), Fall 1864						
Natives	39%	26%	0%	33%	5%	144
Irish Immigrants	57%	29%	0%	13%	1%	229
Germans	38%	30%	0%	23%	10%	261
Other Immigrants	39%	35%	0%	21%	5%	109
Nationwide	29%	47%	.56%	12%	11%	231,918
Milwaukee (Wards 1–4, 6, 8–9), September 1864						
Natives	N/A	65%	0.85%	31%	3%	17
Irish Immigrants	N/A	86%	0%	3%	6%	37
Germans	N/A	42%	0.13%	39%	13%	783
Other Immigrants	N/A	63%	0%	26%	11%	99
Nationwide	N/A	66%	.78%	17%	16%	165,759

Source: "Descriptive Book of Drafted Men," 1st Ohio Draft District, Entry 4559, vol. 8; "Descriptive Book of Drafted Men," 1st Illinois Draft District, Entry 5576, vol. 57; "Descriptive Book of Drafted Men," 1st Wisconsin Draft District, Entry 6172, vol. 3; *War of the Rebellion*, ser. 3, 5:733–35 (for nationwide figures). The Cincinnati totals represent only wards 1–5, 7, 9–11, 13, and 17. For wards 6 and 8, the draft ledger did not list the nativity of the recruits, while the pages in the ledger set aside for wards 14, 15, and 16 were left blank. Of the 38 Cincinnatians from the sampled wards who were held to service in this draft, only 5 went willingly. The other 33 were men who failed to report but were arrested soon afterward by the city's especially vigilant provost marshal. The four Chicago wards examined were the only ones whose draft is recorded in detail in the district's ledger. Milwaukee figures include all wards except 5 and 7, whose draft figures could not be found in the ledger. The Milwaukee figures do not include two Irish immigrants who were arrested in 1865 for failing to report and whose status after arrest was unclear. The total number of men who failed to report in these Milwaukee wards was 647. The "nationwide" figures for Cincinnati and Chicago differ from each other because the Cincinnati draft was part of a relatively small conscription held by only a few states in the spring of 1864. The Chicago draft was held in the fall of that year, when virtually every state conducted a draft. The autumn 1864 draft was also the first conducted after Congress eliminated the option of commutation. The Milwaukee "nationwide" figures differ from the Chicago figures because the Milwaukee ledger did not include the nativity of those who failed to report—therefore, the Milwaukee nationwide figures, like those in Table 2, do not include draftees who did not report.

draft; in fact, in most cases they contributed less (both in terms of joining the army and providing substitutes) than did other drafted Americans.

It is important to acknowledge that there were some significant variations to these trends. In a few cities, such as Lowell and Buffalo, immigrants were held to service at a rate equal to or slightly higher than natives. There were also sometimes great disparities within a single draft district. In the northern Maine hamlet of Golden Ridge, for example, nine of the thirty-eight draftees were held to serve in the army, a proportion four times higher than that of the city with the highest held-to-service rate. Yet in the subdistrict that precedes Golden Ridge in the Maine draft ledger, every one of the fifty-seven draftees failed to report! Such wild variations were most common in isolated rural areas, where substitutes were hard to find, farmers were too poor to pay for commutation, and many undoubtedly believed that their remote residences would protect them from the provost marshals.[15]

There was also variation between drafts. This study has focused on the draft that took place in the summer of 1863 because that was the draft that most often sparked claims of unfairness to the poor. But many states with large immigrant populations were exempt from the draft in 1863 because they had filled their quotas with volunteers. These states were required to hold drafts in 1864, however, and the results do not always comport with the data from 1863. Table 8 presents the results of the first drafts held in Cincinnati, Chicago, and Milwaukee, three Midwestern cities dominated by immigrants. The results in Cincinnati do not differ much from the other cities examined thus far—few residents, no matter what their nativity, were forced into the army as a result of the draft. But in Chicago and Milwaukee, German immigrants entered the army at a much higher rate than natives. It is hard to know how to interpret these figures, though, for when one compares the Chicago and Milwaukee numbers to the national averages, it turns out that the Germans in Chicago and Milwaukee were not being held to service at a particularly high rate. Rather, natives in these cities were entering the army at a rate far below the national average.[16]

---

15. Draft of Aug. 1863, "Descriptive Book of Drafted Men," 4th Maine Draft District, Entry 559, vol. 38, subdistricts 50 (the townships of Madawaska, Daigle, and Dion) and 51 (Golden Ridge). For Lowell and Buffalo, see Tables 1 and 2.

16. At first glance, the rate at which Germans were held to service in Chicago and Milwaukee appears to be quite high, as we have seen that on average 3 percent of draftees were held to service in 1863. But from the summer of 1863 to the fall of 1864, the nationwide failed-to-report rate more than doubled, from 13 percent to 29 percent. Perhaps to compensate, draft officials in 1864 gave far fewer exemptions than they had previously. With the commutation option eliminated and the price of substitutes in the East climbing rapidly, the percentage of draftees held to service in the fall of 1864 was nearly four times higher than in 1863.

The drafts in these three cities were peculiar for other reasons as well. First, almost every person held to service in Cincinnati was put in that position because he was arrested after failing to report. Otherwise, the percentage of citizens forced into service there would have been minuscule. Second, while the proportion of citizens who could buy their way out of the army fell dramatically in most of the country after the option to pay commutation was eliminated for all but conscientious objectors, huge numbers of draftees from all socioeconomic backgrounds were still able to afford substitutes in Chicago and Milwaukee. To understand this anomaly, one needs to remember that immigrants far outnumbered natives in these two cities. With so many noncitizen immigrants in these locales exempt from the draft but willing to serve as substitutes, these towns never experienced the shortage of substitutes that faced so many eastern states in 1864. As a result, while relatively few eastern immigrants hired substitutes or entered the army themselves as a result of the draft in 1863, Germans in these two midwestern cities supplied more than their fair share of recruits and substitutes to the northern cause in 1864.[17]

SUBSTITUTES

In fact, it was the North's substitutes, not its draftees, who were disproportionately immigrants. If this truth has been underappreciated, it is probably because so little is known about the Civil War substitute; there are few other Civil War soldiers about whom we know so little. No books, dissertations, or theses focus on the subject. The first article focusing on substitutes—those in East Texas—only appeared in 2005. One book on the draft does contain a chapter on substitution, but it deals primarily with the mechanics of the system and does not examine who risked their lives in this capacity. The dearth of scholarship on substitutes is especially surprising when one considers that three-quarters of the men who entered the army as a result of the 1863 draft were substitutes.[18]

17. Why the Irish did not contribute as much as the Germans in these cities is unclear. Although the Irish in the West were more likely than those in the East to have the economic means to buy substitutes, they lacked the political motivation to do so.

18. Mary L. Wilson, "Profiles in Evasion: Civil War Substitutes and the Men Who Hired Them in Walker's Texas Division," *East Texas Historical Journal* 43 (2005): 25-38; Murdock, *One Million Men*, 178-96. Mack Walker, "The Mercenaries," *New England Quarterly* 39 (1996): 390-98, focuses on the diplomatic repercussions of a recruitment drive in Germany that brought foreigners to fill the quotas of one Massachusetts draft district. Geary, *We Need Men*, makes only passing reference to substitutes, while Lonn, *Foreigners in the Union Army and Navy*, has a whole chapter on the draft but nothing significant about substitutes.

The federal government mandated that draft officials record the same demographic information for substitutes as for those held to personal service, but, as we have seen, the amount of information actually logged in the draft registers varied enormously, and draft officials were typically even more careless recording information about substitutes than about draftees. Nonetheless, enough draft districts did collect detailed information on their substitutes to allow us to determine what kind of individual became a substitute in the North. Whether one looks in cities or in rural areas, in the East or in the West, substitutes were overwhelmingly foreign-born. In the Fifth Draft District of New York, for example, comprising four wards on the East Side of New York City, immigrants made up 77 percent of the 1863 substitutes, a figure significantly higher than their proportion of the general population. Eighty-four percent of the substitutes hired in the Third Massachusetts Draft District, which comprised half the city of Boston, were also foreign-born, about double the newcomers' representation in the draft-age population there. The same was true in cities with few immigrants. In Concord, New Hampshire, for example, where only 7 percent of the 1863 draftees were foreign-born, 74 percent of the substitutes were immigrants. Even in rural areas with tiny immigrant communities, newcomers also dominated the ranks of the substitutes. In the Eighth Pennsylvania Draft District, where immigrants made up less than 5 percent of the population, the foreign-born constituted 60 percent of the 1863 substitutes. In the Third Draft District of Vermont, another region where very few immigrants lived, they made up 64 percent of the substitutes. And in rural eastern New Hampshire, where the foreign-born population was very small, 77 percent of the 1863 substitutes had been born abroad. Of all the cities examined whose ledgers listed the nativity of substitutes, only Chicago's were not disproportionately dominated by immigrants.[19]

One can imagine how residents of the North's big seaboard cities might have found immigrants to serve as substitutes, but how did those living in rural districts with few foreign-born residents manage to hire them? Recruiting was the predominant method. When residents of rural Deerfield, Massachusetts, could not locate enough substitutes to meet the demand, for example, they found them in Washington, D.C. Towns in New Hampshire hired brokers in Canada

19. "Descriptive Book of Drafted Men," 5th New York Draft District (wards 7, 10, 13, and 14), Entry 1613, vol. 12; "Descriptive Book of Drafted Men," 3d Massachusetts Draft District, Entry 877, vol. 17; "Descriptive Book of Drafted Men," 1st New Hampshire Draft District, Entry 645, vol. 14, subdistricts 6–9 and 20–23; "Descriptive Book of Drafted Men," 8th Pennsylvania Draft District, Entry 2999, vol. 29; "Descriptive Book of Drafted Men," 3d Vermont Draft District, Entry 783, vol. 7; 1st Illinois Draft District, Entry 5576, vol. 57.

to furnish substitutes. Representatives of rural districts had done the same thing earlier in the war in order to find men to fill their voluntary enrollment quotas and the quotas set in local "militia drafts." Newspapers of the era overflowed with advertisements seeking substitutes, and men desiring to hire themselves often traveled great distances to take such work.[20]

In rare cases, the draft ledgers note the residences of substitutes, confirming that the immigrants who dominated the substitutes' ranks often ventured quite far when seeking such employment. For example, only about one in five substitutes hired in 1863 in the 8th Draft District of Pennsylvania in eastern Pennsylvania was a district resident. Another one-fifth lived in other parts of Pennsylvania, but approximately 15 percent had come from Ohio (mostly Cincinnati) to take this work, another 15 percent from New York City, and another 15 percent from Maryland (mostly Baltimore). Some of these Pennsylvania substitutes came from as far as Washington D.C., Indianapolis, Chicago, and Memphis. In the western Massachusetts draft district, where there was a shortage of substitutes, only about one-quarter of those who agreed to serve as substitutes resided in the district. About 15 percent lived in other parts of the Bay State, while approximately 20 percent came from New York State, another 20 percent from the rest of the United States, and another 20 percent from abroad, primarily Canada.[21]

Although a full examination of Northern substitutes does not fall under the purview of this study, one other notable characteristic of Northern substitutes seems worth considering because it relates to the preponderance of immigrants in their ranks: that is, the startling number of sailors who hired themselves out as substitutes. One might not be surprised to find that there were more sailors than followers of any other occupation among substitutes in the port city of Boston. One out of every six substitutes there was a seaman, a figure many times higher than their representation in the city as a whole, and 81 percent of these sailor-substitutes were immigrants.[22]

---

20. Emily J. Harris, "Sons and Soldiers: Deerfield, Massachusetts, and the Civil War," *Civil War History* 30 (1984): 163, 169; Thomas R. Kemp, "Community and War: The Civil War Experience of Two New Hampshire Towns," 52, in Maris A. Vinovskis, ed., *Toward a Social History of the American Civil War: Exploratory Essays* (New York: Cambridge Univ. Press, 1990); Eugene C. Murdock, *Patriotism Limited, 1862–1865: The Civil War Draft and the Bounty System* (Kent, Ohio: Kent State Univ. Press, 1967), 31–33; Murdock, *One Million Men*, 188–195.

21. "Descriptive Book of Drafted Men," 8th Pennsylvania Draft District, Entry 2999, vol. 29; "Descriptive Book of Drafted Men," 10th Massachusetts Draft District, Entry 981, vol. 17.

22. "Descriptive Book of Drafted Men," 3d Massachusetts Draft District, Entry 877, vol. 17. It is generally difficult to determine the number of sailors who might call a city like Boston their home because they were typically at sea when the censuses were taken.

Sailors also made up a disproportionate percentage of the substitutes beyond eastern seaports. In rural eastern New Hampshire, where farmers, laborers, and shoemakers predominated, sailors constituted one-fifth of the substitutes, more than any other occupational grouping. In the state's river towns of Manchester and Concord, where few sailors were drafted, one-third of the substitutes were seamen. In those two towns, three times as many sailors signed up to serve as substitutes as did laborers, the second largest occupational group in the cities' substitute ranks. Even in landlocked Berks County, Pennsylvania, sailors constituted one out of every six substitutes, ranking second there, just behind laborers. In each of these districts, 85 percent of the sailor-substitutes were immigrants. These figures may indicate that we have severely underestimated the economic dislocations that the war caused to Northerners employed in the maritime industry. Or sailors may have been so badly paid that they leapt at the chance to instantly make a large sum of money by hiring themselves out as substitutes.[23]

In the end, then, it turns out to be true that the draft drew disproportionately large numbers of immigrants into the army, but not in the manner previously imagined. Very few immigrants were forced by the draft to serve in the army, and immigrants were much less likely than natives to contribute to the war by hiring a substitute or paying a commutation fee. That the poor were unfairly pressed into service as a result of the conscription is partially true, however, because native-born unskilled workers were disproportionately represented in the ranks of those held to service in 1863. This was true both in urban areas and in the countryside. But in most locales, the rural native-born entered the army more often than their urban counterparts. Rural draftees were also less likely to successfully claim an exemption than urban draftees, less likely to fail to report when drafted, and more likely to hire a substitute or pay the commutation fee.

Immigrants, it turns out, had far more agency in controlling their draft fate than most observers—either then or now—have imagined. The foreign-born skillfully employed a variety of strategies to avoid forcible military service. For some, this merely involved claiming an exemption. For others, it meant taking out loans from friends, neighbors, or co-workers. And for others still, it meant choosing to ignore the draft call and live with the real possibility of arrest and imprisonment (a significant burden that must have weighed heavily on the minds

---

23. "Descriptive Book of Drafted Men," 1st New Hampshire Draft District, Entry 645, vol. 14. "Descriptive Book of Drafted Men," 8th Pennsylvania Draft District, Entry 2999, vol. 29. Many of the sailor-substitutes were deployed in the Union navy, though this fact is not discussed in Michael J. Bennett, *Union Jacks: Yankee Sailors in the Civil War* (Chapel Hill: Univ. of North Carolina Press, 2004).

of those who chose this course). About half the soldiers who entered the army as a result of the 1863 draft were immigrants, but the overwhelming majority of these foreign-born soldiers enlisted voluntarily as substitutes. They *chose* to join the army, gambling that the benefits of substitution fees and enlistment bonuses were worth the risk of disease, injury, or death that might await them.

Immigrants throughout Civil War–era America perceived nativism all around them. They complained of discrimination in housing, in the courts, in the workplace, in politics, and even in the army.[24] The riots that broke out across the North when the draft was implemented, riots instigated primarily by immigrants, indicated that the foreign-born believed that the conscription system would be unfair to them as well. Once the names had been drawn and the case of each draftee considered, however, the result proved far different than the newcomers had imagined. Very few immigrants were forced into the army as a result of the draft. Native-born citizens on the bottom rungs of the North's socioeconomic ladder, especially unskilled workers living in the countryside, were the only ones driven disproportionately into military service by the conscription law. We still know frustratingly little about the 119,954 conscripts and substitutes who agreed to enter the Union army under the Conscription Act of 1863.[25] Understanding their motivations and contributions to the Northern war effort will enable us to better appreciate the complicated means by which Lincoln managed to hold the North and its armies together until they could finally manage to subdue the Southern revolt.

---

24. Kevin J. Weddle, "Ethnic Discrimination in Minnesota Volunteer Regiments During the Civil War," *Civil War History*, ser. 3, 5:730–39.

25. The figure for the total number of soldiers raised by the draft law of 1863 comes from *War of the Rebellion*, ser. 3, 5:730–39.

Welfare, Dissent, and Nationalism

"The Cry of the Sufferers"
The Problem of Welfare in the Confederacy

PAUL D. ESCOTT

The Confederacy has captured the interests of hundreds of historians over the years, yet, some aspects of its history have been neglected. While scores of books deal with the armies, famous generals, and grand issues of strategy and government policy, relatively few probe the internal problems which plagued the South.[1] During the war, southern society underwent a severe testing which brought many latent conflicts to the surface. Bitter controversies and class resentments often prevailed on the homefront. Mass poverty gripped southerners in an ever-tightening vise. Many of the South's oldest traditions crumbled before unprecedented forces, and southerners embraced a cluster of new ideas in an effort to solve their problems. This inner story, the internal history of the Confederacy is important, for it can teach us much about the southern social and political systems.

One of the most crucial factors in this inner history is the existence of poverty in the Confederacy. In addition to its external problems, the new nation

---

The quotation in the title is from the Edgefield, S.C., *Advertiser*, November 12, 1862. A slightly different version of this chapter was presented by the author at the Duquesne History Forum in October, 1975.

1. Among the best of those which do are: Bell Irvin Wiley, *The Plain People of the Confederacy* (Baton Rouge, 1943); Charles W. Ramsdell, *Behind the Lines in the Southern Confederacy*, edited with an introduction by Wendell H. Stephenson (Baton Rouge, 1944); and Emory M. Thomas, *The Confederacy as a Revolutionary Experience* (Englewood Cliffs, N.J., 1971).

faced a major welfare problem. As southerners struggled against destitution, they revealed interesting facets of their political values, and as the problem remained unsolved, its effects spread widely and influenced other events. This chapter attempts to accomplish two things: first, to present some new findings on Confederate welfare activities; and second, to show that the problem of welfare was a central problem in the Confederacy, one which boiled up from the lowest levels of society to affect politics at high levels. Specifically, the chapter will suggest that many state rights controversies in the latter part of the war actually had their origin in the problem of welfare.

The Civil War caused major dislocations in the southern economy and plunged hundreds of thousands of Confederate citizens into poverty. The causes of this domestic disaster were many. For years the South had depended on northern or European manufacturers for its supply of many commodities, and the Federal blockade threw an unprepared region back onto its own resources. Within the South, the system of transportation and distribution was gravely deficient, so much so that perishable foods rotted at depots and many supplies which were available never reached their destination. Speculation and hoarding were also a problem. From the first days of the war greedy speculators snapped up stocks of scarce items in order to make immense profits later, and frightened citizens hoarded food.[2] Naturally the tremendous destructiveness of the war also had a severe impact on the South.

But when one descends from the level of macro-economics to the level of individuals, one finds that the reason for a great amount of poverty was simple: there was a serious shortage of labor in many communities and families, particularly in non-slaveholding rural areas. An early warning of this problem came at the outset of the war. Artisans and craftsmen played key roles in a rural society, and the War Department was inundated with petitions seeking the discharge of craftsmen who had volunteered. Citizens explained that they needed their blacksmith, who kept farming tools in repair, or their miller, who ground their grain into flour and meal, or their tanner, wheelwright, or potter.[3] Conscription

---

2. See Mary Elizabeth Massey, *Ersatz in the Confederacy* (Columbia, S.C, 1952), pp. 17, 20–21.

3. For example see Wm. B. Mason and forty-five others to Jefferson Davis, received Sept. 20, 1861, Letters Received, Confederate Secretary of War, 1861–1865, letter # 5555-1861, National Archives Microfilm Publication M 437, roll 10, frames 160–62 (hereafter cited in the form, M 437, 10/160–62). Similar letters may be found in M 437, 23/0523–0526, 25/398–404, 34/1–2, 39/1914–1917, 44/44–51, 47/1226–1231, 50/644–647, 63/976–980, and 66/754–760.

aggravated this problem, and it brought suffering directly into many homes. Non-slaveholding yeomen families often depended on one man—the husband, father, and breadwinner. When the man from such a family went into the army, the woman left behind had more work to do than any single individual could manage. With children to supervise and household chores to perform, she found that she could not grow enough to support herself and her children. A Georgia woman appealed to the Secretary of War to discharge her husband because, "I can't manage a farm well enough to make a surporte," and an elderly parent in Virginia wrote of his son, "if you dount send him home I am bound to louse my crop and cum to suffer."[4] Help from neighbors and children could not remedy the situation, and poverty descended on untold thousands of family farms.

The extent of suffering was staggering. Before the end of 1861 newspapers everywhere expressed outrage at rising prices and asked how poor people were supposed to survive. By September, 1862, the *Atlanta Daily Intelligencer* bleakly observed that "want and starvation are staring thousands in the face."[5] In 1863 a journal in the hill country of Georgia ran a headline which bluntly asked, "What shall we do for something to eat?"[6] Throughout the South editors admonished their readers to "Relieve the Destitute" or "Think of the Poor."[7] State leaders testified that the reports of privation were not exaggerated. Governor Vance of North Carolina wrote that conscription had swept off "a large class whose labor was, I fear, absolutely necessary to the existence of the women and children left behind," and South Carolina's Governor Bonham opposed the call-up of state troops from a non-slaveholding region on the grounds that it would cause "great suffering next year, and possible starvation."[8] Some idea of the dimensions of poverty can be grasped from the fact that at the end of the war more than a quarter of Alabama's white citizens were on relief.[9] To these should be added

---

4. Mrs. L. Bonnel to Seddon, May 4, 1864, and Joseph B. Bowles to Gov. Letcher of Virginia, Sept. 12, 1861, Letters Received, Confederate Secretary of War, 1861-1865, letters # 395-B-1864 and 5336-1861, M 437, 120/508-10 and 10/163-64.

5. Atlanta, *Daily Intelligencer*, Sept. 4, 1862. See also the Edgefield, S.C., *Advertiser* of Mar. 5, 1862 for this comment: "The duties of war have called away from home the sole supports of many, many families.... Help must be given, or the poor will suffer."

6. Rome, Ga., *Weekly Courier*, Nov. 12, 1863.

7. Atlanta *Daily Intelligencer*, Mar. 20, 1863, and Edgefield, *Advertiser*, Oct. 8, 1862.

8. Vance to Jefferson Davis, Mar. 31, 1863, *OR:* Ser. IV, Vol. II, 464-65; Bonham to James Seddon, June 2, 1864, *Ibid.*, Ser. I, Vol. XXXV, Pt. II, 519-20.

9. From a message of the Governor of Alabama, quoted in *Appleton's American Annual Cyclopedia*, 1865, p. 16. The author has found no evidence of blacks on the relief rolls in the Confederacy.

untold numbers of free blacks and slaves who apparently did not receive a share of the insufficient relief materials available.

Such problems produced desperation and a determined search for solutions. Sudden poverty was a shock to the formerly self-reliant yeomen, and it caused many changes. For one thing, class resentments grew rapidly. Accustomed by years of pro-slavery rhetoric to the idea that all whites were equal, common citizens asked why they should have "to suffer while the rich has aplenty to work for them," and spokesmen for the yeomen demanded that the "wealthier classes ... practice, for awhile, the rigid self-denial that the poor are compelled to practice."[10]

More to the point here, harsh realities wrought a transformation of traditional political values. Abandoning ideas of limited government, southerners demanded that the authorities undertake new responsibilities and provide relief.[11] Newspapers urged the Confederate government to combat rising prices by passing a law against speculation.[12] One journal, the *Atlanta Daily Intelligencer*, even declared that it would "bless the day" when martial law was declared, since military authorities often established a system of price regulation.[13] Ordinary citizens, in their letters to the Richmond administration, revealed that they expected the Confederacy to take control of many areas of life and regulate the economy for the common good. Numerous letters assumed that the central government was operating the railroads, although it had taken care to leave them in private hands.[14] Early in 1862, when the War Department seized scarce grain from a large distillery in Richmond, public support was enthusiastic. A Virginia Congressman who visited his constituency at this time wrote that he "found the People from Richmond to this place proclaiming with one Voice ... that the Government has taken a step in the right direction" and that they wanted this policy extended to "all things which enter in to the Consu[m]ption of our Army and the families."[15] A Georgian who read about the action in Richmond promptly wrote the War Department and urged the administration to take the same step

---

10. Elizabeth Leeson to Seddon, July 22, 1863, Letters Received, Confederate Secretary of War, 1861-1865, letter # 299-L-1863, M 437, 100/664-666; Rome *Weekly Courier*, Oct. 31, 1862.

11. Charles W. Ramsdell was one of the first to recognize the significance of this transformation. See Ramsdell, *Behind the Lines in the Southern Confederacy* (Baton Rouge, 1944), pp. 40 and 82.

12. *Daily Richmond Examiner*, Dec. 1, 1862.

13. Atlanta *Daily Intelligencer*, Apr. 6, 1862.

14. See Letters Sent, Confederate Secretary of War, 1861-1865, M, 522, r 11 5.

15. Fayette McMullen to Gov. John Letcher of Virginia, Feb. 17, 1862, Historical Society of Pennsylvania.

in his state and county to avert a shortage of bread.[16] Newspapers in South Carolina and Georgia also greeted such actions with praise or captions reading "Well done! Well done!"[17] Relief, not political principles, was paramount in the minds of many suffering southerners, and they wanted all levels of government to use their powers to respond to people's needs.

The states responded quickly; indeed, they established during the war the most extensive system of welfare which the South had ever had. Initially the states passed laws to suspend the collection of debts and allowed soldiers certain exemptions from taxes. Between November, 1861, and March, 1862, seven southern states adopted relief laws. These first measures typically relied on county governments to distribute funds raised by a special tax, and the counties selected agents who began a long struggle against poverty. When it became apparent that the counties could not handle the task alone, most of the legislatures assumed additional responsibilities for relief.[18] The lawmakers passed appropriations ranging up to $6,000,000 and redoubled their search for revenue. In some cases they adopted a tax-in-kind and distributed food as well as money—in 1863 Georgia's legislature purchased 97,500 bushels of corn to be distributed to the poor in sixteen hard-hit counties.[19] State governments also bought scarce items such as salt, medicines, cloth, and cotton and wool cards.[20]

Nor was this all. The states also limited cotton production and encouraged the planting of food crops, prohibited distilling to conserve corn, and offered inducements to citizens who would manufacture needed items. When such inducements failed, some governors turned the penitentiaries into factories and manufactured cloth, shoes, baking soda, and medicines. Louisiana's Governor Henry Allen displayed special ingenuity in establishing state-run factories, and the executives of North Carolina and Georgia led the way in developing export-import operations which provided their states with goods that were in short supply.[21] As a result of these vigorous efforts, the states were able to mitigate the suffering among their citizens, and state leaders won a great reserve of gratitude.

---

16. H. Hall to Judah Benjamin, Feb. 21, 1862, Letters Received, Confederate Secretary of War, 1861-1865, letter # 56-H-1862, M 437, 50/174-75.
17. Edgefield *Advertiser*, Mar. 12, 1862, and Atlanta *Daily Intelligencer*, Feb. 16, 1862.
18. Ramsdell, *Behind the Lines*, pp. 25 and 62-67.
19. *Acts of the General Assembly of the State of Georgia Passed in Milledgeville at the Annual Session in November and December, 1863; also Extra Session of 1864* (Milledgeville, 1864), pp. 8 and 67.
20. May Spencer Ringold, *The Role of the State Legislatures in the Confederacy* (Athens, 1966), p. 80.
21. *Ibid.*, pp. 48-52.

What of the Confederacy? What was its response to the problem of widespread poverty? Until now, historians have concluded that the Confederacy played no part in relief operations. E. Merton Coulter, who wrote the volume on the Confederacy for the distinguished History of the South series, flatly asserted that the central government played no role whatsoever. "Although ... state and local governments aided relief," says Coulter, "the Confederate government never dared to venture into that field."[22] There is evidence, however, that the Richmond administration definitely was involved in relief activities, and although the data are not complete, this paper will describe these activities and attempt a preliminary estimate of their significance.

The Confederacy approached the problem of poverty in an indirect way, with many halting steps. Jefferson Davis and his administration were slow to recognize poverty as a major internal problem which demanded their attention, and they tended to respond to it in a piecemeal way. Not until the latter stages of the war did the administration develop a system capable of providing substantial aid to the poor. As a result, the relief activities of the central government evolved gradually and took many different forms.

Sometimes the Confederacy merely supported private charity. On behalf of a committee of ministers, for example, who were trying to obtain wood and coal for the poor of Richmond in December, 1862, Secretary of War James Seddon wrote to the president of the Richmond and Danville Railroad and urged him to do whatever he could to further the ministers' goal.[23] Deterioration of the South's railroads eventually forced the War Department to stop supporting private shipments by rail, but officials did grant other privileges to charities. In 1863 Secretary Seddon assured citizens' relief associations in Columbus, Georgia, and Fayetteville, North Carolina, that he would exempt from impressment all supplies which they purchased for the poor and the families of soldiers. Seddon required them, however, to limit purchases to a "reasonable amount of supplies" and to guard against "the abuses to which such permits is liable."[24]

In certain cases—and those probably were few in number—the government exempted men from service so that they could go home and farm their own land.

---

22. E. Merton Coulter, The *Confederate States of America, 1861-1865* (Baton Rouge, 1950), p. 424.

23. Seddon to Lewis E. Harvie, Dec. 12, 1862, Letters Sent, Confederate Secretary of War, 1861-1865, M 522, 5/181. In this letter Seddon did not waive the government's claim for priority on shipments.

24. For example, see Seddon to Congressman Hines Holt, Apr. 22, 1863, and Seddon to G. W. Williams, Nov. 5, 1863, Letters Sent, Confederate Secretary of War, 1861-1865, M 522, 7/36-37 and 8/384.

In December, 1862, President Davis suspended conscription in a mountainous section of North Carolina where hunger threatened, and he once urged Mississippi's governor to allow 200 state militia men to return to their homes for the spring planting.[25] The Exemption Act of May 1, 1863, gave Confederate officials another means to alleviate individual cases of poverty, for one clause of that act authorized the President to grant exemptions "in districts . . . deprived of white or slave labor indispensable to the production of grain or provisions" and when required by "justice, equity, and necessity."[26] According to the Assistant Secretary of War, this power was used to aid the destitute or large families which had several members in service.[27]

The Confederate government also provided direct relief. The exemption law of February 17, 1864, enabled the Richmond administration to earmark certain amounts of food for relief of the poor. Under this law the Confederate Congress attempted to reduce popular resentment over the exemption of overseers by requiring planters who wished to keep their overseers to furnish a certain quota of food to the government. Planters had to promise under bond that they would supply meat in the ratio of 100 pounds of bacon and 100 pounds of beef for each ablebodied slave. This meat plus surplus grain and other provisions had to be sold to the government or to soldiers' families at established, low prices. In addition this act gave the President and his Secretary of War broad discretionary authority to exempt or detail individuals "on account of public necessity, and to insure the production of grain and provisions for the army and the families of soldiers."[28]

Armed with this law, the Confederate government assumed a responsibility for providing food to feed the poor. In August, 1864, the War Department instructed its commissaries to purchase no more than half of the surplus from bonded planters "and to leave the remainder for the persons who purchase on behalf of the families of soldiers."[29] County relief agents looked to the government to provide food for the poor from this source, and disabled veterans or

---

25. Governor Vance to Davis, Dec. 19, 1862, *OR*, Ser. IV, Vol. II, 246-48, and Vol. III, 845-47; Davis to Governor Pettus, Apr. 4, 1863, in Dunbar Rowland (ed.), *Jefferson Davis: Constitutionalist; His Letters, Papers, and Speeches*, (Jackson, Mississippi, 1923), V, 468.

26. An Act to repeal certain clauses . . . , in James Matthews, (ed.), *Statutes at Large of the Confederate States of America, third session, first Congress, 1863* (Richmond, 1864), pp. 158-159.

27. James A. Campbell to Representatives W. P. Chilton and David Clopton, Jan. 29, 1864, Letters Sent, Confederate Secretary of War, 1861-1865, M. 522, 7/41-42,

28. Matthews (ed.), *Statutes at Large*, fourth session, first Congress, 1863-1864, pp. 211-15.

29. General Orders, No. 69, 1864, issues on Aug. 27, 1864, in General Orders of the Confederate Adjutant and Inspector General's Office, 1861-1865, T 782, 1/301-02 (hand-numbered frames within 1864).

soldiers' wives rejoiced when they received permission to purchase from the bonded planters.[30] As a general rule, only large producers obtained exemptions to raise provisions under the 1864 act, but a ledger of agricultural details in Virginia revealed that a small proportion of the bonded farmers probably were poor men. This record book described the reason for their exemption as "Care of Private Necesity," their bond was small, and only if they produced a surplus did they have to furnish food to the government.[31]

The Confederate activity which held the most potential for relief related to the tax-in-kind. In April, 1863, Congress passed a law which empowered the government to take a tenth of most kinds of farm produce. The purpose of this law was to provide food for the armies, and the government established a corps of new officials to administer the law. The Treasury Department appointed 1,440 appraisers, and the War Department dispatched 2,965 agents throughout the South to collect the crops.[32] For each state the President appointed a Controlling Quartermaster to oversee the collection of the tax-in-kind, and under him were several post quartermasters, one for each congressional district. Directing the entire operation from Richmond was Assistant Quartermaster General Larkin Smith. In only a few months this organization began to function, and the Confederacy collected great quantities of food from the South's farmers. Smith reported that from July through November, 1863, his agents accumulated crops valued at $5,189,087.25, and Smith anticipated even larger collections in the future.[33] Ironically, it was the efficiency of the tax-in-kind agents which drew the Confederacy into relief activities.

By 1863 county relief agents had reached their wits' end trying to feed the poor. The county courts had raised taxes, raided the school funds, and issued large quantities of bonds, but then they found that they could no longer obtain food. The Clerk of Superior Court in Wayne County, North Carolina for example,

30. Wm. M. Hannah to Seddon, Letters Received, Confederate Secretary of War, 1861-1865, letter # 427-H-1864, M 437, 130/351-55; James Rivers to Seddon, Nov. 4, 1864, letter # 242-R-1864, M 437, 140/178-80.

31. "Agricultural Detail Book, Virginia, 1864-1865," Record Group 109, ch. I, vol. 236, National Archives, Washington, D.C. Of the 454 cases enumerated in this ledger, 17 were noted "Care of Private Necessity," and several more which did not have this description carried such small bonds that the individuals involved probably were small farmers.

32. For the text of the law, see Matthews (ed.), *Statutes at Large*, third session, first Congress, 1863, pp. 115-26; Paul P. Van Riper and Harry N. Scheiber, "The Confederate Civil Service," *Journal of Southern History*, XXV, (Nov., 1959), 454-57.

33. C.S.A., War Dept., "Communication from the Secretary of War," (transmitting a report by the Assistant Quartermaster General in charge of the tax-in-kind, Larkin Smith), Jan. 19, 1864, Library of Congress, Rare Book Room.

reported that "the Agents who were appointed by the Court to purchase food for the families of soldiers in this county have been unable to purchase an adequate supply of corn." Officials in nearby Duplin County found that "no corn or other grain can be obtained."[34] Suddenly, through the operation of the tax-in-kind, the Confederate government held great quantities of food and was the obvious source to which to turn. From first one state and then another, local officials applied to the Secretary of War for permission to buy some of the tax-in-kind. They asked also to pay only the prices established as fair by the assessors who worked under the impressment act, for these prices were far below the level of the market.[35] The Georgia legislature endorsed this idea and called on its governor to pressure the Richmond administration into cooperating with the plan.[36]

At first Secretary of War Seddon refused to sell any of the tax-in-kind for relief purposes because he feared that to do so would reduce army rations and stimulate "numberless applications" which he could not meet.[37] But within a month he relented, and on November 27, 1863, he directed officials from two counties in North Carolina to apply to that state's Controlling Quartermaster for aid.[38] Larkin Smith drew up regulations which authorized the Controlling Quartermaster in each state to sell food to county authorities who would certify that the food was needed for the poor and could be obtained in no other way.[39] It is clear that under this system the Confederacy extended some aid at least until the fall of 1864, for in September of that year the Controlling Quartermaster of Alabama set aside 10,000 bushels of corn "for the use of the indigent soldiers families of Randolph County."[40] Unfortunately, the extent of this system cannot

34. Wayne County, N.C., Clerk of Superior Court, Minutes, Court of Pleas and Quarter Sessions, Jan. 14, 1864, p. 416; Duplin County, N.C., Minute Docket, Court of Pleas and Quarter Sessions, Jan. 1864, p. 557, North Carolina Department of Archives and History, Raleigh, N.C. Similar information is in the court minutes for Cumberland, Johnston, Sampson, and Wake Counties.

35. C.S.A., War Dept., "Communication from the Secretary of War," (transmitting a report by the Assistant Quartermaster General in charge of the tax-in-kind, Larkin Smith), Jan. 19, 1864, p. 4, Library of Congress, Rare Book Room.

36. *Acts of the General Assembly of the State of Georgia . . . November and December, 1863; also Extra Session of 1864*, p. 109. The date of this resolution is Nov. 18, 1863. Two days earlier the legislature passed a similar resolution requesting Georgia's congressmen to work for the same object.

37. Seddon to Gov. Bonham of S.C., Oct. 16, 1863, *OR*, Ser. IV, Vol. II, 875-877.

38. Seddon to S. W. Cole, and Seddon to Wm. E. Draughon, Nov. 27, 1863, Letters Sent, Confederate Secretary of War, 1861-1865, M 522, 8/147-148.

39. C.S.A., War Dept., Instructions to be observed by officer and agents receiving the tax-in-kind, March 29, 1864, Library of Congress, Rare Book Room. See especially p. 13.

40. Receipt signed on Sept. 30, 1864, by Major George W. Jones, Controlling Quartermaster of the state of Alabama, among Major Jones' records in Compiled Service Records of Confederate and General Staff Officers, & Nonregimental Enlisted Men, National Archives Microfilm Publication 331, Roll 143.

be determined, for the tax-in-kind records of the Confederate government appear to have been lost.[41]

For a number of reasons, however, it seems unlikely that the Confederacy was able to meet the needs of its citizens through relief based on the tax-in-kind. First, it is important to note that under Larkin Smith's regulations the maximum amount of food which could be sold to any county was merely the amount which that county had furnished as tax.[42] This did little to solve the problem of reduced production. Harvests fell severely in many nonslaveholding counties due to a shortage of labor, unfavorable weather, or the destruction of war. Selling back the tax-in-kind would not make up the deficiency. Second, as the military situation grew more desperate, the Confederate government had to subordinate virtually all its efforts to supplying and strengthening the army, and its relief activities probably suffered as a result. In February, 1864, for example, Congress empowered the army to take up to half of any family's yearly supply of meat. The next month the War Department refused to sell any bacon from the tax-in-kind to a county in Virginia.[43] With such stringent measures in effect, it is unlikely that the government was releasing much food for relief. An earlier study detailing the situation in one state concluded that local officials were unable to obtain the food they needed from whatever source.[44]

The records of Orange County, North Carolina, furnish an example of the inadequacy of Confederate aid. Hard-pressed county officials were struggling against rising prices and scarce crops when Larkin Smith inaugurated Confederate relief from the tax-in-kind later in 1863. County's officials quickly took advantage of this system, and a modest amount of grain was distributed to the poor through

---

41. In the National Archives the tax-in-kind records are not found with the records of the Quartermasters Department, where they should be filed, and neither the author nor a member of the Archives staff could locate them. Relevant documents which did come to light were scattered among correspondence of the War Department or in the Compiled Service Records of the Controlling Quartermasters. Some relevant documents may also be scattered among state archives, and the author will be happy to supply details to other researchers.

42. C.S.A., War Dept., Instructions to be observed by officers and agents receiving the tax-in-kind, March 29, 1864, p. 13, item 84, Library of Congress, Rare Book Room.

43. General Orders of the Confederate Adjutant and Inspector General's Office, 1861–1865, General Orders, No. 39, 1864, March 24, 1864, T 782, 1/96–97 (hand-numbered frames within 1864); E. Burk to J. F. Johnson, Mar. 5, 1864, Letters Received, Confederate Secretary of War, 1861–1865, letter # 288-B-1864, M 437, 120/146–148.

44. William Frank Entrekin, Jr., "Poor Relief in North Carolina in the Confederacy," unpublished master's thesis, Duke University, 1947, pp. 102 and 105. See also pp. 22–26. Entrekin was unaware of any Confederate relief measures.

the first three months of 1864. The Confederacy also allowed Orange County to "borrow" this grain and pay for it at a later date. But by the end of 1865, the supply of aid had dried up. Harvests were poor, reducing any surplus, and the Controlling Quartermaster for North Carolina proved less sympathetic than he had been before. Despite the fact that county agents had scoured the state for grain and had been trying to buy supplies in South Carolina for a year, Major Fuiger directed the county to renew its search in eastern North Carolina. There county agents found that the Confederacy was taking "three fourths of all the surplus corn... for the use of the Army." This fact and Union military action "absolutely close[d] the corn market." With no alternatives left, Orange County could only renew its plea in the name of 600 women and 800 children who needed food.[45]

The effects of the South's unsolved welfare problems were widespread. One of these was to generate state rights controversies, which increased markedly in 1864 and seemed more broadly based and defiant than at any previous period in the war. This resurgence had its origin in the poverty and suffering which gripped the South rather than in differences over constitutional theory. As Frank Lawrence Owsley showed many years ago there were real conflicts over constitutional theory in the early days of the Confederate government. But the experience of war soon led southerners to make "a complete break with their traditions and their whole political philosophy" and to demand that government assume new responsibilities. Strong action to meet the South's crisis and help the needy won the approval of most Confederates.[46] By 1864 both the Richmond administration and the states had left narrow ideas of limited government far behind. Though neither had found a solution to the deteriorating conditions of life, the states continued to try, and in this simple desire to relieve their hard-pressed citizens, state leaders often found themselves opposing the programs of the central government. The Davis administration constantly demanded more from people who had given their all, and frequently the states alone could protect such people from utter destitution. Responding to their constituents' needs, state leaders attempted to shield their citizens from further sacrifice, and when they

---

45. See "County Corn Regulations," Dec. 11, 1863; reports from Millers in the county; minutes of meeting of County Court, Jan. 4, 1865; statement by W. Strayhorn, CSA Commissary Agent, Dec. 14, 1864; minutes of Jan. 4, 1865, meeting, all in Orange County, Provisions for Families of Soldiers, 1863–1865, North Carolina Division of Archives and History.

46. Ramsdell, *Behind the Lines*, p. 40. See also John Brawner Robbins, "Confederate Nationalism: Politics and Government in the Confederate South, 1861–1865," (Ph.D. dissertation, Rice University, 1964) and Curtis Arthur Amlund, *Federalism in the Southern Confederacy* (Washington, D.C.: 1966).

came into conflict with Confederate programs, they raised the familiar cry of state rights as justification. Thus, the quarrels over state rights in 1864 were a symptom of the welfare problem rather than an independent cause of difficulties.

The controversy over shipping regulations provided a clear example of this situation. To gain more vital materials, the Davis administration claimed one-half of the space on all outgoing ships, except those owned completely by the states.[47] Unfortunately, the states customarily leased ships rather than owning them, and several governors relied on the cargoes of these ships to supply the needy among their constituents. When the central government took the space for its cargo, state relief programs suffered. As the Atlanta *Daily Intelligencer* pointed out, Davis' regulations hurt Georgia, Mississippi, Alabama, and North Carolina.[48] The governors of these states organized a protest against the Confederate regulations on the grounds that they infringed state rights. An angry controversy ensued with abundant state rights rhetoric, but the crux of the matter was the welfare problem.[49]

Other issues which had their roots in the problem of poverty also ranged state executives against the central government. During 1864 the governors of North and South Carolina opposed further calls for troops because they feared that these calls would inevitably produce suffering. In this case, Governor Vance of North Carolina resorted to constitutional arguments and asserted the power of his state legislature to stop enrollments.[50] Distilling also brought governors into conflict with the Richmond administration. With hunger widespread, southerners were enraged that scarce corn was used to make whiskey for the armies, and state officials invoked state laws against the practice. Three governors pressed their laws against Confederate authority in an effort to save food for the poor.[51]

The clearest example of the way welfare problems generated state rights rhetoric came from Alabama. Thomas Watts, an Alabama leader, had served for eighteen months as Jefferson Davis' Attorney General, and in that office he issued several legal opinions which expanded the powers of the administration

---

47. *OR*, Ser. IV, Vol. III, 10-11, 28-29, 42-43, 113-14, 78-80, 80-82, 303-04, 380-81, 439, 442, 928-29, 948-53.

48. Atlanta *Daily Intelligencer*, July 1, 1864.

49. See the sections of *OR* cited in footnote 37 plus Rowland (ed.), *Jefferson Davis*, VI, 297-98, 336, 400-01, and James D. Richardson, (ed.), *A Compilation of the Messages and Papers of the Confederacy, Including the Diplomatic Correspondence, 1861-1865*, (Nashville, 1906), I, 466-70 and 505-13. Governors Brown and Vance led the challenge.

50. *OR*, Ser. I, Vol. XXXV, Part II, 519; *ibid.*, Ser. IV, Vol. III, 307.

51. *Ibid.*, Ser. IV, Vol. III, 23-24 and 875-80.

and stressed the supremacy of the national government.[52] Then, late in 1863, Alabama voters chose Watts as their governor, and by 1864 he reemerged as a champion of state rights. Watts opposed further enrollment of troops because it would damage agricultural production. He accused the Confederacy of taking old men and young boys "from their crops . . . and placing them in camps to do nothing, and let their crops be destroyed."[53] Watts also tried to preserve exemptions for some of his state's citizens, although he knew these weren't allowed. Each time he blustered about state rights and even threatened to "resist . . . with all the forces of the state."[54] Here again, internal problems were emerging in the guise of state rights.

The poverty which gripped the South was a central problem for Confederate leadership, for its effects were myriad. Southerners both inside and outside the government knew that soldiers' anxiety about their families contributed greatly to the desertion which decimated the armies. Widespread poverty powerfully stimulated the disaffection which grew throughout the war and always was strongest in the hilly, non-slaveholding regions. Class consciousness sprang up among the yeomen as their standard of living fell precipitously. In fact, a host of significant developments inside the Confederacy lead back to the welfare problem, for it is a key to the internal history of wartime South.

---

52. Rembert W. Patrick, *Jefferson Davis and his Cabinet* (Baton Rouge, 1944), p. 306.
53. *OR*, Ser. IV, Vol. III, 463-64.
54. *Ibid.*, pp. 820 and 848.

Dissent in the Confederacy
The North Carolina Experience

Marc W. Kruman

Since 1925, when Frank L. Owsley published his seminal book, *State Rights in the Confederacy*, historians have been aware that white southerners during the Civil War were not a united people fighting selflessly to preserve a way of life. Owsley identified substantial opposition to the Confederate government among state rights advocates. He believed that in order for the Confederacy to mount a successful war effort, it needed to centralize decision-making. But the insistence of southern politicians that their cherished theories of state rights be implemented caused constant bickering between the Confederate and state governments and ultimately paralyzed the Confederate war effort. In the end, Owsley concluded, the Confederate States of America "died of state rights."[1]

Other historians have emphasized different reasons for popular hostility to the Confederate government. Albert Burton Moore, for example, pointed to the disaffection that grew out of the enactment of the conscription laws. Georgia Lee Tatum catalogued a number of causes of disloyalty in the Confederacy: persistent unionism, the conscription laws, impressment, the tax-in-kind, the suspension of the writ of habeas corpus, and the economic suffering caused by the war. Bell I. Wiley suggested that class legislation, like the exemption from

---

1. Frank L. Owsley, *State Rights in the Confederacy* (1925; reprint ed., Gloucester, Mass., 1961), esp. p. 1.

the draft of a man to oversee twenty or more slaves, generated discontent among "plain folk."[2]

Such interpretations dwell upon the symptoms of dissent in the Confederacy but overlook the underlying causes. They virtually ignore the one cause of opposition to the Confederate government that preoccupied contemporaries. Antagonists of the Confederate government feared that it was becoming a "central military despotism," intent upon robbing the people of their liberty. One might dismiss these fears as political propaganda, but they were repeated too frequently in private correspondence to be regarded as such. It is also tempting to slight such anxieties as mere rhetorical devices designed to cover up more practical objections to individual policies of the Confederate government. To be sure, conscription aroused opposition among those men who did not want to fight, and the tax-in-kind antagonized farmers who hated heavy taxes. But those measures and others also generated deeper fears for the survival of popular liberty.[3]

Those fears reflected the inheritance of more than a century of English and American political belief. Eighteenth-century Americans feared that liberty, their liberty, would be crushed by power, usually the power of government. They portrayed liberty as fragile and passive, power as aggressive and unrelenting. Liberty was always under siege, always threatened. Citizens of the early republic sought the preservation of liberty in the constitutional republican governments of the states and nation. If the republic survived and remained strong, freedom would be protected. But they were also aware that past republics had been relatively short-lived. Hence, Americans remained sensitive to threats to republican government and the liberty it protected. Historians have identified the expression of those fears in the political struggles of the 1790s, in the decision to declare war in 1812, and in the nullification crisis.[4]

---

2. Albert Burton Moore, *Conscription and Conflict in the Confederacy* (New York, 1924); Georgia Lee Tatum, *Disloyalty in the Confederacy* (Chapel Hill, 1934), esp. pp. 3-23; Bell I. Wiley, *The Plain People of the Confederacy* (Baton Rouge, 1943), esp. pp. 36-69. More recent analyses of Confederate dissent that follow these traditional lines of interpretation include: Stephen E. Ambrose, "Yeoman Discontent in the Confederacy," *Civil War History* 8 (1962): 259-68; Paul D. Escott, "Southern Yeomen and the Confederacy," *South Atlantic Quarterly* 77 (1978): 146-58; and idem, *After Secession: Jefferson Davis and the Failure of Confederate Nationalism* (Baton Rouge, 1978).

3. Those fears have been dismissed by most historians. For a typical example, see E. Merton Coulter, *The Confederate States of America, 1861-1865* (Baton Rouge, 1950), pp. 386, 389-90, 393. Three historians have taken those fears more seriously: John Christopher Schwab, *The Confederate States of America, 1861-1865* (New York, 1901), pp. 186-228; David Donald, "Died of Democracy," in David Donald, ed., *Why the North Won the Civil War* (Baton Rouge, 1960), pp. 79-90; and John B. Robbins, "The Confederacy and the Writ of Habeas Corpus," *Georgia Historical Quarterly* 55 (1971): 83-101.

4. Bernard Bailyn, *The Ideological Origins of the American Revolution* (Cambridge, Mass., 1967);

During the 1820s and 1830s, the equality of white men became inextricably linked to the concept of liberty. Men, they believed, who were not the equals of other citizens were not truly free. This ideological commitment to the preservation of republican government and white liberty and equality shaped the contours of political debate in the decades before the Civil War. All of the major parties—Democratic, Whig, American, and Republican—portrayed themselves as the best defenders of freedom. Only by electing us, they each contended, can despotism be averted.[5] Thus, on the eve of the Civil War, the threat that power posed to liberty remained as real to Americans as it had to their fathers and grandfathers. It is in this historical context that popular fears for the survival of liberty developed in the Confederacy. But the nature of those fears, how and why they grew, and how they were expressed and ultimately resolved still require explanation. North Carolina, with a deserved reputation as a state hostile to the Confederate central government, offers an excellent case study of the rise of opposition among white southerners to that government. An examination of the ideological foundations of North Carolinians' hostility toward the central government and of the political context in which it developed reveals why the government aroused such widespread fear and anger among its loyal citizens.[6]

In the winter of 1860-61, after Abraham Lincoln had been elected president and the seven states of the deep South had seceded from the Union and formed the Confederate States of America, North Carolinians remained firmly attached to the Union. On February 28, 1861, a slight majority of North Carolina voters defeated a referendum calling for a convention to consider secession. At the same time they elected an overwhelming majority of unionists to the proposed convention.[7]

Gordon S. Wood, *The Creation of the American Republic, 1776-1787* (Chapel Hill, 1969); John R. Howe, "Republican Thought and Political Violence of the 1790s," *American Quarterly* 14 (1967): 147-65; Roger H. Brown, *The Republic in Peril: 1812* (New York, 1964); and Richard B. Latner, "The Nullification Crisis and Republican Subversion," *Journal of Southern History* 43 (1977): 19-38.

5. Michael F. Holt, *The Political Crisis of the 1850s* (New York, 1978); J. Mills Thornton III, *Politics and Power in a Slave Society: Alabama, 1800-1860* (Baton Rouge, 1978); and Rush Welter, *The Mind of America, 1820-1860* (New York, 1975), pp. 77-249.

6. For other more traditional interpretations of dissent in Confederate North Carolina, see Horace W. Raper, "William W. Holden and the Peace Movement in North Carolina," *North Carolina Historical Review* 31 (1954): 493-516; A. Sellew Roberts, "The Peace Movement in North Carolina," *Mississippi Valley Historical Review* 11 (1924): 190-99; and Richard E. Yates, "Governor Vance and the Peace Movement," *North Carolina Historical Review* 17 (1940): 1-25, 89-113.

7. Marc Wayne Kruman, "Parties and Politics in North Carolina, 1846-1865" (Ph.D. diss., Yale University, 1978), pp. 215-33.

However, public opinion shifted dramatically from strong unionism to almost unanimous support for secession after April 15, the day that Lincoln called for troops to suppress the rebellion in the lower South. North Carolina unionists and secessionists had long opposed any attempt to "coerce" the seceded states. They warned the North that any attempt to compel the return of those states to the Union would cause North Carolina's secession.[8] North Carolinians rejected coercion by the North primarily because they perceived it as an attempt to subjugate the South, to suppress the liberties of free men, to deny men the right to govern themselves. If the federal government could force a restoration of the Union, could it not compel North Carolinians to accede to other kinds of demands? As one secessionist put it, coercion changed "the issue . . . from the Negro to that of a question of popular liberty."[9]

As news of Lincoln's proclamation spread, steadfast unionists became secessionists. W. N. H. Smith, a Whig member of Congress and a strong unionist, wrote to his colleague Zebulon Vance: "The Union feeling *was strong* up to the recent proclamation. This War Manifest Extinguishes it, and resistance is now on every mans lips and throbs in every bosom. . . . Union men are now such no longer."[10] Several weeks after Lincoln called for troops, Josiah Cowles, a Yadkin county Whig politician and a slaveholder, explained to his son why his views had changed: "I was as strong a union man as any in the state up to the time of Lincolns proclamation calling for 75000 volunteers. I then saw that the south had either to submit to abject vassallage or assert her rights at the point of the Sword." Cowles reminded his son that he had opposed coercion, "believing it to be virtually a distruction to liberty."[11] The transformation of Josiah Cowles's

---

8. For example, see Raleigh *Register*, Jan. 19, 1861; Raleigh *North Carolina Standard*, Apr. 3, 1861; and Asa Biggs to Lawrence O'Bryan Branch, Feb. 5, 1861, Lawrence O'Bryan Branch Papers, Manuscripts Room, Duke University, Durham, N.C. (hereafter referred to as Duke).

9. C. B. Harrison to Lawrence O'Bryan Branch, Dec. 2, 1860, Branch Papers, Duke; also see Raleigh *Register*, Mar. 6, 1861. For other implications of a coercive policy, see C. Q. Lemmonds, *Speech of C. Q. Lemmonds, Esq. on the Convention Bill, Delivered in the House of Commons, January 17, 1861* (Raleigh, 1861); also see Raleigh *Register*, Jan. 19, Apr. 10, 1861; and Raleigh *Standard*, Feb. 27, 1861; John Gilmer to William Seward, Mar. 8, 1861, in Frederic Bancroft, *The Life of William H. Seward*, 2 vols. (1899; reprint ed., Gloucester, Mass., 1967), 2:547; and Mrs. Eliza Thompson to Benjamin S. Hedrick, Mar. 21, 1861, Benjamin Sherwood Hedrick Papers, Duke.

10. W. N. H. Smith to Zebulon B. Vance, Apr. 26, 1861, in Frontis W. Johnston, ed., *The Papers of Zebulon Baird Vance*, one vol. to date (Raleigh, 1963), 1:99. The original spelling, syntax, and punctuation have been retained for all quotations.

11. Josiah Cowles to Calvin J. Cowles, June 3, 1861, Calvin J. Cowles Papers, Division of Archives and History, Raleigh, N.C. (hereafter referred to as NCDAH). Also see the letters from Josiah to Calvin dated Apr. 19 and May 1, 1861, both in Cowles Papers, NCDAH.

attitude toward the Union reflected the changes of thousands of other North Carolinians. The press and politicians proclaimed that the incipient war would be fought in the name of popular liberty.[12] On May 20, 1861, delegates to a state convention unanimously adopted an ordinance of secession and ratified the Provisional Constitution of the Confederate States of America.[13]

North Carolinians entered a war that they expected to win quickly, and they assumed that such a war would leave intact their traditionally aloof relationship with the central government. But as it became apparent that the war would last more than a few months, some southerners came to appreciate the need to centralize the war effort and to strengthen the central government enough to curb disloyalty. Would North Carolinians now accept a stronger, more centralized government, one that would almost inevitably infringe on popular liberties? Should they surrender some cherished liberties, they asked themselves, in order to obtain independence from the northern despots? And if they gave up some of their liberties for the duration of the war, would they be able to regain them afterward? The answers North Carolinians gave to these questions played a significant role in the development of their attitudes toward the Confederate government.

The attitudes of North Carolinians toward the centralization of governmental authority and the subsequent infringements on individual liberty can be traced by examining the views of the major political group in the state—the Conservative party. The Conservatives, composed mostly of former members of the Whig party and of persons who had been unionists up to Lincoln's proclamation, began to act publicly as a political party in late 1861 and won massive victories over the Democratic party, which had dominated the state's politics for more than a decade, in the gubernatorial and legislative elections of 1862. Though seriously rent by factionalism after 1862, the party captured nine of the state's ten congressional seats in 1863 and provided both gubernatorial candidates in 1864. Loyal to the Confederacy, the Conservatives nevertheless attacked many Confederate policies.[14] Their attitudes toward the preservation of liberty and toward various measures of the Confederate government mirrored the attitudes of most North

---

12. Raleigh *Register*, May 8, 1861; Raleigh *Standard*, Apr. 24, 1861; also see the proceedings of a public meeting held in Robeson County, in Fayetteville *Observer*, Apr. 29, 1861; Governor Henry Clark's message to the General Assembly, in *Observer*, Aug. 19, 1861; and the editorial of the Wilmington *Journal*, May 2, 1861.

13. Joseph Carlyle Sitterson, *The Secession Movement in North Carolina* (Chapel Hill, 1939), pp. 240-49.

14. On the Conservative party, see Kruman, "Parties and Politics in North Carolina," pp. 246-74, 295-307.

Carolinians and revealed how opposition to the Confederate government grew in North Carolina.

Conservatives, adhering to the ideas of their revolutionary ancestors and of antebellum politics, defined liberty to mean freedom from an arbitrary government. Governments had to act within the limits set by freedom's "chosen instruments—the constitution and the laws."[15] A free man was the equal of all other free men, protected from arbitrary arrest and imprisonment and from unduly heavy taxation. Within the bounds of law, he was able to express himself freely and to own property unmolested.

A man who was not free was a slave. Slavery meant more to white North Carolinians than a system of forced labor for blacks; it was a social and political concept indicating a person's submission to the arbitrary will of another. They believed that a white man deprived of his liberties was just as much a slave as the black bondsman. Black slavery was only the most extreme example of slavery. But the presence of black slaves was important because it constantly reminded white North Carolinians just what it meant to be enslaved.[16] Black slavery also reinforced a belief in the fragility of their own liberty. Unless they protected liberty constantly and carefully, it would be destroyed. "We must retain our self-possession, and our liberties, too, in the progress of this war," wrote one Conservative, "or we will look in vain for them at its close."[17]

Conservative sensitivity to threats to popular liberty reflected not only a response to actions of the Confederate government, but also a persistence of antebellum beliefs. Antebellum political dialogue revolved around the promotion and protection of the freedom and equality of North Carolina white men. The major political issue in the state from 1848 until the mid-1850s was the Democratic party's advocacy of the elimination of the fifty acre requirement for senatorial electors, a measure the party called "equal suffrage." In response to the Democratic proposal, Whigs from the underrepresented western part of the state argued that only increased western representation in the state legislature,

---

15. Governor's Message, Nov. 17, 1862, in *The War of the Rebellion: A Compilation of the Official Records of the Union and Confederate Armies*, 127 books and index (Washington, 1880-1901), ser. 4, 2:188 (hereafter referred to as *Official Records*).

16. James C. Johnston to Zebulon B. Vance, Mar. 10, 1863, Governor's Papers, NCDAH. On the relationship of slavery and freedom in American history, see Edmund S. Morgan, "Slavery and Freedom: The American Paradox," *Journal of American History* 59 (1972): 5-29.

17. Fayetteville *Observer*, Apr. 7, 1862; also see William A. Graham's speech to the secession convention opposing the enactment of a test oath, in Raleigh *Standard*, Jan. 8, 1862.

through the adoption of the "white basis," would make white North Carolinians truly free and equal. Later the entire Whig party claimed that the same benefits could be derived from taxing slaves on an ad valorem basis. The promotion of white equality and freedom was also the goal of politicians in both parties when they defended the right of southerners to settle with their slaves in federal territories. And politicians based their defense of slavery on the grounds that the debasement of black people promoted equality and freedom among whites. On such issues, politicians spoke to the white North Carolinian's fear of having his equality and freedom abridged. In our hands, partisans declared, white liberty and equality are safe.[18]

The threat to liberty and equality and to the republican government which was their guardian came from the aggressive, expansive power of government officials. "All encroachments [on liberty]," warned one Conservative editor, "are sure to begin with and eminate from our rulers." If checks were not placed on the power of rulers, they would concentrate power in their hands and use it to destroy the liberties of the people.[19] Therefore, the people needed specific safeguards for their liberties. First, they demanded that civil power always be supreme over military power. This axiom of English political thought had particular relevance to southerners at war. Because the strength of the military necessarily increased during wartime, it seemed possible that the military power would become supreme. Therefore, Conservatives argued that it was "necessary to hold in check that propensity which war is always likely to bring fourth—a military rule to override the civil power."[20] For this reason, Conservatives were especially sensitive to any encroachments of the military on the civil power.

A strong state government was the second safeguard of the people's liberties. It could serve as a buffer between the people and the arbitrary will of the central government. Because they considered the state as the major defender of their freedom, North Carolinians were acutely aware of all the central government's infringements on the power and rights of the states.

Jefferson Davis first raised the specter of a strong military government in March

---

18. Kruman, "Parties and Politics in North Carolina," pp. 20-26, 41-75, 116-67, 203-12.

19. *Salisbury Carolina Watchman*, Apr. 28, 1862; also see Raleigh *Standard*, Jan. 8, 1862.

20. James J. Philips to Zebulon B. Vance, Oct. 29, 1863, Governor's Papers, NCDAH. For a few examples of the repeated demands that the civil power remain supreme over the military power, see Raleigh *Standard*, Sept. 17, 1862; Apr. 22, Aug. 26, and Oct. 21, 1863; S. S. Bingham to James G. Ramsay, Sept. 8, 1863, James Graham Ramsay Papers, Southern Historical Collection, University of North Carolina at Chapel Hill; Nathaniel Boyden to Zebulon B. Vance, Mar. [n.d], 1863, and James M. Leach to Vance, Mar. 5, 1864, both in Zebulon Baird Vance Papers, NCDAH.

1862, when he asked Congress to enact a law permitting the conscription of white men between the ages of eighteen and thirty-five. Since most soldiers in the Confederate army had volunteered for one year, their enlistment would end that April. Davis argued that conscription was needed to prevent the army's collapse and to maintain some continuity in its membership.[21] Although the bill passed easily in the Confederate Congress, men of all political persuasions in North Carolina were reluctant to accept the need for conscription. Their state had provided more than its quota of soldiers. Why, North Carolinians asked, should they have to contribute more men when other states were not meeting their requirements? If many more men were drafted, the few remaining men in nonslaveholding areas of the state would be unable to cultivate sufficient crops to feed the people.[22]

More important than those complaints was the fear that conscription represented the first step toward military despotism. If the central government and the military alone decided when and how many troops were needed and then took sole responsibility for recruiting them, it would be but a small step for the military thus to attain complete ascendancy in the South. Upon hearing of Davis's request for a conscription law, Congressman Thomas S. Ashe wrote to a friend: "It is said by [its] friends . . . to be the only means of saving the country, but I must confess I fear [it] will be the inauguration of a strong military government."[23]

By assuming complete control over recruitment, the Confederate government apparently infringed on the powers of the states. Richard Puryear, who had been a member of the Confederate Provisional Congress, worried that the doctrine of state rights "is repudiated and trodden under foot and germs of consolidation is already springing up on its ruins. Consolidation leads to despotism—and further than this I would not lift the veil." Because conscription strengthened the military and weakened the state government, Puryear continued, it threatened the people's liberty. "The people are jealous of their rights and many begin to fear that their rulers have designs upon their liberty. Amidst the difficulties which surround us and the dangers which threaten us nothing should be done to increase their fears and apprehensions. And what is better calculated to do this than this conscription?"[24] Despite Conservative apprehension over the loss of civil liberty, as the need for the conscription law became evident, they

21. Moore, *Conscription and Conflict*, pp. 13-14.
22. Fayetteville *Observer*, May 19, 1862.
23. Thomas S. Ashe to Kemp P. Battle, Apr. 1, 1862, Battle Family Papers, Southern Historical Collection.
24. Richard C. Puryear to Henry Toole Clark, Apr. 23, 1862, Henry Toole Clark Papers, Duke.

grudgingly acquiesced to it. But they warned that "we are in the very midst of perils, no not only from the common enemy, but also from those whom we have delegated to transact our public business."[25]

Similar fears were aroused by the suspension of the writ of habeas corpus. The Confederate Congress first authorized the president to suspend the writ from February 27 to October 13, 1862, and then extended authorization to February 13, 1863.[26] Davis used that authority in Salisbury, North Carolina, site of a Confederate prison. Those actions excited fears of arbitrary arrests by military authorities. Conservative Governor Zebulon B. Vance, in his message to the General Assembly in November 1862, feared that once the writ was suspended "no man is safe from the power of one individual. He could at pleasure seize any citizen of the State, with or without excuse, throw him into prison, and permit him to languish there without relief—a power that I am unwilling to see intrusted to any living man."[27] The possibility of arbitrary arrests became a reality in the fall of 1862, when Confederate authorities arrested the Reverend R. J. Graves on grounds of disloyalty and removed him to Richmond's Confederate prison, Castle Thunder. Upon learning of his case, the General Assembly passed a resolution instructing the governor to demand Graves's release. Although Vance obtained the prisoner's freedom, Graves's arrest had frightened persons like the editor of the Raleigh *Standard*, who worried that it "is a gross violation of the Constitution and Bill of Rights of this State, and of the first principles of liberty."[28] The military arrests of men like Graves impelled Tod R. Caldwell, attorney and Conservative party leader, to write that "no man, even tho he is clothed with a little brief military authority should be allowed to trample the laws under his feet and set himself up as superior to law & the law making power." He warned that "if something is not done to crush out this tyranny, we had as well confess ourselves slaves, for we are truly no better than slaves."[29]

The suspension of the writ and the subsequent arrests of North Carolina citizens also excited apprehension about the independence of the state's judiciary. Conservatives regarded an independent judiciary as critical to the protection of liberty. Only judges neither bound to the authorities nor indebted to them for

25. Salisbury *Carolina Watchman*, Apr. 28, 1862.
26. Thomas B. Alexander and Richard E. Beringer, *The Anatomy of the Confederate Congress: A Study of the Influences of Member Characteristics on Legislative Behavior, 1861-1865* (Nashville, 1972), pp. 169-71.
27. *Official Records*, ser. 4, 2:188.
28. Raleigh *Standard*, Dec. 17, 1862.
29. Tod R. Caldwell to James G. Ramsay, Nov. 30, 1863, Ramsay Papers, Southern Historical Collection; also see James C. Johnston to Zebulon Vance, Mar. 10, 1863, Governor's Papers, NCDAH.

favors could check governmental encroachments on liberty.[30] Such independence seemed threatened in mid-1863 when Secretary of War James A. Seddon attempted to obstruct the judicial process. Seddon blamed the desertion of North Carolina troops on the general belief that the state courts had declared the conscription law unconstitutional and asked the governor to use his influence to restrain the judges.[31] Vance, who considered an independent judiciary "the only hope of freedom in times of passion & of violence," indignantly refused. "An upright judge," he wrote, "must deliver the law as he conceives it to be, whether it should happen to comport with the received notions of the military authorities or not. I must therefore most respectfully decline to use my influence in restraining or controlling that co-ordinate branch of the government which [is] . . . in great danger of being overlapped and destroyed by the tendency of the times."[32]

The controversies surrounding several cases before the state supreme court in the spring and summer of 1863 confirmed fears of central government subversion of the judiciary's independence. In October 1862, Congress had passed a second conscription act, which extended the eligibility of white males to age forty-five. Under the first act, John W. Irwin had hired as a substitute a man between the ages of thirty-five and forty-five. The War Department determined that Irwin's substitute could now be conscripted, leaving Irwin without a representative in the army and therefore liable to conscription himself. Military authorities arrested Irwin for draft evasion. Upon Irwin's request, state supreme court Chief Justice Richmond Pearson, who maintained that the second law did not pertain to substitutes, granted a writ of habeas corpus and ordered Irwin freed.

Believing Pearson's decision erroneous, Secretary Seddon refused to release the prisoner. This action led to a heated exchange of letters between the secretary and the governor and eventually to Vance's order that the state militia prevent Confederate authorities from rearresting men released on writs of habeas corpus. In the interest of military efficiency, Vance and Seddon eventually reached a compromise regarding such men, but the conflict itself indicated to North Carolinians that the Confederate authorities were undermining judicial independence.[33] In August 1863, the chief justice cautioned Vance "that the

---

30. Zebulon B. Vance to John H. Haughton, Aug. 17, 1863, Vance Papers, NCDAH.
31. James A. Seddon to Zebulon B. Vance, May 23, 1863, in Official Records, ser. 1, 51, pt. 2:714.
32. Zebulon B. Vance to James A. Seddon, May 25, 1863, in ibid., p. 715.
33. The Irwin case is discussed in J. G. deRoulhac Hamilton, "The North Carolina Courts and the Confederacy," *North Carolina Historical Review* 4 (1927): 369-72; and Richard E. Yates, *The Confederacy and Zeb Vance* (Tuscaloosa, 1958), pp. 53-56. Also see Memory F. Mitchell, *Legal Aspects of Conscription and Exemption in North Carolina, 1861-1865* (Chapel Hill, 1965).

independence of the judiciary cannot be maintained, unless all encroachments are met with firmness."[34]

By mid-1863, the threats to the state's judiciary, the arbitrary arrests, the suspension of the writ of habeas corpus, and the conscription laws had convinced many North Carolinians that the Confederate government was becoming what Congressman Burgess S. Gaither called "a consolidated military despotism."[35] Their fears were increased by the apparently arbitrary impressment of goods by the army and by the implementation of a ten percent tax-in-kind for farmers, many of whom were just barely subsisting on their harvests. The appointment of a nonresident to administer the tax-in-kind seemed further evidence of the central government's intentions.[36]

North Carolinians expressed their discontent at almost one hundred meetings held in all parts of the state in July and August of 1863. At these meetings they urged North Carolinians to unite to "declare whether they shall be freemen or slaves." They complained of the central government's unfair treatment of North Carolina. They also praised the independence of the state's judiciary and Vance's defense of it. Judicial decisions, said the participants at one meeting, "will be disrespected by none but oligarchs, tyrants, despots, and haters of republican liberty." The meetings also lauded the state's soldiers for their sacrifices and bravery. "But," they added, "if the civil law is not maintained, and if civil liberty is not to be the great result of this contest, then will these services have been offered in vain." They also called for the initiation of peace negotiations with the North. With the congressional elections only a few months off, the participants at most meetings either nominated candidates or proclaimed their refusal to support anyone not committed to the commencement of peace negotiations.[37]

After an appeal from Governor Vance on September 7, no additional protest meetings were held, but the discontent persisted and deepened.[38] In the November congressional elections, voters elected nine conservatives.[39] During the months following the elections, it appeared to more and more North Carolinians that, through a new conscription act, another suspension of the writ of habeas

---

34. Richmond M. Pearson to Zebulon B. Vance, Aug. 11, 1863, Governor's Papers, NCDAH.
35. Burgess S. Gaither to Zebulon B. Vance, Apr. 24, 1863, Vance Papers, NCDAH.
36. See Raper, "William W. Holden," p. 499.
37. Raleigh *Standard*, July 29, Aug. 5, 12, and 19, 1863.
38. Frank Moore, ed., *The Rebellion Record: A Diary of American Events with Documents, Narratives, Illustrative Incidents, Poetry, etc.*, 11 vols. (New York, 1861–68), 7:497–98.
39. Kruman, "Parties and Politics in North Carolina," pp. 301–7.

corpus, and a renewed attack on the judiciary, the Davis administration sought to fasten the chains of a military despotism on the people.

In December 1863, Congress abolished the substitute law, which had permitted men liable to conscription to hire substitutes. The new law explicitly made those principals subject to conscription.[40] The law itself aroused opposition because it seemed to be a repudiation of the government's "contract" with the principals, and it precipitated another round of conflict between the state supreme court and the War Department. The law apparently affected less than one hundred men, so it was not the pervasiveness of its impact that caused complaint. Those men who had bought their way out of fighting elicited little sympathy. But many Conservatives objected to the government's repudiation of its obligations, for if the government could ignore one agreement with its citizens it could ignore others. Congressman James M. Leach wrote to Governor Vance that while the people had no immediate interest in the substitute law, "the fear with them is that if the Government rides over this law it will over others, & that civil rights & civil & personal liberty will depart the land."[41]

The substitute law also renewed the Confederate government's conflict with the judiciary. Chief Justice Pearson, believing the new law unconstitutional, granted writs of habeas corpus to all principals who requested them. Partly in response to decisions like Pearson's, Congress once again empowered President Davis to suspend the writ; thereupon, Pearson declared that the suspension of the writ was inapplicable to the principals. Vance warned Secretary Seddon that if the Confederate government attempted to rearrest men free on writs, he would call out the militia to protect them. Seddon replied that those already discharged would be allowed to remain free, but all further writs would be ignored.[42]

While the state and Confederate governments were arguing over Pearson's decisions, in February 1864 Congress passed a new conscription law. The act lowered the conscription age from eighteen to seventeen and raised it from forty-five to fifty. The new conscripts, organized under control of the Confederate government for local defense, would free reserved state troops for conscription into the general army.[43] This act seemingly contravened the right of a sovereign state to maintain "troops for war." Without such troops, the states and their citizens would be wholly dependent for their protection on the central government. Vance worried

---

40. Moore, *Conscription and Conflict*, pp. 44–45.
41. James M. Leach to Zebulon B. Vance, Mar. 8, 1864, Vance Papers, NCDAH.
42. Hamilton, "North Carolina Courts," pp. 389–99; Yates, *The Confederacy*, pp. 56–62.
43. Moore, *Conscription and Conflict*, p. 308.

that the implementation of the act would leave "this State ... powerless, without the shadow of military organization to enforce obedience to law." It would be "contrary to the genius of our new government," he wrote to Secretary Seddon, "to reduce a Sovereign State to [a] dangerous and humiliating condition."[44] Attorney and Conservative leader Augustus Merrimon warned Vance not to give up the troops to the central government. "If you allow the whole fighting population of the state to be taken, you will be a mere formal officer and the state a formal organization, without power, subject to the insults and tyrany of President Davis and his subordinates."[45] One member of the state's Home Guard lamented: "If what few troops the State claims are given up, we will be reduced to a *'miserable Dependency.'* You can see, no doubt, that we are all fast approaching a central military Despotism."[46]

The most ominous of all the central government's action was Congress's renewed authorization of the suspension of the writ of habeas corpus from February 15 to August 1, 1864. North Carolinians believed, with some justification, that the act was aimed at them. Davis had advocated the suspension because of the need to suppress disloyal meetings (like those held in North Carolina) and to overcome the objections of local judges (like Chief Justice Pearson) to the substitute law.[47]

The power Davis would amass from the suspension of the writ troubled North Carolina Conservatives. In a private meeting between the state's congressional delegation and the president, Senator Edwin Reade told Davis that North Carolinians disapproved of the suspension because it clothed Davis with dictatorial power. When Davis said that he would not abuse the power, Reade replied that "I had not intimated that he would, but that the people of North Carolina were unwilling to trust anyone with the power."[48] Upon learning of the passage of the suspension law, Governor Vance warned Davis, if the bill "be strictly within the limits of the Constitution, I imagine the people of this state will submit to it, so great is their regard for law. If it be adjudged, on the contrary, to be in violation of that instrument and revolutionary in itself, it will be resisted."[49]

44. Zebulon B. Vance to James A. Seddon, Apr. 4, 1864, copy, Governor's Papers, NCDAH.
45. Augustus S. Merrimon to Zebulon B. Vance, Feb. 22, 1864, Vance Papers, NCDAH.
46. S. E. Westry to Kemp P. Battle, Mar. 3, 1864, Battle Family Papers, Southern Historical Collection.
47. Alexander and Beringer, *Anatomy*, pp. 171-72.
48. Edwin G. Reade to Zebulon B. Vance, Feb. 10, 1864, Vance Papers, NCDAH.
49. Zebulon B. Vance to Jefferson Davis, Feb. 9, 1864, copy, Governor's Papers, NCDAH.

The suspension impelled some Conservatives to ask what, after all, were southern war aims. In a letter to Senator William Graham, Richard Puryear pleaded: "I hope you will never adjourn until you have restored the writ of habeas corpus, and placed our lives, our property and our liberties beyond the reach of Despots." If North Carolinians were to lose their liberties, it would not matter who won the war. "The people of this state—all loyal, all true to the South, willing to fight and die for liberty, . . . never will wear the chains of a foreign or Domestic tyrant. . . . We shall have first to forget the deeds of our forefathers, and lose all appreciation of the blessings they bequeathed to us. Then we shall be fit subjects for Slavery, and it matters not whether our Master be a Northern or a Southern tyrant."[50] Conservative R. D. Whitley agreed that the attainment of Confederate independence would be a pyrrhic victory without the writ to protect personal freedom. In a letter to his congressman, he wrote that "the Habeas Corpus Suspension act that unbounded Streach of Power unknown to Republican Governments all seem to agree will soon leave nothing worth fighting for."[51]

The suspension of the writ of habeas corpus, combined with the substitute and conscript laws and Confederate defiance of the decisions of the chief justice of the supreme court, convinced North Carolina Conservatives that they faced an impending military dictatorship. The central government had repudiated its obligations by abolishing substitution, had subverted the state's judiciary by ignoring the chief justice's decisions regarding the law, and threatened the sovereignty of the state with its new conscription law. Then Congress authorized the president to suspend the writ of habeas corpus, subjecting personal liberties to arbitrary abuse.

By early 1864, the future of liberty seemed bleak. In late February, Augustus Merrimon reported from Asheville "that the people are really alarmed, greatly alarmed for the safety of their liberties under our forms of government. They are indeed alarmed, and I confess there is cause for the alarm, and believe me when I tell you, this very alarm, but too well founded, is going far towards precipitating the South upon a fearful doom."[52] In January, Congressman James T.

---

50. Richard C. Puryear to William A. Graham, May 10, 1864, in J. G. deRoulhac Hamilton and Max R. Williams, eds., *The Papers of William Alexander Graham*, 6 vols., to date (Raleigh, 1961-), 6:101-2.

51. R. D. Whitley to James G. Ramsay, Apr. 18, 1864, Ramsay Papers, Southern Historical Collection.

52. Augustus S. Merrimon to William A. Graham, Feb. 22, 1864, in Hamilton and Williams, *The Papers of William Alexander Graham*, 6:28; also see Merrimon to Zebulon B. Vance, Feb. 22, 1864, Vance Papers, NCDAH.

Leach asked Senator William Graham: "What shall we do to stay the hand of a military despotism more to be dreaded than death itself; is not the priceless gem of civil and religious liberty worth the risk of rescueing it from the hands of the wicked dynasty that is now shaping our ruin?"[53] In April 1864, the president of the Council of State, Fenner B. Satterthwaite, urged the governor to speak out against the suspension of the writ of habeas corpus. "It may," he wrote, "be instrumental in saving civil liberty, for I confess that I am alarmed myself at the rapid strides which have been made towards a Military Despotism."[54]

Some alarmed Conservatives argued that North Carolina should take formal steps to protect herself and her citizens from that threat. They determined that the legislature should call a state convention, so that the state could act in her sovereign capacity to defend herself. According to Conservative editor William W. Holden, such a convention would seek an armistice with the North and, at the same time, would "protect the State against the encroachment of arbitrary power. It would see to it that the proud head of the State was bowed to no despot. It would insist that the civil law should prevail in all cases." A convention would also "demand that the Congress and the military shall respect that civil law and the inalienable rights of our people."[55] Petitioners throughout the state pleaded with Governor Vance to convene the legislature so that it could call a convention, because they viewed "with indignation & alarm the encroachments of Congress & the executive on the Sovereignty of the State & the constitutional rights of the citizens, which neither plighted faith, the sanctity of contracts nor the gauranties of the constitution serve to restrain. . . . The inevitable tendency . . . unless speedily checked is the overthrow of civil liberty, & the establishment of a military despotism."[56]

Another leader of the convention movement, Thomas Settle, a former Democratic Speaker of the State Senate and a Douglas Democrat in 1860, charged that "the Confederate government is completely controlled by bad, desperate men, who in violation of plain laws and the Constitution are usurping to themselves powers by which they can destroy not only private rights but States rights, and

---

53. James T. Leach to William A. Graham, Jan. 6, 1864, in Hamilton and Williams, *The Papers of William Alexander Graham*, 6:3.

54. Fenner B. Satterthwaite to Zebulon B. Vance, Apr. 18, 1864, Governor's Papers, NCDAH. Also see Daniel L. Russell, Jr., to Edward J. Hale, Jan. 12, 1864, in Edward Jones Hale Papers, NCDAH, but see Hale's reply of Jan. 16, 1864, ibid.

55. Raleigh *Standard*, Jan. 19, 1864, quoted in Raper, "William W. Holden," pp. 506-7.

56. A copy of the petition was enclosed in M. Masten et al. to Thomas Settle, Jr., Jan. 7, 1864, Thomas Settle Papers, No. 2, Southern Historical Collection.

finally clothe Jefferson Davis with more power than is now possessed by any crowned head in Europe." Writing in January 1864, Settle cautioned that if the recently proposed legislation regarding taxation, the currency, conscription, and the suspension of the writ of habeas corpus were adopted (and they were), then "the rights of persons and property will be completely destroyed & we will all find ourselves at the mercy of tyrants." Political decisions, he said, had reached the most basic level. North Carolinians would have to determine whether "white men will remain free."[57] Conservatives like Settle and Holden thought North Carolinians could preserve their freedom only by calling a convention.

Historians who have examined the purposes of the convention movement, agreeing with the assessment of Governor Vance, have seen it an effort to achieve a reconstruction of the Union.[58] It is true that reconstructionists supported the proposal and that if a convention had been called to defend the rights of the state and its people, it may have found no defense against the encroachments of the Confederate government except through reunion with the North. But because reconstruction was a logical culmination of the convention movement does not mean that it was the goal of convention advocates. On the contrary, the evidence cited above suggests that many Conservatives were trying to extricate themselves from an almost inextricable situation. They wanted to protect their freedom and seek an honorable peace, but in the Confederacy. State Treasurer Jonathan Worth advised Vance not to attack convention supporters as reconstructionists *"intending* to withdraw the State from the Confederacy. I presume very few favor a convention for this purpose."[59] Other convention supporters declared that a convention would be able to seek an honorable peace. If those efforts failed, "it can in no case injure, but would greatly strengthen the cause, for in that event, we would fall back united, upon the Cannon & the sword with redoubled courage & energey, as the last & only alternative."[60]

Other Conservatives, led by Governor Vance, rejected the idea of calling a convention because they believed that it would lead to reconstruction rather than to an honorable peace. Men like Vance persisted in their effort to preserve the rights and liberties of North Carolinians, but they opposed anything that seemed to hint at reconstruction. State legislator C. D. Smith expressed those Conservatives' fears of reunion: "All we who have battle[d] nobly for Habeas

---

57. Thomas Settle, Jr., to Masten et al., Jan. 14, 1864, ibid.
58. See Raper, "William W. Holden," p. 498; and Yates, "Governor Vance," pp. 4, 21–25, 104–6.
59. Jonathan Worth to Zebulon B. Vance, May 1, 1864, Vance Papers, NCDAH.
60. Proceedings of public meeting, Caldwell County, Feb. 8, 1864, Governor's Papers, NCDAH.

corpus in N Carolina, must naturally feel great trepidation in regard to linking our destiny with a government that has made a clean breast of it. Moreover, I am strongly inclined to the belief that our return at this juncture would be a voluntary submission to the worst of slavery."[61]

The split in the Conservative party over the convention question broadened into open political warfare in March 1864, when William Holden announced himself as a candidate opposed to the reelection of Governor Vance. Holden argued that Vance had inadequately protected popular liberty in North Carolina and, indeed, had only a lukewarm commitment to its protection. Only a state convention, Holden argued, could protect the state and its citizens from the overweening power of the Confederate government. He denied that the calling of a convention would lead to reconstruction. Hence, Vance's opposition to the convention was, in Holden's eyes, opposition to the establishment of safeguards for the threatened liberty of the people.[62] While the candidates spent much of the campaign discussing the merits of the convention, each devoted substantial time to proving that he was the better defender of civil liberty. The campaigners expressed the fears of North Carolinians that they were losing their freedom, and, by so doing, they simultaneously reinforced those fears.

Vance began his reelection campaign in February 1864 with a speech to the citizens of Wilkesboro, in the mountainous northwest corner of the state. He vigorously defended the righteousness of the southern cause and attacked the proposal for a convention. He also upset his Conservative supporters by what seemed to them to be an apologia for the suspension of the writ of habeas corpus.[63] John H. Haughton, one of the governor's political confidantes advised him to answer the serious charge that he had endorsed "that justly odious law suspending the great writ of Habeas Corpus."[64] Council President Satterthwaite informed Vance that "the *only* ground of complaint against you is the *fear* of some of your friends that . . . you are yielding two much to the Richmond administration, and have not taken that *decided* opposition to the serious encroachments, which has been made upon the *rights* and *liberties* of the people. That is the ground upon which Mr. Holden and his friends assale you." He suggested that Vance "take the very highest ground in favour of 'Constitutional liberty.' Express your

---

61. C. D. Smith to James G. Ramsay, Nov. 17, 1863, Ramsay Papers, Southern Historical Collection; also see Zebulon B. Vance to Edward J. Hale, Jan. 22, 1864, Hale Papers, NCDAH.

62. Raleigh *Standard*, May 25, 1864.

63. James M. Leach to Zebulon B. Vance, Apr. 27, 1864, Vance Papers, NCDAH.

64. John H. Haughton to Zebulon B. Vance, Apr. 23, 1864, Governor's Papers, NCDAH.

opinion boldly upon the policy of the suspension of the writ of habeas corpus." Satterthwaite assured Vance that "it would remove every ground of suspicion and Complaint against you! it would take 'all the wind out [of] Mr. Holden sale' and he would be compelled to withdraw, and give you his support or be so badly beaten in the race as never to raise his head again."[65]

Accepting the advice of Haughton, Satterthwaite, and others, Vance "boldly" defended the sacred writ of habeas corpus in a major speech delivered before three thousand people in Fayetteville on April 22, in his message to the General Assembly on May 17, and thereafter on the stump.[66] In his message, which occupied four and one-half columns of the Fayetteville *Observer*, Vance's denunciation of the suspension of the writ of habeas corpus covered two full columns.[67] His new tactic succeeded.[68] The Reverend A. W. Cummings reported to Vance that while traveling his circuit in the mountains he had talked with many people about the election. "Two weeks ago Holden would have received a majority of votes within my bounds." In one precinct he had found all but one man supporting Holden. "I am from that country to day," he wrote in early May. "I am happy to find a great change going on among the people all in your favor. It arises from what they learn to be your opinions and action upon the Habeas Corpus, and the continuance of the war."[69] After Vance's message was delivered to the General Assembly, Jonathan Worth, who sympathized with Holden, declared: "I see no cause to H[olden] for continuing in the field, and I think V[ance]'s friends who were becoming alienated have generally expressed their satisfaction."[70]

While Vance portrayed himself as a friend of liberty and of peace, he argued that the convention would produce neither. A state convention, he declared, could do nothing that the legislature could not, except take the state out of the Confederacy. That would lead North Carolina into a war with the Confederacy and ultimately back into the Union. A return to the Union would not mean a restoration of freedom, Vance declared, but rather "the destruction of everything."

---

65. Fenner B. Satterthwaite to Zebulon B. Vance, Apr. 18, 1864, ibid.
66. Fayetteville *Observer*, Apr. 25 and May 23, 1864.
67. Ibid., May 23, 1864.
68. James M. Leach to Zebulon B. Vance, Apr. 27, 1864, Vance Papers, NCDAH.
69. A. W. Cummings to Zebulon B. Vance, May 9, 1864, ibid.
70. Jonathan Worth to J. J. Jackson, May 30, 1864, in J. G. deRoulhac Hamilton, ed., *The Correspondence of Jonathan Worth*, 2 vols. (Raleigh, 1909), 1:309. When Worth learned that Vance was about to shift his position on the suspension of the writ, he urged Holden to withdraw from the race. Worth to Holden, Apr. 23, 1864, ibid., pp. 306-8.

A vote for Holden, Vance and his supporters argued, was a vote for continued war and for a return to northern despotism.[71]

Underlying Vance's attack on Holden was the charge that Holden was disloyal to the Confederacy. Only a month before the election, Vance Conservatives discovered the existence of a secret unionist organization, the Heroes of America. The organization existed, as did unionism in parts of the state, but the exposure of the organization just weeks before the election was surely no coincidence. Vance's supporters widely publicized the existence of the Heroes during July, the month before the election, and though most did not charge Holden with being a member of the organization, they did try to associate him with it and with unionist sentiment in the state.[72]

Vance ran a masterful campaign. Between February and May he changed the issues of debate in the campaign. In February, he had been on the defensive because of his apparently lukewarm defense of the liberties of North Carolinians. Vance eliminated that issue by coming out vigorously in defense of the writ of habeas corpus. By early summer, the issue had become the loyalty of William Holden and the aims of the convention movement. By the end of July, Holden spent much of his time denying that he was a member of the Heroes of America or that he wanted North Carolina to make a separate peace with the Lincoln administration.[73] Vance, in effect, gave the electorate what it desired. He defended the liberties of the state's citizens while demanding that southerners continue their armed struggle for independence. And he contended that the convention would do nothing to protect liberty or promote peace but, instead, would lead to a bloody war with the other Confederate states and to submission to the despotic North.

Soldiers and civilians came to the polls and gave Vance a massive victory. He won 80 percent of the total vote, 87.9 percent of the soldier vote, and 77.2 percent of the civilian vote. Holden obtained a majority in only three of the state's counties. In twenty of the counties unoccupied by the Union army, Holden obtained less than fifty votes.[74] Vance's victory represented a popular commitment to a position that ultimately proved untenable. The intense opposition to conscription, the suspension of the writ of habeas corpus and other acts indicated the unwillingness of North Carolinians to accept the centralization of governmental

71. Fayetteville *Observer*, Apr. 25 and May 23, 1864.
72. Ibid., July 4, 11, 18, and Aug. 1, 1864.
73. Raleigh *Standard*, July 27, 1864.
74. These figures were calculated from data supplied by the Inter-University Consortium for Political Research, Ann Arbor, Michigan.

operations necessary for an effective war effort or to allow any incursions on their rights. But they rejected the alternative of returning to the old Union, where the Lincoln administration had snuffed out liberty. In the end, they could only assume a negative stance and fight to preserve civil liberty in the South.

The fears for liberty excited by the Confederate government among North Carolinians and other white southerners rested upon a firm historical foundation. Inheriting many of the political beliefs and fears of the American revolutionaries, southerners were prepared to divine the worst of motives in the government's actions. Those fears were exacerbated further because the war brought a central government in contact with most people for the first time. Before the war, the vast majority dealt with the federal government only through the postmaster. The war brought conscription, arbitrary arrests of civilians, the central government's apparent subversion of the judiciary, the impressment of private property, heavy taxes, and the suspension of the writ of habeas corpus. Southerners viewed those drastic actions with horror and asked whether the government had designs on their liberty.

The anxieties of North Carolinians and other white southerners were paralleled in the North, yet the contours of dissent in the two regions differed. A comparison of the Union and the Confederacy reveals why dissent assumed distinctive forms and why North Carolinians were especially sensitive to threats to their liberty. Recent historians have argued that northern popular discontent with the Lincoln administration was limited by the existence of a two-party system there. The partisan desire to defeat the Democratic party helped to unite even discontented Republicans behind Lincoln's policies. And the existence of a strong Republican organization, ready to denounce even a hint of Democratic disloyalty, moderated Democratic actions.[75]

The Democratic party played an additional role in shaping and moderating dissent in the North. Just as North Carolina Conservatives attacked and distrusted the apparently despotic Davis administration, so too did northern Democrats fear the Lincoln administration.[76] But the Democrats, with an effective national

---

75. The most important statements of this thesis are: David M. Potter, "Jefferson Davis and the Political Factors in Confederate Defeat," in Donald, *Why the North Won the Civil War*, pp. 91-112; and Eric L. McKitrick, "Party Politics and the Union and Confederate War Efforts," in William Nisbet Chambers and Walter Dean Burnham, eds., *The American Party Systems: Stages of Political Development* (New York, 1967), pp. 117-52.

76. On Democratic fears, see Joel H. Silbey, *A Respectable Minority: The Democratic Party in the Civil War Era, 1860-1868* (New York, 1977), pp. 62-88.

organization, could hope to oust Lincoln in 1864. They offered northerners the traditional means by which Americans protected their liberty, voting for the opposition party.[77] Voters in North Carolina and other Confederate states were offered no such alternative. Because North Carolina Conservatives had ties with no national party, they could not hope to neutralize Davis, and because he was serving one six-year term, they could not remove him. Conservatives saw no way to rid themselves of the threat of despotism through the ballot box. North Carolina Conservatives were thus left with two unsatisfying choices. A small portion moved unwittingly in the direction of disloyalty to the Confederacy and reconstruction of the Union; the larger portion was left to complain bitterly and impotently of the threat to their freedom.

The absence of a national two-party system shaped the attitudes of North Carolinians toward the Confederate government; so too did the presence of a statewide two-party system. While North Carolinians had evinced much anxiety about the exercise of power by the Confederate government, they had accepted the exercise of considerable power by the state government. Under Governor Vance, for example, the state engaged in blockade running, clothed its troops, and effectively enforced the conscription laws.[78] The acceptance of state power derived less from an ideological commitment to state rights than from the state's party system. The party system provided an effective mechanism for removing from power those rulers who threatened popular liberty. After all, the voters had overwhelmingly elected Conservative Zebulon Vance in 1862 and thereby rebuked the Democratic party, which had controlled the state government since 1850 and which was associated with the Davis administration.

While the Democratic party remained an effective opponent, it moderated the positions assumed by the Conservatives; but when it declined in strength in 1863, the need to preserve Conservative unity also declined.[79] That trend culminated in the gubernatorial campaign of 1864, in which the two Conservative adversaries sought to outdo each other in their attacks on the Davis administration and in their defense of freedom. The moderation of 1862 was gone. Therefore, North Carolinians may have reaffirmed their loyalty to the cause of southern independence by voting for Vance, as Vance himself believed, but the election

---

77. On this point see Holt, *The Political Crisis of the 1850s* (New York, 1978), esp. pp. 37-38; Kruman, "Parties and Politics in North Carolina," esp. pp. 198-245.

78. Yates, *The Confederacy and Zeb Vance*, pp. 34-35, 68-84; Glenn Tucker, *Zeb Vance: Champion of Personal Freedom* (New York, 1965), pp. 216-38.

79. Kruman, "Parties and Politics in North Carolina," pp. 295-307.

campaign exacerbated the hostility which North Carolinians felt toward the Confederate government.

While the structure of politics shaped the way in which North Carolinians responded to the Confederate government, that response was also influenced by a nonpolitical factor, the state's geographic location. Although the enemy occupied part of the state's coastline and threatened the mountain counties on the Tennessee border, North Carolina was one of the southern states most isolated from military action. As an interior state, North Carolina was more susceptible to the demands of the Confederate government than other states. For example, North Carolina and two other states paid about two-thirds of the total produce collected under the tax-in-kind.[80] At the same time, the need for measures like the tax-in-kind, conscription, and the suspension of the writ of habeas corpus were not readily apparent to North Carolinians because the enemy posed no immediate threat. Thus, North Carolinians were called upon to make more sacrifices than were people in other states at a time when they least perceived the need for such an effort.[81]

Those geographic and political factors combined to make North Carolinians especially alert to any incursions on their liberty. By 1864, most had come to feel that the Confederate government was seeking to establish a military despotism and rob them of their liberty. They agreed with merchant Leander S. Gash when he wrote to Governor Vance: "Gradually the last vestige of freedom is departing from us. We all feel it. None of us feel that we have the manhood we once had. It is humiliating yet it is so."[82]

During times of crisis, societies often reveal the inner fears and tensions that are less evident in peaceful, stable times. The crisis of war laid bare the American fear, northern and southern, that their freedom was in jeopardy. While the political structure of the states and nations and the location of the states influenced the way people responded to the behavior of the central governments, the fear for liberty remained central to the thinking of Americans. The North Carolina experience may have been extreme in the extent to which those fears were developed and expressed, but in its extremity it revealed most fully the fears of the American people.

---

80. Schwab, *Confederate States*, p. 297.

81. This interpretation was influenced by Alexander and Beringer, *Anatomy of the Confederate Congress*, esp. pp. 320-22, 336-37; and by Professor William L. Barney's comments on my paper, "The Rise of Opposition to the Confederate Government in North Carolina" (Presented before the Annual Meeting of the Southern Historical Association, Atlanta, Ga., 1976).

82. Leander S. Gash to Zebulon B. Vance, Sept. 7, 1863, Governor's Papers, NCDAH.

Disaffection, Persistence, and Nation
Some Directions in Recent Scholarship on the Confederacy

Gary W. Gallagher

Thirty years have passed since Emory M. Thomas's *The Confederate Nation, 1861–1865* appeared on the historiographical landscape. Some of its themes had been present in his earlier *The Confederacy as Revolutionary Experience*, and together the two books heralded the emergence of a major figure in the field.[1] Factors weakening the Confederacy loomed larger than evidence of Rebel persistence or strength in the scholarly literature at that time, but Thomas took seriously the idea of national sentiment in the seceding states. When defeat apparently stalked the slaveholding republic in the spring of 1862 and "their national experiment seemed almost a failure, Confederate Southerners began to respond to their circumstances by redefining themselves—or, more precisely, by defining themselves as a national people." The cruel pressures of war obliged them to "define themselves in deeds. Accordingly the Confederacy acted out its national destiny." Destiny took Rebel armies to Appomattox and Durham Station, final stops on a road marked by catastrophic human and material loss, class struggle, debates about civil liberties, and wrangling over a "state rights political philosophy" that

---

I am pleased to thank T. Michael Parrish, Aaron Sheehan-Dean, and Joan Waugh for careful and very helpful readings of this essay.

1. *The Confederate Nation* and *The Confederacy as a Revolutionary Experience* were published in 1979 (New York: Harper and Row) and 1971 (Englewood Cliffs, N.J.: Prentice Hall) respectively. *The Confederate Nation* was part of the New American Nation series.

gave way as pressures mounted to establish "a centralized, national state." In the end, "ex-Confederates who accepted defeat and reunion were often unable to accept the consequences of being a vanquished people."[2]

David Williams's *Bitterly Divided: The South's Inner Civil War* traverses much of the same ground as Thomas's work, offering a convenient point of departure to consider the trajectory of recent scholarship on the Confederacy. The author or editor of four previous books dealing with various aspects of Confederate history, Williams complains that generations of historians have emphasized the war "waged with the North" rather than exploring how the "South was torn apart by a violent inner civil war, a war no less significant to the Confederacy's fate than its more widely known struggle against the Yankees." Resolutely focused on that "inner civil war," *Bitterly Divided* creates an impression of overwhelming internal fracturing that renders the presence of U.S. armies strangely irrelevant. Across a chaotic home front, men and women of the "plain folk" join black and native minorities, arraying themselves against selfish slaveholders who somehow manage to fight a four-year war while also avoiding direct military service. "Most responsible for the Confederacy's creation," the planter class "excused themselves from the draft in various ways, then grew far too much cotton and tobacco and not nearly enough food. Soldiers went hungry, as did their families back home. Women defied Confederate authorities by staging food riots from Richmond, Virginia, to Galveston, Texas. Desertion and draft evasion became commonplace.... Many deserters joined guerrilla bands..., which controlled vast areas of the southern countryside." Native Americans also "increasingly resisted Confederate authority," and African Americans, especially slaves, did their best to undermine the war effort. "From its beginnings, the Confederate cause lacked support from a majority of southerners," concludes Williams, and that, "to a great extent, explains why it was lost."[3]

Two questions come immediately to mind regarding *Bitterly Divided*. First,

---

2. Thomas, *Confederate Nation*, 298-99, 306. Thomas was indebted to other scholars who considered the Confederacy a nation that inspired obvious devotion among many of its citizens. See, for example, Charles P. Roland, *The Confederacy* (Chicago: Univ. of Chicago Press, 1960), and Frank E. Vandiver (Thomas's mentor at Rice Univ.), *Their Tattered Flags: The Epic of the Confederacy* (New York: Harper's Magazine Press, 1970). "Elaboration upon the Confederacy's weaknesses has often obscured her formidable strength," writes Roland, adding: "The Confederacy was born of an authentic Southern urge for independence ... lived briefly and in bitter tribulation ... [and] was destroyed by an authentic Northern urge to retain the Union" (194-95).

3. David Williams, *Bitterly Divided: The South's Inner Civil War* (New York: New Press, 2008), 1-2, 5, 241.

does it make a fresh contribution methodologically, evidentially, or analytically? This can be answered with a simple no—though, quite remarkably, a starred review in *Publisher's Weekly* predicted the book "will be a revelation even to professional historians" because Williams pulls together "the latest scholarship with his own research" to expose "the deep, often murderous divisions in Southern society." With Williams's "long overdue work" at hand, enthused this individual, "the history of the Civil War will never be the same again."[4] *Bitterly Divided* cites no manuscripts, includes fewer than ten references to the *Official Records*, quotes from only a handful of other published primary materials, and relies overwhelmingly on secondary materials that emphasize Confederate disaffection. Anyone conversant with scholarship on Confederate society from the 1920s to the mid-1940s, the 1970s and 1980s, or the last dozen years—perhaps most especially with Williams's own earlier books—will find no surprises.[5]

The second obvious question concerns where this book fits within recent literature on the Confederacy. Because it rests on a secondary foundation, it must be considered synthetic. But what kind of synthesis? Will readers find a state-of-the-field assessment regarding the war's impact on civilians, the presence (or absence) of national sentiment in the Confederacy, the relationship between government and citizen, the complex ways in which class and gender and race played out amid seismic strains, and the importance of military campaigns that literally destroyed much of the economic, political, and social fabric of the region? Once again, the answer must be no. More an extended polemical essay than anything else, *Bitterly Divided* simply ignores a substantial body of recent scholarship that does not support its arguments. It depends on anecdotal testimony, leaves critical definitions unsettlingly vague, and marshals apparently impressive but ultimately confusing numbers to substantiate a hoary class-driven argument about why the Confederacy failed.

4. Review of David Williams's *Bitterly Divided: The South's Inner Civil War, Publisher's Weekly* 255 (June 23, 2008): 47. Blurbs on the jacket typically claim much for the book. Howard Zinn predictably applauds the class-based analysis, claiming that it "demolishes, with powerful documentation, the myth of a united Confederacy"; Lee W. Formwalt finds Williams's "evidence from nearly every corner of the South" decisive in proving "the Lost Cause was lost before it ever began."

5. *Bitterly Divided* draws very heavily on its author's previous work, citing it more than 200 times in 567 endnotes. Williams's other titles include *Rich Man's War: Class, Caste, and Confederate Defeat in the Lower Chattahoochee Valley* (Athens: Univ. of Georgia Press, 1999); *Johnny Reb's War: Battlefield and Homefront* (Abilene, Tex.: McWhiney Foundation Press, 2000); *Plain Folk in a Rich Man's War: Class and Dissent in Confederate Georgia*, ed. with Teresa C. Williams and R. David Carlson (Gainesville: Univ. Press of Florida, 2002); and *A People's History of the Civil War: Struggles for the Meaning of Freedom* (New York: New Press, 2005).

Although he remarks more than once that dissent in the Confederacy remains an underappreciated dimension of the conflict, Williams admits that this "important story ... has in recent years become something of a cutting-edge topic among historians." This last statement is true as far as it goes—though the implication that earlier historians failed to explore dissent surely is misleading. Internal fissures serve as the interpretive touchstone of a rich body of older work, a brief review of which reveals that *Bitterly Divided* plows in deep existing furrows. As early as 1867, editor Edward A. Pollard of Richmond's *Examiner* denied that northern manpower and resources had settled the issue. "The great and melancholy fact remains," Pollard observed in *The Lost Cause*, "that the Confederates, with an abler Government and more resolute spirit, might have accomplished their independence." Indeed, he asserted in language much like Williams's, history offered no example of a nation so large as the Confederacy suffering defeat "by any amount of military force, *unless where popular demoralization has supervened.*"[6]

In 1937, while Margaret Mitchell's pro-Confederate epic *Gone with the Wind* sold in huge numbers, pioneering African American historian Charles H. Wesley challenged the Lost Cause narrative of noble Rebels struggling against impossible odds. "Historians of the Confederacy have based their works mainly upon the military subjugation of the South and the heroic actions of its defenders and have neglected the contributing social factors," maintained Wesley in *The Collapse of the Confederacy*. Internal conflict should figure prominently in any explanation of Confederate defeat, Wesley insisted, because there "was no solidarity of interest among the Southern people." They lived in "a stratified society based mainly upon two sharp class lines, those who owned slaves and those who did not own slaves. The owners of slaves constituted the ruling class. Jealous of the security of the ruling class, the common folk shirked the call to war."[7]

Twenty-eight years later, Carleton Beals reprised much of Wesley's argument in *War within a War: The Confederacy against Itself*. "This book is about those people who resisted, because of their love for the Union, or civil rights, or because they believed the struggle to be a 'rich man's war, poor man's fight,'" wrote Beals, who featured "mountain people," opponents of conscription, African Americans, and

---

6. Williams, *Bitterly Divided*, 6; Edward A. Pollard, *The Lost Cause: A New Southern History of the War of the Confederates* (New York: E. B. Treat, 1867), 728-29 (emphasis in original).

7. Charles H. Wesley, *The Collapse of the Confederacy* (Washington: Associated Publishers, 1937), 167, 83-84. Wesley's book, with an introduction by John David Smith, was reprinted in 2001 by the University of South Carolina Press.

others at odds with the Confederate government. Beals lamented how "stories of those who refused to conform to the patriotic slogans of the Confederacy and suffered their own Golgotha, who resisted vigilante terrorism rarely paralleled in history, have largely been lost."[8]

Two historiographical waves established a durable framework within which many advocates of internal failure have examined the Confederacy. Between the mid-1920s and the mid-1940s, a number of scholars joined Wesley to mount a powerful collective assault on Lost Cause mythology.[9] Although they sometimes deployed simplistic class models to support the idea of a rich man's war and a poor man's fight, their findings contributed importantly to topics such as conscription, state rights as a divisive ideology, desertion, persistent unionism, resistance among slaves (what W. E. B. Du Bois called "The General Strike"), class tensions, and corrosive guerrilla warfare. The fact that all major titles by these authors have been reprinted at least once suggests their continuing influence.[10]

A flurry of studies in the 1970s and 1980s, spurred in part by the new social history's emphasis on people outside the traditional power structure, expanded on the earlier literature. Some of this work can be read as a direct or indirect response to Thomas's *The Confederate Nation, 1861-1865*.[11] Authors and editors drove home

---

8. Carleton Beals, *War within a War: The Confederacy against Itself* (New York: Chilton, 1965), v–viii. Page 2 of the book offers a map of the Confederacy, delineating vast areas of "armed resistance before the end of 1863." Williams includes neither Wesley's nor Beals's book in his bibliography.

9. Among the most important titles are Albert Burton Moore, *Conscription and Conflict in the Confederacy* (New York: Macmillan, 1924); Frank L. Owsley, *State Rights in the Confederacy* (Chicago: Univ. of Chicago Press, 1925); Bessie Martin, *Desertion of Alabama Troops from the Confederate Army: A Study in Sectionalism* (New York: Columbia Univ. Press, 1932); Georgia Lee Tatum, *Disloyalty in the Confederacy* (Chapel Hill: Univ. of North Carolina Press, 1934); W. E. B. Du Bois, *Black Reconstruction: An Essay toward a History of the Part which Black Folk Played in the Attempt to Reconstruct Democracy in America, 1860-1880* (New York: Harcourt, Brace, 1935); Roger W. Shugg, *Origins of Class Struggle in Louisiana: A Social History of White Farmers and Laborers during Slavery and After, 1840-1875* (Baton Rouge: Louisiana State Univ. Press, 1939); Bell I. Wiley, *The Plain People of the Confederacy* (Baton Rouge: Louisiana State Univ. Press, 1943); Charles W. Ramsdell, *Behind the Lines in the Southern Confederacy* (Baton Rouge: Louisiana State Univ. Press, 1944). Williams cites the titles in this note more than sixty times.

10. Several of these books find contradictory forces at work in the Confederacy. Moore, for example, details "friction, confusion, and dereliction" in the operation of conscription and describes the Confederacy in 1865 as "a house divided against itself." Yet his concluding paragraph alludes to "the heroic devotion of the masses" and what he terms "unsurpassed sacrifice and heroism of the Southern armies and civilian population" (Moore, *Conscription and Conflict*, 353, 361).

11. The essays in Harry P. Owens and James J. Cooke, eds., *The Old South in the Crucible of War* (Jackson: Univ. Press of Mississippi, 1983), present a lively debate between Thomas and several other scholars on the topic of Confederate nationalism. For example, Lawrence N. Powell and Michael S. Wayne's "Self Interest and the Decline of Confederate Nationalism," which looks at planters along the lower Mississippi River, charges: "Selfishness appears to have been their dominant trait, self-interest their only creed" (30).

the point that no one should think of the Confederacy as a society united across boundaries of region, class, race, and gender. In a category by itself was *Why the South Lost the Civil War*, by Richard E. Berenger, Herman Hattaway, Archer Jones, and William N. Still—a detailed and thoughtful, if not ultimately persuasive, brief for the centrality of internal causes of Confederate failure. This prize-winning study attributed defeat to the impact of southern religion, an absence of nationalism, and, despite a level of commitment that absorbed the deaths of approximately one-quarter of all military-age white males in the Confederacy, weak popular will.[12] Armstead L. Robinson's posthumous *Bitter Fruits of Bondage: The Demise of Slavery and the Collapse of the Confederacy, 1861-1865*, though published in 2004, belongs with late-1970s to mid-1980s scholarship. It closes with this epitaph for the failed slaveholding republic: "Confederate States of America / 1861-1865 / Died of Class Conflict."[13] As a group, these studies supplemented and extended scholarship from the 1920s-1940s by positing, among other things, a class-driven dialectic between self-interested slaveholders and increasingly unhappy yeomen and poorer citizens that severely compromised the Confederate war effort.

Drew Gilpin Faust weighed in on the topic of Confederate nationalism at the end of the 1980s. Suggesting that the "creation of Confederate nationalism was the South's effort to build a consensus at home, to secure a foundation of popular support for a new nation and what quickly became an enormously costly war," she identifies religion as critical to a conception of nation predicated on defining Confederates as God's chosen people. Faust also notes the centrality of slavery to the Confederate consciousness and warns against working backward from Appomattox to yoke discussions of nationalism to those about why the Rebels

---

12. In addition to *Why the South Lost the Civil War* (Athens: Univ. of Georgia Press, 1986), important titles from the 1970s and 1980s include Paul D. Escott, *After Secession: Jefferson Davis and the Failure of Confederate Nationalism* (Baton Rouge: Louisiana State Univ. Press, 1978); Steven Hahn, *The Roots of Southern Populism: Yeoman Farmers and the Transformation of the Georgia Upcountry, 1850-1890* (New York: Oxford Univ. Press, 1984); John Cimprich, *Slavery's End in Tennessee, 1861-1865* (Tuscaloosa: Univ. of Alabama Press, 1985); Malcolm C. McMillan, *The Disintegration of a Confederate State: Three Governors and Alabama's Home Front, 1861-1865* (Macon, Ga.: Mercer Univ. Press, 1986); Clarence L. Mohr, *On The Threshold of Freedom: Masters and Slaves in Civil War Georgia* (Athens: Univ. of Georgia Press, 1986); Fred Arthur Bailey, *Class and Tennessee's Confederate Generation* (Chapel Hill: Univ. of North Carolina Press, 1987); Stephen V. Ash, *Middle Tennessee Society Transformed, 1860-1870: War and Peace in the Upper South* (Knoxville: Univ. of Tennessee Press, 1988); George C. Rable, *Civil Wars: Women and the Crisis of Southern Nationalism* (Champaign: Univ. of Illinois Press, 1989). Williams cites the titles in this note several dozen times.

13. The "Publisher's Note" for Robinson's book explains that the manuscript "was made up of three parts, completed in 1982, 1984, and 1991, respectively." The University Press of Virginia received the manuscript in 1996, the year after the author's death (Robinson, *Bitter Fruits of Bondage*, xvii, 283).

failed. Her conclusions, however, stress the ultimate weakness of nationalistic sentiment in the southern republic.[14]

Substantive work describing (though not always primarily concerned with) Confederate disaffection continued into the early and mid-1990s. Key titles from LeeAnn Whites and Drew Gilpin Faust develop themes relating to tensions among women of different classes, between women and men, and between women and the Confederate state. In her study of North Carolina women, Victoria E. Bynum describes their tipping the balance of power "between warring men" in the region. "By waging a war to save slavery at the expense of nonslaveholders," she argues, "the Confederacy lost the allegiance of many men and women of the North Carolina yeomanry. The defiance exhibited by women who rioted or harbored deserters attests to the unpopularity of a war that did not serve the interests of the overwhelming majority of its people and that ultimately could not be won without their support."[15] Other books explore political and social warfare in Texas and locate among small farmers and laborers in northeastern North Carolina, as "in many parts of the South," a belief that the Confederacy waged a "rich man's war and a poor man's fight ... to secure the property of slaveholders."[16]

The more recent "cutting-edge" literature on internal dissent Williams mentions has appeared at a steady rate over the past dozen years. A full discussion lies beyond the scope of this essay, but some trends are evident. It has long been a commonplace that the hill country and mountains of the Confederacy functioned as centers of antiwar and anti-Davis administration activity.[17] An

---

14. Drew Gilpin Faust, *The Creation of Confederate Nationalism: Ideology and Identity in the Civil War South* (Baton Rouge: Louisiana State Univ. Press, 1988), 6-7, 22, 42, 60, 84. The book offers Faust's revised Walter Lynwood Fleming Lectures at Louisiana State University.

15. LeeAnn Whites, *The Civil War as a Crisis in Gender: Augusta, Georgia, 1860-1890* (Athens: Univ. of Georgia Press, 1995); Drew Gilpin Faust, *Mothers of Invention: Women of the Slaveholding South in the American Civil War* (Chapel Hill: Univ. of North Carolina Press, 1996); Victoria E. Bynum, *Unruly Women: The Politics of Social and Sexual Control in the Old South* (Chapel Hill: Univ. of North Carolina Press, 1992), quotation 149-50.

16. James Marten, *Texas Divided: Loyalty and Dissent in the Lone Star State, 1856-1874* (Lexington: Univ. Press of Kentucky, 1990); Richard B. McCaslin, *Tainted Breeze: The Great Hanging at Gainesville, Texas 1862* (Baton Rouge: Louisiana State Univ. Press, 1994); Wayne K. Durrill, *War of Another Kind: A Southern Community in the Great Rebellion* (New York: Oxford Univ. Press, 1990), quotation 241. McCaslin places a notorious vigilante action against unionists within the context of contentious politics in North Texas between 1860 and the immediate postwar period.

17. See, for example, James G. Randall and David Donald, *The Civil War and Reconstruction*, 2d ed. (Boston: D. C. Heath, 1961), chap. 14. The most widely adopted textbook for many years, this volume draws on literature from the 1920s-1940s; points to problems for the Confederacy in the uplands of Alabama, Arkansas, and Texas; and claims that across "the great Appalachian mountain region opponents of the Confederacy were probably in the majority throughout the war" (264).

array of recent scholarship has examined the war in Appalachia, confirming deep divisions in mountainous regions but also finding evidence of strong support for the Confederacy. Works on North Carolina, Virginia, Tennessee, and Georgia create a composite picture affirming John C. Inscoe and Gordon B. McKinney's observation that "within the southern highlands, the war played out in very different ways for western North Carolinians than it did for East Tennesseans or north Georgians or western Virginians or Eastern Kentuckians." The authors might have added that within each of these five populations the variety of reactions to the war and its trials also defy easy characterization.[18]

Several books examining unionism in the Confederacy further the work of pioneers such as Georgia Lee Tatum. Generations of scholars have known that such sentiment existed in many places, often hindered the Confederate war effort, and frequently brought harsh consequences to the unionists. Although no one can give a firm number for unionists, their presence and impact has been brought into sharper relief at the state, local, and individual levels. Historians have conducted a successful search for unionists beyond the strongholds of western Virginia and East Tennessee, where allegiance to the Union broke up one state and posed crippling problems to the Richmond government in another, without appreciably changing the overall picture of the relationship between unionism and Confederate failure. Thomas G. Dyer's *Secret Yankees: The Union Circle in Confederate Atlanta* provides a case in point. It confirms the presence of a few unionists in the city but likely has prompted many readers to wonder about that fact's larger meaning. In a similar vein, Dale Baum labels Texas unionists after the fall of Vicksburg "admittedly a small group" of mostly "quiescent 'reconstructionists'" who thought the state should "negotiate a separate agreement with President Abraham Lincoln."[19]

---

18. Examples of the literature on Appalachia include Kenneth W. Noe and Shannon H. Wilson, eds., *The Civil War in Appalachia: Collected Essays* (Knoxville: Univ. of Tennessee Press, 1997); Noel C. Fisher, *War at Every Door: Partisan Politics and Guerrilla Violence in East Tennessee, 1860–1869* (Chapel Hill: Univ. of North Carolina Press, 1997); W. Todd Groce, *Mountain Rebels: East Tennessee and the Civil War, 1860–1870* (Knoxville: Univ. of Tennessee Press, 1999); John C. Inscoe and Gordon B. McKinney, *The Heart of Confederate Appalachia: Western North Carolina in the Civil War* (Chapel Hill: Univ. of North Carolina Press, 2000), quotation 8; Martin Crawford, *Ashe County's Civil War: Community and Society in the Appalachian South* (Charlottesville: Univ. Press of Virginia, 2001); Brian D. McKnight, *Contested Borderland: The Civil War in Appalachian Kentucky and Virginia* (Lexington: Univ. Press of Kentucky, 2006); Jonathan Dean Sarris, *A Separate Civil War: Communities in Conflict in the Mountain South* (Charlottesville: Univ. of Virginia Press, 2006).

19. In addition to *Secret Yankees* (Baltimore: Johns Hopkins Univ. Press, 1999), important titles include Baum's *The Shattering of Texas Unionism: Politics in the Lone Star State during the Civil War Era* (Baton Rouge: Louisiana State Univ. Press, 1998), quotation 233–34; Daniel E. Sutherland, ed.,

Germane to any internal weakness argument, Confederate debates about enrolling slaves in the army and the possible impact of class on military operations have invited recent attention. Bruce Levine's discussion of disputes in 1864–65 regarding the arming of slaves exposes fissures among slaveholders and between them and many nonslaveholders. Michael D. Pierson's treatment of Fort Jackson's fall in the spring of 1862, a pivotal event in the Federal campaign against New Orleans, identifies class, ethnicity, and union sentiment—rather than the more obvious U.S. land- and waterborne forces—as major components in the Confederacy's failure to hold on to its largest city and busiest port.[20]

Tackling a subject often placed high on any list of factors that undid the Confederacy, Mark A. Weitz has updated Ella Lonn's classic study of desertion. Although few, if any, historians would claim desertion had no effect on Confederate fortunes, Weitz sets up as straw targets those who focus on the majority of Confederate soldiers who remained in the ranks "rather than what they see as a minority who lost hope." Unable to revise upward Lonn's figure for overall desertion, Weitz observes that what "makes the quantitative data confusing is that the numbers simply cannot be reconciled with the letters, diaries, official reports" and other materials that suggest desertion severely damaged the Confederacy. Frustrated by this, he finesses the problem. "The story goes beyond the numbers that can be derived from the available records," he assures readers; more than that, he falls back on a widely held but problematical assumption that triumphant Union soldiers must have possessed a stronger sense of nationalism than vanquished Confederates, who hailed from "a region dominated by localism." In a fine example of reading backward from Appomattox, Weitz observes: "This study is possible because the South did lose the war. The reality of defeat begs the question of why. Part of the answer to whether desertion hurt

---

Guerrillas, Unionists, and Violence on the Confederate Home Front (Fayetteville: Univ. of Arkansas Press, 1999); William W. Freehling, *The South versus the South: How Anti-Confederate Southerners Shaped the Course of the Civil War* (New York: Oxford Univ. Press, 2001); John C. Inscoe and Robert C. Kenzer, eds., *Enemies of the Country: New Perspectives on Unionists in the Civil War South* (Athens: Univ. of Georgia Press, 2001); James Alex Baggett, *The Scalawags: Southern Dissenters in the Civil War and Reconstruction* (Baton Rouge: Louisiana State Univ. Press, 2003); Elizabeth R. Varon, *Southern Lady, Yankee Spy: The True Story of Elizabeth Van Lew, a Union Agent in the Heart of the Confederacy* (New York: Oxford Univ. Press, 2003); Victoria E. Bynum, *The Free State of Jones: Mississippi's Longest Civil War* (Chapel Hill: Univ. of North Carolina Press, 2003); Margaret M. Storey, *Loyalty and Loss: Alabama's Unionists in the Civil War and Reconstruction* (Baton Rouge: Louisiana State Univ. Press, 2004).

20. Bruce Levine, *Confederate Emancipation: Southern Plans to Free and Arm Slaves during the Civil War* (New York: Oxford Univ. Press, 2006); Michael D. Pierson, *Mutiny at Fort Jackson: The Untold Story of the Fall of New Orleans* (Chapel Hill: Univ. of North Carolina Press, 2008).

or crippled the Confederate war effort lies in accepting that precise numbers are impossible."[21]

These works on Appalachia, unionism, slavery, desertion, and other subjects spotlight fissures within the Confederacy but tell only part of the story.[22] There is a second edge to literature from the past dozen years or so that cuts a very different way. It arose in the mid- and late 1990s to challenge elements of the "internal weakness" school of interpretation—a school that had long since gained supremacy in the field of Confederate home-front studies. Readily acknowledging internal tensions and war weariness, a number of historians, and I count myself among them, detect substantial evidence of national sentiment, willingness to sacrifice amid war weariness, steadfastness among soldiers, agreement about questions relating to slavery and race, awareness of class inequities that prompted measures to address them, cohesion around cultural symbols, and preference for the Confederacy, whatever its flaws, over return to a United States governed by Abraham Lincoln and emancipationist Republicans.[23] In

---

21. Mark A. Weitz, *More Damning than Slaughter: Desertion in the Confederate Army* (Lincoln: Univ. of Nebraska Press, 2005), ix, xvi–xviii. David M. Potter's essay on nationalism in *The South and the Sectional Conflict* (Baton Rouge: Louisiana State Univ. Press, 1968), which describes hierarchies of shifting loyalties, can be read as a persuasive counter to Weitz's nationalism/localism formulation. Weitz focused solely on Georgia in his earlier *A Higher Duty: Desertion among Georgia Troops during the Civil War* (Lincoln: Univ. of Nebraska Press, 2000).

22. Other titles devoted to social, political, and military turbulence in the Confederacy include Jon L. Wakelyn, *Confederates against the Confederacy: Essays on Leadership and Loyalty* (Westport, Conn.: Praeger, 2002), which uses a biographical approach; and David J. Eicher, *Dixie Betrayed: How the South Really Lost the Civil War* (Boston: Little, Brown, 2006), which echoes Frank L. Owsley's pioneering book in claiming state rights "destroyed the Confederacy." (Owsley's book does not appear in Eicher's notes or bibliography.) See also Steven Elliott Tripp, *Yankee Town, Southern City: Race and Class Relations in Civil War Lynchburg* (New York: New York Univ. Press, 1997); William Warren Rogers Jr., *Confederate Home Front: Montgomery during the Civil War* (Tuscaloosa: Univ. of Alabama Press, 1999); Robert R. Mackey, *The Uncivil War: Irregular Warfare in the Upper South, 1861–1865* (Norman: Univ. of Oklahoma Press, 2004); and Jacqueline Jones, *Saving Savannah: The City and the Civil War* (New York: Knopf, 2008). Jones focuses on evidence of anti-Confederate thought and action in the territory surrounding Savannah. The index includes subheadings under "Confederate States of America" for conscription, desertion, and mutinies among Confederate soldiers—but none for any category relating to white support for the Confederacy.

23. For examples of this literature that deal with the Confederacy as a whole, see Gary W. Gallagher, *The Confederate War* (Cambridge, Mass.: Harvard Univ. Press, 1997); Robert E. Bonner, *Colors and Blood: Flag Passions of the Confederate South* (Princeton, N.J.: Princeton Univ. Press, 2002); Anne Sarah Rubin, *A Shattered Nation: The Rise and Fall of the Confederacy, 1861–1868* (Chapel Hill: Univ. of North Carolina Press, 2005); Jason Phillips, *Diehard Rebels: The Confederate Culture of Invincibility* (Athens: Univ. of Georgia Press, 2007). Bonner states that "Confederate flags helped to focus patriotic emotions from the early days of the secession crisis in 1860 past the moment of military defeat in 1865." Because the Confederates lost, he believes, "it has been harder to see how patriotic symbols

these studies, most Confederates—as opposed to most southerners, who included white and black people in the four loyal slave states and black residents in the Confederacy—displayed resilience in the face of powerful U.S. armies and naval forces and developed feelings of national community that had antebellum roots and carried over into the postwar years.[24]

All these books deal with class tensions to a greater or lesser degree, reminding readers that discovering such stresses in Confederate society is roughly equivalent to finding sand on a beach. Every society in every place at every time manifests class friction. The interesting question is not whether it exists, but whether it shapes events decisively. Stephen V. Ash's book on occupied regions of the Confederacy affords a useful example. Ash's narrative includes many instances of class-driven confrontation and posturing. It also shows that U.S. military officers recognized the existence of class divisions in the Confederacy and, in company with unionists, sought to exploit them by turning "poor whites" against the elites. Yet despite some "sensational episodes," decides Ash, "the conflict that they evidenced was singularly muted. Of all the struggles that convulsed the occupied South—including those of Rebels versus Yankees, secessionists versus Unionists, and whites versus blacks—the struggle of the propertied versus the propertyless was the most restrained."[25]

Virginia and the principal army that defended it have been well served by this second edge of the literature. Scholars have applied a range of analytical tools and approaches to portray a state that endured horrendous social and economic

---

were powerful sources of cohesion within the wartime South" (3). For the postwar role of women as Confederate nationalists, see Caroline E. Janney, *Burying the Dead but Not the Past: Ladies' Memorial Associations and the Lost Cause* (Chapel Hill: Univ. of North Carolina Press, 2008), esp. chaps. 1-3.

24. In a misguided effort to get the Confederacy right on slavery, a marginal literature avers that many African Americans willingly supported the Rebel war effort—including as soldiers. For examples of this mutation of Lost Cause–era "loyal slave" arguments, see Charles Kelly Barrow, J. H. Segars, and R. B. Rosenburg, eds., *Forgotten Confederates: An Anthology about Black Southerners* ([Atlanta, Ga.]: Southern Heritage Press, 1995); Richard Rollins, ed., *Black Southerners in Gray: Essays on Afro-Americans in Confederate Armies* (Murfreesboro, Tenn.: Southern Heritage Press, 1994); J. H. Segars and Charles Kelly Barrow, comps., *Black Southerners in Confederate Armies: A Collection of Historical Accounts* (Atlanta: Southern Lion Books, 2001). For a more scholarly, though still controversial, treatment, see Ervin L. Jordan Jr., *Black Confederates and Afro-Yankees in Civil War Virginia* (Charlottesville: Univ. Press of Virginia, 1995), esp. chaps. 10-11. For amusement (unintended by the author), see Richard G. Williams Jr., *Stonewall Jackson: The Black Man's Friend* (Nashville, Tenn.: Cumberland House, 2006).

25. Stephen V. Ash, *When the Yankees Came: Conflict and Chaos in the Occupied South, 1861–1865* (Chapel Hill: Univ. of North Carolina Press, 1995), 192-93. Ash also demonstrates that nonslaveholding unionists often disliked Yankees and black people even more than they disliked slaveholders.

disruption, experienced sometimes crippling internal strife (a big chunk of the state, after all, broke away in 1863), yet maintained an impressive fight against Federal military power for most of the conflict. Family ties, a foe perceived as brutally threatening, fears of racial disruption, and conceptions of manhood and womanhood, among many other factors, promoted a sense of Virginian/Confederate identity. William Blair details efforts at all levels of government to relieve sufferings among poor Virginians, concluding: "If anything, planters and owners of large farms had more complaints with the government than the 'rebellious' common folk as 1864 progressed." In a study of southeastern Virginia, Brian S. Wills uncovers "strong evidence" that "flies in the face of those who contend that ... [Confederate] nationalism never truly emerged or faded quickly with adverse military results." Aaron Sheehan-Dean helpfully observes that white Virginians, slaveholders and nonslaveholders alike, did not react to the conflict as might be expected by twenty-first-century observers. "The Confederate experience teaches us to evaluate skeptically the ways that we understand and explain people's motivations," he notes, "especially those that involve armed conflict.... In the Civil War, the harder the North fought, the more vigorously the Confederacy resisted."[26]

The bulwark of that resistance was Robert E. Lee's Army of Northern Virginia, the subject of important books by J. Tracy Power and Joseph T. Glatthaar. Based on exhaustive research in manuscripts, both present a force that overcame obstacles of all kinds, including truly staggering losses, to retain its lethal power until late in the contest. Glatthaar constructed a statistical sample of the roughly 200,000 men who served in its ranks to produce by far the most sophisticated analysis to date of any Civil War army, manipulating his data to reveal a great deal about soldiers' wealth, slaveholding status, casualties, and rates of desertion.

---

26. William Blair, *Virginia's Private War: Feeding Body and Soul in the Confederacy, 1861–1865* (New York: Oxford Univ. Press, 1998), quotation 7; Peter S. Carmichael, *The Last Generation: Young Virginians in Peace, War, and Reunion* (Chapel Hill: Univ. of North Carolina Press, 2005); Brian Steel Wills, *The War Hits Home: The Civil War in Southeastern Virginia* (Charlottesville: Univ. Press of Virginia, 2001), quotation 256; Richard R. Duncan, *Beleaguered Winchester: A Virginia Community at War, 1861–1865* (Baton Rouge: Louisiana State Univ. Press, 2007); Aaron Sheehan-Dean, *Why Confederates Fought: Family and Nation in Civil War Virginia* (Chapel Hill: Univ. of North Carolina Press, 2007), quotation 195. See also William G. Thomas, "Nothing Ought to Astonish Us: Confederate Civilians in the 1864 Shenandoah Valley Campaign," in *The Shenandoah Valley Campaign of 1864*, ed. by Gary W. Gallagher (Chapel Hill: Univ. of North Carolina Press, 2006), 222–56. Analyzing the impact of Maj. Gen. Philip H. Sheridan's crushing victories, Thomas describes the Valley's population as chastened but resolute: "Despite this reversal and their astonishment at it, Confederate civilians in the Shenandoah Valley held fast to their desperate, losing cause, hoping, praying, and believing that they would not be forsaken" (250).

"Undermanned, underfed, poorly clothed, and inadequately equipped," he states, "the Army of Northern Virginia kept a significantly larger and better-resourced Union army at bay for almost four years. Its success was so great that in the minds of Northerners and Southerners alike it came to symbolize the vitality of the Confederate States."[27] Chandra Manning's study of Civil War soldiers also allots some attention to Lee's army. Echoing other authors, she identifies shared beliefs about race and slavery that crossed class lines as critical to prolonging the war amid escalating demands by the nation and by the men's families.[28]

Although Virginia has been more thoroughly examined than any other state, scholars have not ignored evidence of persistent support for the Confederacy elsewhere. A few examples will suggest the tenor of this work. Jacqueline Glass Campbell effectively disputes the long-held notion that Sherman's campaigns in Georgia and the Carolinas left behind a broken population willing to capitulate at any price. Civilians initially cast down by Confederate inability to stop Union destruction, she shows in analysis similar to Sheehan-Dean's, often became more determined to resist subjugation by what they saw as a savage enemy. A study of Company A of the 5th Alabama Infantry maintains the war strengthened ties between soldiers and their friends and relatives on the home front, nourishing a sense of community that combined loyalty to locality, state, and nation. In the wiregrass region of Georgia, argues Mark V. Wetherington, nonslaveholding farmers and craftsmen had self-interested reasons for supporting the Confederacy. The feared Union victory because it would subject them and the rest of the Confederate states to emancipation and other Republican measures. Finally, a pair of essays by Keith S. Bohannon and Rod Andrew Jr.,

---

27. J. Tracy Power, *Lee's Miserables: Life in the Army of Northern Virginia from the Wilderness to Appomattox* (Chapel Hill: Univ. of North Carolina Press, 1998); Joseph T. Glatthaar, *General Lee's Army: From Victory to Collapse* (New York: Free Press, 2008), quotation 471-72. Glatthaar's six-hundred-man sample allows him to move beyond the time-honored practice of reading as many letters and diaries as possible and then drawing inevitably impressionistic conclusions. A companion volume to *General Lee's Army* will present Glatthaar's data in the form of charts and graphs.

28. Chandra Manning, *What This Cruel War Was Over: Soldiers, Slavery, and the Civil War* (New York: Knopf, 2007). Unlike Power and Glatthaar (and following a well-established tradition), Manning finds little evidence of nationalism among Confederate soldiers, emphasizing instead localism, family, and slavery/race (she sees U.S. soldiers as more likely to embrace Union/nation and to commit unselfishly to emancipation). On Lee's army and civilian morale, see also Lisa Laskin, "'The Army Is Not Near So Much Demoralized as the Country Is': Soldiers in the Army of Northern Virginia and the Confederate Home Front," in *The View from the Ground: Experiences of Civil War Soldiers*, ed. by Aaron Sheehan-Dean (Lexington: Univ. Press of Kentucky, 2007), 91-120; Gary W. Gallagher, *Lee and His Army in Confederate History* (Chapel Hill: Univ. of North Carolina Press, 2001), chaps. 1-4.

on reenlistments in the Army of Tennessee in the winter of 1864 and Georgia's congressional elections in 1863 respectively, reveals a welter of attitudes about the war but highlights resolve among Confederates in the army and behind the lines. Intriguingly, Andrew contends that voters often replaced incumbents "with men who had served at the front and been wounded in combat and now called for a greater commitment to the war effort"—a phenomenon he interprets as "an expression of evolving Confederate nationalism."[29]

The editors of a collection of essays on the final phase of the Confederate experience affirm that civilian morale remained in flux and "was never so uniformly depressed as hindsight would have it." Contesting what might be called the Appomattox syndrome (circular reasoning that the war had to end in Confederate defeat because the war ended in Confederate defeat), the editors conclude: "An air of inevitability has clung too long to the Confederacy's final months." One essayist responds to Drew Gilpin Faust's famous suggestion that disaffection among women may well explain "why the Confederacy did not endure longer." Jean V. Berlin acknowledges that women had grounds for unhappiness with their government, the enemy's armies, and even their own military defenders, but "to suggest that they hastened or postponed defeat is to ignore the complex interplay of Confederate ideology, religion, domestic politics, and military events in late 1864 and 1865." The women "focused their rage and disappointment solely on the North," states Berlin, "not on the institutions that failed them at home. And it would be this preoccupation with defeat at the hands of a demonized North, combined with a refusal to examine the failures of their beloved Confederacy, that would keep these women trapped among the ghosts of the past."[30]

---

29. Jacqueline Glass Campbell, *When Sherman Marched North from the Sea: Resistance on the Confederate Home Front* (Chapel Hill: Univ. of North Carolina Press, 2003); G. Ward Hubbs, *Guarding Greensboro: A Confederate Company in the Making of a Southern Community* (Athens: Univ. of Georgia Press, 2003); Mark V. Wetherington, *Plain Folk's Fight: The Civil War and Reconstruction in Piney Woods Georgia* (Chapel Hill: Univ. of North Carolina Press, 2005); Keith S. Bohannon, "'Witness the Redemption of the Army': Reenlistments in the Confederate Army of Tennessee, January–March 1864," and Rod Andrew Jr., "The Essential Nationalism of the People: Georgia's Confederate Congressional Election of 1863," both in *Inside the Confederate Nation: Essays in Honor of Emory M. Thomas*, ed. by Lesley J. Gordon and John C. Inscoe (Baton Rouge: Louisiana Univ. Press, 2005), 111-27, 128-46, quotation 143. For a treatment of Sherman's campaigns that suggests it crushed Confederate civilian will, see Russell F. Weigley, *A Great Civil War: A Military and Political History, 1861-1865* (Bloomington: Indiana Univ. Press, 2000), 390-96. Excellent testimony from the ranks of Hubbs's Alabama company is in Hubbs, ed., *Voices from Company D: Diaries by the Greensboro Guards, Fifth Alabama Infantry Regiment, Army of Northern Virginia* (Athens: Univ. of Georgia Press, 2003).

30. Mark Grimsley and Brooks D. Simpson, introduction, and Jean V. Berlin, "Did Confederate Women Lose the War? Deprivation, Destruction, and Despair on the Home Front," both in *The*

Imprecise definitions of key terms and questionable use of statistics can lead to confusion for those who navigate in Confederate interpretive waters. Descriptive terms such as "poor folk," "common folk," "plain people," and "the yeomanry" sometimes seem to be synonymous, other times not. Selfish planters most often dominate class-based arguments, but other slaveholders occasionally join them to take advantage of poorer Confederates. Is it as simple as slaveholders versus nonslaveholders (as Charles H. Wesley suggested more than seventy years ago)? The amorphous wealthy against equally amorphous poorer people? A single note in *Bitterly Divided*, number 11 on page 252, encapsulates the problem. It informs readers that different historians have defined yeomen as "small farmers and herdsmen" who owned no slaves, "up to four slaves," or, in South Carolina, as many as "eleven or twelve slaves." Anyone owning twelve slaves in 1860, it scarcely seems necessary to point out, surely resided in the middle or upper-middle class and should not be lumped together with nonslaveholders. Poor whites worked land that they did not own, but "plain folk" or "common folk," Williams continues, could embrace poor whites, yeomen, skilled artisans (or mechanics), and small merchants—producing a category so elastic as to possess little analytical value. Such imprecision, which marks many studies, can abet rhetoric about class conflict but seldom sheds light on anything as complex as the Confederate home front.

Projections of stark and often ill-defined class divisions mask critical factors at play in society and politics. Most obviously, racial attitudes united most Confederates across classes and geographical areas—something addressed in the 1920s by U. B. Phillips's "central theme" and in the early 1970s by George M. Fredrickson's application of "herrenvolk democracy." Does this mean nonslaveholders nursed no grudges against wealthier slaveholding neighbors? Of course not, but the former also were determined to maintain white supremacy and manifested widespread acquiescence in slavery as in institution that controlled black people and promised many white people economic gain and social status. As Edward A. Pollard commented after the war, slavery's true value to the white South lay as "a barrier against a contention and war of races."[31]

Collapse of the Confederacy, ed. by Grimsley and Simpson (Lincoln: Univ. of Nebraska Press, 2001), 11, 188. Other contributors to this collection include William B. Feis, George C. Rable, and Steven E. Woodworth. For Faust's quotation, see her "Altars of Sacrifice: Confederate Women and the Narratives of War," *Journal of American History* 76 (Mar. 1990): 1228.

31. Pollard quoted in U. B. Phillips, *The Course of the South to Secession*, ed. by E. Merton Coulter (New York: D. Appleton-Century, 1939), 163. See Phillips's "The Central Theme of Southern His-

Yankee victory would place fundamental racial order at risk, a threat that hardened Rebel resolve, across class lines, to resist. A telling example came in North Carolina's gubernatorial election of 1864, which at a time of pronounced war weariness in the state produced an overwhelming vote for Zebulon B. Vance over peace candidate William Woods Holden. "Vance's campaign and election matter," states one recent treatment, "because they highlight the role of racial fear in suppressing disaffection, in smoothing the tensions inherent in Confederate patriotism, and in keeping enlisted men committed to the war when the Confederacy violated some of its very reasons for being." Holden's identification with the unionist Heroes of America society, a group hoping for Confederate defeat and a return to the United States (and thus, in voters' minds, to emancipationist Republican rule), contributed to Vance's receiving more than 77 percent of civilian votes and 13,209 of 15,033 cast by soldiers.[32]

Politics in the Confederacy also pitted members of the same class against one another. Many of Jefferson Davis's most bitter opponents shared his status as a large slaveholder, and Confederates of all social strata locked horns with each other over impressment, taxes, conscription, arming slaves, and abridgements of civil liberties. "Those speaking for national unity and their libertarian opponents (not to mention moderates searching for some middle ground)," remarks George C. Rable, "all claimed to be the true defenders of a genuine Southern republicanism as well as a nascent Confederate nationalism." Intrigued by a central state that required passes to travel and arrested several thousand civilians, Mark E. Neely Jr. discusses rancorous conflict regarding civil liberties but concludes that "most Confederate citizens reconciled themselves to the restrictions on freedom typical of modern wars. Their experience mirrored that of the northern society with which they were at war." Proximity to U.S. armies and their destabilizing

---

tory" in the same volume, 152-65, and George M. Fredrickson, *The Black Image in the White Mind: The Debate on Afro-American Character and Destiny, 1817-1914* (New York: Harper and Row, 1971), 60-70. Phillips first offered his thoughts about a "central theme" in 1928 at a meeting of the American Historical Association in Indianapolis.

32. Chandra Manning, "The Order of Nature Would Be Reversed: Soldiers, Slavery, and the North Carolina Gubernatorial Election of 1864," in *North Carolinians in the Era of the Civil War and Reconstruction*, ed. by Paul D. Escott (Chapel Hill: Univ. of North Carolina Press, 2008), 118-19; William C. Harris, *William Woods Holden: Firebrand of North Carolina Politics* (Baton Rouge: Louisiana State Univ. Press, 1987), 150-53. Holden alleged that the soldier vote had been manipulated, but Harris believes an honest tally undoubtedly would have given Vance a majority. Inscoe and McKinney, *Heart of Confederate Appalachia*, argue that the peace movement regained momentum shortly after the election (161-63).

effect on slavery rather than class interests guided debates about arming slaves, suggests Philip D. Dillard in a comparative piece, with Texans opposing and Virginians supporting the proposal in the war's last phase. For Dillard, the "selection of independence over slavery by those who had seen and felt the full effect of war provides an eloquent statement about the strength of Confederate nationalism."[33]

Paul D. Escott also engages how Confederate society dealt with the presence of an enemy's military forces. Among the best and most influential scholars of dissent, he charts the exponential growth of central power as the Davis government sought to parry successive U.S. offensives. "The interests of the nation took precedence over the rights of the individual," Escott observes in a cautionary tone: "Measures necessary to reach military goals prevailed over accustomed norms, beliefs, and political philosophy. A central lesson from the Confederate experience is that war is a potent, corrosive agent of societal change that gains in power as the scope of fighting on the battlefield increases." Revisiting his earlier argument that profound disaffection spread after two years' fighting brought hardship to the home front, Escott attributes Confederate survival into the fourth spring of the conflict to "the coercive application of power by the central government, including military power." Thus did civil society "become militarized in the Confederacy."[34]

For scholars writing about the Confederacy, no definitions require greater exactitude than "Confederate" and "southern." The frequent conflation of these terms, David Williams aptly notes, leads to a "firmly embedded misconception" that masks the presence of anti-Confederate white southerners. Yet *Bitterly Divided*—preeminently an exploration of problems *within* the Confederacy—often blurs the line by using southerners living in the United States to bolster arguments

---

33. George C. Rable, *The Confederate Republic: A Revolution against Politics* (Chapel Hill: Univ. of North Carolina Press, 1994), 2-3; Mark E. Neely Jr., *Southern Rights: Political Prisoners and the Myth of Confederate Constitutionalism* (Charlottesville: Univ. Press of Virginia, 1999), 2-6, quotation 6; Philip D. Dillard, "'What Price Must We Pay for Victory?' Views on Arming Slaves from Lynchburg, Virginia, and Galveston, Texas," in Gordon and Inscoe, *Inside the Confederate Nation*, 316-31, quotation 328. See also Jaime A. Martinez, "The Slave Market in Civil War Virginia," in *Crucible of the Civil War: Virginia from Secession to Commemoration*, ed. by Edward L. Ayers, Gary W. Gallagher, and Andrew J. Torget (Charlottesville: Univ. of Virginia Press, 2006), 106-35, which makes this observation about the wartime market in slaves: "Until the very end of the Civil War, white Virginians continued to believe in the economic and social vitality of the institution of slavery, and whenever possible they participated in a sales and hiring market fully dependent on their level of confidence in Confederate independence" (131).

34. Paul D. Escott, *Military Necessity: Civil-Military Relations in the Confederacy* (Westport, Conn.: Praeger Security International, 2006), xiv, 176.

about internal weakness in the breakaway republic.[35] "If the nearly half-million southerners who served in the Union military had been with the Confederates," Williams states, "the opposing forces would have been almost evenly matched." Unwary readers might take this as stunning proof that calamitous numbers of its own citizens took up arms against the Confederacy. How did Williams arrive at his figure? Richard N. Current estimates 104,000 white men from the Confederacy donned blue uniforms (72,000 of them from Tennessee or western Virginia). Approximately 100,000 black men living in the Confederacy also served in U.S. military forces—bringing the total to just more than 200,000. Loyal slave states and the District of Columbia contributed another 209,502 white and 44,988 black soldiers. Even this broadest definition of "the South" yields a number lower than Williams's estimate—which also does not acknowledge 75,000 white men from loyal slave states who fought in the Confederate army.[36]

For an instructive contrast, readers should consult William W. Freehling's examination of anti-Confederates in the South. Freehling scrupulously defines the South as the whole that encompassed the Confederacy as its largest part. This book often is labeled a direct response to my *The Confederate War;* however, Freehling remarks in his preface that the two address different populations—mine the white people in the Confederacy (with brief attention to a few pro-Confederate Kentuckians and Marylanders) and his the white and black residents of the fifteen slave states. The two books clearly demonstrate why precise definitions of "Confederate" and "southern" (and their other forms) are so important. "If all the Slave South's inhabitants had emulated Confederate state whites," Freehling concedes, "southern battlefield commitments would have trumped home-front defections."[37]

Other recent readings of Confederate enlistments reveal a quite remarkable mobilization. Between 775,000 and 825,000 Confederate men probably served in their nation's armies—a number determined by subtracting the loyal slave

---

35. The closing sentence in chapter 1 sets a typical tone: "It was clear even in the early days that the disunited Confederacy was in for a two-front war: one against the North, the other against its own people." The first sentence in chapter 2 reinforces the idea that Williams is writing about the eleven states that left the Union: "As the excitement of summer faded into fall, home-front opposition continued to undermine the Confederate war effort." The final chapter offers this: "By the winter of 1864-65, most common folk were too busy fighting off Confederates to worry about the Yankees" (Williams, *Bitterly Divided*, 7, 52–53, 236).

36. Ibid., 7, 245; Richard Nelson Current, *Lincoln's Loyalists: Union Soldiers from the Confederacy* (Boston: Northeastern Univ. Press, 1992), 217–18; Frederick H. Dyer, *A Compendium of the War of the Rebellion* (Des Moines, Iowa: Dyer Publishing, 1908), 11.

37. Freehling, *South Versus the South*, xii–xiii.

states' 75,000 from the generally accepted total of 850,000–900,000. These soldiers came from a population that in 1860 contained 984,475 white men between the ages of seventeen and fifty (the expansive definition of "military age" adopted by the last Confederate conscription legislation). More reached draft age as the war unfolded, but the percentage placed in uniform remains impressive. "Between 1861 and 1865," observes one scholar, "almost 70 percent of Virginia's white men between the ages of fifteen and fifty served in Confederate forces. Calculating the figure using only those sections of Virginia controlled by the Confederacy, and thus reachable by enlistment and conscription agents, boosts the level to nearly 90 percent of eligible men." Another study finds that in early 1864 "Virginia had roughly 93 percent of all males of military-age either in the army or committed to war-related work."[38]

Percentages probably were lower in some Confederate states; many men in the ranks would have preferred to be elsewhere, others were absent without leave for a variety of reasons, and desertion rates might have approached 15 percent for the war (spiking in the spring of 1862, when conscription went into effect, and again beginning in late 1864).[39] Still, Confederate mobilization far exceeded that in the United States and, at least until the last months of the conflict, scarcely supports a portrait of massive popular disengagement.

That mobilization encompassed all classes. Few clichés have proved more durable than the "rich man's war / poor man's fight" formulation. Lacking solid statistics, historians too often fall back on assertions and anecdotes. *Bitterly Divided*, for example, insists that "so few men of means served that soldiers in Virginia sarcastically grumbled that it was easier for a camel to go through the eye of a needle than for a rich man to enter Camp Lee [a gathering point for recruits]."[40] Many poorer Confederates did grumble about class favoritism regarding military service,

---

38. Sheehan-Dean, *Why Confederates Fought*, 13; Blair, *Virginia's Private War*, 125; Thomas L. Livermore, *Numbers and Losses in the Civil War in America, 1861–1865* (1900; repr., Bloomington: Indiana Univ. Press, 1957), 20–22. Sheehan-Dean estimates the average enlistment rate in northern states to be 35 percent. Edward L. Ayers's comparative study of Franklin County, Pennsylvania, and Augusta County, Virginia, reveals the disparity in rates of enlistment: "Augusta, like the South as a whole, sent a higher proportion of its men into the service at each step of the war." By the end of 1862, Augusta had mobilized "almost double the rate relative to population" (Ayers, *In the Presence of Mine Enemies: War in the Heart of America, 1859–1863* [New York: Norton, 2003], 291–92).

39. Joseph T. Glatthaar estimates that desertions totaled just more than 14 percent in the Army of Northern Virginia: "In Lee's army, desertion was a problem, but it became critical after Lincoln's re-election, and it was reflective of all sorts of other problems" (Glatthaar, *General Lee's Army*, 532nn1,5). See also Gallagher, *Confederate War*, 31–32, 181n21.

40. Williams, *Bitterly Divided*, 57. Williams remarks that the initial conscription act offended

but this should not be taken as proof that slaveholders shirked their duty. Relying on records rather than anecdotal evidence, Joseph T. Glatthaar demonstrates that members of the slaveholding class were overrepresented in the Army of Northern Virginia in terms of both enlistments and casualties. The volunteers of 1861—nearly half of the total who served in the army during the war—"were 42 percent more likely to own slaves themselves or to live with family members who owned slaves than the general population." Those who entered service in 1862—another third of the total—arrived "having accumulated more wealth and owning more slaves [than enlistees in 1861], although the differences were not that pronounced." Many ties bound nonslaveholding soldiers to their more privileged comrades. "Untold numbers of enlistees rented land from, sold crops to, or worked for slaveholders," remarks Glatthaar: "For slaveholder and nonslaveholder alike, slavery lay at the heart of the Confederate nation."[41]

Because surviving Confederate records contain many vexing gaps, pinning down statistics and determining exactly what they indicate always will be challenging. A few last words about desertion are pertinent in this regard. Mark A. Weitz explains the difficulty of settling on definitive numbers, a problem compounded by the need to fathom how best to read surviving records. Once again, *Bitterly Divided* helps identify the issue. "Had it not been for the two-thirds of soldiers who were absent by September 1864," observes Williams, "the Confederacy might well have been able to offset the North's population advantage.... Together with hundreds of thousands more who actively and passively resisted the Confederacy, it was southerners themselves as much as anyone else who were responsible for Confederate defeat." This text doubtless would leave many, or even most, readers with an impression of catastrophic desertion by the early autumn of 1864.[42]

---

poorer Confederates because "monied men could simply pay an expensive commutation fee to the government in lieu of service. Or they could hire a substitute." Leaving aside that commutation fees were never part of Confederate conscription, it is true that substitution alienated poorer men—a circumstance that in late 1863 led Congress to get rid of it and make all who had purchased substitutes liable for service. (Williams neglects to mention this congressional response.) Some who had paid substitutes challenged the new law, but the "highest courts of the States and the Confederate district courts generally rejected the depositions of the principals" (Moore, *Conscription and Conflict*, 43-45).

41. Glatthaar, *General Lee's Army*, 19-20, 202-3, 403, 532n21. Glatthaar further estimates that between 6 and 8 percent of Lee's army were conscripts, less than a quarter of whom "either owned or lived with parents who owned slaves." This percentage was much closer to the overall rate of slaveholding in the Confederacy. The example of "rich men" risking their lives in the forefront of battle almost certainly inspired many "poor men" to fight with determination—a topic awaiting close study through letters, diaries, and other evidence.

42. Weitz, *More Damning than Slaughter*, ix-xi; Williams, *Bitterly Divided*, 242. Brig. Gen. John S. Preston, superintendent of the Confederate Bureau of Conscription, reported to the secretary of

Desertion unquestionably grew in severity as the war headed into its final nine months, but a closer look at the critical evidence—inspection returns—muddies the picture. The "consolidated abstract from returns of the Confederate Army on or about December 31, 1864" gives these numbers: Present for Duty, 154,910; Aggregate Present, 196,016; Aggregate Present & Absent, 400,787. These totals might seem to suggest that only 38.7 percent of the men were ready for duty and that the rest must have gone off somewhere. In fact, the first two categories (roughly one-half of the whole) include those literally present as well as all men detailed for duty elsewhere, under arrest in camp, sick in field hospitals, and in other categories. In the third category, the absent would include prisoners of war, men on furlough, and those in general hospitals due to illness or battlefield wounds—categories that do not necessarily support a portrait of class tensions ripping apart the armies.[43]

The August 19, 1864, inspection report for the 10th South Carolina Infantry of Brig. Gen. Arthur M. Manigault's brigade of the Army of Tennessee pinpoints the difficulty of extracting unequivocal numbers from manuscript sources. The report lists 208 men present for duty; 255 as the aggregate present, with 39 of them on special, extra, or daily duty and 8 sick; and 529 as aggregate present and absent, with 14 on detached service, 2 on leave, 156 absent sick, and 7 absent without authority. The sum of 255 + 14 + 2 + 156 + 7 equals only 434—95 short of 529. The report also has a column for prisoners of war listing another 96 men, producing a grand total of 530, one more than the aggregate present and absent (perhaps the clerk was tired or not very good at arithmetic). Some of those on detached service, on leave, or absent sick could have deserted and the regiment not yet known it; some of the 96 prisoners also could have taken the oath or joined the United States Army to fight Indians on the frontier. But without doubt many (most?) of the 274 or 275 soldiers not among the "present" or "aggregate present" should be reckoned loyal soldiers.[44]

---

war in February 1865 that just more than 33,000 deserters had been returned to the army during the course of the war. These men do not figure in Williams's calculations. (*The War of the Rebellion: A Compilation of the Official Records of the Union and Confederate Armies*, 128 vols.[Washington, D.C.: GPO, 1880-1901], ser. 3, vol. 5:711; hereafter cited as *OR*).

43. *OR*, ser. 4, vol. 3:989. U.S. returns for the same period are: Present for Duty, 495,899; Aggregate Present, 605,360; Aggregate Present & Absent, 936,996. (ser. 3, vol. 1:1034.) An alternate way to deploy statistics would be this: on June 30, 1864, after the massive casualties of the Overland campaign, the Army of Northern Virginia reported approximately 65,000 men present for duty—far more than were present in the wake of the Pennsylvania campaign a year earlier (ser. 4, vol. 3:520). I am indebted to Keith S. Bohannon, Joseph T. Glatthaar, Robert K. Krick, James H. Ogden III, and Carol Reardon for sharing their expertise regarding the complexity of returns.

44. James H. Ogden III to Gary W. Gallagher, Oct. 29, 2008 (e-mail). The material and analysis

Recent scholarship on the Confederacy resembles inspection returns that can be mined to support very different interpretations. Those such as David Williams interested in class conflict and other internal rupturing will be amply rewarded, but so will those seeking soldiers and civilians who persevered in the face of far greater human and material loss than that endured by any other group of white Americans. How should the evidence be judged? What are the relative meanings of Richmond's bread riots in the spring of 1863 and Rebel doggedness in the wake of the Overland campaign's grisly butcher's bill the following year? Does it matter that slaveholders probably entered military service in disproportionate numbers? Or should the focus be on the perception among some poorer Confederates that wealthier citizens could find ways to stay out of uniform? It has long been apparent that the abundance of firsthand accounts will support almost any interpretation. The key lies in playing it straight with bountiful literary evidence, doing the best possible job with incomplete official documents, and going where the preponderance of testimony and other materials points rather than cherry-picking quotations and facts to suit an argument.

Fruitful areas of inquiry beckon. Joseph T. Glatthaar's painstaking statistical work on the Army of Northern Virginia should be replicated with the Army of Tennessee, Trans-Mississippi forces to the extent possible, and other groups of Confederate soldiers. That would foster a discussion regarding, among other things, the degree to which Lee and his famous command played a singular role vis-à-vis the Confederate people's relationship with their nation. Similarly, more comparative regional work might shed light on the relative importance, as building blocks of Confederate national sentiment, of such factors as rates of slaveholding and how badly U.S. armies disrupted social and economic life. Substantive rather than impressionistic analysis of the workings of state and national slave impressment and other controversial measures also would be very helpful, as would greater care in resisting the temptation to equate unhappiness with Confederate policies with a desire to return to the United States.[45] The role of U.S. military forces remains vexingly underappreciated—as a factor in both

---

regarding the 10th South Carolina Infantry supplied by Ogden, a National Park Service historian at Chickamauga and Chattanooga National Military Park, includes a copy of the inspection report. Ogden notes that the terms "present for duty," "aggregate present," and "aggregate present and absent" were "frequently interpreted differently at the time"—which further complicates their use.

45. Jaime A. Martinez's forthcoming study of slave impressments in Virginia and North Carolina will make a good start on this topic. It will offer substantive analysis of rates of impressment by county and region, reactions among slaveholders to governmental policies, and the complex web of relations between military officers and state politicians.

depressing and strengthening Confederate morale and as the most transformative influence on the institution of slavery.

The time also has come to move beyond a binary approach to questions of disaffection, commitment to the nascent nation, and the like. The American Revolution presents a valuable comparative model in this respect, and historians would do well to keep in mind that many citizens fell into a category between the Confederate equivalents of Patriots and Loyalists. This nebulous group occupied "an ambivalent position," as one scholar has put it, manifesting fluctuating loyalties while always trying to do "what was best for themselves and for their families." A segment of the population "difficult to discern and even more difficult to quantify," these people certainly deserve closer attention. As with so many aspects of Confederate history, the impact of Union military forces likely played a significant role in shaping behavior and attitudes among people hoping to maintain some type of neutrality.[46]

This essay should leave no doubt about the volume and quality of work on the Confederacy. The continuing influence of the Appomattox syndrome remains evident, though the past few years have witnessed a powerful challenge to the idea that internal weaknesses quickly sapped Confederate energy and virtually guaranteed U.S. triumph. The pace of publishing in the field shows no sign of slackening, with important recent and forthcoming studies from Daniel E. Sutherland on the centrality of guerrilla warfare, John Majewski on attitudes toward political state building, Stephanie McCurry on a political transformation among the Confederacy's disenfranchised, and Kenneth W. Noe on soldiers who enlisted after 1861, to name but four.[47] These books will add to an imposing

---

46. David Brown, "North Carolinian Ambivalence: Rethinking Loyalty and Disaffection in the Civil War Piedmont," in Escott, *North Carolinians in the Era of the Civil War and Reconstruction*, 8. For a comparative look at nationalism in revolutionary America and the Confederacy, see Benjamin L. Carp, "Nations of American Rebels: Understanding Nationalism in Revolutionary North America and the Civil War South," *Civil War History* 48 (Mar. 2002): 5–33.

47. See Daniel E. Sutherland, *A Savage Conflict: The Decisive Role of Guerrillas in the American Civil War* (Chapel Hill: Univ. of North Carolina Press, 2009) and John Majewski, *Modernizing a Slave Economy: The Economic Vision of the Confederate Nation* (Chapel Hill: Univ. of North Carolina Press, 2009). For a preview of themes in McCurry's book, see her essay titled "Gender and the Politics of Subsistence in the Civil War South," in *Wars within a War: Controversy and Conflict over the American Civil War*, ed. by Joan Waugh and Gary W. Gallagher (Chapel Hill: Univ. of North Carolina Press, 2009). Majewski argues that southern opposition to a strong central government in the prewar years was closely linked to struggles against northern legislative dominance and that state rights sentiment weakened rapidly as Confederates sought to build their own nation. Noe's book will challenge many conventional views, including that post-1861 enlistees were more likely to desert

literature that has accumulated since Emory M. Thomas wrote *The Confederate Nation, 1861–1865*. That justly honored book has enjoyed a very long run, but the time has come for someone to undertake a new synthesis.[48]

---

or refuse to fight than comrades who joined earlier. Like many other scholars, Noe finds agreement across class lines regarding slavery and race.

48. For a tribute to Thomas and his scholarship, see Gordon and Inscoe, *Inside the Confederate Nation*.

Literature and Society

For the Good, the True, and the Beautiful

Northern Children's Magazines and the Civil War

JAMES MARTEN

"What has been gained by all the fighting?" young William asks Uncle Rodman in a story from *Our Young Folks* in the summer of 1865. Uncle Rodman lays aside his newspaper, removes his spectacles, and solemnly tells William and his sister Susie, "I am very glad to hear you express a wish to know more about the conflict that is now closing. It has been the great event of this century, and you ought to have a clear general idea of its origin and results." Four years ago, "it was not to be expected that you should understand what so many grown people failed to appreciate. But you are older now, and the terrible meaning of the war is clearer to us all than it was then." The subsequent dialogue explains the folly of Southern secession and the righteousness of the Northern victory. Its certainty in the right of the Union cause, its emphasis on the evils of slavery and slaveholders, and the earnest romanticism of its patriotism reflect the attitudes developed in Civil War–era children's magazines.[1]

While the editors and writers of children's magazines did take on war-related topics, they continued to utilize formats and embrace assumptions that had shaped children's literature for decades. Stories and articles promoted the principles of hard work, obedience, generosity, humility, and piety; provided moral guidance and examples of the benefits of family cohesion and the consequences

---

1. J. T. Trowbridge, "The Turning of the Leaf," *Our Young Folks* 1 (June 1865): 399.

of the absence of such order; and furnished mild adventure stories, innocent entertainment, and instruction. The values thus expressed were valuable anytime, of course, but were absolutely necessary at times of crisis—especially during a war being fought to defend exactly those noble traits. Works of fiction and nonfiction alike—"the incidental work of leading British and American authors, and the major work of some incidental writers of Victorian prose and poetry," in the words of John Morton Blum—stressed character and framed the world in moral terms. E. Douglas Branch unsympathetically characterized the tone of much of prewar children's literature when he described the story-telling scenarios of Peter Parley (Samuel G. Goodrich) in his books on history, geography, and nature: "a kindly old gentleman, marvelously well-informed, talking to an inquisitive set of little prigs." Authors of stories and novels as well as schoolbooks for children combined a faith in virtue with the confidence in the American political and economic systems; patriotism and good deeds and hard work and unselfishness together would guarantee individual success and national honor.[2] Much of the content of wartime children's periodicals reflected these antebellum concerns.

Yet they also moved from the antebellum reluctance to discuss politics, military affairs, and race relations in order to rally children to the Union war effort. Anne Scott MacLeod has shown that the "relentless moralizing" in children's literature between 1820 and 1860 tended to focus on self-improvement—especially temperance—and pacifism; the antislavery movement, on the other hand, was controversial. "Children's fiction was seldom chosen as a vehicle for the heavy burden of the national debate over slavery" because publishers simply could not afford to alienate important segments of the book-buying public. The dozens of best-selling books by Jacob Abbott "reflected little of that era's controversy or ferment for reform." When Abbott and others featured African Americans in their stories and novels, even the most sympathetic characters were burdened by stereotypes and by the condescension and patronizing attitudes of clearly more intelligent white characters. Surprisingly, perhaps, literature distributed

---

2. John Morton Blum, ed., *Yesterday's Children: An Anthology Compiled from the Pages of Our Young Folks, 1865-1873* (Boston: Houghton Mifflin, 1959), xiii; E. Douglas Branch, *The Sentimental Years, 1836-1860* (1934; reprint, New York: Hill and Wang, 1965), 312; J. Merton Englad, "The Democratic Faith in American Schoolbooks 1783-1860," *American Quarterly* 15 (Summer 1963): 191-99; Carol Billman, "McGuffey's Readers and Alger's Fiction: The Gospel of Virtue According to Popular Children's Literature," *Journal of Popular Culture* 11 (Winter 1977): 614-19; John H. Westerhoff III, *McGuffey and His Readers: Piety, Morality, and Education in Nineteenth-Century America* (Nashville: Abingdon, 1978); John G. Cawelti, *Apostles of the Self-Made Man* (Chicago: Univ. of Chicago Press 1965), 104-8.

by the American Sunday School Union avoided the issue of slavery. Children's magazines, according to John B. Crume, "asked no more of their . . . readers than that they behave themselves."³

The same caution applied to military subjects. As *The Student and Schoolmate* noted in August 1862, most Northerners had "only a few years ago . . . looked with a feeling bordering upon contempt on military matters." Public satire of military institutions prevailed; "a military company was senseless pageant to be enjoyed only by little boys and stupid men." It seemed that the militia system in Massachusetts would be abolished by public apathy, if not by law. The rebellion changed everything, however. "When Fort Sumter was bombarded, the military spirit rose to a tremendous pitch of enthusiasm," and society became more accepting of military uniforms and parades and training.⁴

Similarly, the war helped to transform periodical literature for children. Not only did children's magazines provide information about the war through accounts of battles and of life in the army, short biographies of leading generals and politicians, and entries on war-related trivia and statistics, but they also encouraged children to get involved in the Northern war effort by inspiring them with tales of bravery and patriotism, showing them how they could contribute to Union victory, and explaining the causes and history of the war in its political and moral contexts. The war furthered the transition in children's magazines described by R. Gordon Kelly, who argues that from their initial appearance in the 1780s through the 1840s, religious themes and imagery predominated over pleasure in the content of children's journals; by the 1860s, however, a "more relaxed attitude" had taken hold, with far less emphasis on conversion. After the Civil War, magazines dedicated themselves to "wholesome entertainment."⁵

The effects of the war on juvenile periodicals can be traced through six of the leading commercial magazines published in the North during and just after the

---

3. Anne Scott MacLeod, *A Moral Tale: Children's Fiction and American Culture, 1820-1860* (Hamden, Conn.: Archon Books, 1975), 104-16; Mary E. Quinlivan, "Race Relations in the Antebellum Children's Literature of Jacob Abbott," *Journal of Popular Culture* 16 (Summer 1982): 27-36; Donnarae C. MacCann, "The White Supremacy Myth in Juvenile Books About Blacks, 1830-1900" (Ph.D. diss., University of Iowa, 1988), 48-125; Anne M. Boylan, *Sunday School: The Formation of an American Institution, 1790-1880* (New Haven: Yale Univ. Press, 1988), 85; John B. Crume, "Children's Magazines, 1826-1857," *Journal of Popular Culture* 6 (Spring 1973): 698-707. See also John C. Crandell, "Patriotism and Humanitarian Reform in Children's Literature, 1825-1860," *American Quarterly* 21 (Spring 1969): 3-22.

4. "The Implements of War," *The Student and Schoolmate* 11 (Aug. 1862): 253-57.

5. R. Gordon Kelly, *Mother Was a Lady: Self and Society in Selected American Children's Periodicals, 1865-1890* (Westport, Conn.: Greenwood Press, 1974), 4.

war. Although they all shared similar goals and formats, subtle differences in tone differentiated them. *Merry's Museum*, which appeared under several names during its thirty-two-year career, was first published in 1841 and, during the war, was edited by John N. Stearns. Through columns like "Robert Merry's Chat with His Friends" and "Aunt Sue's Scrap-Bag," in which kindly advice was tendered and readers were encouraged to correspond with "Robert Merry" as well as with other readers, the *Museum* created a cozy, familiar community of readers who called themselves "cousins." (Other magazines also attempted to create such a sense of family, although less successfully; *The Student and Schoolmate* included a section called "The Teacher's Desk," while *Our Young Folks* called its games and correspondence section "Round the Evening Lamp.") Grace Greenwood's *The Little Pilgrim*, which came out in 1853 and lasted until 1868, took its name from John Bunyan's *Pilgrim's Progress*. Published by Leander Lippincott—Greenwood was the pen name of his wife, Sara J. C. Lippincott—it emphasized, perhaps more than the other magazines, middle-class morality and piety. *The Student and Schoolmate* was the product of the 1855 merger between *The Student and Young Tutor* with the *The Schoolmate*, and it survived several more mergers and name changes after the Civil War before its demise in 1872. Its editor, Oliver Optic (William T. Adams), was a prolific writer of children's books who stressed a temperate life-style and unquestioning patriotism. *Forrester's Playmate* began publication in Boston in 1854 and went through several name changes—including *Youth's Casket and Playmate*—before merging with the *Student and Schoolmate* in 1867. It featured the fewest articles and stories on the war, although its "Chat with Readers and Correspondence" section frequently included editorial remarks or letters related to wartime issues. Ticknor and Fields began publishing *Our Young Folks* in January 1865; its trio of editors—J. T. Trowbridge, Lucy Larcom, and Gail Hamilton—were well-known children's authors, and their magazine, despite its relatively brief eight-year career, was the first of the great postwar children's periodicals. According to Richard L. Darling, *Our Young Folks* "set the standard" for the increasingly secular and entertaining magazines of the latter third of the nineteenth century. Finally, *The Little Corporal* appeared during the first summer after the war and lasted until its absorption by *St. Nicholas* in 1875; its mascot was a boy dressed in a Zouave uniform and brandishing a sword and a pike. Although its content resembled other children's magazines of the period, the tone of its first few volumes was decidedly militaristic. Its motto demonstrated the mingling of the traditional concerns of children's journals with the military metaphors of which its editors were fond: "Fighting Against Wrong, and for The Good, the True and the Beautiful."[6]

These half-dozen magazines offered information, opinions, or war-related trivia in virtually every type of feature: short stories, nature sketches, travel articles, and "declamation" pieces, which in *The Student and Schoolmate* included symbols for the appropriate gestures and emphases. Words and picture games and songs often revolved around the war and Northern political principals. Illustrated rebuses asked readers to construct phrases based on a series of pictures or symbols that stood for words or sounds that, when combined, would phonetically create the correct answer. Some merely referred to images of battle: "Cannoneers delight in shooting their balls into the enemy's lines." Others were much more politically oriented: "We propose to make our flag shelter the oppressed wherever it waves," and "In the cause of Independence our forefathers sanctified their lives and fortunes. Let us aim to hand down to latest posterity the priceless heritage of the Union, cemented by their richest blood." Enigmas combined coded phrases with fill-in-the-blank questions on a wide variety of subjects, including the war: "They are for my Union though the last man should die," "Negro slavery is an institution the South did prize, Now dead and buried forever it lies," and "Secession rears its hideous, gory head, O'er fields of dying and the dead."[7]

The Little Corporal contained elaborate rebuses, called "picture stories," that often went on for several verses. One devoted half of its stanzas to the Civil War and challenged readers to deduce the following:

"They fall upon the falling South,
American eagle at the cannon's mouth; they rush upon the last redoubt.
The eagle grasps the flag about,
For Union and for victory!—The war is past—the fight is done—
The great rebellion overthrown!
The conquering eagle smooths her wings, And safely back each hero brings.
To Union and to Liberty!"

6. For an excellent analysis of this durable children's magazine, see Patricia Ann Pflieger, "A Visit to Merry's Museum; or, Social Values in a Nineteenth-Century American Periodical for Children" (Ph.D. diss., University of Minnesota, 1987). R. Gordon Kelly, ed. *Children's Periodicals of the United States* (Westport, Conn.: Greenwood Press, 1984), 285-91, 427-35, 329-41, 277-82; Richard L. Darling, *The Rise of Children's Book Reviewing in America 1865-1881* (New York: R. W. Bowker, 1968), 44.

7. *Our Young Folks* 1 (Apr. 1865): 287, 285; ibid. (Feb. 1865): 151; ibid. (May 1865): 350-51.

The Student and Schoolmate offered similar activities as well as a song on the last page of each issue; many of the latter were patriotic hymns that heralded the United States as the God-chosen home of Freedom. A typical example, "A Song of Hope," referred to the conflict that continued to ravage "the land that God was keeping, / Freedom's hope and home to be." Lacking specific images of the war, it nevertheless confidently asserted that "the Lord is watching o'er us, / He will lead through strife to peace." A later offering, "On to Richmond!" proclaimed that

> "Should coming days be dark and cold,
> We will not sigh or murmur,
> For Grant has said, with courage bold,
> 'We'll fight them here all summer.'"

The children's magazines did not ignore humor; *Our Young Folks* punished its readers with war-related jokes like "Why should soldiers never meddle with nutcrackers? Because they make shells burst on the kernel (Colonel)." In an 1860s version of "Kids say the darndest things" *The Little Pilgrim* had a section called "Anecdotes and Sayings of Children," which sometimes included comments by three to six year olds on the war. A little girl who had skinned her head, knees, and arms in a fall looked sadly at her wounds and said to her mother, "Oh dear! what dreadful times these war times are!" Another, revealing a small cut on her hand, explained, "I been to war, and fell down on a bullet, and it bleeded." One youngster, browsing through the battle scenes—replete with dead soldiers—published in *Harper's Weekly*, said, "Isn't it a pity, mamma, that so many men were wasted?" A picture in the same magazine of the "Dead Drummer-boy" inspired militaristic Eddie to declare that, when his father went to war, he would accompany him "as the *Dead Drummer Boy.*"[8]

Oliver Optic's *The Student and Schoolmate* presented dozens of vignettes and statistics—often in a section called "Curious and Amusing"—that targeted children's insatiable appetite for war trivia. In January 1862, readers learned, for instance, that Gen. Nathaniel Banks's division had sent 98,000 letters during one two-month period and that the U.S. flag waved in a portion of every Rebel state except

---

8. *The Little Corporal* 4 (May 1867): 80; Mrs. M. B. C Slade, "A Song of Hope," *The Student and Schoolmate* 13 (Jan. 1864): 32; L. Adams, "On to Richmond!" ibid. 14 (Aug. 1864): 64; "Round the Evening Lamp," *Our Young Folks* 1 (Feb. 1865): 151; *The Little Pilgrim* 8 (Dec. 1861): 163; ibid. 10 (July 1863): 97; ibid. 9 (Jan. 1862): 13; ibid. 10 (Aug. 1863): 111.

Alabama and Arkansas. Other entries informed children that the government paid sixteen dollars for each rifled musket it bought from the Springfield armory and that one young lady near Boston had already knitted one hundred pairs of mittens for soldiers during the first nine months of the war. In the spring of 1864, readers learned that the new commander of Union armies, General Grant, had been a wood-hauler only six years before. Brief entries told of children playing amidst the shelling of Vicksburg and of the scion of a wealthy New England family who walked seven miles each day as the mail-carrier for the 17th Connecticut.[9]

Two years into the war, Oliver Optic referred to the "cheap patriotism" reflected in the drum-beating and flag-waving of the early days of the war and applauded the deeper, more confident, and more sustained patriotism of both the army and the public. This seriousness was reflected in the scores of stories and articles that presented in a rather matter-of-fact way the nuts and bolts of life in the army and provided other war-related information of interest to their readers. *Merry's Museum* offered a biography of Gen. George B. McClellan late in 1861, as well as a description of common artillery pieces and their projectiles. Even "Aunt Sue" devoted a column of her "Scrap-Bag" to military insignia to help her readers "distinguish a Major-General from a First-Lieutenant and a Captain from a Corporal" and, later, described a line of battle. Charles C. Coffin offered readers of *The Student and Schoolmate* a series of "Letters from the Army" that provided matter-of-fact information about military matters. "A Walk Through the Camp" related methods of preparing and eating meals and warming tents and stressed the importance of soldiers of receiving and sending letters. "How an Army Lives" focused on foraging parties—which not only punished traitors but provided rations for soldiers—and on the "gay time" that followed the return of foragers to camp. "A Battle" described a skirmish between a brigade or two of Confederates and Yankees in Virginia; although Coffin provides a few tactical details and two small maps, he emphasizes the confusion and violence witnessed by the common soldiers. He ends on an ominous note: "Perhaps, one of these days if the war should continue, you will be found in the ranks ready to do what you can for your country." Another series appeared in the same journal about two years later. Called "Campaigning," it began with several articles that discussed the differences between companies, regiments, brigades, divisions, corps, and armies; another displayed the ways in which those units would be

---

9. *The Student and Schoolmate* 11 (Jan. 1862): 35; ibid. 11 (Feb. 1862): 71; ibid. 13 (Mar. 1864): 95; ibid. 12 (Oct. 1863): 312; ibid. 12 (Mar. 1863): 85.

deployed in battle. Later entries offered more exciting fare—the adventures of a daring squad of Union soldiers.[10]

The juvenile press went far beyond providing minutiae about the war. Although it would be too much to argue that children's writers in the North actually encouraged underage boys to join the army, many stories portrayed the extent to which a few children displayed their loyalty to the Union. Several threw their protagonists—often twelve years old or less—into battles or other dangerous situations and ranged in length from a paragraph about a fourteen-year-old hero on the USS Cumberland to full-blown short stories and serials. In "The Little Prisoner," young James is finally allowed by his widowed mother to become a drummer boy of an Ohio regiment. He proves his mettle at the Battle of the Wilderness, where he is also bayonetted—not seriously—by a Rebel intent on robbing the body of a friend of his father's. A kindly black woman takes him to an abandoned plantation nearby where she nurses him back to health, reads the Bible with him, and tells him about her long-lost son, who had been "sold South" years before but miraculously appears just as James is captured by John Mosby's raiders. The author describes the famous partisan as "manly" but cautions that the "stormy, unbridled passions, and ... cruel, inflexible disposition" ingrained in this slaveholder made him an oppressive commander and an unworthy enemy. Eventually, Mosby releases James, who returns home to his mother, revealing how "God dealt with a little boy who trusted in and prayed to him." A similar tale—purportedly a true story—has another twelve-year-old Yankee drummer boy, Robert, captured at the Battle of Chancellorsville, at which he cares for both wounded Union and Confederate soldiers. He encounters Robert E. Lee, who had "none of the smaller vices, but all of the larger ones; for he deliberately, basely, and under circumstances of unparalleled meanness, betrayed his country, and, long after all hope of success was lost, carried on a murderous war against his own race and kindred." Marse Robert treats the hero patronizingly and responds angrily when Robert declares, "I came out here, sir, to help fight the wicked men who are trying to destroy their country." Robert

---

10. "Teacher's Desk," ibid. 12 (June 1863): 189; "Major Gen. George B. McClellan," *Merry's Museum* 11 (Nov. 1861): 115-16; Wilforley, "A Summer Trip Eastward," ibid. (Dec. 1861): 138-41; "Aunt Sue's Scrap-Bag," ibid. 11 (Oct. 1861): 117; "Aunt Sue's Scrap-Bag," ibid. 12 (Sept. 1862): 88-89; Charles C. Coffin, "Letters from the Army," *The Student and Schoolmate* 11 (Feb. 1862): 55-58; ibid. (Mar. 1862): 90-93; ibid. (Jan. 1862): 16-19; "Campaigning," ibid. 14 (July 1864): 21-22; ibid. (Aug. 1864): 47-48; ibid. (Oct. 1864): 108-10; ibid. (Dec. 1864): 175-78; ibid. 15 (Feb. 1865): 39-42; ibid. (Apr. 1865): 117-18.

ends up in Libby Prison, where he survives a nasty fever, studies his lessons with a "good Colonel," and rediscovers one of the patients he had nursed during the battle, a seventeen-year-old Confederate who kindly helps him escape. This reversal of the magazine's usual presentation of Rebel perfidy is nevertheless true to form. Young, poor whites are not to blame for the carnage, at least in the war-stricken South presented in the juvenile press; "after all . . . it is true that the same humanity beats under a gray coat that beats under a blue one."[11]

A "Declamation" piece from *The Student and Schoolmate* portrayed a fifteen-year-old drummer boy who died from exposure the night after the battle at Fort Donelson. The six-stanza poem ended with the injunction,

"And there let him rest, on the battle-field fearful.
Where heroes, in thousands, repose at his side;
And we'll think on his doom with a feeling less tearful,
To know that for justice and freedom he died."

Another example of courageous piety was found in the fortitude of Eddy, a thirteen-year-old drummer boy at Gettysburg who loses his arm—enduring the amputation without chloroform—but proudly upholds a promise to his mother that he "wouldn't drink nor swear use tobacco nor play cards." He could never have kept that promise, he says, "if I hadn't known that 'Jesus is my Captain.'" The editor of *Forrester's Playmate* encouraged "old Playmates" who had joined the army to report on their experiences. "I *shouldn't* like to know many are fighting in the rebel army, if there be possibly a single one," he cautioned, but he did "want to know how many there are in arms against rebellion and treason."[12] A number of old "playmates," as well as former correspondents of *Merry's Museum* and *The Student and Schoolmate*, wrote of their army experiences.

Another major genre of stories and articles showed children of all ages actively participating in the war effort by acting out their more violent patriotic impulses, finding ways to support the troops or the families of soldiers, or taking on heavy responsibilities at home. In one common scenario, little boys drill with wooden swords and broomsticks and charge a group of girls who had giggled

---

11. Ibid. 11 (June 1862): 211; *Our Young Folks* (Jan. 1865): 33-37; ibid. (Apr. 1865): 240-44; ibid. (May 1865): 327-39; ibid. (July 1865): 462-65; ibid. (Sept. 1865): 600-608.

12. J. C. Hagen, "The Drummer-Boy of Fort Donelson," *The Student and Schoolmate* 12 (Sept. 1863): 278-279; Cousin Mabelle, "The Drummer Boy at Gettysburg," *The Little Corporal* 1 (Nov. 1865): 67-68; *Forrester's Playmate* 22 (Feb. 1864): 160.

at their efforts. In a similar story, a score of boys struggle to organize their own company of Zouaves; in their case, battle is nearly joined with a competing company who fortunately retreat in the face of superior numbers. In both stories, the children strive for authenticity in their equipment, uniform, and military demeanor. Young ladies also get into the act, but in gender-appropriate ways. A little girl named Nelly, inspired by her wounded and convalescing brother's stories of the United States Sanitary Commission, resolves to create a hospital for various wounded animals; she is the nurse, while the gardener's son is the surgeon. She builds a tiny ambulance with the Sanitary Commission emblem on the side and proceeds to treat a fly trapped in a spider's web—she calls it "a black contraband"—and a gray snake, even though it is obviously a Rebel. Her efforts cheer her brother to recovery and convince other children in the neighborhood to refrain from hurting innocent animals in the future.[13]

Other stories not only encouraged children to support the war directly but also provided lessons in humility and generosity. Gertrude, "The Discontented Girl," agrees to "scrape lint" for bandages but spends most of her time playing with a neighbor's parrot and complaining about her burden; she produces very little lint. Edgar, her older brother, arrives and scolds her for her attitude. "You don't want to belong to the rebel side, do you?" he asks. She says no, of course, to which he replies, "When I hear you talk so, I feel very sorry, and I say to myself, 'Gerty is a rebel, Gerty wants to secede.'" The parrot picks up the refrain and squawks the words to everyone who comes near, shaming Gerty into doing her duty. In "The Cloud with the Silver Lining," a little girl named Kate eagerly looks forward to attending a Sanitary Fair. When a downpour keeps her at home, she mopes around the house until a tiny beggar appears at the door. The daughter of a soldier killed in the war, all she has left to remember him is a uniform button. Kate and her mother give her food and clothing, and Kate presents her with the money she had saved to spend at the fair. A Sanitary Fair also enters into "The Two Christmas Evenings," by Lydia Marie Child, in which a family of well-off children receive Christmas presents with which they quickly become bored. Shamed into action by their father, they plan to give up their presents next year and to donate the money to the needy. This mushrooms into a series of performances (tableaux, speeches on liberty and patriotism) and sales of handicrafts

---

13. Christie Pearl, "The Fort and How it was Taken," *The Student and Schoolmate* 11 (Aug. 1862): 273-74; "The Yankee Zouaves: A Story for Boys," *The Little Pilgrim* 9 (Oct. 1862): 133-34; Louisa May Alcott, "Nelly's Hospital," *Our Young Folks* 1 (Apr. 1865): 267-77.

that eventually raise two hundred dollars for the local orphan asylum and for books and toys for black children in South Carolina.[14]

One children's magazine, *The Little Corporal*, appeared as the result of the most ambitious effort by Northern children: raising money for soldiers by selling pictures of "Old Abe, the War Eagle," mascot of the 8th Wisconsin. Children could earn commissions in "The Army of the American Eagle" by selling postcard-sized reproductions of the famous bird; a dollar's worth of sales earned a corporal's commission, ten dollars a captain's, one hundred a colonel's, four hundred a major-general's and so on. By July 1865, ten thousand children from around the country had raised fifteen thousand dollars for the Northwestern Sanitary Fair. Alfred L. Sewell, the Chicago lawyer who had organized the campaign, was inspired by the "precious letters . . . sweet heart-words, and . . . earnest patriotism" of the legions of boys and girls who joined his army and began publishing *The Little Corporal* in July 1865. After the war, Sewell continued to encourage benevolence among his subscribers; he asked them to provide subscriptions for poor war orphans at the Soldier's Orphan Home in Madison, Wisconsin, and, later, to orphans around the country.[15]

In the fictional world of the Civil War home front, children contributed in more private ways, too. In "A Box for the Soldier," a family of children place carefully chosen presents in a package for their father in the army. Nuts and apples are gathered from a hill where they and their father had played; one son sends his favorite knife while another sends a crudely whittled gun, sword, and cannon; the older daughters knit mittens and socks, while the youngest sews a sleeping cap "to keep his precious head from the frosty ground." All of the items would establish a sentimental link between the father and each of his children along with easing his life in the army. Their grandmother provides the most meaningful present, however; she sends the family Bible to her son, "the very Bible his father read out of; the Bible I've read out of for fifty years; the Bible that he himself read out of when a child. No other is like it nor *can be*—to me and to him too. And he'll never want it more than now, when he's every day

---

14. "The Discontented Girl," *The Little Pilgrim* 9 (Nov. 1862): 150-51; *Our Young Folks* 1 (Dec. 1865): 557-61; ibid. 2 (Jan. 1866): 2-13.

15. *The Little Corporal* 1 (July 1865): 1-3. A more detailed account of "Old Abe's" career and of the fund-raising campaign appeared in "The Veteran Eagle and what the Children Did," *The Little Corporal* 3 (Dec. 1866): 88-90. See also "The Veteran Eagle," *Our Young Folks* 2 (Oct. 1866): 616-22; *The Little Corporal* 2 (Feb. 1866): 30; "Soldiers' Orphans and the Poor: A Proposition," ibid. 4 (Jan. 1867): 13.

looking death so close in the face." "It seems to me," she concludes, "that God himself will go to my son, with that blessed book." The children solemnly and tearfully agree that "Grandmother has sent the *best* thing."[16]

Obviously, one prominent feature of life on the children's home front was the loss of loved ones. The deaths of fathers and brothers brought emotional and material burdens and often forced children to take on responsibilities normally filled by adults. "Renny's Uniform," which appeared in *Merry's Museum*, featured a young boy forced to break the news of his father's death to his mother. Dozens of other stories and poems echoed with the pathos of loss. "The Soldier's Baby" shows an infant sleeping as its mother weeps beside the cradle. "Death's cannon rattle" had claimed her husband and the baby's father. The author fails to provide a particularly uplifting ending:

> The baby is sleeping,
> Good angels are keeping
> Watch over its bed.
> Too young to know sorrow
> Or life's woes to borrow.
> Must learn some to-morrow,
> Its father is dead

In "Home-News in Battle-Time," a "Declamation" piece published in *Forrester's Playmate*, a dying soldier begs a friend to read a letter received that day from home. It contained the usual news

> "how baby ... Had learned to walk; how Tom had won the prize
> At school, last term; how he, the dear one, far away,
> Was prayed for nightly; how, with straining eyes,
> They waited his return, as for a festal day."

Apparently comforted with the letter's mundane familial news, when death came to the wounded soldier, he uttered "Good-night, my dears!"; his comrades buried the letter with him.[17]

---

16. "Mrs. Phebe H. Phelps, "A Box for the Soldier," *The Student and Schoolmate* 13 (Mar. 1864): 71–74. In "The Clouds that Rained Gold" (*The Little Corporal* 3 [Sept. 1866]: 37–38) children were warned that it was well and good to scrape lint of knit stockings for the soldiers as long as they also performed their normal duties around the household.

17. Pflieger, "A Visit to Merry's Museum," 147; C. Chauncey Burr, "The Soldier's Baby," *The*

"The Soldier's Little Boy" is not only the most maudlin example of a child filling an adult role, it also doubles the tragedy of wartime loss. The poem, which appeared in *The Little Pilgrim* in August 1863, depicted "little Willie" dying of an unnamed disease. "Who will care for you now, mother," he asks. The

> pain of leaving you here alone
> Is the sharpest pain I have;
> For I know you will never smile again,
> And no little boy will be nigh
> To wipe the tears on your cheek away,
> And whisper—"Dear mother, don't cry!"

Since his father's death at Antietam, "I did what I could . . . But my hands were young and weak." Despite his sorrow at leaving his mother alone, like a good Victorian Christian boy, he was

> not afraid to die . . .
> For the fear of death is past;
> But mother—oh, mother, you must not grieve,
> We'll meet again by and by—
> Where every tear shall be wiped away—
> Father, you, and I.

Equally tearful was the poem "The Soldier's Little Daughter," which told of a seven-year-old girl whose mother is dead, whose father is away in the army, and who is forced to beg from door to door. The narrator feeds her and brings her into his house; as she eats she asks plaintively, "And is it true as people say / That the war is ended—nearly?" Coincidentally, the Samaritan reads from a newspaper a list of recent casualties, which, not surprisingly, includes the little girl's father. He breaks the news to the girl, takes her sobbing into his arms, and swears to bring her up as one of his own, to

> Teach her to hold as sacred trust,
> Her patriot father's doom;

Student and Schoolmate 12 (Aug. 1863): 239; "Home-News in Battle-Time," *Forrester's Playmate* 23 (July 1864): 120.

Teach her to pray that from his dust
Freedom's fair flower may bloom.[18]

Less sensational was the serial "The House that Johnny Rented," which appeared in *The Little Corporal* during the first summer after the war. It told the story of the White family, whose minister father goes off to become a chaplain in the Union army, leaving the invalid mother and several children—including twelve-year-old Johnny—to fend for themselves. Forced to leave the parsonage in which they had lived for many years, Johnny finds the family a smaller but equally pleasant cottage to rent; there the children raise a garden, help their mother, fret about their father (who returns home on sick leave for a time), and help educate a contraband boy brought home by the Reverend White. The children are obedient and cheerful, they patriotically bad-mouth Confederate generals Lee and Beauregard, and they typically find that racial differences are less important than they previously thought.[19]

Finally, Northern juvenile magazines sought to instill an 1860s version of "political correctness" by defining Union War aims, establishing the centrality of slavery in causing the war, and recognizing the humanity of the former slaves. The Uncle Rodman who appeared in J. W. Trowbridge's "The Turning of the Leaf" summarized this political dogma: "In a word, children, slavery was the cause of the war; and God permitted the war in order that slavery might be destroyed." He goes on to stress the moderation of the Lincoln administration and intolerance of Southern slaveowners, who had "grown arrogant, conceited, overbearing . . . determined to destroy the government they could not control." Obviously, according to Uncle Rodham and dozens of other politically knowledgeable characters in children's stories, "the rebellion was a stupendous piece of folly, as well as stupendous wickedness." The benefits of the American political system, argued *Merry's Museum*, made "rebellion in such a country as this . . . the highest of crimes, because without excuse, and we all fervently desire to see it put down by every means." From his "Teacher's Desk" in *The Student and Schoolmate*, Oliver Optic proclaimed after Lincoln's assassination, "What a glorious spectacle is presented to the civilized world in the simplicity yet perfection of our form of government," in which the humble rise to great power, meet unrivaled chal-

18. Holly Clyde. "The Soldier's Little Boy," *The Little Pilgrim* 10 (Aug. 1863): 110; "The Soldier's Little Daughter," *The Student and Schoolmate* 11 (Apr. 1862): 131.

19. Emily Huntington Miller, "The House that Johnny Rented," *The Little Corporal* 1 (July 1865): 7-9; ibid. (Aug. 1865): 19-21; ibid. (Sept. 1865): 42-45.

lenges, and then, when "withdrawn from mortal sight to higher duties above," be replaced by an equally humble but also equally qualified successor. Throughout the war, Optic had included "Declamation" pieces aimed at inspiring patriotism and support for the war effort among his readers. Most were excerpts from the speeches of prominent Americans; they included the famous Tennessee Unionist "Parson" Brownlow's rebuke of Southern secessionists, Massachusetts governor John Andrew's salute to "Our Heroic Dead," Gen. Benjamin F. Butler's soliloquy on "Loyalty," Edward Everett's oration at Gettysburg, Gen. George McClellan's speech at West Point, and even Alexander Stephens's impassioned argument against secession at the Georgia convention in January 1861.[20]

The Student and Schoolmate also published in each issue brief playlets, or "Dialogues," many of which dealt with patriotic and war themes. In August 1862 a satire of the sectional conflict appeared called "The Comedy of Secession." Set in the "Union Seminary" for girls, its main characters included "Madame Columbia," the principal, and "Madame Britannia, a neutral old Lady, fond of giving advice," "La Belle France, fascinating, but cautious," the "Goddess of Liberty, a popular belle," and a bevy of students with names like "Georgiana," "Mary Land," "Vermont," "Little Rhody," "K. Tucky," and so on. The scene opens with Madame Columbia complaining about the behavior of a half dozen young ladies who "have become exceedingly rebellious, and threaten to leave—secede, they call it—without reason or justice, and contrary to the wishes of their fathers and mothers." Another half dozen "are sulky and impertinent, and I don't know whether they will stand by the rules of the school or join the malcontents." Much of the play consists of Madame Columbia lecturing the wayward "young ladies" on their irresponsibility, the good the seminary has done for them, and the shame they will bring on their ancestors. Nevertheless, the girls begin planning their own school, the "Confederate Seminary," where "J. Davis" will be principal, "Beauregard" dancing master, and "Wigfall" chaplain. The rebels are interrupted in their plotting by Goddess Liberty, who Miss Caroline tries to convince to come over to their seminary. When Liberty asks why they are leaving, the latter replies, "Because our rights have been trampled upon." To which Liberty retorts, "Nonsense! You mean if you cannot be the greatest toad in the puddle, you will set the river on fire." Accusations fly,

---

20. Trowbridge, "Turning of the Leaf," 399; "The Home Society," *Merry's Museum* 45 (June 1863): 164-65, quoted in Pflieger, "A Visit to Merry's Museum," 190; "Teacher's Desk," *The Student and Schoolmate*, 15 (June 1865): 190; ibid, 11 (Dec. 1862): 422-23; ibid. 12 (Feb. 1863): 56-57; ibid. (July 1863): 215-16; ibid. 13 (Mar. 1864): 88-89; ibid. 14 (Sept. 1864): 85-86; ibid. (Dec. 1864): 182-84.

Madame Britannia and La Belle France try to pick a fight with Madame Columbia, and the "Northern" girls rally around their principal. Although eleven young ladies eventually exit in a huff, "Miss Tennie" returns after a severe "whipping" and the company closes by singing the "Star Spangled Banner."[21]

A dialogue more directly aimed at instilling a spirit of sacrifice appeared in November 1863, four months after the bloody draft riot in New York City. "Avoiding the Draft" displayed the untoward self-pity of a well-to-do woman contemplating the vulnerability of her beloved son Walter to the "dreadful draft." She is put to shame by her Irish washerwoman, Bridget, who asks for a day off in order to prepare her "old man" for his trip to the army. A family friend adds to her shame when he arrives with the news of his and Walter's "prize" in the draft lottery; "this is no time for men to fall back," he declares, "Think of the glorious victories we have gained, and how much depends upon the future." Mrs. Brown still resists, but in the face of Walter's enthusiasm, she finally consents to his going. "It is to be a great trial," she admits, "but I must bear it; go, and let your country never have reason to blush for you."[22]

A pep talk in the form of a poem appeared during the uncertain fall of 1864. Bayard Taylor's "Looking Back!" responded to Copperheads and other proponents of peace. "What! hoist the white flag when our triumph is nigh? . . . crouch before Treason? make Freedom a lie?" Appealing to the memories of the heroes and martyrs of the Union, Taylor concedes that cowardice and treason threatens the Old Union. Yet he concludes with the oath,

> By the God of our Fathers! this shame we must share,
> But it grows too debasing for freemen to bear,
> And Washington, Jackson, will turn in their graves
> When the Union shall rest on two races of slaves.[23]

Part of the Northern gospel argued that the South had gone to war at the instigation and in the best interest of only a few aristocratic slaveholders. J. W. Trowbridge's "The Turning of the Leaf" characterized Rebel leaders as "confident that they could override Northern freemen as they had so long overridden their black slaves," deceiving and misleading "the ignorant masses" into going

---

21. "The Comedy of Secession," *The Student and Schoolmate* 11 (Aug. 1862): 279-28; ibid. (Sept. 1862): 314-19.
22. "Avoiding the Draft," ibid. 12 (Nov. 1863): 346-48.
23. Bayard Taylor, "Looking Back!" *Forrester's Playmate* 23 (Sept. 1864): 181.

to war under the banner of secession. Yet not all Southerners were so deluded; "there was a large class of loyal Unionists in the South, who loved the old government, and opposed secession," only to be driven from their homes and killed for their beliefs. *Merry's Museum* stressed the basic loyalty of most Southerners, who helped Yankees by nursing their wounds and aiding their escapes from Southern prisons. The single Rebel soldier whose background is described in a *Museum* war story is a victim of the tyrannical slaveocracy. Trowbridge played variations on his theme in a series of travelogues that appeared in *Our Young Folks* during the last months of the war and the two years that followed. The articles generally featured sites and battlefields in the South, but the first visit was to Camp Douglas, the Union prisoner-of-war camp in Chicago. The author guides the child "visitors" through the clean, orderly, well-managed camp, presenting the stern but fair commandant, the proficient guards, and the good-natured and healthy inmates. The most important political point—aside from contrasting the kind treatment of Confederate prisoners with the horrible treatment of Federal prisoners in the South—is that most of the men in the prison are delighted to be safely away from the war. They are well treated and many have taken the loyalty oath to the United States. In fact, most are actually very much like Northerners, "differing . . . only as they are warped by slavery or crushed by slaveholder." As many as a quarter of the prisoners had been forced into the Confederate army against their wills. The article ends with the conclusion of the war, but subsequent travelogues continued the theme of generally good-hearted Southerners led by a tiny coterie of slaveowners into a war few of them favored. Several travelogues by the same author offered similar accounts of Confederate cruelty toward Yankees and Southern Unionists combined with the realization that many—perhaps most—Southerners had only reluctantly supported the Confederacy and that they had suffered as well.[24]

Another important element in the political education of children was their introduction to the group over whom the war was being fought—Southern blacks. Several authors and correspondents combined their readers' politicization with

---

24. Trowbridge, "The Turning of the Leaf," 400; "Left on the Field," *Merry's Museum* 50 (Oct. 1865): 99; ibid. (Nov. 1865): 136, in Pflieger, "A Visit to Merry's Museum," 191; "A Visit to Camp Douglas," *Our Young Folks* 1 (Apr. 1865): 252-60; ibid. (May 1865): 291-300; ibid. (June 1865): 357-60; "Battle-Field of Fredericksburg," ibid. 2 (Mar. 1866): 163-70; "Richmond Prisons," ibid. 2 (Apr. 1866): 298-304; "A Tennessee Farm-House," ibid. 2 (June 1866): 370-76. Trowbridge also published a book for adults describing his travels in the South, *The South: A Tour of its Battle-fields and Ruined Cities* (Hartford: Stebbuis, 1866).

an attempt to awaken their social responsibilities by describing the conditions and needs of refugee blacks in terms with which Northern white children could identify. G. N. Coan wrote of the thousands of freedmen crowding Norfolk, Virginia, in the spring of 1864, many of whom "are as white as any of you are, with blue eyes and straight hair, or pretty auburn ringlets." Color had not made them slaves, but the "African blood in their veins had doomed them to suffer the cruelty of the auction block" where "mothers and children [were] torn asunder by their cruel masters, never to see each others' faces again." The little ones among the freedmen love to go to school and learn quickly; "could you see their eyes sparkle and their faces shine with delight, as they sing their little songs (such as you sing), and hear them answer questions from the Bible, I am sure you would be delighted, and think they were anything but stupid." They constantly present their teachers with simple gifts and frequently express their love for President Lincoln and "Uncle Sam." The letter concludes with a request for help. "Now, dear children, can you not do something for these poor little ones? There are still hundreds of them who cannot go to school for want of comfortable or decent clothing: will you not send them some of your old dresses, quilts, sacks, or shoes, so that they may be able to go to school, and learn to read the word of God, and thus become good men and women?" Another appeal for aid in the *Little Pilgrim* assured readers that former slave children "love [the *Little Pilgrim*] and his pretty stories, very much" but also stressed that many of the recently freed blacks "are ignorant and debased." They needed help in the form of clothes, schools, books; the correspondent urged friends of the *Little Pilgrim* to "whisper a sweet, pleading whisper in the ear of each and every dear friend . . . to send all they can spare," convince rich parents or uncles or aunts to send money, and to contribute toy and candy money to the cause of the freed children.[25]

Christie Pearl's "The Contraband" offered a fictional account of children who not only respond to a newspaper's call for clothing for the freed slaves but also find that there are wrong and right ways of demonstrating concern for the less fortunate. At first, the half-dozen or so children of a solidly upper-middle-class family treat the call for aid flippantly, eagerly casting off clothes that are too small, too ugly, too impractical to keep. Along the way, they imagine the improbable and entertaining sight of the contrabands wearing the "dickeys" and bracelets and old hats they plan to pack into the barrel and rejoice that by clearing out

---

25. G. N. Coan, "Correspondence," *Little Pilgrim* 11 (June 1864): 81-82; Clara C. Clark, "An Appeal," ibid 9 (July 1862): 93.

their closets of unwanted clothing they will be able to buy new wardrobes. Their father interrupts the fun with "a loud 'Ahem!'" and asks sternly, "are there any things there that you want or need?" When they reply that there is not, he lectures them, "Then you have not given properly. Your clothes may keep the 'contrabands' warm, but they will bring no additional warmth to your own hearts. You must make sacrifices in order to reap the benefit of giving." Promptly and properly chagrined, the children repack the aid barrel with warm, practical clothes—some of them the children's favorites—as well as a doll and a top. A note attached to the former reads, "My dear little 'Contraband':—Whoever you may be, we send you our doll with all her clothes. If she don't keep you warm outside, she'll make you as heart warm, we guess."[26]

The images of blacks as rather pitiable creatures was also reflected in the words of a little girl reported by her mother to *The Little Pilgrim*. The daughter, after hearing about some "very poor and distressed ... colored children" living nearby, pleaded in her prayers, "Oh God, you have made these poor children *black*, and now will you please make white people kind to them." More heart warming, perhaps, was "Christmas, After All," which also featured well-off children achieving a high, if rather smug, level of selflessness. Unable to come up with a "grand" way to celebrate Christmas, the children listen to a story from their African American servant, Aunt Thula, who tells them about her daughter Peely, now a grown woman of thirty-five, who was supposed to be freed when her master died. After his death, however, his heirs moved many of the slaves they inherited to Tennessee, including Peely. The children pool their resources and give Thula enough money to buy her daughter out of slavery. On Christmas day, the nuts and candy they find in their stockings taste better knowing Peely was no longer a slave; pleased with herself, one girl declares, "It was a good Christmas, because it wasn't a selfish Christmas."[27]

While most references to African-Americans were to the unfortunate but enthusiastic contrabands, a story that appeared in *Forrester's Playmate* in early 1864 actually relates an incident between the narrator and a free black living in the North. One evening while playing, the narrator and several of his "playfellows" begin harassing Jim Dick, a young black boy playing with them, by calling him "'negro,' 'blackamoor,' and other ill names." Jim leaves the group, "very much

---

26. Christie Pearl, "The Contraband," *The Student and Schoolmate* 11 (Feb. 1862): 45–48.
27. "Anecdotes and Sayings of Children," *The Little Pilgrim* 9 (Sept. 1862): 125; "Christmas, After All," ibid. 9 (Apr. 1862): 50–52.

hurt at our conduct." Nevertheless, when the narrator asks to borrow Jim's ice skates a few days later, Jim lends them willingly. When the white boy returns the skates, he finds Jim sitting before his Bible, "with tears in his eyes." He then "kindly and meekly" says, "Do not call me blackamoor again." Although it took place a number of years before the war, the narrator remembers that "these words went to my heart; I burst into tears, and from that time I resolved I would never again be guilty of abusing a poor black." Many lessons could be learned from this little vignette, the author argued; do not use insulting names or mock others; have a forgiving spirit and control your anger; and "do not undervalue any for the color of skin, or the shape of their bodies, or the poverty of their condition, for we are as God made us." "Black George" struck a similar note. It tells of the author's girlhood friend George, a young black living in New York many years before. One day, his white guardian—who had purchased the boy, freed him, and sent him to school—spots him scrubbing his skin raw with soap and sand. "Oh, sir!" George exclaims, "the black wont come off! What *did* God make me so for?" Mr. Rich assures the distressed little boy, "God did make you so, and whatever He has made is good. You need never be ashamed of your skin, for God loves you just as well as though it were white, and we shall love you, too, if you are a good boy." Just to make sure readers got the message of racial sensitivity, the last line intones "Children, never call a black boy a 'nigger' again." *Our Young Folks* told of a slave boy named "Dog Carlos" who, fed up with abuse from his younger master Harry and threatened with a whipping when he is caught coming out of a forbidden prayer meeting, runs away and joins Sherman's men as they march through the area. The author gently reminds his readers that they must not judge Harry too harshly, "or plume yourself as being so much better, unless you are quite certain that, if you had a boy or a dog all to yourself, and were sure that papa and mamma would either know nothing or say nothing about it, you would not cuff and strike him when you were very much out of humor, as I have seen certain little Northerners do to their brothers, and sisters, and pets."[28]

Occasionally, very different images of freedom appeared. Stories in *Merry's Museum* tended to portray black characters as stereotypes, complete with nearly incomprehensible dialects, and as vehicles for providing comic relief. A story

---

28. "Jim Dick; or the Best Revenge," *Forrester's Playmate* 23 (May 1864): 45-46; "Black George," *The Little Pilgrim* 9 (June 1862): 80; "Dog Carlos," *Our Young Folks* 1 (Oct. 1865): 644-51. For Jacob Abbott's treatment of sympathetic black characters—in which young African Americans persevere in the face of discrimination and name calling—see Quinlivan, "Race Relations in the Antebellum Children's Literature of Jacob Abbott," 27-36.

from the *Little Pilgrim* provides a reminder of the standards of grateful obedience expected of children—especially recently freed slaves. A little boy calling himself George Washington had attached himself to an army unit stationed at City Point, Virginia. The soldiers gave him clothes, dressed him up, and gave him a job helping the cook. They also made him something of a pet as well as the object of practical jokes, such as painting his face as he slept. The author, apparently rather puzzled that such treatment was not acceptable to young George, reports that he was a "good boy" for a while but soon got "lazy" and began stealing and was sent out of camp. "Had he been a good little contraband," the narrator concludes sternly, "he would have had a good home."[29]

It is impossible, of course, to trace the effects of juvenile magazines on the political development of Civil War-era children. Subscription lists have vanished and virtually no memoirist refers to having read any of the periodicals mentioned above. Yet thousands of children did read these magazines, and, if political scientists who study the politicization of children are correct, they internalized at least some of the values and ideas that were promoted in the stories and poems and games and editorials of their youth. John Morton Blum suggests that *Our Young Folks*—and, by extension, other children's periodicals—"gave direction and possibly also courage to children, whatever their place of residence, who did their reading in New England's lingering twilight." It transmitted New England culture in particular and American culture in general to the generation that came of age after 1880, providing not only a complement to their formal education but also socialization and politicization to American values and assumptions.[30]

One reader of such magazines was young Theodore Roosevelt, who, although he was less than three when the Civil War began, was swept up in the war, playing a game he called "Running the Blockade" and wearing his own colorful Zouave uniform. Driven by his poor health as a youngster, by his father's decision to hire a substitute to take his place in the army, by the exploits of Southern uncles and other relatives in the war, and by his later acquaintance with many of the leading generals of the Union armies, Theodore came to see war as a noble enterprise, as an opportunity for glory and as the vehicle for personal, moral reformation. He hated cowardice, loved the "strenuous life," and

---

29. Pflieger, "A Visit to Merry's Museum," 185-87; "The Little Contraband," *The Little Pilgrim* 13 (Feb. 1866): 18.

30. R. W. Connell, *The Child's Construction of Politics* (Melbourne: Melbourne Univ. Press, 1970), 43-49; Fred I. Greenstein, *Children and Politics* (New Haven: Yale Univ. Press, 1965), 71-72; Blum, *Yesterday's Children*, xv.

admired military discipline and military leaders.[31] The entire era of the Civil War and Reconstruction had an extraordinary impact on Roosevelt's character and interests and view of the world, but it must not be overlooked that among young Theodore's favorite reading material was the magazine *Our Young Folks*. Few other connections between wartime experiences and postwar attitudes can be so directly established, much less attributed to children's reading habits. Yet magazines like Roosevelt's childhood favorite surely played an important role in the incorporation of children into the world wrought by civil war. Applying familiar themes and formulae to exciting and frightening new situations, they helped explain the war—its causes, its conduct, and its ultimate meaning—to the sons and daughters and nieces and nephews and brothers and sisters of the Northern soldiers fighting it.[32]

---

31. Kathleen Dalton, "Theodore Roosevelt and the Idea of War," *Theodore Roosevelt Association Journal* 7 (Fall 1948 1): 6-12.

32. Far fewer children's magazines appeared in the Confederacy than in the Union states. Shortages of paper and printing facilities and a deteriorating economic situation plagued Southern publishers throughout the war. As a result, only a few issues of a handful of Southern magazines survive to the present. Nevertheless, they complement Northern magazines in their presentation of patriotic narratives and images. The two longest-running periodicals were the *Child's Index* and the *Deaf Mute Casket*. Samuel Boykin published the former as a hard-shell Baptist Sunday school paper, while the North Carolina Institution for the Deaf and Dumb and the Blind published the latter. Other short-lived publications included the *Children's Guide*, a Methodist Sunday school paper, and the *Child's Banner*, another religious publication out of Salisbury, North Carolina. Although their religious content was more prominent than in typical Northern magazines, they, too, provided stories and articles that explained the war to children and showed the ways that children were involved in the war. See Sarah Law Kennerly, "Confederate Juvenile Imprints: Children's Books and Periodicals Published in the Confederate States of America, 1861-1865" (Ph.D. diss., University of Michigan, 1956), 250-312.

The Sentimental Soldier in Popular Civil War Literature, 1861–65

ALICE FAHS

> These Hospitals, so different from all others—these thousands, and tens of twenties of thousands of American young men, badly wounded, all sorts of wounds, operated on, pallid with diarrhea, languishing, dying with fever, pneumonia, etc., open a new world somehow to me, giving closer insights, new things, exploring deeper mines than any yet, showing our humanity (I sometimes put myself in fancy in the cot, with typhoid, or under the knife) tried by terrible, fearfulest tests, probed deepest, the living soul's, the body's tragedies, bursting the petty bonds of art. To these, what are your dramas and poems, even the oldest and tearfulest?
> —Walt Whitman

"Oh! it is great for our country to die," began a poem published in the *Boston Transcript* on May 28, 1861; "Bright is the wreath of our fame; glory awaits us for aye." "It is well—it is well thus to die in my youth, / A martyr to freedom and justice and truth!" proclaimed the narrator of the October 1861 *Southern Monthly* poem "The Dying Soldier."[1] At the start of the Civil War, numerous popular poems and songs

---

  1. James G. Percivial, "It Is Great For Our Country To Die," in *The Rebellion Record: a Diary of American Events, with Documents, Narratives, Illustrative Incidents, Poetry, etc.*, ed. Frank Moore, 11 vols. (New York: G. P. Putnam, 1861–63; D. Van Nostrand, 1864–68), 1:105; *Southern Monthly* 1 (Dec. 1861): 249.

Civil War History, Vol. XLVI No. 2 © 2000 by The Kent State University Press

both North and South offered variations on the classical adage *dulce et decorum est pro patria mori*, imagining the subordination of individual interests to the needs of the nation.[2] Diarists, too, approvingly noted the patriotic sentiments of such literature: Caroline Cowle Richards of Canandaigua, New York, for instance, reported in May 1861 that it seemed "very patriotic and grand" to hear departing soldiers singing '"It is sweet, Oh, 'tis sweet, for one's country to die.'"[3]

Yet by 1862, and then in increasing numbers as battle deaths mounted during 1863 and 1864, popular poems and songs that asserted the importance and individuality of the ordinary soldier acted as a counterpoint to literature that stressed the subordination of individual interests to the needs of country. Hundreds of sentimental stories, songs, and poems focused intently on the individual experiences of the ordinary soldier on the battlefield and in the hospital, especially imagining that soldier's thoughts at the moment of death. As the mass movements of armies increasingly defined the war, and the outcome of battle was increasingly mass slaughter, an outpouring of sentimental literature fought against the idea of the mass, instead singling out the individual soldier as an icon of heroism.

An examination of wartime sentimental soldier literature, part of an extensive popular war literature that both explored and shaped the meanings of the war, forces a reassessment of a long-lived paradigm of the cultural history of the war. In 1965 George M. Fredrickson wrote in *The Inner Civil War*, his influential study of Northern intellectuals and their responses to the war, that during the war "a process of natural selection was occurring which was giving more relevance to impersonal efficiency than to pity or compassion." At the same time, because "there were clear limitations to what could actually be accomplished for the relief of the wounded and dying, a stoical and fatalistic sense of the inevitability of large-scale suffering was also being inculcated. Implicit in both developments was a challenge to those antebellum humanitarians who believed that sympathy was the noblest of emotions and that all suffering for which human beings could be held responsible was unacceptable and called for immediate relief."[4]

---

2. Similarities between Northern and Southern wartime poetry and songs far outweigh their differences. Thus a study of popular literary culture during the war buttresses Reid Mitchell's assertion that a "shared American culture" can be found in the experiences of soldiers during the war. See Reid Mitchell, "'Not the General but the Soldier': The Study of Civil War Soldiers," in *Writing the Civil War: The Quest to Understand*, eds. James M. McPherson and William J. Cooper (Columbia: University of South Carolina Press, 1998), 88.

3. Caroline Cowles Richards, *Village Life in America 1852–1872 including the Period of the American Civil War as Told in the Diary of a School-Girl* (New York: Henry Holt, 1913), 131.

4. George M. Fredrickson, *The Inner Civil War: Northern Intellectuals and the Crisis of the Union* (New York: Harper and Row, 1965), 90.

In Fredrickson's account, Northern intellectuals during the war turned away from the anti-institutionalism of the antebellum era to embrace new values of centralization and organization within American life.

Fredrickson provided an acute analysis of the experiences of many Northern intellectuals, especially those who sought to organize the care of wounded soldiers under the auspices of the Sanitary Commission. But while he confined his analysis to a small but influential group of intellectuals, other writers have assumed that a new adherence to ideologies of impersonal efficiency, centralization, organization, and consolidation characterized a wide swath of Northern culture during and after the war.[5]

This chapter argues that sentimental soldier literature offers a corrective to this "organization thesis" governing the cultural history of the war.[6] In doing so it points to popular literature, both widely distributed and widely read and shared, as an important but often neglected part of the cultural and intellectual history of the war.[7] Popular war poetry, for instance, was not only declaimed on

---

5. See David S. Reynolds's account of a wartime transition from an ethos of individualism and sentimentalism in his *Walt Whitman's America; A Cultural Biography* (New York: Alfred A. Knopf, 1995), 431-32. In Reynolds's account, which cites Fredrickson, Whitman's "individualistic, anti-institutional bias" was a "holdover from the fifties." See also Eric Foner, *The Story of American Freedom* (New York: W. W. Norton, 1998); Lori D. Ginzberg, *Women and the Work of Benevolence: Morality, Politics and Class in the Nineteenth-Century United States* (New Haven: Yale University Press, 1990). Most recently, Jeanie Attie has taken issue with Ginzberg's version of the organization thesis in *Patriotic Toil: Northern Women and the American Civil War* (Ithaca: Cornell University Press, 1998). Examining the work of local aid societies, Attie has found that by the middle of the war Northern women resisted the call from the U.S. Sanitary Commission to centralize their relief efforts, and turned increasingly instead to the U.S. Christian Commission, which had a focus on the religious and physical needs of individuals.

6. Fredrickson's "organization thesis" was influenced by the work of Allan Nevins, whom Fredrickson cited in the introduction to the 1993 revised edition of *The Inner Civil War* (Urbana: University of Illinois Press, 1993), ix. The seventh and eighth volumes of Nevins's epic *Ordeal of the Union* announced this thesis explicitly in their subtitles: volume 7 was "The Organized War," while volume 8 was "The Organized War to Victory." Nevins wrote: "To organize armies, to organize the production of arms, munitions, clothing, and food, to organize medical services and finance, to organize public sentiment—all this required unprecedented attention to plan, and an unprecedented amount of cooperative effort. The resultant alteration in the national character was one of the central results of the struggle." (See Allan Nevins as quoted in James M. McPherson, "Introduction," *Ordeal of the Union*, 4 [1971; rpt., New York: Collier Books, 1992], vi-vii.) The particular trajectory of Civil War cultural history has given Nevins' thesis a prominence it has long since lost in political, social, and military histories of the war.

7. In this article "popular literature" refers to a wide and inclusive range of Civil War literature intended to appeal to a large public. Such literature cannot simply be summarized with the label of "low" to distinguish it from "high" literature. Instead, publications such as *Harper's Weekly*, or songsheets distributed to hundreds of thousands of people, often occupied a middle ground that

numerous public occasions as part of what Kenneth Cmiel has called a culture of "democratic eloquence," but was also exchanged widely among newspapers both North and South.[8] Such poetry was part of an understanding of the war as a public literary event: far from literature being separate from the experience of the war, it was accepted as an appropriate, expected, and often deeply felt part of that experience. Popular war songs, too, were part of this public culture of war: "piled up by the gross on counters for sale," according to Oliver Wendell Holmes, they were "dinned in our ears by all manner of voices until they have made spots on our ear-drums like those the drumsticks made on the drum-head."[9]

An analysis of the ideology of this popular war literature shows that an insistence on the individual, personal meanings of the war was far more prevalent than is usually recognized, and that it was an important counterpoint to developing ideas of the war as new forms of system and organization in American life. A study of popular literature thus helps to provide a fuller cultural history of the war, at the same time reminding us that ideas were developed during the war not just in the writings of intellectuals, but in a broad array of popular cultural forms as well. Within this wide-ranging popular literature—and among a broad reading public—a sentimental insistence on the importance of sympathy and individual suffering became the most potent mode of discussing and coping with the wounding and killing of soldiers during the war. Far from sentimental individualism having been discarded during the war, it received new energy within the realm of popular literature.

The insistence on the individual soldier within popular literature did not mean that he was depicted in the "realistic" mode of late-nineteenth-century social realism, with its insistence on the primacy of "fact" and a mimetic depiction of social conditions.[10] Instead, the sentimental soldier of popular wartime literature was

---

incorporated elements of both "high" and "low." The high-low dichotomy was in fact shaped in the late nineteenth and early twentieth centuries to categorize and organize cultural authority, and must be used with caution in assessing mid-nineteenth-century culture. On this, see Lawrence Levine, *Highbrow/Lowbrow: The Emergence of Cultural Hierarchy in America* (Cambridge, Mass.: Harvard University Press, 1988). There has been no systematic study of the popular culture of the Civil War. But for the Mexican War, see Robert W. Johannsen, *To the Halls of the Montezumas: The Mexican War in the American Imagination* (New York: Oxford University Press, 1985).

8. Kenneth Cmiel, *Democratic Eloquence: The Fight over Popular Speech in Nineteenth-Century America* (New York: Morrow, 1990).

9. Oliver Wendell Holmes, unpublished 1865 lecture, "The Poetry of the War," Huntington Library.

10. On realism see Eric J. Sundquist, ed., *American Realism: New Essays* (Baltimore: Johns Hopkins University Press, 1982).

conventionalized and typologized, presented within a framework of sentimentalism that insisted on the primacy of emotion and sentiment as a form of "reality." Both a popular mode of thought and language of expression in mid-nineteenth-century America, sentimentalism emphasized emotion as central to the individual's life. For sentimentalists, powerful feelings structured individual identity—but not as the bursts of solitary rapture or the intimate communion with nature earlier celebrated by English Romantics, or, in a different key, by American Transcendentalists. Sentimentalists celebrated sympathy, not self-communion; they portrayed experiences of emotion as social events rooted in human relationships, legitimized through being witnessed by or communicated to another.[11]

Because sentimentalism stressed the social—and potentially transformative—nature of emotion, sentimental literature often included deathbed scenes in which a character's impending death had a powerful impact on the lives of witnesses. The most famous of all antebellum sentimental deathbed scenes, for instance, Little Eva's lingering death in Harriet Beecher Stowe's 1852 *Uncle Tom's Cabin*, was portrayed as a profoundly social act, with one after another of the characters in the novel receiving guidance and inspiration through their last contact with her. Her death was conceived of as deeply spiritual as well. *Uncle Tom's Cabin* was written within an explicitly Christian framework—what one scholar has called the "Sentimental Love Religion" of sacrifice, suffering, and redemption that in the mid-nineteenth century increasingly offered a stirring, personalized alternative to the sometimes grim rigors of Calvinism. Within this emotive religion, the bodily sufferings and deaths of little Eva and, especially, Uncle Tom, were crucial elements of a redemptive Christian national parable, in which the exercise of a sacred domesticity would redeem the nation from the sin of slavery. A vast antebellum popular literature shared Stowe's concern with the Christian-influenced themes of sacrifice, suffering, and redemption—especially through the vehicle of the suffering body.[12]

---

11. On the social nature of sentimentalism, see Karen Halttunen, *Confidence Men and Painted Women: A Study of Middle-Class Culture in America, 1830-1870* (New Haven: Yale University Press, 1982). On sentimentalism as a mode of thought and language, see especially Barton Levi St. Armand, *Emily Dickinson and Her Culture: the Soul's Society* (New York: Cambridge University Press, 1984); Jane Tompkins, *Sensational Designs The Cultural Work of American Fiction, 1790-1860* (New York: Oxford University Press, 1985); Christine Bold, "Popular Forms I," in *The Columbia History of the American Novel*, gen. ed. Emory Elliot (New York: Columbia University Press, 1991).

12. Barton Levi St. Armand uses the term "Sentimental Love Religion" in *Emily Dickinson and Her Culture*. See Jane Tompkins, "Sentimental Power: Uncle Tom's Cabin and the Politics of Literary History" in *Sentimental Designs* for a discussion of Little Eva's death and Victorian sentimentalism.

With the coming of war, the wounded, dying, and dead bodies of soldiers became the vehicle for a new sentimentalism that fused patriotism and Christianity.[13] Walt Whitman, who became a hospital visitor in Washington, D.C., in 1862, reflected upon the experiences and deaths of soldiers in letters, notebooks, and articles, as well as in a group of poems ultimately published in 1865 as *Drum-Taps*. His poem "A Sight in Camp in the Day-Break Grey and Dim," for instance, explicitly associated the dead body of a soldier with Christ. After examining a corpse outside a hospital tent with "a face nor child, nor old, very calm, as of beautiful yellow-white ivory," the narrator directly addressed the body:

Young man, I think I know you—I think this face of
yours is the face of Christ himself;
Dead and divine, and brother of all, and here again he lies.[14]

Sentimentalism provided a way of making sense of the bodily sacrifices of soldiers within an explicitly Christian framework. It also allowed wartime writers to cope with a central problem posed by the war: the shocking anonymity of suffering and death undergone by ordinary soldiers far from home. This was an aspect of war that many Americans found unbearable. They simply could not accept that soldiers' suffering and death would go unsung and unmourned. As George William Curtis noted in *Harper's Monthly* in June 1862, during the first year of war there had been many "leaders" in the army whose "heroic names and acts" were "repeated and remembered with joy and pride." But Curtis reminded his readers that there were many "unnamed heroes" as well, who "marched with no less lofty purpose" and who fought "with the same bravery" as their leaders. "When we count our treasures," Curtis urged, "let us remember the unnamed, the devoted sons and brothers and husbands and lovers, who have obeyed the call of their country" and "have marched to battle and to death, knowing that their fall must be unknown to all but those whose homes it would darken, and whose hearts it would break."[15] In March 1862 the *Southern Monthly* also urged its

13. On the history of death in American culture, see Gary Laderman, *The Sacred Remains: American Attitudes Toward Death, 1799–1883* (New Haven: Yale University Press, 1996).
14. Walt Whitman, "A Sight in Camp in the Day-Break Grey and Dim," in *Walt Whitman's Drum-Taps (1865) and Sequel to Drum-Taps (1865–66). A Facsimile Reproduction*, ed. F. DeWolfe (Gainesville, Fl.: Scholars' Facsimiles and Reprints, 1959), 46.
15. George William Curtis, "Editor's Easy Chair," *Harper's New Monthly Magazine* 25 (June 1862): 123. See also Curtis's comments on the "unrecorded heroism of the private soldier, who, in this war at least, so often sacrifices as much as many an officer whose name is blazoned in our current history." *Harper's New Monthly Magazine* 25 (Oct. 1862): 709. In an 1864 lecture Grace Greenwood

readers to remember the "unlaureled heroes," who "fall undecked with victory's splendors."[16] In both North and South, writers not only asserted the importance of remembering *all* "fallen soldiers" during the war, but also assigned literature a central role in accomplishing this task.

Many writers during the war expressed their indignation that soldiers' deaths occurred among strangers, or that soldiers might be nameless or unknown in death. The idea that there might be "unknown soldiers" as an inevitable aspect of warfare only took hold in the wake of World War I; the Tomb of the Unknown Soldier was dedicated in 1921. During the Civil War, in contrast, many writers protested against the idea that soldiers were alone or even anonymous when they died. Whitman, for instance, wrote at length to his mother in 1864 of "one poor boy" who "groaned some as the stretcher-bearers were carrying him along—& again as they carried him through the hospital." Though "the doctor came immediately," it "was all of no use," for the soldier had died at the hospital gate. "The worst of it is too," Whitman said, that he was entirely unknown—"There was nothing on his clothes, or any one with him, to identify him—& he is altogether unknown—Mother, it is enough to rack one's heart, such things—very likely his folks will never know in the world what has become of him—poor poor child, for he appeared as though he could be but 18."[17] Louisa May Alcott, too, registered indignation and sorrow at the solitary death of a soldier in her 1863 *Hospital Sketches*. Her narrator, Nurse Tribulation Periwinkle, had just gone to get a drink of water for a patient, but when she came back,

> something in the tired white face caused me to listen at his lips for a breath. None came. I touched his forehead; it was cold: and then I knew that, while he waited, a better nurse than I had given him a cooler draught, and healed him with a touch. I laid the sheet over the quiet sleeper, whom no noise could now disturb; and, half an hour later, the bed was empty. It seemed a poor requital for all he had sacrificed and suffered,—that hospital bed, lonely even in a crowd; for there was no familiar face for him to look his last upon; no friendly voice to

---

asked, "But who shall number and name the great host of fiery young leaders, and the glorious thousands of the rank and file,—the mighty, melancholy multitude of brave men slain in battle, buried from hospitals, martyred in prisons!" Grace Greenwood, *Records of Five Years* (Boston: Ticknor and Fields, 1867), 135.

16. Guy, "Unlaureled Heroes," *Southern Monthly* 1 (Mar. 1862): 559.

17. Walt Whitman to Louisa Van Velsor Whitman, March 29, 1864, in *The Correspondence*, ed. Edwin Haviland Miller, "Collected Writings of Walt Whitman," 6 vols (New York: New York University Press, 1961-69), 1:205.

say, Good bye; no hand to lead him gently down into the Valley of the Shadow; and he vanished, like a drop in that red sea upon whose shores so many women stand lamenting. For a moment I felt bitterly indignant at this seeming carelessness of the value of life, the sanctity of death.[18]

For both Alcott and Whitman, it was a cultural affront that wartime death occurred outside of the framework of sentimental norms that emphasized a tender, emotive parting from family and friends.[19]

Many of the most popular poems of the war attempted to provide exactly that tender, emotive death. "Somebody's Darling," for instance, first published in the South but reprinted widely in both North and South, counseled the reader/witness to take a final, tender parting of an anonymous soldier who had just died in the hospital:

Kiss him once for *somebody's* sake;
Murmur a prayer, soft and low;
One bright curl from the cluster take—
They were somebody's pride, you know.[20]

Likewise, John Reuben Thompson's popular "The Burial of Latané," first published in the *Southern Literary Messenger* of July and August 1862, imagined a tender funeral among sympathetic strangers for a slain Confederate captain:

A brother bore his body from the field,
And gave it into strangers' hands, that closed

---

18. Louisa May Alcott, *Hospital Sketches* (1863; rpt., Cambridge, Mass.: Belknap Press, 1960), 36–37.

19. See also "Lines by a Private Soldier," *Spirit of the Fair*, April 12, 1864, p. 77. In this poem, the narrator acknowledged the problem of mass, anonymous death:

To be buried alone, alone—
Even that is an honor rarely shown;
In a common grave
Lie many brave
We have no means of knowing;
Their hopes and fears are forever hid
In the cold ground—some ill-carved box lid
Their regiment only showing.

20. T. C. De Leon, ed., *South Songs: From the Lays of Later Days* (1866; rpt., Westport, Conn.: Greenwood Press, 1977), 67.

The calm blue eyes, on earth forever sealed,
And tenderly the slender limbs composed:
Strangers, yet sisters, who, with Mary's love,
Sat by the open tomb, and weeping, looked above.[21]

As with Whitman's "A Sight in Camp in the Day-Break Grey and Dim," the poem made an explicit connection between the body of the dead soldier and the body of Christ.

Hundreds of popular songs and poems during the war grappled with the fact of mass, anonymous death by creating idealized deaths for soldiers, especially by giving voice to dying soldiers' thoughts. "Dying soldier" poems had been published during the Mexican War, too, as Robert W. Johannsen has pointed out: D. W. Belisle's "The Dying Soldier to His Mother" was but one example of war poetry that portrayed dying soldiers' thoughts.[22] But during the Civil War this sentimental poetry exploded in popularity. Published throughout the war in the North and South, these poems and songs were ubiquitous, with songs in particular sometimes selling hundreds of thousands of copies. In October 1864, for instance, an ad in *Harper's Weekly* claimed that the song "Who Will Care for Mother Now?" had in "less than one year attained the unprecedented sale of over half a million copies."[23]

These "dying soldier" poems have traditionally been dismissed as "mere" sentimentality, but that view obscures the importance of these poems within Civil War culture, allowing little means of analyzing the meanings of the war they shaped both North and South. It is useful to note that at the time of the war, even as a number of Northern intellectuals questioned the efficacy of sentimental humanitarianism, several commentators asserted the cultural value of these sentimental poems. In an 1865 lecture on "The Poetry of the War," for instance, Oliver Wendell Holmes reflected on the "ballads and sentimental pieces which are numbered by the thousand," and which are "piled up by the gross on counters" for sale, and concluded that "There is a genuine and simple pathos in many of

---

21. John Reuben Thompson, "The Burial of Latané," in De Leon, *South Songs*, 20–21. For a discussion of popular painting inspired by this poem later in the war, see Drew Gilpin Faust, *Mothers of Invention: Women of the Slaveholding South in the American Civil War* (Chapel Hill: University of North Carolina Press, 1996), 188–89.

22. Johannsen, *To the Halls of the Montezumas*, 212. A variety of forms of popular war literature during the Civil War—including sensational novels, sentimental and patriotic poems, and wartime humor—had antecedents in the Mexican War.

23. Ad by Sawyer and Thompson, Music Publishers, in *Harper's Weekly* (Oct. 8, 1864).

them. I do not know whether it sounds scholarly and critical and all the rest, but I think there is more nature and feeling in some of these [songs] than in very many poems of far higher pretensions and more distinguished origin." Holmes told his audience that "if I should read the familiar lines 'Dear Mother, I've come home to die,' and could read them as they ought to be read, you may be very sure that the light would trouble a good many eyes before it was finished."[24]

Holmes's comments indicate the significance of these poems and songs for a Civil War audience: not only did they portray the dying thoughts of soldiers, thereby countering the brutal anonymity of death, but they also allowed an imagined form of communication between the imagined soldier and his listener—in reality a reader on the home front. While these poems imagined the soldier as an emotive and sympathetic figure, they also by implication imagined the listener/reader on the home front as similarly emotive and sympathetic. Thus these poems imagined tight links between home front and battlefront, links that were in fact usually broken by the soldier's death far from home.

Dying soldier poems did not so much deny the deaths of soldiers as perform the difficult cultural task of making often anonymous deaths meaningful. It was widely assumed during the war that soldiers' deaths held great meaning; the idea that such deaths might be senseless only fully emerged in the wake of World War I. Yet it was also widely assumed that soldiers' deaths gained meaning only through the creation of appropriate representations—whether funeral rituals, monuments, or poems—that could memorialize the fallen soldier appropriately.

Thus it makes sense that in a war of unprecedented slaughter, in which ultimately more than six hundred thousand men died, there were an unprecedented number of poems, too, that over and over again imagined the dying thoughts of soldiers. The task of making soldiers' deaths meaningful required constant effort; the sentimental meaning of the soldier's life could not be generated once, but needed to be recreated over and over again. Hundreds of dying soldier poems were the result, in both North and South.

Many of these began with a brief account of a soldier's death from a newspaper, and then elaborated upon that account in the poem that followed. "You'll Tell Her, Won't You?" for instance, published in the *Richmond Dispatch* of October 4, 1862, prefaced the poem with a brief quotation from a witness who had described a soldier's last moments. "Shot through the lungs," the soldier "clasped a locket to his breast and moved his lips till I put down my ear and listened for

---

24. Holmes, "The Poetry of the War."

his last breath—'You'll tell her, won't you?'" The witness commented that 'Tell who or what I could not ask, but that locket was the picture of one who might be wife, sweetheart, or sister."[25] This quotation inspired the poem that followed—a common device for poems and songs throughout the Civil War.

The subsequent poem, however, no longer accepted the soldier's whispered last moments, but instead imagined an eloquent dying speech for him:

> You'll tell her, won't you? Say to her I died
> As a brave soldier should—true to the last,
> She'll bear it better if a thought of pride
> Comes in to stay her, the first shock o'er past!
>
> You'll tell her, won't you? Show her how I lay
> Pressing the pictured lips I loved so well;
> And how my last thoughts floated far away,
> To home and her, with love I could not tell.
>
> You'll tell her, won't you?—not how hard it was
> To give up life—life for her sake so dear;
> Nay, nay, not so! Say it 'twas a noble cause,
> And I did die for it without a tear.
>
> You'll tell her, won't you? She'll be glad to know
> Her soldier stood undaunted, true as steel,
> His heart with her, his bosom to the foe,
> When the blow struck no human power could heal.
>
> You'll tell her, won't you? Say, too, we shall meet
> In God's Hereafter, where our love shall grow
> More holy for this parting, and more sweet,
> And cleansed from every stain it knew below.[26]

This poem touched on a number of motifs that underlay "dying soldier" poetry during the war: the concern for a loved one at home; the desire for and memory

---

25. "You'll Tell Her, Won't You?" *Daily Richmond Dispatch*, Oct. 4, 1862.
26. Ibid.

of home itself; the soldier's acceptance of death in a "noble cause"; the desire to communicate his last thoughts to his loved one; and his assurance that his sacrifice would receive a heavenly reward. All of these were considered appropriate deathbed or dying thoughts, and numerous poems reiterated them during the war. In this poem, as in many others, such imagined thoughts acted as an explicit form of compensation for the difficult truth that the dying soldier often had no time to compose the well-wrought sentences and the final thoughts that were considered an appropriate part of Victorian death.[27]

Like so many dying soldier poems, "You'll Tell Her Won't You?" concentrated not on the martial identity of the soldier but on his identity as an individual tied to family and home.[28] Indeed, surprisingly few battle poems achieved real popularity during the war, despite the fact that, as Charles Royster has pointed out, numerous Civil War readers enjoyed—apparently without ever understanding its bitter irony—Tennyson's 1854 ballad "Charge of the Light Brigade,"[29] with its galloping lyrics of a doomed British cavalry brigade during the Crimean War:

> Cannon to right of them,
> Cannon to left of them,
> Cannon in front of them
> Volleyed and thundered;
> Stormed at with shot and shell,
> Boldly they rode and well,
> Into the jaws of Death,
> Into the mouth of hell
> Rode the six hundred.[30]

While several poets imitated Tennyson's ballad, and numerous poets wrote battle poems during the war, no ballad or poem of comparable popularity emerged during the war to celebrate the heroics of battle. The most popular Civil War poems

---

27. See also Cuba, "The Dying Soldier," *Southern Illustrated News* (May 7, 1864): 137.

28. On the importance of the soldier's ties to home, see especially Reed Mitchell, *The Vacant Chair: The Northern Soldier Leaves Home* (New York: Oxford University Press, 1993).

29. Charles Royster, *The Destructive War: William Tecumseh Sherman, Stonewall Jackson, and the Americans* (New York: Knopf, 1991), 257-58.

30. Alfred, Lord Tennyson, "The Charge of the Light Brigade," in M. H. Abrams et al., eds., *Norton Anthology of English Lit*, 2 vols. (New York: W.W. Norton, 1968), 2:898-99. One of many poems that imitated Tennyson's poem during the war was George H. Boker's "The Second Louisiana," in "Poetry and Incidents," *Rebellion Record*, 7:3.

and songs, on the contrary, turned away from battle and imagined the thoughts of individual soldiers.

Among those imagined thoughts, by far the most prevalent involved the soldier's mother. In 1865 Oliver Wendell Holmes commented that he had "obtained from several vendors" in Boston and in New York "copies of the songs most largely sold to soldiers and others." There was "one little fact" about these "that must find its way to every heart": "What thought was most constantly present with those who were hurrying to the conflict, who were fainting on the march, who were bleeding on the battle-field, who were languishing in prisons? These were the men who were doing the hardest work that falls to manhood. And out of thirty-three songs lying before me, selected by different vendors as the most popular according to their sales, no less than fourteen find their inspiration in the sacred name of *mother*."[31]

Mother Would Comfort Me, a song with words and music by Charles Carroll Sawyer, was typical of the genre. As was true of many Civil War songs, it began with an explanatory note: "A soldier in one of the New York regiments, after being severely wounded, was taken prisoner; and after lying in the hospital for a number of days, he was told by those who were in attendance that 'they could do no more for him,' that he must die." For a few moments the poor fellow seemed in deep thought; reviving a little, he turned slowly toward those near him, and after thanking them for the kind manner in which they had treated him during his sickness, a sweet smile passed over his pale face, and with a firm voice he said, 'Mother would comfort me, if she were here.' These were his last words." The song itself elaborated on this theme, representing the dying soldier's thoughts and especially stressing the soldier's loneliness, his distance from home, and the fact that he was "unknown":

Wounded and sorrowful, far from my home,
Sick among strangers, uncared for, unknown;
Even the birds that used sweetly to sing
Are silent, and swiftly have taken the wing.
No one but Mother can cheer me today,
No one for me could so fervently pray:
None to console me, no kind friend is near—
Mother would comfort me if she were here.[32]

31. Holmes, "The Poetry of the War."
32. Charles Carroll Sawyer, *Mother Would Comfort Me* (Brooklyn, N.Y.: Sawyer and Thompson, 1863). Sheet Music Collection, Special Collections, Duke University.

The reiteration of thoughts of mother reminds us that the Civil War occurred within a maternal culture that celebrated soldiers' connections to their mothers as an appropriate feminization of their characters. The emphasis on mother was an intertwined social and cultural reality: soldiers often spoke and wrote of their mothers, at the same time that it was widely perceived as appropriate that they do so. In a small "Hospital Note Book" that Walt Whitman carried with him, for instance, he noted about a "poor unfortunate boy" shot for desertion on June 19, 1863, that "he was very fond of his mother"; "he tried to get away to see his mother"; and again, "he was dotingly fond of his mother."[33] Numerous hospital visitors noted soldiers' concern for their mothers.

During the war the concept of manliness included feminized components that late in the century would be excised from new concepts of masculinity.[34] On appropriate occasions it was considered manly to show emotion, even to cry. Indeed, in a wide variety of popular poems weeping was presented approvingly as a tribute to a dead comrade. At the same time, within a culture of domesticity that tightly bound not only women but also men to their homes, the soldier's imagined longings for home were also deemed highly appropriate and represented not only in poems and songs, but also in numerous popular engravings. "I'm thinking of my distant home, / That Eden spot of earth to me, / And something comes across my eyes / I do not care my men should see!" were lines of Viola's "By the Camp Fire," published in 1863 in the *Southern Illustrated News*.[35] The widely reprinted Currier and Ives engraving "The Soldier's Dream of Home" showed a soldier sleeping on the ground while thinking of his wife and children on the home front. Caroline A. Mason's much reprinted poem "The Soldier's Dream of Home" also imagined a soldier longing for his wife and three children:

> Oh, my very heart grows sick, Alice,
> I long so to behold
> Rose with her pure, white forehead,
> And Maud, with her curls of gold;
> And Willie, so gay and sprightly,
> So merry and full of glee;

---

33. Walt Whitman, unpublished Hospital Note Book, Huntington Library.
34. See Mitchell, *The Vacant Chair*. For the late nineteenth century, see especially Gail Bederman, *Manliness and Civilization: A Cultural History of Gender and Race in the United States, 1880-1917* (Chicago: University of Chicago Press, 1995).
35. Viola, "By the Camp Fire," *Southern Illustrated News* (Apr. 11, 1863): 7.

Oh, my heart *yearns* to enfold ye,
My "smiling group of three!"[36]

Soldiers as well as civilians were moved by this poem. One soldier wrote to Mason that his own family was an "almost exact copy of the picture you have painted." "Such lines as yours," he said, "carry with them many a blessing as they are read by the exiled soldier—self exiled as many of us are, away from home, kindred and friends, especially from the dear ones of his heart."[37]

Expressions of longings for home, but especially for mother, were part of a shared popular literary culture in both the North and South. In February 1863, for instance, *Frank Leslie's Illustrated Newspaper* published "A Soldier's Letter," which began, "Dear Mother—in my lonesome tent, / With battle-whispers on the air, / I weave some pleasant dreams of home, /And wish myself a moment there."[38] The next year, the same poem was published in the *Magnolia Weekly* as Southern in origin. The contributor of the poem said that "the following beautiful and touching lines were enclosed to his mother by a young Lynchburger," who was represented as composing the poem in May 1863 shortly before "his fall in battle."[39]

Striking about the manly universe of such poetry was the virtual absence of fathers. While at the beginning of the war much popular poetry and prose spoke with reverence of Revolutionary forefathers and the need to emulate them, sentimental soldier literature rarely mentioned actual fathers. Indeed, in many popular poems soldiers' fathers were portrayed as dead, so that the imagined social universe of the war sidestepped the patriarchal authority invested in family altogether.[40] There was a compelling reason for this: war demanded that soldiers be loyal to a new patriarchal authority, the state, as expressed in the popular enlistment poem, "We are coming Father Abraham, three hundred thousand more." With the state imagined as a new "father," the family was redefined in sentimental soldier poetry as the province of republican mothers who "gave" their sons to the state.

36. Caroline A. Mason, "The Soldier's Dream of Home," in *Lyrics of Loyalty*, ed. Frank Moore (New York: George P. Putnam, 1864), 139-41. Mason was an established poet on the eve of the war who had published a volume of poems, *Utterance*, in 1852.
37. H. B. Howe to Caroline A. Mason, Mar. 22, 1863, Briggs Family Papers, ser. 3, Schlesinger Library, Radcliffe College. Howe reported reading Mason's poem in the *Anti-Slavery Standard*.
38. "A Soldier's Letter," *Frank Leslie's Illustrated Newspaper*, Feb. 7, 1863.
39. *Magnolia Weekly*, Dec. 3, 1864.
40. On the portrayal of patriarchal authority during the Revolutionary era, see Jay Fliegelman, *Prodigals and Pilgrims: the American Revolution against Patriarchal Authority, 1750-1800* (New York: Cambridge University Press, 1982). For a psychohistory claiming that Lincoln had "powerful patricidal desires" against the revolutionary fathers, see George Forgie, *Patricide in the House Divided: A Psychological Interpretation of Lincoln and His Age* (New York: Norton, 1979), 284.

Mothers, not fathers, were imagined in popular poetry to have authority over their sons' enlistment in the war, as in *Harper's Weekly*'s March 1862 "Mother, May I Go?" by Horatio Alger Jr.: "I am eager, anxious, longing to resist my country's foe: / Shall I go, my dearest mother? tell me, mother, shall I go?"[41] And Oliver Wendell Holmes confessed to "some weakness about the eyes" in reading Nancy A. W. Priest's "Kiss Me, Mother, and Let Me Go," an enlistment poem reprinted in numerous collections during the war.[42]

A soldier's entire career could be charted through popular poems and songs that affirmed his connection to his mother. One of the most popular songs of the war, for instance, was *Just Before the Battle, Mother*, which imagined a soldier's thoughts turning to his mother the night before a battle:

Just before the battle, Mother,
I am thinking most of you,
While upon the field we're watching,
With the enemy in view . . .

Farewell, Mother, you may never
Press me to your heart again;
But O, you'll not forget me, Mother,
If I'm number'd with the slain.[43]

In addition, from early in the war numerous popular songs imagined a soldier's dying thoughts turning to his mother, including Charles Carroll Sawyer's *Who Will Care For Mother Now?* ("Soon with angels I'll be marching, / With bright laurels on my brow, / I have for my country fallen, / Who will care for mother now?"); *The Dying Volunteer* ("Come mother, dear mother, oh! come to me now; / My soul wings its flight, I would see thee once more, / Again I would feel thy dear hand on my brow"); *The Dying Soldier or Kiss me good night Mother* ("But mother, your kiss turns the darkness to light; / Kiss me good night, mother, kiss me good night"); *Is That Mother Bending O'er Me?* ("Is that mother?—Is that mother bending o'er me, / As she sang my cradle hymn—/ Kneeling there in tears before me? / Say! my sight is

---

41. Horatio Alger Jr., "Mother, Can I Go?" *Harper's Weekly* 6 (Mar. 22, 1862), 187.
42. Holmes, "The Poetry of the War."
43. George F. Root, *Just Before the Battle, Mother* (Chicago: Root and Cady, 1863), Sheet Music Collection, Special Collections Library, Duke University.

growing dim."); and Henry C. Work's *Our Captain's Last Words* ("Strangers caught his parting breath, / Laden with the murmur 'mother' / Last upon his lips in death. / 'Mother!' 'Mother!' / Last upon his lips in death.")[44] Many of these songs circulated throughout both the Union and the Confederacy.

With their frequent evocation of a physically passionate attachment to mother that recaptured the experience of infancy and childhood, such songs imagined soldiers as boys rather than men. As Oliver Wendell Holmes commented in 1865, "these were *boys* then who fought our battles, boys at heart, if not always, as they often were, in years and growth."[45] Many soldiers during the Civil War were literally boys: according to estimates made by Bell Irvin Wiley, for instance, 1.6 percent of Union soldiers were under eighteen years old. Still, the point remains that, according to Wiley, "the great mass" of Union soldiers, 98 percent, "were neither very old nor very young, but fell in the eighteen-to-forty-five group." James M. McPherson has commented that the median age of soldiers was 23.5. Yet imagining soldiers as "boys"—a usage, tellingly, that arose during the war—was so commonplace during the conflict that it suggests a distinct cultural unease with the idea of soldiers as full-grown men separated from the maternal culture of home.[46]

While numerous wartime accounts, including soldiers' own letters, indicate that soldiers intensely longed for home, a simultaneous reality was a culture-wide denial that those who fought for their country should be defined as men. Such denial suggests perhaps a widespread fear that soldiers as "men" were a frightening entity, especially in a mass that subordinated individuality to national needs. Sentimental literature operated against this wartime development, creating

---

44. Charles Carroll Sawyer, *Who Will Care for Mother Now?* (Brooklyn: Sawyer and Thompson, 1863); *The Dying Volunteer* (New Orleans: Louis Grunewald, 1865); Edward Clark, *The Dying Soldier or Kiss me good night Mother* (Boston: Oliver Ditson, 1861); J. C. Johnson, *Is That Mother Bending O'er Me?* (Boston: Oliver Ditson and Company, 1863); Henry C. Work, *Our Captain's Last Words* (Chicago: Root and Cady, 1861). See also A. B. Chandler, *I've Fallen in the Battle* (New Orleans: Louis Grunewald, 1864); Ednor Rossiter, *I Loved That Dear Old Flag the Best* (Philadelphia: Lee and Walker, 1863); and Thomas Manahan, *Bear this gently to my Mother* (New York: Horace Waters, 1864). Sheet Music Collection, Special Collections Library, Duke University.

45. Holmes, "The Poetry of the War."

46. Bell Irvin Wiley, *The Life of Billy Yank: The Common Soldier of the Union* (Indianapolis: Bobbs-Merrill, 1951), 299, 303; James M. McPherson, *Ordeal by Fire: The Civil War and Reconstruction* (2d ed., New York: McGraw-Hill, 1992), 355. "Nearly two-fifths of soldiers were 21 or younger at the time of enlistment," according to McPherson. But of course this also means that a majority of soldiers were not "boys." The first usage of "boys" to mean soldiers in American history occurred in 1861. See *A Dictionary of American English On Historical Principles*, (Chicago: University of Chicago Press, 1936), 1:300.

domesticated individual soldiers characterized by tender feelings and yearnings for home. This literature emphasized that those who fought in the war were not professional soldiers but "citizen-soldiers," with the emphasis on "citizen." Certainly many sentimental writers during the war preferred to find the essence of American manhood not on the battlefield but in the hospital, a place where men often were perceived as "boys" and where an inevitable process of reduction took place. Eben Hannaford, for instance, who published "In Hospital after Stone River" in the January 1864 *Harper's Monthly*, remembered recovering from a wound in a hospital as a process of infantilization. Describing the weeks of his recovery, he evoked the "infantile weakness" of his condition and "the utter prostration of all the powers of mind and body that form the glory and the strength of manhood." When a male nurse sang the *Battle Cry of Freedom*, Hannaford found that early wartime memories "came surging back over my poor, weak, disordered brain, in a wild, sweeping rush of feeling, which I was powerless, utterly, to control."[47]

Yet it was precisely the powerless condition of soldiers in the hospital that many sentimental writers celebrated as the essence of American manhood. Whitman, for instance, wrote that "I find the best expression of American character I have ever seen or conceived—practically here in these ranks of sick and dying young men."[48] To Ralph Waldo Emerson, Whitman wrote that "I desire and intend to write a little book out of this phase of America, her masculine young manhood, its conduct under most trying of and highest of all exigency," and added that in Washington he saw "America, already brought to Hospital in her fair youth."[49]

For Whitman, as Betsy Erkkila has pointed out, the hospital became a metonymic figure for the nation at war.[50] But as was true for many other sentimental writers, the nation at war did not mean the "traditionally masculine polarity of militarism, violence, and aggression," but instead was closer to the "traditionally feminine polarity of nurturance, compassion, and love."[51] It was precisely because the hospital "softened" the aggressive masculinity associated with war that many observers found their ideal of manhood in the hospital. It was a commonplace during the war, as William Howell Reed pointed out in his *Hospital Life in the Army of the Potomac*, that "suffering subdues and softens any nature, however rough; and that there is an influence all the time in the hospital

---

47. Eben Hannaford, "In Hospital after Stone River," *Harper's New Monthly Magazine* 28 (Jan. 1864): 264–65.
48. Whitman, *Correspondence*, 1:69.
49. Walt Whitman to Ralph Waldo Emerson, Jan. 17, 1863, in *Correspondence*, 1: 69.
50. Betsy Erkkila, *Whitman the Political Poet* (New York: Oxford University Press, 1989), 206.
51. Ibid., 199.

to bring out what is purest and noblest in the heart."[52] "Many a soldier," Reed said, "is like a September chestnut,—the outside is hard, and sharp, and shut up; but the inside is soft, and sweet, and good."[53]

Because he clung to these sentimentalized ideals in wartime, it has sometimes been suggested that Whitman was little more than a holdover from a feminized antebellum culture of sentimentalism. But this view underestimates the hold of a powerful sentimental culture during the war. It also wrongly presupposes that the war was primarily understood as "masculinized" in its own time, when in fact ideas of the Civil War as a "masculinized" war only coalesced in the 1880s and 1890s.[54] Finally, this view ignores the outpouring of literature—whether poems, songs, stories or books—during the war that celebrated a sentimentalized soldier. As Miss Dunlap argued in her 1864 *Notes of Hospital Life*, "our army is no 'Corporation without a soul,'" but instead "a collection of beating hearts, throbbing pulses, and straining nerves, which ask and need our love."[55] The poem "Dying in the Hospital," published in July 1863 in the *Continental Monthly*, was one of many wartime verses that asserted the soldier's yearning for love:

> I am dying, mother, dying, in the hospital alone;
> With a hundred faces round me, not a single one is known;
> And the human heart within me, like a fluttering, wounded dove,
> Hungers with a ceaseless yearning for one answering word of love.[56]

The idea that the individual soldier in the hospital needed the love and tenderness of those on the home front became a commonplace during the war. In an 1864 *New York Times* article, for instance, Whitman wrote that "the American soldier is full of affection and the yearning for affection. And it comes wonderfully grateful to him to have this yearning gratified when he is laid up with painful wounds or illness, far away from home, among strangers. Many will think this merely sentimentalism, but I know it is the most solid of facts."[57]

---

52. William Howell Reed, *Hospital Life in the Army of the Potomac* (1866; rpt., Boston: W. V. Spencer, 1891), 141. Reed noted this common belief, but in the wake of war also asserted that "still, the men who lie there are only average men" (141-42).

53. Reed, *Hospital Life*, 153.

54. Alice Fahs, "The Feminized Civil War: Gender, Northern Popular Literature, and the Memory of the War, 1861-1900," *Journal of American History* 85 (Mar. 1999): 1461-94.

55. *Notes of Hospital Life from November, 1861 to August, 1863*. (Philadelphia: J. B. Lippincott, 1864), xiii.

56. Mary E. Nealy, "Dying in the Hospital," *Continental Monthly* 4 (Aug. 1863): 229.

57. "Hospital Visits," *New York Times*, Dec. 11, 1864, rpt. in *The Complete Writings*, 7:126.

At the same time, numerous writers noted that hospitalized soldiers displayed a tenderness that sometimes surprised them. William Howell Reed, for one, noted that "it is surprising to see what tender spots there are in the hearts of some of our roughest men," and recounted the time a female nurse sang "a plaintive little song, 'Just before the battle, mother,' then the most popular song in the army, and reproduced in a hundred different ways by the soldiers or by the bands." "There was perfect stillness in the ward, the melody melted into that exquisite air, 'I'm lonely since my mother died.' Nearly every man had raised himself on his elbow to catch these notes. Some were wiping their eyes, and others, too weak to move, were hiding their emotion, which still was betrayed by the quivering lip, and the single tear as it fell, but was not wiped away."[58] Miss Dunlap in *Notes of Hospital Life* also argued for the tenderness of the soldier, saying that "it is often asserted that the sight" of "constant suffering and death, so hardens and accustoms the men to the fact, that they do not appear to feel it in the slightest degree. My own observation has led to a directly opposite conclusion."[59]

Thousands of soldiers' wartime letters, plus the reminiscences of hundreds of hospital visitors, indicate that the hospitalized soldier's tenderness, yearning for love and longing for home were "the most solid of facts." Of interest here, however, is not so much that the wounded soldier in hospital yearned for affection, but that the literary figure of that same wounded soldier became, much like the figure of the dying soldier on the battlefield, an icon of American nationalism. This nationalism did not subordinate the individual to the demands of the Union or Confederacy, as early in the war; instead, the tender, individualized nationalism of sentimental literature located the essence of the nation's meaning in the individual bodies of wounded soldiers.

Louisa May Alcott's *Hospital Sketches* created such an icon in the depiction of the lingering death of John, a "brave Virginia blacksmith." Published in 1863, Alcott's "sketches" drew from a collection of letters detailing her six weeks of experience as a nurse at the Union Hotel Hospital in Georgetown. First published in the *Commonwealth* before reprinted in book form by James Redpath, her letters attracted a great deal of notice. As Alcott noted with delight in her journal, "Much to my surprise they made a great hit, & people bought the papers faster than they could be supplied."[60] Alcott's sketches captured public atten-

---

58. Reed, *Hospital Life in the Army of the Potomac*, 140.
59. *Notes of Hospital Life*, 39.
60. Joel Myerson and Daniel Shealy, eds., *The Journals of Louisa May Alcott* (Boston: Little, Brown, 1989), 118.

tion as interest in the hospitals grew—a trend reflected in a variety of popular literature. As Whitman noted in 1864, "as this tremendous war goes on," public interest "gathers more and more closely about the wounded, the sick, and the Government hospitals."[61]

In Alcott's fictionalized *Hospital Sketches* the sentimental drama of the dying soldier took center stage in a way that readers found immensely appealing. The centerpiece of the book was "A Night," a chapter in which the narrator, Tribulation Periwinkle, witnessed the lingering death of John, represented as an ideal type of American manhood, combining both feminine and masculine traits. "A most attractive face he had, framed in brown hair and beard, comely featured and full of vigor," with a mouth "grave and firm, with plenty of will and courage in its lines," and a smile "as sweet as any woman's." At first, however, Nurse Periwinkle did not recognize John's tender side, and found his manliness disquieting. She "was a little afraid of the stately looking man, whose bed had to be lengthened to accommodate his commanding stature; who seldom spoke, uttered no complaint," and "asked no sympathy." It was only when John inadvertently revealed his feminine, tender side, through crying, that Periwinkle responded to him fully. "I had forgotten," Periwinkle said, "that the strong man might long for the gentler tendance of a woman's hands, the sympathetic magnetism of a woman's presence, as well as the feebler souls about him." Noticing John looking "lonely and forsaken" she saw "great tears roll down and drop upon the floor." Now she was able to respond to him not as a self-sufficient man, but as a boy: "my fear vanished, my heart opened wide and took him in," and she gathered "the bent head in my arms, as freely as if he had been a little child."[62]

Periwinkle's account stressed John's boyish qualities. Although he was almost thirty, and "the manliest man" among the patients Nurse Periwinkle cared for, he also said "'Yes, ma'am,' like a little boy"; and "his eyes were child's eyes, looking one fairly in the face." As Periwinkle's account made clear, it was only through recognizing John's powerless, enfeebled, boyish qualities that she could fully celebrate him as a soldier. Afraid of the manly man, she was tender and compassionate with the homesick, yearning boy. It was this side of the soldier that her readers celebrated, too. As a surgeon at the Union Hospital wrote to her, "these papers have revealed to me much that is elevated, and pure, and refined in the soldiers' character, which I never before suspected. It is humiliating to

---

61. Walt Whitman, "Hospital Visits" *New York Times*, Dec. 11, 1864, rpt. in *Complete Writings of Walt Whitman*, 7:101.
62. Louisa May Alcott, *Hospital Sketches*, 1863, rpt., (Cambridge: Belknap Press, 1960) 49-51.

me to think that I have been so long among them with such a mental or moral obtuseness that I never discovered it for myself."[63]

Imagining John as a sentimental soldier allowed Alcott to create a meaningful death for him. He settled his affairs by having Periwinkle write a farewell to his family, said good-bye to a comrade by kissing each other "tenderly as women," and, after suffering greatly at the last, saw "the first red streak of dawn" and "seemed to read in it a sign of hope of help, for, over his whole face there broke that mysterious expression, brighter than any smile, which often comes to eyes that look their last." This last evocation of the dawn, a conventional mode of rendering sentimental death, allowed Alcott to suggest that John's sufferings might be the vehicle to ultimate redemption, thus keeping John's death within the parameters of the "sentimental love religion."[64]

At the same time, imagining John as a sentimental soldier allowed Alcott, like other sentimental writers during the war, to claim possession of the soldier through special knowledge of his real nature and needs. This possessive relationship to the soldier was a theme running through the writings of sentimental authors, who claimed knowledge of the tender, often elevated qualities of the soldier that neither the government, nor sometimes even soldiers themselves, possessed. As Whitman wrote, "I know what is in their hearts, always waiting, though they may be unconscious of it themselves."[65]

This sense of special knowledge also provided witnesses to soldiers' suffering with an additional cachet when it came to publishing their hospital experience. In doing so, they tapped into the widespread sentimental belief that the suffering body should "speak" or communicate its pain in public through retelling these stories. Hannah Ropes, for instance, a nurse who was Louisa May Alcott's superior at Union Hotel Hospital, hoped in the winter of 1862 that the Boston *Advertiser* "would send me a *good price*" for excerpts from her journal.[66] Also in late 1862, Charles Edward Lester, a prolific antebellum writer of popular biography and history who had been visiting hospitals in Washington, D.C., sent the Philadelphia publisher G. W. Childs a proposal for a book "on a subject which nobody has treated to any extent." To be called "Heroism in the Hospital," his proposed work "would abound in scenes of personal heroism in the midst of

---

63. *American Publishers' Circular and Literary Gazette* 1 (Sept. 1863), 346.
64. Alcott, *Hospital Sketches*, 56–57.
65. Whitman, *Correspondence*, 1:262.
66. Hannah Ropes, *Civil War Nurse: The Diary and Letters of Hannah Ropes*, ed. John R. Brumgardt (Knoxville: University of Tennessee Press, 1980), 108.

sufferings indescribable." Lester planned to speak of "*1st the heroism of soldiers during painful operations*—which by the concurrence of our veteran surgeons exceeds all they ever before witnessed in civil or military or believed to be possible," and "2—The heroism of the Soldier *dying from wounds, operations, or disease.*"[67] The "main object of the work," he said, "will be to carry the brave & suffering soldier's *heart*, back to his home—to show how deep and unquenchable is the *amour patriae* in the young hero's breast." Yet it would "by no means be a book of horrors," he reassured his publisher. "It will rather be characterized by tenderness of sympathy." If he was "not entirely deceived," Lester said, "Heroism in the Hospital" could be "made a popular book." After all, he concluded, "heroism & feeling will forever be the most attractive features of popular books, & this little work I speak of has both in abundance."[68]

These attitudes underscore the confidence on the part of a number of writers that representations of the war would be popular with a widespread reading public. This confidence also underlay a wide-ranging book project that Walt Whitman proposed to James Redpath in late 1863. After the success of Alcott's *Hospital Sketches* the previous summer, Whitman proposed "a book of the time, worthy [of] the time—something considerably beyond mere hospital sketches—a book for sale perhaps in a larger American market—the premises or skeleton memoranda of incidents, persons, places, sights, the past year." Whitman especially had "much to say of the hospitals," including "many hospital incidents" that "will take with the general reader." He concluded that his book "should be got out *immediately*. I think an edition, elegantly bound, might be pushed off for books for presents etc. for the holidays, if advertised for that purpose. It would be very appropriate. I think it a book that would please women. I should expect it to be popular with the trade."[69]

Neither Ropes nor Whitman published their proposed books during the war.[70] But anecdotal evidence indicates that Alcott's book appealed to a variegated reading public who found in it reflections of the sentimental war they desired. Henry

67. Ibid.
68. Charles Edward Lester to George W. Childs, Nov. 6, 1862, Dreer Collection, Historical Society of Pennsylvania, Philadelphia. Lester's work was eventually published, although in a drastically altered form, as *The Light and Dark of the Rebellion* (Philadelphia: George W. Childs, 1863).
69. Whitman, *Correspondence*, 1:171-72.
70. Ropes died in January 1863 from illness caught while she nursed soldiers. See Ropes, *Civil War Nurse*, 122-26. Redpath wrote to "Friend Whitman" that there was "a lion in the way" of his project—money. Horace Traubel, *With Walt Whitman in Camden, January 21 to April 7, 1889* (Philadelphia: University of Pennsylvania Press, 1953), 415.

James Sr. responded to this aspect of Louisa May Alcott's *Hospital Sketches* when he wrote to tell her "how much pleasure" he had taken in her "charming pictures of hospital service," and "how refreshing he found the personal revelation there incidentally made of so much that is dearest & most worshipful in woman."[71] At the same time, at least one intriguing piece of evidence suggests that soldiers themselves sometimes enjoyed Alcott's representations of their hospital experiences. The nurse Amanda Akin Stearns recorded in her diary of December 6, 1863 that "when evening came" she sat next to one of her soldier patients "to keep him from feeling lonely and dispirited" at a time when "thoughts of home came very sweet and its comforts seemed very far off." She then "read aloud a chapter from Miss Alcott's 'Hospital Sketches,' "which seemed to entertain a number very much, particularly my sensible John," who said "he did not see where such an interesting book came from; he had not been able to get such and would like to buy it."[72] Such a comment raises the intriguing possibility that soldiers' own views of their hospital experiences may have been shaped by wartime popular literature.

Sentimental literature discussing the hospitalized moved heroism from the battlefield to hospital. A.S. Hooker's "Hospital Heroes," published in 1863 in *Frank Leslie's Illustrated Newspaper*, denied that "all the heroes" were on the battlefield, instead asserting that "our hospitals are full of heroes," who "uncomplaining die." As Mrs. H. wrote in her 1867 *Three Years in Field Hospitals of the Army of the Potomac,* Union soldiers endured "suffering with a heroism which exceeds even the bravery of the battle-field." William Howell Reed, too, noted this "harder heroism of the hospital."[73]

Moreover, such literature ascribed heroism to the ordinary soldier, not to the officers who had been celebrated in early wartime literature. Lester, for instance, titled one of his chapters "The Real Heroes of the War—The Rank and File in the Hospital." Alcott, too, chose an ordinary soldier to become her iconic hero of the war. She "consoled myself with the thought that, when the great muster roll was called, these nameless men might be promoted above many whose tall monuments record the barren honors they have won."[74] As Miss Dunlap wrote

---

71. *American Publishers' Circular and Literary Gazette* 1 (Sept. 1, 1863): 346.
72. Amanda Akin Stearns, *The Lady Nurse of Ward E* (New York: Baker and Taylor, 1909), 102.
73. A. S. Hooker, "Hospital Heroes," *Frank Leslie's Illustrated Newspaper,* Oct. 3, 1863; Mrs. H., *Three Years in Field Hospitals of the Army of the Potomac* (Philadelphia, J. P. Lippincott, 1867), 47; Reed, *Hospital Life in the Army of the Potomac,* 47.
74. Alcott, *Hospital Sketches,* 36-7.

in her 1863 *Notes of Hospital Life*, "at the opening of the war" she had thought "that the finer feelings of our nature were exclusively the property of the higher classes." But two years as a nurse in a military hospital, "where men appear mentally as well as physically in 'undress uniform,'" had shown her "the utter fallacy of such a theory." Now, in fact, she did "not hesitate to affirm" that she had "seen there as much unwritten poetry, tender feeling, aye, and love for the beautiful," as she had "ever witnessed among the same people gathered together at any time, or in any place."[75] Dunlap dedicated her volume "to the Privates of the Army of the United States," whose daring in danger; patience in privation; self-sacrifice in suffering; and loyalty in love for their country, have given to the world a noble example, worthy of all imitation." Another nurse simply said "the heroes are in the ranks."[76]

This literary process of redefining heroism occurred throughout the North and South. In 1863 the *Southern Punch* printed "Private in the Ranks," a poem that claimed "Deserving most, too oft forgot, a high-toned nation's thanks," was "one of nature's noblemen—the private in the ranks."[77] In another piece the *Southern Punch* protested against the use of the phrase "common soldiers" to "distinguish the rank and file, from uncommon soldiers—officers." "Let us have no more of this," the magazine urged. "These 'common soldiers' constitute the flower and chivalry of the South."[78] And in Augusta Jane Evans's *Macaria*, near the end of a lengthy account of the hospital death of a young private named Willie, the narrator urged that her compatriots remember that "we are indebted for Freedom" to the "uncomplaining fortitude and sublime devotion of the private soldiers of the Confederacy, not less than to the genius of our generals and the heroism of our subordinate officers."[79] Early in the war numerous poems and memorial volumes had celebrated such "martyred" officers as Elmer Ellsworth, Theodore Winthrop, and Nathaniel Lyon, ignoring the deaths of privates. But increasingly during the war popular literature insisted on a democratization of heroic death—and by extension a democratization of the nation itself.

75. *Notes of Hospital Life*, xii.
76. *Notes of Hospital Life*, dedication page; Ropes, *Civil War Nurse*, 58. See also p. 74 for Ropes's claim that privates "were really the heroes of the war."
77. "Private in the Ranks," *Southern Punch* 1 (Aug. 22, 1863), 7.
78. "Common Soldiers," *Southern Punch* 1 (Oct. 24, 1863), 2.
79. Augusta Jane Evans, *Macaria; or, Altars of Sacrifice*, ed. Drew Gilpin Faust (1864; rpt., Baton Rouge: Louisiana State University Press, 1992), 390. The account of Willie's death offers an interesting comparison with Alcott's description of John's death. See *Macaria*, 382-83.

In "The Hero without a Name," the Confederate poet W. S. Hawkins reflected on his own wartime shift in ideas of what constituted heroism, writing: "I loved, when a child, to seek the page / Where war's proud tales are grandly told," before mentioning such boyhood heroes as Sir Launcelot and Light-Horse Harry. "But little I hoped myself to see," the narrator continued, "a spirit akin to these stately men." "Yet, I've seen in the wards of the hospital there, / A hero, I fancy, as peerless of soul." This hero, a wounded soldier and a pale-faced boy, suffered "through the day's long pain and gloom," yet "he never makes a moan!" The narrator concluded that "somehow I think, when our lives are done, / That this humble hero—without a name—/ Will be greater up there, than many a one / Of the high-born men of fame."[80]

Adulation of the ordinary soldier occasionally crossed class and ethnic lines. Northern hospital visitors and nurses who "discovered" the ordinary soldier sometimes wrote of Irish or German soldiers, for instance, though they maintained ethnic stereotypes in their writing, particularly in associating Irish soldiers with what one author labeled "Irish humor." Alcott wrote humorously of caring for a "withered old Irishman, wounded in the head," who offered her the blessing, "May your bed above be aisy darlin', for the day's work ye are doon!" Likewise, she spoke of a "big Prussian, who spoke no English," with whom she shared an "irrepressible laugh" after taking care of a recalcitrant fellow patient. William Howell Reed, too, spoke of "a young German, a noble fellow," who "had been in every battle of the Army of the Potomac." Within him were "smoldering those old fires of liberty which had allured him to this country, and finally into the strife; and he was there fighting for a cause which he believed to be his cause, as it was the cause of every oppressed people on earth."[81]

While praise for the ordinary soldier within Northern popular literature sometimes crossed ethnic lines, such adulation rarely crossed racial lines, although African American soldiers were a vital military presence in the North after 1862. Walt Whitman was one of the few hospital observers who mentioned his care of and interest in black soldiers. In an 1864 *New York Times* article he claimed, "Among the black soldiers, wounded or sick, and in the contraband camps, I also took my way whenever in their neighborhood, and I did what I could for them." However, in a letter to his mother he was more candid, saying "I went once or twice to the Contraband Camp, to the Hospital, etc. but I could

---

80. Col. W. S. Hawkins, "The Hero without a Name," *South Songs*, 33–37.
81. Alcott, *Hospital Sketches*, 31, 47; Reed, *Hospital Life in the Army of the Potomac*, 146–47.

not bring myself to go again—when I meet black men or boys among my own hospitals, I use them kindly, give them something, etc.," but "there is a limit to one's sinews & endurance & sympathies."[82] Certainly Whitman did not provide the detailed, individualized accounting of black soldiers that he provided for white soldiers. The individualized sentimental soldier was coded as white in Northern popular literature.

Additionally, popular literature rarely had a place for "bad" soldiers. Such individuals appeared only as a strange rupture in texts that otherwise clung to the notion of the "worthy" soldier. Alcott's *Hospital Sketches*, for instance, suggested the possibility of "bad" soldiers, but only as momentary contrasts to her noble blacksmith John, not as subjects in their own right. Railing against John's impending death, Alcott commented that "such an end seemed very hard for such a man, when half a dozen worn out, worthless bodies round him, were gathering up the remnants of wasted lives, to linger on for years perhaps, burdens to others, daily reproaches to themselves."[83] Yet these "worthless" bodies did not appear elsewhere in her text, which otherwise maintained the fiction of her subjects' worthiness. The sentimental soldier was above all pure of heart; other soldiers existed as little more than ruptures in otherwise seamless narratives.

For countless writers during the war, it was not the soldier marching with his regiment or fighting alongside his comrades who fired the imagination, but instead the lonely, isolated soldier, sometimes *in extremis*. Poems about picket guards, for instance, were among the most popular soldier poems of the war both North and South, and yet they imagined a soldier away from his regiment rather than as a member of it. The Northern poem "The Picket-Guard," for instance, also often called "All Quiet Along the Potomac Tonight" and widely popular both North and South, spoke of the "quiet along the Potomac to-night, / Where the soldiers lie peacefully dreaming":

There's only the sound of the lone sentry's tread
As he tramps from the rock to the fountain,
And thinks of the two in the low trundle-bed,
Far away in the cot on the mountain.
His musket falls slack; his face, dark and grim,
Grows gentle with memories tender,

82. Walt Whitman, "Hospital Visits," *New York Times*, Dec. 11, 1864, rpt. in *The Complete Writings of Walt Whitman*, 7:127; Whitman, *Correspondence* 1:115.
83. Alcott, *Hospital Sketches*, 50–51.

As he mutters a prayer for the children asleep,—
For their mother,—may Heaven defend her!

A Southern version of this poem, Carrie Bell Sinclair's "All Quiet Along the Savannah To-night," also imagined a Confederate sentinel whose "visions of loved ones flit over his soul" as he wandered "back home in his dreams." As was true of so many sentimental soldier poems published during the war, both "The Picket-Guard" and "All Quiet Along the Savannah To-Night" made clear that the soldier retained a primary connection to home. "The Picket-Guard" also stressed the soldier's extreme vulnerability: "Was it moonlight so wondrously flashing? / It looked like a rifle: 'Ha! Mary, good-bye!' / And the life-blood is ebbing and plashing."[84]

Likewise, a separate "The Picket Guard," published in March 1862 in the *Richmond Dispatch*, imagined a guard "at his lonely post" who felt "the foe's first deadly brunt" and died.[85] Such poems were part of a popular literature that vicariously embraced the violence of war, as Charles Royster has pointed out.[86] But this embrace did not necessarily mean a shallow celebration of violence; rather, the many sentimental soldier poems published in wartime sought to comprehend and make sense of the violence of war individual by individual, and life by life—a task that grew ever more formidable over the course of the conflict.

This effort required a form of imaginative sympathy that deepened the war's meanings for observers, as they found in the bodies of wounded and dying soldiers a new and revelatory way of comprehending country. In sentimental soldier literature, it was not an abstract notion of country that made the individual deaths of soldiers meaningful, but the reverse: the suffering and deaths of soldiers themselves provided a new way of understanding a previously abstract nationhood. "For herself the lesson of the day had not been unfolded in vain," commented a character in Alice B. Haven's "One Day," a *Harper's Magazine* story of one woman's

---

84. "The Picket-Guard," in Richard Grant White, *Poetry Lyrical, Narrative and Satirical of the Civil War* (1866; rpt., New York: Arno Press, 1972), 120. The authorship of "The Picket Guard" was contested, with both Northern and Southern authors claiming to have written it. Their dispute only served to underline the many commonalities between Northern and Southern popular culture. Carrie Bell Sinclair, "All Quiet Along the Savannah To-Night," Laura Waldron Papers, Special Collections Library, Duke University; "The Picket Guard," 120.

85. "The Picket Guard," *Richmond Dispatch*, Mar. 20, 1862, in the M. J. Solomons Scrapbook, Special Collections Library, Duke University. See also Rosa Wild, "On Guard," *Southern Illustrated News* (Feb. 7, 1863): 3, whose opening line is "I'm watching now at my lonely post."

86. Royster, *The Destructive War*, 232–95.

visit to an army hospital. "She had seen all now. Loss, suffering—weary hearts, brave, hopeful hearts—" and, in the death of one soldier, "the drama's close." She knew that this suffering and loss "was but a tithe of the crimson harvest of War; that all over her country, in the dull walls of city hospitals, in the white tents pitched by wood and coast and stream, such scenes were daily transpiring. Her country!" she concluded. "Not only in the portion to which we are learning to limit our devotion, but in that where the wind of all this whirlwind was sown, strong men were bearing the anguish of pain and death, and women the heavier burden of suspense and breaking hearts; and she went out of the sunshine of her own undimmed life into the shadow of theirs, and so fulfilled the law of Divine sympathy and love."[87] Through such sympathy, expressed in hundreds of short stories, poems, and songs during the war, both Northerners and Southerners continued to insist on the importance of the individual, not the organization, in American life.

---

87. Alice B. Haven, "One Day," *Harper's New Monthly Magazine* 25 (Oct. 1862): 669.

Contributors

WILLIAM Y. THOMPSON (1922–2013) was professor and chair, Department of History, Louisiana Tech University.

ROBERT H. BREMNER (1917–2002) was professor of history, Ohio State University.

WENDY HAMAND VENET is professor of history, Georgia State University.

MELINDA LAWSON is senior lecturer and director of public history, Union College.

JO ANN CARRIGAN is professor of history emerita, University of Nebraska, and professor of public health emerita, University of Nebraska Medical Center.

JOHN S. HALLER is professor of history emeritus, Southern Illinois University, Carbondale.

EMILY J. HARRIS is vice president, Metropolis Strategies, Chicago.

DANIEL E. SUTHERLAND is distinguished professor of history, University of Arkansas.

EUGENE C. MURDOCK (1922–1992) was professor and chair, Department of History, Marietta College.

MARTIN CRAWFORD is professor of history emeritus, Keele University, UK.

TYLER ANBINDER is professor of history, The George Washington University.

PAUL D. ESCOTT is Reynolds Professor of history, Wake Forest University.

MARC W. KRUMAN is professor and chair, Department of History, Wayne State University.

GARY W. GALLAGHER is John L. Nau III Professor of history, University of Virginia.

JAMES MARTEN is professor and chair, Department of History, Marquette University.

ALICE FAHS is professor of history and director of the Humanities Honors Program, University of California, Irvine.

Index

Abbott, Jacob, 280
abolition, 37, 47, 70; Women's National Loyal League petitioning for, 34, 44. *See also* emancipation
abolitionism, and feminism, 41-42, 41-43, 51, 52
abolitionists, 33-34, 41, 49; split over women *vs.* black suffrage, 50-51; women as, 34, 38 (*see also* Women's National Loyal League)
Adams, William T. *See* Oliver Optic
African Americans: animosity toward, 51, 70-71; belief in deterioration of race, 115-18; body measurements of, 105-10, 106; discrimination against, 118, 219-20; effects of freedom studied in, 110-15; explanations for believed inferiority of, 112-15; fitness as soldiers, 108; free, 144, 147, 297-98; hospitalized, 326-27; mortality rates of, 110-11, 115; political rights for, 47, 49-50; portrayals in children's literature, 280, 295-99; slavery's effects on physiology of, 106, 109-10; studies of physiology of, 118; suffrage for, 42-43, 47, 49, 51, 64; undermining Confederate war efforts, 253; in Union army, 68, 70-72, 102-3, 107-8, 199, 269; Union Leagues and, 70-71, 76-77; Women's National Loyal League and, 38-39, 47
Agassiz, Louis, 105
Alabama, white citizens on relief in, 219
Albany, New York: responses to draft in, 193, 194, 203; Sanitary Fair in, 14, 16
Albany Army Relief Bazaar, 16
Alcott, Louisa May, 307-8, 320-24, 326-27

Allen, Henry, 221
American Anti-Slavery Society, 39
American Bible Society, 23
American Board of Commissioners of Foreign Missions, 23
American Equal Rights Association, 49
American Woman Suffrage Association, 51, 52
Anderson, Robert, 8
Andrew, John, 293
Andrew, Rod, Jr., 264-65
Anthony, Susan B.: moderating radicalism, 46-47, 52n47; organizing women abolitionists, 34-35; speaking for feminism, 41-42, 47, 51-52; split with male abolitionists, 50-51; Women's National Loyal League and, 36, 37-39, 41-42, 44
anthropologists, body measurements by, 102
anthropometry. *See* body measurements
antislavery societies, network of, 35-36
Appalachia, support for Confederacy in, 259
Army of Northern Virginia, 165, 263, 270n39, 271
Army of Tennessee, 265
Army of Virginia, 141
Ash, Stephen V., 262
Ashe, Thomas S., 237
Ashe County, North Carolina, 171; casualties from, 177-78; companies from, 172-75; demographics of, 168-69, 178-81; diversity in economies of, 184-85; residential districts of volunteers from, 181-82, 185; volunteering for regular *vs.* community companies in, 175-76; volunteers from, 170, 176-81
Ashurst, William, 74

Aspinwall, William H., 67
Astor, John Jacob, 11
Astor, Mrs. John Jacob, 71
asylums, funding for, 22–25
Atkinson, Thomas P., 112
Attie, Jeanie, 303n5
Ayers, Edward L., 270n38

Bache, Alexander Dallas, 102, 105
Baltimore, Sanitary Fair in, 14, 15–16
Bangor, Maine, 192, 203
Banks, Nathaniel P., 95, 97, 99
Barrows, E. S., 107–8
Barton, Clara, 30
Baum, Dale, 259
Baxter, J. H., 107, 117
Beals, Carleton, 255–56
Beckert, Sven, 70
Beecher, Henry Ward, 5–6, 39–40
Belisle, D. W., 309
Bell, John, 169
Bellows, Henry W., 5, 7, 10, 40; on duty, 76, 79; in New York League, 64, 66–67; Sanitary Fairs and, 14, 18; U.S. Sanitary Commission under, 29, 102
Belmont, August, 64–65
benevolent societies, major, 23–25, 42
Berenger, Richard E., 257
Berlin, Jean V., 265
Bernstein, Iver, 76
Billings, Franklin, 11
Bitter Fruits of Bondage: The Demise of Slavery and the Collapse of the Confederacy (Robinson), 257
Bitterly Divided: The South's Inner Civil War (Williams), 253–55, 266, 270
Blackwell, Antoinette Brown, 36
Blackwell, Henry, 51
Blevins, Albert, 165
Blevins, Alfred, 164–66, 184, 185
Blevins, Felix, 164–65
Blevins, Horton, 164–65
blockade, Federal, 88, 218
Bloomer, Amelia, 38
Bloor, Alfred J., 9, 13
Blum, John Morton, 280, 299
body measurements, 102; analyses of, 106, 118; conclusions drawn from, 106–8, 107–8; goals of, 101, 109; instruments of, 104–5, 107; post mortem, 110, 113; by Provost Marshal General's Bureau, 107–8; racial differences in, 101, 113; by U.S. Sanitary Commission, 104–7, 115–16; uses of data from, 115–16, 118
Bohannon, Keith S., 264–65
Boker, George Henry, 62–63
Bonham, Governor, 219
Bonner, Robert E., 261n23
Boston, 67–68; responses to draft in, 192–93, 198, 211–12; Sanitary Fair in, 9–10; Union Leagues in, 55–56, 67–69
Boston Sanitary Commission, 9
Boston Union Club, 68–69
bounties, commutation payments supporting, 159
Bowen, James, 96
Bower, George, 168–69
Boyden, Nathaniel, 171
Boykin, Samuel, 300n32
Boyle, Hugh, 187
Brace, Charles Loring, 24
Bragg, Thomas, 174
Branch, E. Douglas, 280
Brimmer, Martin, 68
Britain, contributions to Sanitary Fair from, 11
Brooklyn Sanitary Fair, 10
Brown, Gratz, 50
Brownlow, "Parson," 293
Bryan, T. B., 5
Bryant, William Cullen, 8
Buffalo, New York, 193, 209
Bull Run, Battle of, 124, 138
Bullock, Alexander H., 78
Bundy, Ryburn, 147
Burgwyn, Henry King, Jr., 175
burials, after battles, 151
Burt, W. J., 112–13
bushwhackers, 147–48, 177
business, 29, 59; leaders in Union Clubs, 56, 66–68; leaders' ties to South, 60–61, 67–68, 169; preservation of Union's importance to, 61–62
Butler, Benjamin F., 77, 95, 293; credited with preventing yellow fever epidemics, 97–99; on New Orleans expecting yellow fever, 88–89; praise for, 6, 97; trying to prevent yellow fever epidemics, 90–94
Bynum, Victoria E., 258

Cabot, Mary, 36
Cadwalader, George, 71
Caldwell, Tod R., 238
Camp Douglas (Chicago), 5
Camp Henry (Culpeper County), 138
Camp Miller (Deerfield, Massachusetts), 127
Campbell, Jacqueline Glass, 264
Cedar [or Slaughter's] Mountain, Battle of, 148-52
census data, racial differences in death rates based on, 111
Chaillé, Stanford E., 97-98
charity, 24; Confederacy supporting private, 222; Sanitary Commission *vs.* Christian Commission on, 29-30
Chase, Salmon P., 16
Chicago: draft of immigrants *vs.* natives in, 208, 209; Sanitary Fairs in, 4-7
Chicago Soldiers' Home, 5, 7
Child, Lydia Maria, 34
children, 279; encouraged to help freed slaves, 296-97; participation in philanthropy, 22, 289; politicization of, 299-300; relations with soldier fathers, 289-90; supporting Union war efforts, 287-89
children's magazines: Civil War in content of, 283, 289-90; Civil War references in, 283-84; in Confederacy, 300n32; death and loss in stories of, 290-92; drummer boys as heroes in, 286-87; effects of Civil War on, 281-82; explanations of Civil War in, 279, 281, 292, 300; goals of, 282, 286, 292-93, 299-300; influence of, 299; information about Union army in, 285-86, 287; moralizing in, 288, 296-98; portrayals of blacks in, 295-99; portrayals of slaveholders in, 294-95; promoting patriotism, 280-84, 293; religion in, 281, 284; Sanitary Fairs in, 288-89; values in, 279-80, 299-300
Childs, G. W., 322
Choate, Joseph H., 11
Christian Commission, 28, 31; given profits from Sanitary Fairs, 7, 15-17; Lincoln praising, 13-14; U.S. Sanitary Commission *vs.*, 28-30, 303n6
Christian Commission Fair, 17, 17n7
Cincinnati: response to draft in, 208, 209-10; Western Sanitary Fair in, 7-8

Civil War: cultural and intellectual history of, 303-4; disillusionment with, 60-62, 68, 73, 139, 165-66, 240; dissent in Confederacy causing defeat in, 255, 257; effects of, 23-25, 27, 31, 57-58, 136, 281-82, 290-92; end of, 6-7, 14; enthusiasm for, 124, 166, 170; expectations of quick victory in, 124, 127, 138, 234; explanations for children, 280-81; explanations to children, 279, 281, 300; goals of, 34, 40, 243, 292; legacies of, 135, 249; motives for, 40, 125, 234, 294-95; opposition to, 64; in Philadelphia, 61-62; representations of, 284, 323; shaping meaning of, 309, 310; support for, 56, 62-63, 69-70, 125, 138, 280-81; weariness of, 54-55, 75-76
civilians, 146, 166; abandoning homes, 139, 149; accusations against Confederate army, 144n13, 145n14; caring for wounded, 150-52; confiscations and destruction of property of, 141-45, 153-55; Federal soldiers abusing, 140, 145-46, 153; feeling vulnerable, 139-40; killed in battles, 149; morale of, 26-27, 265; refusal to abandon homes, 149-50; resistance by, 142, 147-48, 263n26, 264; seeing effects of battles, 150-51; states trying to shield from further sacrifice, 227-28
Clark, Henry T., 182
Clark, Perkins, 129
Clark Hare, J. I., 62-63
class, 134, 168; effects on draft, 190, 198, 201, 206-7; in elite *vs.* popular Union Leagues, 59, 59n11; heroism of ordinary soldiers *vs.* officers, 324-26; paying of commutation and, 159-60; in selection of companies' officers, 174-75
class relations, 59, 64-66, 76-77
class tensions, 287; Confederacy divided by, 220, 229, 255, 257-58, 262, 266; impact on military operations, 260, 272; over conscription, 197-98, 270-71
Cleveland, Northern Ohio Sanitary Fair in, 14, 16
Coan, G. N., 296
Cocke, Philip St. George, 138
Coffin, Charles C., 285
Cole, John, 146
Colfax, Schuyler, 7, 16, 29

Colgate, James B., 11
The Collapse of the Confederacy (Wesley), 255
colleges/universities, 25
Colman, Lucy, 36
communities, 129, 282; defense of, 167, 176; effects of battles in, 149; importance of selecting companies' names and officers to, 173-76; independence and interdependence in, 184-85; introduction to war, 137-38; militia organization by, 173-74; postwar erosion of self-sufficiency, 185-86; split over war, 146-47; taking responsibility for war demands, 134-35, 136; town companies recreating feeling of, 127, 174, 264
commutation payment, as option to draft: hostile reception of, 197-98; motives for offering as option, 196-97, 210; wealth's relation to, 161-62, 191-94, 213
Company D, from Deerfield, 127
Concord, New Hampshire, *193*
Confederacy, 241, 292, 300n32; Army of Northern Virginia symbolizing vitality of, 264; civilian morale in, 26-27, 265; class conflict in, 257-58, 267; Conservative party's relations with, 234-35, 250-51; differing definitions of, 269; disillusionment with, 165-66, 230, 265; disloyalty to, 238, 248, 250; dissent in, 227, 254-55, 257, 269n35, 273; divisiveness in, 230, 256; early enthusiasm for, 166, 170; factor uniting, 257, 266-67; farmers bound to provide food to, 223-24; group with fluctuating loyalty to, 274; internal weakness of, 234, 257, 261, 268, 274; judiciary *vs.*, 239-41; lack of majority support for, 253, 257-58; motives of, 263-64; as national community, 252-53, 261-62; nationalism and lack of, 257-58, 260, 264n28, 265; North Carolina's relations with, 240, 244, 247, 250-51; older scholarship on, 256; opposition to, 146-47, 253, 255-56, 258-59, 268; opposition to extended powers of, 231, 240-41, 243-45, 251, 268; poverty in, 217-18, 222, 229; proposed causes of defeat of, 257-61, 265, 271; recent scholarship on, 253-54, 258, 261-63, 273; relief efforts by, 222-23, 225, 227; responses to nearness of Union army, 268;
social history scholarship on, 256-57; states' rights *vs.*, 27-28, 227-28, 230, 237, 241-42; strengths of, 253n2, 261-62; support for, 61, 138, 141, 147-48, 258-59, 264, 269-70, 273; unionism within, 256, 259. *See also* South
The Confederacy as Revolutionary Experience (Thomas), 252
Confederate army, 240; body measurements of soldiers of, 105; casualties of, 257; civilians and, 137, 144n13, 145n14, 150-54; class in, 260; conscription into, 147, 178; desertion from, 239, 253, 260-61, 270-72; difficulty analyzing records of, 271-73; enlistments in, 138-39, 164-66, 269-70; food for, 224-27; local companies in, 172-75; need for more troops, 228-29, 237; passing through Culpeper County, 153, 154, 155; recruitment for, 175-76, 237; reenlistments in, 265; relief for families of, 138, 184, 222, 225; resolve within, 265; selection of companies' names and officers in, 174-76; slaveholders in, 174-75, 181-82, *183*, 253, 271; slaves in, 260; soldiers leaving to care for families, 222-23, 229; struggle for control in, 241-42; volunteers for, 167, 170, 178-79, 255, 269
The Confederate Nation (Thomas), 252, 256-57, 275
Confederates, *vs.* Southerners, 268-69
Congress, U.S.: petition for women's suffrage presented to, 50; women's antislavery petitions introduced to, 35; Women's National Loyal League's petitions to, 34, 44, 48-49
Conscience Whigs, in Boston, 68
conscription, Confederate, 147, 178, 239; class tension over, 253, 270-71; disillusionment with Confederacy and, 230-31, 236-37, 240-41; exacerbating labor shortage, 218-19, 237; exemptions from, 131, 194-96, 198-99, 201, 223, 230-31; farmers avoiding, 204, 223; wealth's relation to, 163, 187, 198-200
conscription, Union, 294; analysis by occupation, 198-201; avoiding, 130-31, 191, 194, 206-7, 209, 210; commutation payments to avoid, 130-31, 159-60; of immigrants, 187-89, 209; immigrants

conscription, Union (cont.)
    avoiding, 213–14; immigrants not drafted disproportionately, 189, 194, 198, 207–9; major calls for, 196, 209; native-born laborers' serving disproportionately, 190, 214; necessity of, 128, 237–38; politics' effects on, 202–3; possible responses to, 190–91, *192–93*, 201–7; record keeping on, 188–91, 211–12; state government managing, 135; substitutes for, 128, 134, 159, 211–12; sufficient volunteers exempting states from, 131–33, 209
Conservative party, of North Carolina, 234–36, 240; acquiescing to need for conscription, 237–38; Democrats *vs.*, 250–51; fear of losing freedom, 235, 237–38; fear of reunion, 245–46; opposition to suspension of habeas corpus, 238, 242–43
Constitution, U.S., as organism of national life, 78
Conway, Moncure, 41
Cooke, Jay, 29
Coons, Martha, 139–40
Coons, Susan, 141
Copperheads, 35, 67, 69, 294
Costello, Richard, 127
Cotton Whigs, in Boston, 68
Coulter, E. Merton, 222
Cowan, Edgar, 35
Cowles, Josiah, 233–34
Cox, Aras B., 174
Crittenden, Catherine, and daughters, 150, 152
crops, 141, 253; destruction of, 142, 150; poor harvests of, 226–27. *See also* taxes, in kind
Crume, John B., 281
Crumpler, Thomas N., 169, 176, 178
Culpeper County, Virginia, 138; Battle of Cedar Mountain in, 148–52; confiscations and destruction of property in, 153–55; effects of battles in, 150–51, 154; preparing for invasion, 139; resistance by civilians of, 142; support for Confederacy in, 147–48, 153; Union occupation of, 140, 141–42, 144, 155; unionists in, 146–47
culture, Northern, 303

Cummings, A. W., 247
Cunningham, R. M., 115
Cunningham, Richard H., 139–40
Curti, Merle, 56–57
Curtis, George William, 149, 306
Cutler, Hannah Tracy, 43, 43n26

Danson, John Towne, 102
Darling, Richard L., 282
Davis, Jefferson, 8n1; Conservatives' attacks on, 250–51; opposition to, 258, 267; opposition to extended power of, 242, 244–45; poverty and, 222–23; on strong military government, 236–37; suspending habeas corpus, 238, 241
death, 302; anonymity of soldiers', 306–10; giving meaning to soldiers', 309–10, 328; heroism of ordinary soldiers' *vs.* officers', 324–25; in sentimental literature, 305, 321–22, 329; soldiers thinking of mothers at, 316–17
Decker, Gottlieb, 131
Deerfield, Massachusetts, 123; casualties from, 129–30, 136; contributing "sons" and "soldiers" to war, 121, 125–26, 136; demographics of recruits of, 131–34; depleted of "sons" to recruit, 131–32, 135; efforts to meet recruiting quotas, 127–28, 131–33; financial burden for war, 124, 135; paying bounties for enlistment, 125–26; paying for draft substitutes, 128, 134; quotas for recruits increasing for, 134–35; recruitment at war meetings in, 126, 132–33; response to draft in, 128–31; return of Fifty-second Regiment to, 128–30; war memorial in, 121, 135–36
defeatism, 55; increasing, 60–62; Union Leagues countering, 72–73, 75–76
democracy, 73, 125, 166, 292–93
Democratic party, 71, 74; exclusion by Union Leagues, 63–64; fear of Lincoln administration, 249–50; in North Carolina, 235–36, 250–51; on suffrage, 50, 64
Dickinson, Anna, 41, 52
Dillard, Philip D., 268
disaster-relief organizations, 22
diseases, deaths from, 177–78
Dix, John A., 11–12
Dodge, William E., 25, 29

Douglas, J. H., 105
Douglass, Frederick: lecturing for Women's National Loyal League, 39, 41, 43; promoting black suffrage, 43; promoting black troops, 71
draft. *See* conscription, Confederate; conscription, Union
draft riots, 71, 74, 188, 198, 294; by immigrants, 129, 214
Drums-Taps (Whitman), 306
Dubois, W. E. B., 52n47
Duncan, William Butler, 67
Dunlap, Miss, 320, 324-25
duty, 167, 171, 288; unconditional loyalty as citizens', 77-79; Union Leagues promoting sense of, 75-76
Dyer, Thomas G., 259
"dying soldier" poems, cultural value of, 309-12

economy, 47; Northern elites' ties to South through, 60-61, 67-68, 169; prewar scarcity in, 22-23
economy, North's, 23-25, 73
economy, South's, 64; Confederate government expected to regulate, 220-21; diversity in Ashe County, 184-85; effects of war on, 185-86, 218; suffering from, 26, 219-20, 230
elections, as means of protecting freedom, 250
Eliot, William Greenleaf, 28
elites, 70, 73; divided by slavery and secession, 60, 62; gaining status through Union Leagues, 69, 72; split over slavery and secession, 66, 67-68; threats to, 59, 64, 74; in Union Leagues, 56, 59, 63, 65, 68, 72; Union Leagues rallying behind war, 62, 67-68, 72
Elliott, Ezekiel B., 104
emancipation, 70; effects studied in African Americans, 112-15; opposition to, 64, 264; thought to increase mortality rates, 110-11; Women's National Loyal League educating public on, 46, 48. *See also* abolition
Emancipation Proclamation: draft donated to Northwestern Sanitary Fair, 4-5; response to, 34, 37, 40, 48, 68
Emerson, Ralph Waldo, 68

Equal Rights Association, 50-52
equality: for African Americans, 37, 47; among free men, 235; of whites, 220, 232, 236; for women, 37, 47
Escott, Paul D., 268
Europe, contributions to Sanitary Fair from, 11
Evans, Augusta Jane, 325
Everett, Edward, 14, 68, 169, 293
Evrie, Van, 111
Ewell, Richard S., 138-40, 142
exile, for refusing to swear allegiance, 142

families: Confederate soldiers', 27, 229; effects of volunteering on, 171, 184; relief for soldiers', 27, 31, 184; in sentimental literature, 311-17
farmers, 4, 258; Confederate, 223-24, 253; conscription and, 202, 204; effects of volunteering on families, 171, 184; erosion of self-sufficiency of, 185-86; nonfarmers vs., 204-6; poor harvests of, 226-27; poverty of Southern yeomen, 218-20; soldiers exempted to home and farm, 222-23; taxes-in-kind on, 224-26, 240
Farnham, Eliza, 36
Farragut, David G., 12
Faust, Drew Gilpin, 257, 258, 265
feminism, 49; abolition and, 34, 41-42; during Civil War, 51, 53; improved public image of, 52-53; in Women's National Loyal League, 37, 42-43
Fenner, Erasmus Darwin, 96-97
Field, Ira, 144
Fifteenth Amendment, 50-52
5th Alabama Infantry, Company A, 264
Fifty-second Regiment, Company D ("The Franklin County Nine Months' Volunteers"), 126-27, 129-30, 132
First Manassas, Battle of, 124, 138
1st North Carolina Cavalry, Company A, 173
Fish, Mrs. Hamilton, 10-11
flags, as symbols of patriotism, 261n23
Foner, Philip, 74
food riots, by Southern women, 253
Forbes, James David, 102
Forbes, John Murray, 68, 74-76
Forest Club, 60
Forrester's Playmate, 282, 287, 290, 297-98

Fort Pillow, massacre at, 15-16
Fort Sumter: Lincoln's call for Federal enlistments after, 167, 169-70, 233; Northern response to, 57, 68, 73, 281
Fourteenth Amendment, 49-52
Fox-Genovese, Elizabeth, 171
France, contributions to Sanitary Fair from, 11
Fransioli, Joseph, 55
Fredrickson, George M., 78, 266, 302-3
free labor, as benefit of war, 76
Freedman's Bureau, 43
Freedman's organizations, 42
freedom/liberty, 234; defending, as North Carolina's highest priority, 248-49, 251; from government, 234-35, 237; government infringements on, 231, 236, 238-40, 267; North Carolina's fear of losing, 235, 244-46; obedience as path to, 79-80; proposals to defend, 236, 244-45; public fear of losing, 231-32, 237, 243, 249, 251; safeguards of, 236, 238-40, 250; white equality linked to, 220, 232, 236
Freehling, William W., 269
Frémont, John C., 46-47
Fuiger, Major, 227
fund-raising, methods of, 22

Gage, Frances D., 41
Gaither, Burgess S., 240
Garfield, James A., 16
Garrison, William Lloyd, 8, 39
Gash, Leander S., 251
Geary, James W., 188, 204n12
gender, 22; feminine components of manliness, 314; masculinity of war counteracted by femininity of hospitals, 318-19, 321
gender roles, 288; separate spheres doctrine and, 33, 36, 42; Women's National Loyal League and, 41, 52n47
General Order No. 107, amending Pope's earlier orders, 142n10
General Orders No. 5, 7, and 11: to squelch civilian resistance, 142-43
gentlemen's clubs, 60
Gentry, James M., 170-71, 177-78, 182
Georgia, elections showing support of Confederacy, 265
Gerhard, Benjamin, 63, 74
Germans, highest rate of military service by, 189, 209

Germany, contributions to Sanitary Fair from, 11
Gibb, Duncan, 116
Gibbs, Wolcott, 64, 66-67, 102
Ginzberg, Lori D., 303n5
Glatthaar, Joseph T., 263-64, 270n39, 271
Gorrell, Joseph B., 153
Goss family, 184
Gould, Benjamin A., 104
government, 40; military, 236-37, 240-41; neither Union and Confederate prepared for war, 27; public fear of, 231-32; seen as threat to freedom, 235, 236, 237
government, Confederate: expansion of, 227, 234; infringements on freedom by, 238-40, 243-44, 248-49; in relief efforts, 221-22; responsibilities of, 220-21, 243; states vs., 227-30, 236, 241-42
government, county, relief by, 221-27
government, Deerfield's, 128, 132-35
government, federal, 66; expansion of, 57-58, 76; lack of public involvement with, 56, 249; lack of public relations department, 57-58; loyalty to, 74, 77-78; states vs., 56, 64; Union Leagues supporting, 62-63, 76. *See also* nation
government, state, 236, 250; relief programs by, 27, 28, 221-22; taking over recruiting responsibility, 135, 136; trying to shield citizens from further sacrifice, 227-28
Graham, William, 244
Grant, Nellie, 15
Grant, Ulysses S., 7, 12, 14, 15n4, 155
Graves, R. J., 238
Greeley, Horace, 40-42
Greenwood, Grace (pen name of Sara J. C. Lippincott), 282
Griffing, Josephine, 43
Grimké, Sarah, 38
Gunther, C. Godfrey, 11

habeas corpus, Confederate suspension, 238; disillusionment with Confederacy for, 230, 240-41; extension of, 242-43; Vance on, 246-47, 246-48
Hale, Edward Everett: "A Man Without a Country" by, 54-55, 80-83; in Union League, 68, 75
Hamilton, Alexander, Jr., 11
Hamilton, Benjamin R., 130

Hamilton, Gail, 282
Hamlin, Hannibal, 16
Hammond, William A., 108
Hancock, Winfield S., 15
Hannaford, Eben, 318
Hardin, James Welborn, 174
Hardin, Joseph, 174
Harris, J. William, 180
Harris, Seale, 112
Harrisburg, Pennsylvania: lack of immigrants in, 199–200; responses to draft in, *192*, 199
Hartzog, John, 174
Haskell, Henry C., 130
Hattaway, Herman, 257
Haughton, John H., 246–47
Havens, Alice B., 328–29
Hawkins, W. S., 326
"held to service": immigrants underrepresented in, 189–90; native-born laborers' contributing disproportionately, 190, 201, 207; responses to, 161n3, 196, 201–7. *See also* conscription, Confederate; conscription, Union
Henry, Joseph, 105
Heroes of America, secret unionist organization, 248
heroism, changing ideas of, 302, 306, 322–26
Herschel, John, 103
Hoes, J. H., 5
Hoffman, Frederick L., 114, 116–18
Hoge, Jane C. (Mrs. A. H.), 4–7
Holden, William W., 244, 246–48, 267
Holmes, Oliver Wendell, 317; in Boston Union Club, 68–69; on cultural value of sentimentalism, 309–10; Sanitary Fair and, 5–6; on war songs, 304, 313
Holmes, William H., 105
home, soldiers' longing for, 317–18, 328
Hooker, Isabella Beecher, 35
Hooker, Joseph, 6
Hookers, A. S., 324
Hosmer, James K., 127
Hospital Life in the Army of the Potomac (Reed), 318–19
Hospital Sketches (Alcott), 320–24, 327
hospitals: civilians caring for wounded in, 5, 150–52; in sentimentalist literature, 317–29
Hovey Fund, 39

Howe, Daniel Walker, 67–68, 78
Howe, Julia Ward, 52
Howe, Samuel Gridley, 102
Hoyt, Mrs. E. O. Sampson, 36–37
Hudson, Matilda, 147
humanitarian reform, prewar, 22
Hunt, Sanford B., 108–9, 115

identity, national, 57; Confederate, 262; "A Man Without a Country" showing importance of, 80–83; Union Leagues promoting, 56, 58
Illinois, support for Women's National Loyal League in, 43–44, 48
immigrants, 59, 64, 88, 326; "alien" draft exemptions for, 195, 199, 201; avoiding draft, 198–99, 213–14; draft dodging by natives *vs.*, 191, 194, 206–7; draft of, 187–88, 213; in draft riots, 129, 214; enlistment of, 133–34; not drafted disproportionately, 189, 194, 198, 207–9; representation in Union army, 188, 189–90; responses to draft, 191, *192–93;* serving as substitutes to draft, 210–12, 214
individualism/anti-instutionalism, antebellum, 303
industrialization, 59, 221
inflation, increasing, 73
Ingersol, Mrs. H. C., 36
Ingersoll, Charles, 62
The Inner Civil War (Frederickson), 302
Inscoe, John C., 169–70, 259, 267n32
institutions, benevolent, 22–24, 26
institutions, public, 25–26
insurance companies, 102, 116, 118
intellectual ability, 108–9
intellectuals, in North: response to war, 302–3; on value of sentimentalism, 309–10
Irish, underrepresented in held to service ranks, 189, 194
Irwin, John W., 239

Jackson, Alexander, 144
Jackson, Thomas J., 140, 142, 148–52
James, Henry, Sr., 323–24
Jay, Mrs. John, 71
Jenkins, J. Foster, 18–19
Johannsen, Robert W., 309
Jones, Archer, 257
judiciary, independent, 238–40, 241, 243

Karge, Joseph, 143
Kelley, William D., 41
Kelly, R. Gordon, 281
Kenzer, Robert, 173-74
Kidd, Benjamin, 115
Kimber, Abby, 45
Kiplinger, Frederick, 131
Klement, Frank, 59n11

labor shortage, 26, 218, 223; in arguments against conscription, 228-29, 237; effects of, 219, 226
labor unions, revived during war, 73-74
Lafayette, Marquis de, 8
Lane, Henry S., 16
Larcom, Lucy, 282
Latham, Jacob, 177-78
Latin America, yellow fever from, 98n28, 99
Leach, James M., 241
Leach, James T., 243-44
Lee, Robert E., 142; Army of Northern Virginia under, 165, 263-64; Battle of Cedar Mountain and, 148-52; portrayals in children's magazines, 286-87
Lester, Charles Edward, 322-23
Levine, Bruce, 260
Lewis, Thomas, 141
liberty. *See* freedom/liberty
Lieber, Francis, 11, 74, 78
Liharzik, Franz, 102
Lincoln, Abraham, 64, 70, 102, 142, 259; call for enlistments after Fort Sumter attack, 167, 169-70, 233; calling for more enlistments, 125-26; opposition to policies of, 167, 170, 249-50; rationale for commutation option, 196-97; Sanitary Fairs and, 4-8, 13-16; Women's National Loyal League leaders and, 46-47
Lincoln, Tad, 7
Linderman, Gerald, 170
Lippincott, Leander, 282
Lippincott, Sara J. C., 282
literature: children's, 279-80 (*see also* children's magazines); sentimental soldier in, 304-5, 319, 321-22; war, 304, 309, 327
The Little Corporal, 282-83, 289, 292
The Little Pilgrim, 282, 284, 291, 296-97, 299
Livermore, Mary A. (Mrs. D. P.), 4-6, 52
Lonn, Ella, 260

Lost Cause narrative, 255-56
love, sentimental soldiers' longing for, 319
Lowell, James Russell, 68
Lowell, Massachusetts, 192, 209
Loyal Publication Society, 75n45
Loyal Women's National League. *See* Women's National Loyal League
loyalty. *See* patriotism

MacLeod, Anne Scott, 280
Madden, Willis, 144
Maine, 201-2, 209
"A Man Without a Country" (Hale), 54-55, 80-83
Manchester, New Hampshire, 193, 213
Manigault, Arthur M., 272
Manning, Chandra, 264
Mars, George, 147
Mason, Caroline A., 314-15
Mason, Mary, 154-55
masses, Union Leagues and, 73-76
May, Abby W., 9
McClellan, George B., 12, 15n4, 293
McCurry, Stephanie, 274
McGuire, Hunter, 152
McKim, Lucy, 33
McKinney, Gordon B., 259, 267n32
McMichael, Morton, 61-63
McPherson, James M., 188, 317
Meade, George Gordon, 155
Mears, J. H., 108
Medical Bureau, and Sanitary Commission, 30
Meigs, Montgomery C., 30
men: feminists and, 49-51; Women's National Loyal League and, 38-40, 46
Merrimon, Augustus, 242-43
Merry's Museum: content of, 285, 290, 292, 295; effects of Civil War on, 282; portrayals of blacks in, 298-99
Mexican War, 309
military: children acting out, 287-88; children's literature and, 281-83; civil power vs., 236, 244, 268
militia, organized by community, 173-74
Miller, J. F., 113-14
Miller family, 184
Milwaukee, 208, 209
Minturn, Robert B., 66-67

Mississippi Valley Sanitary Fair (St. Louis), 14
mixed blood: believed inferiority of, 108-9, 116-17; body measurements of, 104-6
Moore, Albert Burton, 230
Moore, John, 115
morale, 26-27, 265. *See also* Civil War, weariness of; defeatism
mortality rates, African Americans', 110-12, 115-16
Morton, Samuel George, 109
mosquitos, yellow fever transmitted by, 88n2
Mother Would Comfort Me (Sawyer), 313
mothers, in war songs and poems, 313-17
Mumford, Annie, 36
Murdock, Eugene C., 128, 188

Nalle, Thomas B., and family, 152
nation, 83; obligations to and expectations of, 56-57, 79; as path to liberty, 79-80; Union League on, 77-78
National Freedman's Relief Association, 43
National Woman Suffrage Association, 51, 52
nationalism, 55n4, 57; Confederate, 265, 267-68; Confederate lack of, 257-58, 260, 264n28; Union Leagues promoting, 56, 58, 65, 75
Native Americans: body measurements of, 104-7; resisting Confederate authority, 253
nativism, immigrants complaining about, 214
Neely, Mark E., Jr., 267
Nevins, Allan, 303n6
New England Loyal Publication Society, 75
New England Women's Auxiliary, 9
New Haven, Connecticut, *192*, 199, 203
New Orleans: Confederate loss of, 260; filth of, 93, 98; hostile population of, 88-90, 93-94; prevention of yellow fever epidemics in, 88, 90-99; Union occupation of, 88-89; yellow fever epidemics in, 87-90, 96
New York, 161
New York Children's Aid Society, 23
New York City, 44, 74, 160n1, *163*, 211; Sanitary Fair in, 10-13; Union Leagues in, 55-56, 59-60, 64, 70-71
New York League, 64-67, 69

newspapers, 41-42. *See also* abolitionist press
Noe, Kenneth W., 274
Norman, Letitia, 170-71
Norman, William M., 170
North, 34, 83, 146n15; Confederates' resistance to, 263-65; economy of, 23-25, 73; intellectuals' response to war, 302-3; North Carolina considering negotiations with, 240, 244-45, 247-49; North Carolina resisting coercion by, 233-34; response to Fort Sumter attack, 57, 68, 73, 281; Union League support for, 62-63; war weariness and defeatism in, 55, 58, 60-62
North Carolina, 235; concern about extension of government powers, 242-43; Conservative party of, 234-36; considering relations with North, 240, 244-45, 247-48; convention movement in, 240, 244-45, 247-48; fear of losing freedoms, 246, 248-49, 251; relations with Confederacy, 232, 240, 244, 247, 250-51; resisting subjugation of South, 169, 233-34; secession, 164, 167, 169, 233; unionists in, 167, 169, 177, 182, 232-33; war and, 164, 234, 243, 251, 267
North Carolina Cavalry, Fifth Battalion, 173
Northern Democratic party, 61
Northern Ohio Sanitary Fair, in Cleveland, 16
Northerners, susceptibility to yellow fever, 88-89
Northwestern Sanitary Fairs (Chicago), 4-7
Norton, Charles E., 68, 73-75, 78
Notes of Hospital Life (Dunlap), 320, 324-25
Nott, Josiah, 117

oath of allegiance, Southern civilians asked to swear, 142, 146
occupation, Union, 198-201, 212-13
Olmsted, Frederick Law, 64-67, 102
Optic, Oliver (pen name of William T. Adams), 282, 285, 292-93
Orange & Alexandria Railroad, in Culpeper County, 142
"organization thesis," 303, 329
Otis, George A., 113
Our Young Folks, 282, 284, 298-300
Owsley, Frank Lawrence, 227, 230

Parley, Peter (Samuel G. Goodrich), 280
patriotism, 36, 132, 261n23; American *vs.* European, 57-58, 77-78; benefits of unconditional, 79-80; children's magazines promoting, 280-85, 293; effects of draft on, 128-29; "A Man Without a Country" inspiring, 54-55, 80-83; rhetoric in recruitment efforts, 127-28; in sentimental literature, 301-2, 306; Union Leagues redefining, 56, 69-70, 72, 76-78
Payne, Willis, 145, 152
Payne daughters, 147, 149
peace: convention movement seeking, 245, 248; soldiers missing, 165-66
peace movement: Southern, 267n32; Union Leagues refuting, 35
Pearl, Christie, 296-97
Pearson, Richmond, 239, 241
Pervere, Dwight C., 124
Pervere, Horace, 124
Pervere, Rufus, 124
Pervere, Russell, 124
Philadelphia: Sanitary Fair in, 13-14; support for South in, 61-62; Union Leagues in, 55-56, 60, 62-63, 69-71
Philadelphia Club, 60
philanthropy: competition among organizations of, 22-23, 28-29; effects of economic scarcity on, 22-23; efforts to organize, 27-30; increased giving to, 24-25; postwar, 31-32
Philip Nolan, in "A Man Without a Country," 54-55, 80-83
Phillips, U. B., 266
Phillips, Wendell, 39, 41
Pierson, Michael D., 260
Pittsburgh, Sanitary Fair in, 14
poetry: about picket guards, 327-28; similarity of Northern and Southern, 302n2, 310, 325, 327-28; soldiers' deaths idealized in, 306, 309; war, 303-4, 312-17
political rights, African Americans' *vs.* women's, 49-50
politics, 267; contractual expectations of, 56-57, 78, 241, 243; elites in, 29, 59, 70; influence of, 202-3, 249; influences on, 40, 249-50; in North Carolina, 169, 235-36; women's activism in, 42, 44, 48, 52-53; women's participation in, 35, 47, 170-71

Pollard, Edward A., 255, 266
Pomeroy, Samuel C., 16
Pope, John, 141, 148-49, 153; response to civilian resistance, 142-43, 146; soldiers going beyond orders of, 143, 146
popular will, weakness of Confederate, 257
Portsmouth, New Hampshire, 193, 203
Post, Amy, 34, 36, 45
poverty: Civil War increasing relief for, 31; in Confederacy, 217-20, 222-23, 228-29
Power, J. Tracy, 263
presidents, citizens' obligation to support, 79
Priest, Nancy. A. W., 316
prisoners of war, 10, 106, 295
prisons, during war, 25-26
private charities, 23-25
Provost Marshal General's Bureau: anthropometry by, 101, 104, 107-8; records kept by, 190
publication societies, Union Leagues', 56, 70, 74-76
Pugh, Sarah, 45
Puryear, Richard, 237

quarantine, to prevent yellow fever epidemic, 88, 90-92, 97-99
Quetelet, Lambert Adolphe Jacques, 103-4, 118

Rable, George C., 171, 267
race, 101, 292; Confederacy united in attitudes toward, 266-67; differences in body measurements, 102-3, 106-7, 109, 113; differences in death rates, 110-12, 115; equality of, 37, 47; explanations for differences, 114-15
racism: based on wartime anthropometry, 101, 118; Stanton resorting to, 51
railroads: in Culpeper County, 139, 142; Southern, 220, 222
Rappahannock River, 138, 140
Reade, Edwin, 242
Reading, Pennsylvania, 192, 203
Redpath, James, 320
Reed, William Howell, 318-19, 324, 326
relief: for African Americans, 43, 219-20; Confederacy's role in, 221-23, 225, 227-28; extent of need for, 219; for families of Confederate soldiers, 138, 184, 225; food

shortages and, 221, 225–26, 228; state and county governments providing, 221–22
religion, 43, 257; charity and, 23, 29; in children's magazines, 281, 284, 287, 300n32; in sentimental literature, 305, 306, 309
republican motherhood, Stanton appealing to, 36
Republican party, 249; on suffrage, 49–51; Union Leagues supporting, 35, 58–59
Revolutionary War, heritage of, 125
Reynolds, David S., 303n5
Rhodes, James Ford, 18n8
Richards, Caroline Cowle, 302
Richmond, Virginia, 142
rights: contractual expectations of, 56–57, 78; women's, 51. *See also* freedom/liberty
Robinson, Armstead L., 257
Rochester, New York, *193*, 198–99
Roland, Charles P., 253n2
Roosevelt, Theodore, 299–300
Ropes, Hannah, 322
Rose, Ernestine, 36–37
Rosencrans, William S., 15
Rowan, S. C., 12
Royster, Charles, 328
Russia, contributions to Sanitary Fair from, 11
Russell, Ira, 109

sailors, as draft substitutes, 212–13
Sanitary Commission. *See* U.S. Sanitary Commission
Sanitary Fairs, 8, 19; Albany, 16; Baltimore, 15–16; Boston, 9–10; Brooklyn, 10; in children's magazines, 288–89; Cleveland, 16; New York City, 10–13; Philadelphia, 13–14; profits from, 3–4, 9–10, 14, 17–18; spread of, 7, 9, 17; Washington, DC, 16–17
sanitation: Butler improving New Orleans', 91–94, 99; in causes of yellow fever, 89–90, 93, 96; in preventing yellow fever, 91–98
Satterthwaite, Fenner B., 244, 246–47
Sawyer, Charles Carroll, 313, 316
Scranton, Pennsylvania, *193*, 194, 203
secession, 70; divisiveness over, 60, 177; North Carolina and, 169, 232–34
Second Manassas campaign, 148–52
Secret Yankees: The Union Circle in Confederate Atlanta (Dyer), 259

Seddon, James, 222, 225, 239, 241
sentimental literature, 305, 319, 329; anonymity of soldiers' suffering and deaths and, 306–8; cultural value of, 309–10; themes of, 313–18, 326–27
separate spheres doctrine, 36
service, prewar development of, 22
Settle, Thomas, 244–45
Sewell, Alfred L., 289
sexes, equality of, 37
Sexton, Reuben, 165
Seymour, Horatio, 16
Sheehan-Dean, Aaron, 263, 270n38
Shenandoah Valley, 142, 263n26
Sheridan, Philip H., 263n26
Sherman, William T., 7
Simms, Albert Gallatin, 153
Simpson, Matthew, 31
Sinclair, Carrie Bell, 328
Slaughter, Ella, 146
Slaughter, Philip, 145
slaveholders, 40, 258, 260; military service of, 181–82, *183*, 253, 271; "plain people" vs., 76, 253, 255, 257, 266; portrayals in children's magazines, 286, 292, 294–95; raising and leading companies, 174–75
slavery, 235; in children's magazines, 280–81, 292; continued belief in institution of, 236, 268n33; effects of, 40, 109–10, 113–14; elite divided by issue, 60, 67–68; Loyal League educating public on, 40–41; nearness of Union army destabilizing, 139, 143–44, 267–68, 273–74; nonslaveholders' acquiescence to, 266, 271
slaves, 106, 296; Confederate war efforts and, 150, 253; debate about arming, 260, 268; disadvantages of, 108–9; escaping, 143–44, 153; former, 108, 296–97; Union occupation and, 143–45; Union treatment of, 143–45; violence by, 139, 168–69
Smith, Anthony D., 55n4
Smith, C. D., 245–46
Smith, Larkin, 224–26
Smith, W. N. H., 233
social compact: Confederacy seen as repudiating, 241, 243; contractual expectations of, 56–57, 241, 243; contractual expectations of rights in, 56–57, 78; *vs.* society as organism, 78

social history, on Confederacy, 256–57
soldiers: anonymity of, 306–9; as "boys," 317, 321; dying and deaths of, 306–9, 321–22, 328; experiences in sentimental literature, 302, 306; heroism of hospitalized, 322–23, 322–24; home and, 317–18, 328; hospitalized, 317–29; individuals honored, 312–13, 329; masculinity of war counteracted by femininity of hospitals, 318–19, 321; mothers in popular war songs and poems, 313–17; outpouring of benevolence for, 27; sentimental, 302, 304–5, 319, 321–22, 326–27; in sentimental literature, 304, 306–7, 321–22, 329; suffering of, 304, 306–9, 322
soldiers' aid societies, 27, 28, 35, 303n6
Soldiers' Aid Society, Northern Ohio, 16
Somerset Club, 60, 68
songs, war, 302n2, 303–4, 309, 313–17
South, 63, 137, 252; call for enlistments after Fort Sumter seen as threat in, 167, 169–70; economy of, 26, 64; Northern elite ties to, 60–61, 67–68, 70; philanthropy in, 27–28; relief efforts in, 27, 31; resistance in, 142, 233–34, 249; unionists in, 295; war's effects on, 26–27, 167, 217–18. *See also* Confederacy
Southerners: Confederates *vs.*, 268–69; portrayals in children's magazines, 295
Springfield, Massachusetts, 199
Sprout, Alden and Dana, 130, 136
Squires, Edgar P., 132, 136
St. Louis Sanitary Fair, 14–15
St. Nicholas, 282
Stanton, Edwin, 102
Stanton, Elizabeth Cady, 47; abolitionists and, 34–35, 50–51; on African Americans' *vs.* women's rights, 49–50; moderating radicalism, 46–47, 52n47, 53; promoting women's rights, 47, 51, 52; racism and, 51, 104; Women's National Loyal League and, 35–42, 44, 49
State Rights in the Confederacy (Owsley), 230
State Troops Act, recruitment under, 175–76
states' rights: Confederacy *vs.*, 227–28, 230, 237, 241–42; interfering with organization of philanthropy, 27–28
Statistics, Medical and Anthropological of the Provost-Marshal-General's Bureau (Baxter), 107, 117
Stearns, Amanda Akin, 324
Stearns, John N., 282
Stebbins, Henry G., 65
Stephens, Alexander, 293
Stewart, Alexander T., 67
Stewart, William B., 79
Still, William N., 257
Stillé, Charles J., 7, 14, 102
Stone, Lucy, 36, 38, 51–52
Stowell, Charles, 126
Stowell, Cyrus O., 126, 129, 136
Stowell, D. Porter, 140–41
Stowell, Deacon, 132
Stowell, Myron, 126, 136
strikes, increasing during war, 73–74
Stringfellow, Ella S., 146
Strong, George Templeton, 64, 66–67, 73, 76
Stuart, George Hay, 29
The Student and Schoolmate, 282, 285, 287; Civil War trivia in, 284–85; declamation pieces in, 283, 287, 293; praise for Union democracy in, 292–93; war-related playlets in, 293–94
substitutes, to draft, 163n4; commutation option to limit price for, 196–97; Confederacy abolishing, 241, 243, 270n40; immigrants serving as, 210–12, 214; lack of, 199–200, 209; recruitment of, 211–12; sailors as, 212–13; wealth's relation to, 163, 213, 270n40
suffering, in sentimental literature, 304–5, 322, 329
suffrage: African Americans', 42–43, 47, 49, 51, 64; expansion of, 59, 235–36; women's, 42, 43n26, 49–50; women's *vs.* black, 50–51
Sumner, Charles: abandoning fight for women's suffrage, 50; Fourteenth Amendment written by, 49; Women's National Loyal League and, 39, 46, 48; Women's National Loyal League petitions and, 35, 44, 48–49
Sutherland, Daniel E., 274
Switzerland, contributions to Sanitary Fair from, 11
sympathy, virtue of, 304, 328

Tatum, Georgia Lee, 230, 259
taxes: increasing during war, 27, 73, 221; in kind, 224-27, 230-31, 240, 251
Taylor, Bayard, 294
Taylor, John, 145
Taylor, Moses, 67
Tenth Regiment Massachusetts Volunteers, 124
3d United States Regiment, Colored Troops, 71
Thirteenth Amendment, 47-48
30th North Carolina Infantry, 153
34th Regiment, 173
37th North Carolina Regiment, Company K (the "Alleghany Tigers"), 165
37th Regiment, Company A of, 173-74
Thomas, Emory M., 252, 256-57, 275
Thomas, Stephen, 182
Thompson, John Reuben, 308-9
Thorn, Lucy, 145
Tocqueville, Alexis de, 57-58, 166-67
Townsend, Joseph B., 74
transportation, South's, 218, 228
Trowbridge, J. T., 282, 292
Trowbridge, J. W., 294-95
Truth, Sojourner, 51
26th Regiment, Company A: "Jeff Davis Mountain Rifles" of, 173, 176

Uncle Tom's Cabin (Stowe), 305
Union, 57, 267; children supporting war efforts of, 286-88; importance to business interests, 61-62, 66; praise for democracy of, 292-93; preservation of, 61-62, 64, 70; publication societies' literature supporting, 74-76; restoration of, 233-34, 250; support for, 64, 70; supporters in Culpeper County, 146-47; supporters in North Carolina, 167, 169, 177, 182, 232-34
Union army, 264, 303; abuse of Southern civilians by, 140, 145-46, 147-48, 153; African Americans in, 68, 70-72, 102-3, 107-8, 269; body measurements of, 105-6; body measurements of soldiers in, 102-3; brothers and cousins joining together in, 124n4, 126; call for enlistments after Fort Sumter, 167, 169-70, 233; children's relations with fathers in, 289-90; confiscations and destruction of civilian goods by, 140, 142-46, 154-55; conscription for, 128, 134-35; Deerfield contributing "sons" *vs.* "soldiers" to, 121, 122; demographics of soldiers in, 131-34, 317; effects of nearness of, 267-68, 273-74; enlistment quotas in, 134-35, 212; enlistments in, 125-26, 133-34, 270n38, 286; exploiting class tensions within Confederacy, 262; fitness for service in, 108, 195-96; immigrants not overrepresented in, 188; invasions by, 139-40, 251; native-born laborers' contributing disproportionately, 190, 214; occupations by, 88, 144-45, 155; portrayals in children's magazines, 285-87; recruitment for, 69-70, 125-26, 127-28, 131-33, 212; reenlistments in, 132; Southerners serving in, 177, 269; substitutes making up three-quarters of, 210-11; towns raising companies for, 124, 126; treatment of escaped slaves by, 143-44; veterans' return from, 128, 146n15; yellow fever and, 89-90, 94-95. *See also* soldiers
Union Club (Philadelphia), 60, 62-64, 69
Union Leagues, 35, 58; elite *vs.* popular, 59, 59n11, 65; elites regaining status through, 69, 72; facilities of, 63, 65-67; formation of, 64, 68; goals of, 55-56, 58, 72; influence of, 56, 69; membership of, 67, 69; partisan *vs.* nonpartisan, 58-59; political participation by, 70; projects of, 69-70; promoting black troops, 70-72; promoting nationalism, 56, 58; promoting sense of duty, 75-76; publication societies of, 70; redefining patriotism, 70, 72, 76-78. *See also* New York League; Union Club (Philadelphia)
unionism, within Confederacy, 234, 248, 259, 295
Unitarianism, 78
United States Christian Commission for the Army and Navy, 6
unknown soldiers, development of concept, 307
U.S. Army, using anthropometric data, 116
U.S. Sanitary Commission, 8, 11, 64, 288, 303; body measurements by, 101, 103-7, 115; Christian Commission *vs.*, 28-30,

U.S. Sanitary Commission (cont.) 303n6; effectiveness of, 30, 32; end of, 31–32; finances of, 3, 16–17, 18; formation of, 3, 102; Lincoln praising, 13–14; profits from Sanitary Fairs for, 5, 7, 10, 13–18; Sanitary Fairs funding, 3–4; South lacking, 31; trying to organize philanthropy, 28–30; women's roles in, 35, 42

Vallandigham, Clement, 80–83
Van Buren, William H., 102
Vance, Zebulon B., 219, 238–39, 240, 250; on convention movement, 245, 247–48; elections of, 250, 267; on expanded conscription law, 241–42; opposing reunion, 245–46; on suspension of habeas corpus, 241–42, 244, 246–48
Vassar, Matthew, 17
vigilante terrorism, against unionists, 256
Virginia, 270; steadfastness of beliefs in, 262–63, 268n33; support for secession in, 138, 147. *See also* Culpeper County
volunteering, 27; in Ashe County, North Carolina, 167, 170, 177; draft and, 178, 209; effects on families, 171, 184; influences on, 182–84, *183;* lack of studies on, 166–67; motives for, 166, 170, 176, 178; for regular *vs.* community companies, 175–76; residential and kinship ties in, 173–74, 181–82; wealth's effects on, 179–82, *183;* women's role in, 170–72, 316

Wade, Benjamin F., 16
Wagg, Samuel P., 175
Wallace, Lew, 14
Waller, Altina, 184
War Fund Committee of Brooklyn and County of Kings, 10
war journals, sent back to Deerfield, 127
War within a War: The Confederacy against Itself (Beals), 255–56
Warren, Robert Penn, 30–31
Washington, D.C., 16–17, 146
Watts, Thomas, 228–29
wealth, 168; commutation payments and, 159–62, 196–97; determination of districts', 160–61; draft and, 163, 187, 198–200; effects on volunteering, 179–82, *183;* in selection of companies' officers, 174–75
Weitz, Mark A., 260–61
Weld, Angelina Grimké, 36, 38, 40
Weld, Theodore, 41
welfare. *See* relief
Wells, Elisha, 125
Wells, William, 130
Wesley, Charles H., 255
Western Sanitary Commission, 14–15, 30
Western Sanitary Fair (Cincinnati), 7–8
westward expansion, 64
Wetherington, Mark W., 264
Whig party, 61, 68, 234–36
White, Mary, 36
whites, body measurements of, 105–6, 106–7
Whites, LeeAnn, 258
Whitley, R. D., 243
Whitman, Walt, 306, 319, 323; on hospitalized soldiers, 318, 321, 326–27; lamenting unknown soldiers, 307–9
Why the South Lost the Civil War (Berenger, Hattaway, Jones, Still), 257
Wilcher, John, 140
Wiley, Bell Irvin, 188, 230–31, 317
Willard, Fannie, 36
Williams, David, 253–55, 258, 266, 268–71
Wills, Brian S., 263
Wilson, Henry, 49
Wistar, Caspar, 60
Wistar Party, 60, 63
women, 258; activism of, 35, 42, 44, 47–48, 52–53; dissatisfaction with Confederacy, 253, 265; roles in war, 33, 42, 170–72, 219; suffrage for, 42, 43n26, 49–51
Women's Executive Committee, 10–11
women's magazines, 42
Women's National Loyal League, 34; African Americans and, 38–39; educating public on emancipation, 46, 48; educating public on slavery, 40–41; effectiveness of, 48; feminism mixed with abolitionism in, 41–43, 51; first convention of, 36–37; goals of, 35, 39, 47; leaders of, 37–40, 43, 46–47; men and, 38, 46; moderation in, 46–47, 52n47; petitions of, 39, 42–49; public image of, 52;

recruiting for, 35–36, 42–43; resolutions of, 37; Sumner and, 46, 48; support for, 39, 41, 43–44, 48, 52

Women's Relief Association of the City of Brooklyn, 10

women's rights, 34, 51–52; African Americans' put ahead of, 49–50; limited to petitioning, 42, 44; Women's National Loyal League split over, 37

Woodward, Joseph J., 113

Work, Henry C., 317

workers, during war, 73–74

Worth, David, 182

Worth, Jonathan, 245, 247

Wright, Ellen, 33, 34, 39

Wright, Martha, 36

Wyman, Jeffries, 105

Yager, William, 151

yellow fever: causes of, 89–91, 97–98; epidemics in New Orleans, 87–88, 90, 96, 98; limited to two cases under Butler's regime, 92, 95–96; in New Orleans, 88n2, 95–96; Northern doctors unfamiliar with, 94–95; prevention of, 88, 95–99; Union soldiers' fear of, 89–90

Y.M.C.A.s, 29

"You'll Tell Her, Won't You?," 310–12

"Young America" movement, 64

www.ingramcontent.com/pod-product-compliance
Lightning Source LLC
Chambersburg PA
CBHW032016230426
43671CB00005B/103